THE TRANSFOR

Studies in Rural Culture | Jack Temple Kirby, editor

The

University

of North

Carolina

Press

Chapel Hill

and London

The Transformation of Rural Life

Southern Illinois, 1890–1990

JANE ADAMS

Manufactured in the
United States of America

The paper in this book meets
the guidelines for permanence
and durability of the Committee on Production Guidelines
for Book Longevity of the
Council on Library Resources.

Library of Congress
Cataloging-in-Publication Data
Adams, Jane (Jane H.)
The transformation of rural life:
southern Illinois, 1890–1990 /
by Jane Adams. p. cm. — (Studies
in rural culture) Includes biblio-
graphical references (p.) and index.
ISBN 0-8078-2168-3 (alk. paper)
ISBN 0-8078-4479-9 (pbk. : alk. paper)
1. Union County (Ill.)—Social life
and customs. 2. Union County (Ill.)
—Rural conditions.
I. Title. II. Series.
F547.U5A34 1994   94-4176
977.3'99504—dc20   CIP

Jane Adams is associate professor
of anthropology at Southern Illinois
University.

98 97 96 95 94   5 4 3 2 1

I dedicate this book to my

parents, Edward L. and

Lillian Kanet Adams, whose

lives have exemplified love

of the land, respect for people,

delight in the intellect, and a

passion for social justice.

CONTENTS

> We hope that this history . . . will re-
> fresh the minds of its people with mem-
> ories of its past efforts, its dreams, its
> failures and successes. In so doing, it is
> desired that our thinking will be in-
> spired by experiences and opportuni-
> ties, stimulated by forceful personali-
> ties and warned by mistakes of the
> past. There is also a possibility that in
> this [book], some long forgotten and
> unfulfilled potentiality may be pre-
> sented to our minds. If only a small
> portion of this is realized, we may
> become better prepared for accom-
> plishment in community improve-
> ment.—"Introduction," *History of*
> *Cobden*, Cobden Historical Committee

To Refresh the Minds of Its People

It is always difficult, I think, to write books about people who will read them. In the past, anthropologists often had the dubious luxury of writing about people who could not read and perhaps were not even aware of books as a medium of communicating with other people. That day is long past, and now all anthropologists have to assume that at least some of the people they write about will read their work.

This book is somewhat different because it is written not only *about* people who I expect will read it, but it is in part written *for* them, by one of their own.[1] This book is as much autobiography—an attempt to understand my own life course—as it is an exercise in scholarly interpretation. I grew up a few miles from the county this book deals with. My family's farm, although dating only to the early 1940s, is now essentially aban-

xv

The author and her brother, Jim, sit on the foundation of an old barn on their parents' farm, ca. 1947. Oak Ridge School is in background. Author's collection.

doned, the community emptied. I grew up through the transition from relatively self-provisioning to fully commercialized farming, attended a one-room country school, was active in 4-H, and like most of my classmates, left the area as soon as I graduated from high school. I was fortunate to be able to return some twenty years later as a scholar and researcher, to try to make sense of the experiences through which I and all those with whom I shared time and space were formed and which we in part formed. After nearly ten years' research, the memories of the people I have worked with have, in many cases, nearly become my own; the Union County landscape has become superimposed over that of my childhood.

Doing ethnographic and historical research is a humbling experience. As I drive around the roads, I see the layers of experience that have preceded me and that surround me, and of which I will only learn the smallest fragment. Daffodils blooming in early spring mark the site of an abandoned farmhouse. Who lived there? What stories would they have told me? A century-old post-and-beam barn, relic of an earlier agricultural pattern, sags inward. Year by year I watch its decay and final collapse. Unlike the society in which it once functioned, which opened outward into the larger society, the barn sinks into itself, a compact heap of rotted timbers giving rise to mushrooms, a haven for mice and king snakes.

If you have lived in an area for several years, you can read its history in many and varied clues. The washed-out dam of the old pond is where the boys used to swim, before bulldozers and the Agricultural Stabilization and Conservation Service dotted ponds across the farms. A grass waterway snakes down a draw. It was a demonstration project, and all the area's farmers were there, seeing this new way to stop the gullies that devoured the land. An old schoolhouse, now holding junk or hay, still stands forty years after the last class. It was built by the men of the district and was supported by pie suppers and land taxes—taxes that drove many off their farms during the depression years when tax land went for a few dollars an acre (my parents bought our worn-out farm for $11 an acre in 1941). A community center during its useful days as a school, maybe this building was the site of square dances for a few years after consolidation as the people in the area tried to retain a local focus for their social life. Then, as people left or drifted apart, or when the minister who was the spark plug left, the neighboring farmer bought the school and used it to store hay or tools or to pack his fruit. Perhaps a family moved in, and it became a home for a few years. That old building could tell many stories.

There, nearly hidden beneath poison ivy and an overgrown thicket of brush, stands an old log house; each year it gets a little closer to the ground as the bottom logs rot into earth. Wind once whistled under it, sending cold drafts along the floor; snow sifted through the roof shingles, so the kids woke up with their blankets frozen like a mound above them.

A narrow creek bottom might have been planted in onions, then tomatoes. People did backbreaking work over the hot beds and cold frames and weeding the fields. "What good old days?" they say, and yet the nostalgia creeps in, for between the hardship, drudgery, and Mother with the switches that made you work, there are fond memories of the smells of new-plowed earth, of leaves rotting in the woods, of thunderstorms and flooded creeks, of the pungent dust of late summer. There were the picnics, the friendly competitions over who could pick the most blackberries or go deepest into the blackberry bramble barefooted, and the practical jokes that tested your ability to laugh at yourself (knowing you would avenge yourself on your tormenter). There were fishing adventures when the flash flood nearly drowned the whole gang, or when you (a girl) rescued a boastful young man from a snag when his boat capsized.

The landscape encodes memories that always threaten to escape, to disappear. Perhaps people like us, who lack a strong oral tradition, have no other means to store our inchoate memories, and so the landscape takes on a power it may not have for other people in other times or places. Each barn that collapses, every century-old house that burns down, and each bend of the road that is straightened removes a piece of our collective identity, feels like a personal loss, and threatens to undo us even as it is undone. So many of us go to great lengths to preserve our past. Old people shake their heads at the prices their old junk brings at auctions as younger people compete to buy icons of times past. Families mount plaques announcing their farm is a century farm; those with enough money spend inordinate sums restoring fine old houses. And those in love with our heritage may enter political battles with people who do not seem to be infected with this virus of nostalgia, who reflect the older attitude of "progress at all costs," who "never look back" and prefer to tear down the old and build anew.

Such scenes evoke nostalgia in most of the people I have worked with— a complicated nostalgia because no one would, given the option, resurrect the past these relics represent. Are we the first people to be infected with such longings? Do our factories produce nostalgia along with automobiles, televisions, and toilet paper? For there is no discounting the angst many of us feel as we look across our landscapes. Farm families and people who have grown up in rural areas seem caught on the horns of a dilemma: the old way was materially impoverished but far richer socially than the present. Must one quality be lost in order to have the other? Into that unresolved tension nostalgia creeps, a love affair with an imagined past stripped of its suffering and injustices.

It is well to remember that not everyone who grew up on a farm or who lives in one locality much of his or her life feels the deep attachment to the landscape that seems to characterize much of this area. Even more, every individual seems to be of several minds about preserving what is old and building what is new. If young people are going to stay around, after all, they must have jobs, and for jobs there must be new activities. We cannot live out of our past only, no matter how beautiful it has become with the patina of age. Nostalgia can mask passivity in the face of painful and unwanted change; worse, it can cover the complicity we share in having created this present with its threat of ecological catastrophe and its enormous and increasing disparities in wealth and power.

This southern Illinois landscape, with its hills and hollows, its forests and farmlands and orchards, and its small towns and back roads, has a beauty that I suppose every rural area develops, that embeds itself in those who grow up in it, and that places its stamp upon them so no other place, no matter how beautiful and grand, can ever replace it. I frankly love this region, yet I know it is part and parcel of the larger world. The arrogance of power, either actual power wielded by some people over others, or the identification with larger representatives of power, infects as many people here as anywhere. Although the deep gullies that scarred the land in the 1930s have healed, it is largely because the terrain is too rugged to allow people to gain from exploiting the land as they once did, and as many people around the world still do. Those who live in this region are no more free of bigotry than men and women anywhere else in the United

States. For many, the conditions of family and social life often cause, and have in their past configurations caused, a great deal of anguish and suffering. I would act and write in bad faith if I used nostalgia to paper over these realities, if I told our history as I wish it were rather than as I and others have experienced it.

I seek not only to tell the stories of the people who have lived here, but also to comprehend how we came to be the way we are. I understand our past as a constant process of taking certain paths, which inevitably shut off other alternatives. Sometimes those paths were clearly chosen but led to unexpected destinations. Other times, alternatives were simply blocked by actors more powerful than we as individuals, as citizens of a relatively poor, marginal region, or as members of a relatively powerless group. Sometimes we seemed to be traveling at such breakneck speed that alternative routes into the future were bypassed unseen.

Part of my project in writing this book is to try to reimagine the path taken by a specific rural area, by specific farm families, and to try to imagine alternate routes into the future. Perhaps we could have invented a course that would have allowed us our material prosperity without simultaneously impoverishing our social life. Perhaps we could have made different decisions that would have allowed more young people to stay in the area and that would have allowed farming in these hills to remain viable. Perhaps that is what our nostalgia is all about: a sense that, had we known better, we would not have lost so much, even as we gained so much.

I hope I can do justice to the small piece of this fine land I am writing about, and to the stories I have learned from the people who live and have lived in these old hills.

A Note on Methods

Before turning to the meat of this book, the reader may find it helpful to glimpse how I went about learning what I present here. I do not want to present the making of this book as a more orderly process than it in fact was. In 1982 I began research in Union County. My intent was to trace the changes that had occurred within my lifetime, since World War II. I discovered, however, that when I said "history," I was directed to the oldest member of the family, and I found myself learning about the period from the late 1910s on. That was at least as interesting as my original research design, and I allowed myself to be deflected somewhat. Anthropologists are notorious for abandoning their research program as soon as they hit the reality of the field, so I was not disturbed by this turn of events; it simply opened new vistas. Then, in the course of doing some research on the history of county roads for a column I wrote for the local newspaper, I stumbled on a vigorous farmers' movement in 1873. I have always been interested in social movements but, like virtually everyone now living, had no idea that southern Illinois had generated militant agrarian activity. That took me further back in time to try to understand the social milieu out of which that movement arose and its consequences, and led to three articles.[2]

In order to fund my research I worked with the Union County Historical Society and got a grant from the Illinois Humanities Council to document old farmsteads in the county and to study five of these farms in depth. The late Dr. C. W. "Doc" Horrell, a Union County native and retired Southern Illinois University professor, contributed his time to the project and photographed the houses and barns on these five farms; through oral histories and some archival research I reconstructed the histories—brief "biographies"—of these farms and presented the results in a series of slide programs around the county and as articles in the county and regional newspapers. I also worked for some time for the Illinois Crop Reporting Service as a survey enumerator and in that capacity was able to meet and talk with farmers from all over southern Illinois. None of the information gained in these discussions can be used directly in this work, but it allowed me to get a feel for ethnic and regional differences within southern Illinois and to learn informally a great deal about the area.

Out of research funds, in 1986 I joined a public interest group, the Illinois South Project (now Illinois Stewardship Alliance), that was working on the farm crisis and coal issues. For a year, during the height of the farm crisis, I worked on the "front lines," trying to help farmers save their farms, mobilizing community support, and working for government policies that would once again allow family-operated farms to be economically viable. This work was crucial in helping me untangle the alphabet soup of government programs that affect rural communities, in providing understanding of the multiplicity of institutions and individuals that influence the direction of rural America, and in giving insight into the social and personal costs of specific government and corporate policies. Those projects, along with a great deal more research, eventually became my dissertation, four articles on changing farm women's roles, and articles dealing with broader issues of rural policy.[3]

In 1987, at the request of the Union County Historical Society, I also undertook to write a history of the Cobden Peach Festival, which was celebrating its fiftieth anniversary.[4]

After I completed my dissertation, I wrote an article that drew on my research on Latin America.[5] I was struck by the contrast between what was happening with many peasant families and what happened in the United States as the economy industrialized: In much of Latin America, farm women's work intensifies as men leave the farming community for wage labor, leaving women to do virtually all the subsistence production as well as take care of all dependent family members—children, the sick, and the elderly. On American farms, as the economy industrialized after World War II, farm women found themselves with little to contribute to the farm operation and turned to off-farm jobs for cash income. That article was the seed from which this book germinated.

I did not realize, however, that I had planted any seeds; rather, I was ready to consider that project complete. I turned to the nineteenth century, to try to understand the social context of the agrarian movements I had discovered. I plowed that field for two years until a publisher's representative inquired if my article on women (which I was giving at the National Women's Studies Association annual meeting in 1989) was the basis for a book. I could see that there was a lot of interest in the topic, and so I quickly changed plans and resurrected the "completed" project. In summer 1990 I created a field school and enlisted the cosponsorship of Gary Kolb, professor of cinema and photography at SIUC, to document two farms and thus to replicate in greater depth and focus the project I had done six years earlier. The people associated with the Walton farm, just east of Anna, and the Kimber farm, just west of Dongola, allowed us—ten students, two professors, and an archaeologist—to invade their privacy for three weeks during that summer, going through old photographs, mapping, photographing, and questioning. We formally interviewed thirteen individuals who had been connected with the farms as family members or as renters and laborers. In addition I went to the Nimmo School reunion and talked with many people who had lived in the area of the Walton farm and who had worked as seasonal laborers for the Waltons. From genealogical materials supplied by some of these people I was able to reconstruct kin connections among the tenants on the Walton farm and discovered that many of them came from the Woodbury, Tennessee, area.[6] In the first project, I had focused on the changing farming technologies and crop mix and on changes in farmstead architecture and layout. With the larger number of fieldworkers and an archaeologist, we were able to document those changes and also to delve far more deeply into the social relations within the families of owners and renters, and the relations between them. Since we focused on changing women's work, we were also able to get far more detailed information on that, plus develop some data about the differences between more affluent and poorer farmers and tenants.

These projects relied heavily on oral histories (transcribed and deposited with SIUC Morris Library Special Collections), copies of old photographs (also deposited with Special Collections), and mapping current structures. In addition I mined archival sources: microfilm copies of the county paper, Farm and Home Extension Service records, aerial photographs going back to 1938, courthouse records, census reports, memoirs, county histories and atlases, and other published materials.[7]

Finally, I have immersed myself in the recent literature on U.S. women in general and farm women in particular, a field that has burgeoned since the early 1970s, and I have taught several anthropology courses, particularly a graduate course in anthropological theory and method, that have kept me abreast of the intellectual currents that are driving our field. These currents stress the importance of human agency, of people as historical actors. I hope in this book to create a narrative that implicitly places human actors in the flow of historical time. I want to bring together the two dimensions of our reality: that we experience ourselves as self-willed individuals and, at the same time, experience ourselves as caught up in systems and orders beyond our power to control or even, all too often, affect.

This is a difficult project. It makes demands on my writing and thinking abilities that I am not sure I am capable of meeting. More importantly, because this is a book about real people in a real place, I of necessity walk lightly on the substance of their lives. This book is biography and autobiography at the same time that it is historical ethnography; in constructing my story I must therefore take into account not only what is publicly available but also information that, if improperly construed, may hurt or offend real people, people I like and care about. I have stumbled on few skeletons in the course of my work, largely, I suspect, because I have trouble being "nosy" and I tend not to push too hard on closet doors. Every family has skeletons, and what is considered shameful by one member of a family may not be considered shameful to another: the hanging of a man as a horse thief may be a thrilling tale to a person born in 1950 while being a dreadful blot on the family's reputation to her grandmother; a famous outlaw may be claimed as a relative by one family member while being utterly rejected by another. I have tried to exercise tact where I thought feelings might be tender, and I gave the manuscript to some of the people of whom I write so that they could correct errors they found. They saved me from some significant embarrassment, but I am sure other inaccuracies and controversial interpretations remain for which only I am responsible.

Sometimes it has been necessary to write of the unpleasant side of life. It would be dishonest and inaccurate to write about changing women's roles and not deal with issues of illegitimacy, marital infidelity, interpersonal violence, theft, and betrayal. I do not, however, have a great deal of data on these issues, and most of that data comes from my own experience in this area and from conversations with people other than those mentioned by name in this book. It has not been difficult, then, to honestly mask the identities of the people involved in such scandalous events and activities. I have taken the liberty of using anecdotes and bits of information from people throughout southern Illinois, without attribution, when discretion seemed to advise this course.

I hope I have created a work through which the farming people and descendants of farming people of this region can recognize themselves and re-collect their (our) heritage in a way that allows them (us) to create a more humane and equitable future than we have thus far created.

Acknowledgments

This book would not have been possible without the help and support of many people. Most important are those who opened their lives to me, teaching me the history of this region. I owe a special debt to the seven families who allowed me and my students and collaborators to invade their privacy and document their farms: Norbert and Betty Cerny and Elizabeth Cerny; Helen Kimber, Bob Kimber, and Jacquie Eddleman; Edith Rendleman and her sons, Lee Roy and W. P. "Bud"; Helen Sirles and Wayne "Ren" and Betty Sirles of Rendleman Orchards; Bill Rhodes; Rosemary Walton and Barbara and Marlin Throgmorton; and George and Marita Weaver. I participated with the Cerny families—Norbert and Betty and their son Tom, and Richard and Jo and their children Theresa and Eric—in the Smithsonian Folklife Festival in 1990 and am indebted to folklorist Lee Ellen Friedland, who did the fieldwork that led to our participation. Many other people allowed me to tape their memories: Al Basler, Claude Boyd, C. E. "Bud" Braden, Ed Brimm, Agnes Tucker Cash, Myrta Clutts, Wayne Corzine, Clara Davidson, Alvie and Mildred Duty, David and Clara Elder, Albert Flamm, Coy Gertman, Austin and Hazel Halterman, Mary Walton Hill, Ruel Hindman, Bertie and Finis Hunsaker, Floyd and Frances Karraker, Maude Kinder, Gerald and Lorene Lingle, Marjorie and Stella Lingle, Oscar "Dutch" Lingle, Clara Bell Miller, George E. Parks, Wilbern Patterson, Faye and Curtis Smith, Arilla Spiller, Geraldine Stadelbacher, Grant Taylor, Charles Thomas, Glenn Tweedy, Witt and Mary Venerable, and Sybil Tucker Wilson. Data on the Cobden Peach Festival was given by the Cobden Lions Club, Mr. and Mrs. Conrad Baggott, Faye and Donald Ballance, Patrick Brumleve, Richard Cerny, Allie Jane Davis, Mary Flamm, Roger Gray, Melvin Lockard, Wilma Nebughr, Everett Randall, G. Wallace Rich, Arilla Spiller, Lou Stadelbacher, Will Travelstead, and Mr. and Mrs. Jack Williams. The members of the Union County Historical Society (now the Union County Historical and Genealogical Society) were unfailingly helpful, especially Robert and Jane Brown, Pat Brumleve, Pat Meller, and Judy Travelstead. Elaine Rushing has been very helpful, both as a person with a long memory and as a Green Thumb employee at the Union County clerk's office. I owe a debt as well to local historians George E. Parks, with his long memory, and Darrel Dexter.

This does not exhaust the list of people who have shared information that has made its way into this book: A number of people contributed to the histories of the seven farms who were not interviewed on tape; I surveyed nearly 100 farms in the course of a 1983–84 study, and at each farm I learned something of value; many people donated photographs to our growing Southern Illinois Collection (Morris Library, Special Collections) during a 1990 field school; members of the Carbondale Farmers' Market allowed me to participate for a year in their meetings and to observe the market; and others have shared their memories with me. Some of the people to whom I am indebted include Jesse Aldridge, Jenny Anderson, Rodney and Sandy Anderson, Geneva Basler, Robert J. "Bally" Basler, W. A. Bittle, Charles Boswell, Claude and Bertie Boyd, C. E. Braden, Jess and Mable Brimm, Golda Brown, Harold Brumleve, Ted and Marilyn Buila, Dellis Buzbee, Oliver and Mrs. Caldwell, Lela Casper, Tirza Casper, Blanche Cerny, Shirley Chamness, Maryanne and Bruce Chrisman, Earl Clutts, Eldon Clutts, H. R. Clutts, Jr., Mart Clutts, Myrta Clutts, Wayne Corzine, Ken Cruse, John and Jo Cunningham, Martha Dalton, Onida Davis, Thelma DeGamore, Mr. and Mrs. Floyd Dillow, Pearl Dillow, Wayne Dillow, Spike and Judy DuBois, Alvie and Mildred Duty, Edwin "Sonny" Eddleman, Mildred Fink, Albert Flamm, Alice

Fly, Dorris and Grace Garner, Donna Garner, Tom Gatlin, Coy Gertman, Anna Gilliam, Troy Glasco, Charles Glover, Mary Gray, Austin and Hazel Halterman, Bon Hartline, Rhonda Henderson, H. L. Hileman, Mary Beth Hileman, Ruel and Juanita Hindman, Glenn and Murchie Hoffner, Belva Keller, C. J. Keller, Cecil Kelley, Jerry Kennedy, Tom Kimber, Bill and Dee King, Bonnie Krause, Rita and Allen Laminack, Dorris Landreth, Randal Lawrence, Jr., Mary Light, the "Lingle Five"— Gerald, Lorene, Henry, Levi, and Donna—Ruby Lingle, Stella Lingle, Wilber Loyet, Ralph Lyerla, Hazel Lyerla, Virginia Marmaduke, Glen and Doris Middleton, Clara Bell Miller, Elaine Miller, Robert Mowery, Mercedes Mull, Gerald Neher, Charles and Rita Neighbors, Carlos Norton, Carl Nothren, Jim and Nancy O'Connor, Bill Osman, Henry Otrich, P. L. Parr, Judy Pedigo, Margaret Petty, Mev Ponder, Leon Porterfield, Charles Rendleman, Daniel and Beverly Rendleman, Gary Rendleman, Lary Rendleman, Tom and Helen Sanders, Hazel Sauerbrunn, Steve and Roselie Fulia Smith, Susie Boyer Smith, Mildred Smoot, Leroy and Ellen Spalt, Ralph Springs, Charles Stadelbacher, Geraldine (Mrs. Leo) Stadelbacher, Robert and Lou Stadelbacher, Lynn Stevenson, Herman Stokes, Frances Stout, Mathilda Stout, Brenda Sutliff, Patrick Sweeney, Viola Young Tinsley, Fred Toler, Judy Tomkins, Clara Tweedy, Glen Tweedy, James and Mary Tweedy, Jim and Kathy Van Oosting, Mildred Verble, Ray and Ellen Verble, John and Mary Vitt, Bill Wagner, Wesley Walton, Bob West, Homer Wilkins, Doris West Williams, Lela Williams, Myrtle Williams, Mary Wilburn, Caroline Wilson, Jack Yates, Ruby Yates, and Doug Young. Many of the people named here have passed away, making me aware, in a way I was not at the time I spoke with them, of how fleeting our time is here and how precious are the memories they shared with me. I have had uncounted informal conversations with people whose names do not appear here, many of whose names I do not know. To all of these people, I am grateful. One of the things I deeply value about this region is neighborliness—the generosity with which people enter into conversations with acquaintances and strangers—which makes a project such as this possible and living here rewarding.

I have relied heavily on people who oversee many forms of records: Bobby Toler, Union County clerk, and his staff; Matt Page, Union County circuit clerk, and her staff; Miss Bacon, Bob Hafeman, and Gladys Freeze, the librarians at the Stinson Memorial Library in Anna; Teddie Whitacre of the Jonesboro Library; and Patsy Rose Hoshiko and the staff at Shawnee Regional Library. I am also indebted to the librarians and staff at Southern Illinois University Morris Library, especially David Koch, director of Special Collections; Sheila Ryan and Karen Drickamer, curators of manuscripts in Special Collections; map librarians Jean Ray and Harry Davis; and social science librarians James Fox, Charles Holliday, and Walt Stubbs.

Several people have read and helpfully commented on portions of the manuscript, rescuing me from embarrassment by catching some of my more glaring errors. These include Jack Kirby, the series editor; Sonya Salamon; two anonymous reviewers; Jacquie Eddleman; Richard Cerny; Jo Cerny; Norbert Cerny; Betty Cerny; Judy Travelstead (who also, in her capacity as librarian for the *Southern Illinoisan*, searched out facts for me); and Barbara Throgmorton. Any mistakes of fact or interpretation remain, of course, entirely my own.

My intellectual debts are numerous and wide ranging. Despite early involvement in the feminist movement, I began my project far more interested in class relations than in gender and intrafamily relations; I am particularly indebted to women who have been working to reconstruct women's roles in farming and elsewhere, who have encouraged my work. Valerie Yow invited me to present a paper at the 1990 National Women's Studies Association meeting; she has since become a valued friend and colleague. Seena Kohl, Peggy Barlett, and Sonya Salamon all shared their interests with me, encouraging my efforts to maintain a focus on the social relationships in which farm women are embedded. Elizabeth Brumfiel was also very encouraging. I owe a special debt to Laura DeLind, who asked me to participate in a panel on exploitation in American agriculture she organized at the 1991 American Anthropological Association annual meetings. Much academic discourse strips analysis of its political content; Laura provided a venue in which the political implications of our agricultural system could be explored. To a considerable extent, I became able to imagine this book as engaging such issues (which I have engaged outside of academia) because of this session.

I have, in addition, drawn enormous support from people on my campus: Jill Adams, Srimiti Basu, Paula Bennett, Sarah Blackstone, Kay Carr, Kathy Flanagan, Robbie Lieberman, Kathy Ward, and Margaret Winters, members of my feminist pedagogy group, which meets weekly; Jim Allen; Alicia Chavira; Mareena Wright; Mike Batinksi; Carolyn Donow; and the many others with whom I have exchanged ideas.

Because my work entails a considerable amount of historic reconstruction, and because of my interest in farmsteads, I have drawn on the knowledge of and worked with a number of archaeologists: Michael McNerney of American Resources Group, who served as a consultant on the Union County Historical Society's 1983–84 Farmsteads Project; Jeanette Stephens, who was staff archaeologist for my 1992 field school that documented the Walton and Kimber farmsteads; Carol Morrow, Dan Haas, Mary McCorvy, and Mark Wagner, with whom I have swapped lore about the region; and architects Gail White and Robert Swenson. A number of people who are interested in local history have been very helpful, especially Kay Ripplemeyer, who has researched the Colored

Civilian Conservation Corps camp in Pomona, Illinois; Darrel Dexter; George Parks; and Herb Meyer.

Much of my knowledge of agriculture and many of my ideas were formed outside academia, working on the farm crisis with the Illinois South Project (now Illinois Stewardship Alliance). All the people I worked with are, for me, present in these pages. They include (but are not limited to) Tom Anderson, Roger Beck, Susan Denzer, Kate Deusterberg, Gayle Goold, Perry Knop, John Little, June Little, Deonne Orvis, P. L. Parr, Renée Robinson, Charles "Chuck" Snyder, and Allen Williams. In a delightful lunch hour, members of the Illinois Stewardship Alliance board of directors helped me select the photographs included here, helping sort some sixty photographs down to a manageable number. Iowa-based Prairie Fire, with its annual Rural Women's Conference, which I have attended as presenter and as participant, and Nebraska-based Center for Rural Affairs, whose summer institute I was able to attend in 1986, have also been very important in developing alternative perspectives on U.S. agriculture.

Several people have helped me with the actual work involved in assembling the data and the contents of the book: The photographs are here because of the work of Gary Kolb, who codirected the 1992 summer field school in ethnohistoric methods and documentary photography and the subsequent exhibit at the SIUC Museum, Jack Whitlock, director. Jo Ann Nast, then curator of history at the museum, arranged the exhibit, and Allen Harasimowicz installed it. The students in this field school did yeoman work, interviewing, mapping, and working with photographs. They include Elizabeth Durdle, Troy Meyer, Julie Prombo, Ron Rich, Bonita Rubach, Martin Lee Merrill, Andrea Brinkman, Jennifer Daesch, Sarah Fiola, and Dennis Spohrer. Pat McNerney made the original drawings of house plans, and John Richardson (director), Karen Fiorino, and John Vercillo at SIUC Research Photography and Illustration Facility were consistently helpful with drawings and photographs. Graduate assistants Lesa Davis, Christine Gemignani, Jian Li, Mark Wagner, and, especially, Ron Rich helped track down and enter data that appears in this book. C. W. "Doc" Horrell volunteered many hours to photograph the five farms documented in 1983–84, Donna Garner helped photograph farms we surveyed, and Suanna Wilson and her staff at Wilson's Typing Service, especially Rebecca Schwartz, transcribed the interviews.

During the ten years I have been collecting the data on which this book is based, I received financial support from a variety of sources, without which this project could not have been completed. My dissertation research was funded by the Wenner-Gren Foundation for Anthropological Research, an Illinois State Historical Society Fellowship, and University of Illinois Graduate College grants. A major grant from the Illinois Humanities Council (a regranting agency of the National Endowment of the Humanities) allowed me to reconstruct the histories of five Union County farms, and two minor grants allowed me to compile the history of the Cobden Peach Festival and collect data on nineteenth-century agrarian leaders. A summer fellowship from the American Association for State and Local History allowed me to research nineteenth-century agrarian movements in the county. Support from SIUC's College of Liberal Arts, the Department of Anthropology, the College of Communications and Fine Arts, and the Department of Cinema and Photography; the Illinois Humanities Council (with a major and a minor grant); U.S. Forest Service; Southern Illinois Arts; and SIUC Museum Associates made possible the research and exhibit associated with the summer field school. I worked with WSIU-TV to make the results of the 1990 field school available to the public through a half-hour television program, and I have used materials elicited during filmed interviews in this book. Thanks to David Kidd, producer, and Gary Wolf as well as financial support from the Illinois Humanities Council and SIUC Broadcast Services for making this project possible. Finally, my university and department have supported this work with grants and other assistance, including a summer research fellowship and a Graduate College research award; my department made graduate assistants available and supported many of the technical aspects of the project. I am especially grateful to Drs. Jon Muller and Prudence Rice, chairs of the department, and Tedi Thomas, department secretary, without whose support this project would not have been completed.

Last, but by no means least, my daughter, Dawn Roberts, and my parents, Edward and Lillian Adams, have constantly supported and contributed to this project in a myriad of tangible and intangible ways.

CHAPTER I

How I love this dear home in the

rugged Ozarks,

With its mountains of forests, those

stately old parks.

—James W. Thomas, "Monta Rosa"

The Way It Was

As I have talked with people in Union County over the past ten years, in formal interviews and informal discussions, I have become aware that there are two discrete narratives of the past. One recollection stresses the plenty provided by living on a farm: never wanting for or worrying about food, the closeness of neighbors and family, the generosity and honor with which people treated one another, and the respect for hard work. The other account stresses the hardship and poverty associated with farm life: the arduous labor that began at an early age and was frequently enforced with paddles and switches or other punishments, and the injustices inflicted by people of higher social standing or wealth. These narratives, although often told by the same person, often within one interview, are rarely brought together, except perhaps to reflect favorably on past hardships with such comments as "Hard work didn't hurt us any," or to express gratitude that those times are gone and to ask, "What good old days?" This book will retain some of these dualities, presenting both the positive and the negative sides of life, with the understanding that the two are intimately interconnected. The intent is to leave the reader with the question that seems to pervade my interviews: How might it be possible to retain the positive aspects of life as it was lived in the early years of this century, without the negative aspects? What alternative route(s) into the future might be imagined?

I believe that other tensions underlie the dualism people speak about. One pervasive set of values embodies a utilitarian, profit-oriented, future-be-damned attitude toward the land and people. The other values stewardship both of the land and of human relations. This notion of "making a living" aims more at passing on an improved environment to one's heirs than accumulating wealth and power.

Another tension, not so easily pared down into a "this" or "that" contrast, concerns women's relationship to farming. Before World War II, women were important producers of primary agricultural products, particularly dairy and poultry, and they were intimately involved in most aspects of farm life. The story of agricultural technification is in part the story of policymakers' attempts, only partially successful, to remove women from farming and make them full-time homemakers. Perhaps if we as a society had recognized that wives were as much farmers as husbands, we would have made other policy decisions and farming would be differently organized today.

At the same time policymakers have believed, and acted on, a fiction: that farming was done by individual entrepreneurs. This false assumption provided the foundation on which they built all their farm programs. By ignoring farm families' dependence on one another, they created policies that systematically undercut the bonds that tied together neighbors and kin. Some of those bonds people were glad to shed, but many others people experienced as a loss. Had those who developed agricultural policies had a keener grasp of rural social life, perhaps they would have designed their programs differently. Perhaps not. But one aim of this book is to reclaim women's roles in Union County agriculture and to create an account of the social fabric that existed before World War II. The other major aim is to trace changes in the county's social life after World War II in order to understand present relations through a "genealogy" of the past.

The Centrality of Work

Many anthropologists organize their ethnographies around key concepts, "root metaphors," or other cultural forms they see as representing larger processes in the society about which they are writing. I had not originally designed my research or my writing in such a way, but as I have worked with the materials, and with the writings of other people who focus on U.S. farm women, it seems that I have, inchoately perhaps, utilized "work" as the key concept around which I have built my project. I began my research with an assumption that I had to understand the labor process in order to make sense of historical change. Most literature on women indicated, however, that women themselves did not see their work, or the social relations in which it was effected, as central to their identities. The "doctrine of separate spheres" defined women as "homemakers"—consumers, responsible for the family's morality and health, but separated from the "men's world" of work. I found this to be inaccurate. Unlike the women Fink interviewed in Iowa, no woman I interviewed saw her work as a "sideline."[1] Most of the women seemed to identify strongly with their work, which included but was not limited to their family. Edith Rendleman, whose farm I studied and whose memoirs I edited, repeatedly made such statements as, "All I ever knew was to work," "All anybody ever wanted of me was to work," and "I really began to work [when we moved to Sublette farm]." Other women I interviewed spoke at length about the work they did, not only because I asked them about it, which I did, but because work made up most of the substance of their lives, and they were generally highly self-conscious about it, particularly the technical aspects of work—"how we did x."

Historically, people's capabilities as good workers provided one of the primary bases for evaluating their worth. People often evaluated status differences in terms of how people treated those with whom they worked: whether a person was "common" and worked alongside his or her hired hands, or whether she was a "snooty somebody" who was "too good" to do hard labor were, in the early years of this century, important characterizations. Through hard work a poor person could accumulate what Bourdieu terms "cultural capital," with the possibility of vocational advancement and access to financial credit and other means of social and economic mobility.[2] Reciprocally, a wealthy person, by indolence and arrogance, could lose status, with practical consequences of having difficulty recruiting reliable workers and losing access to needed resources. The aphorism "Shirtsleeves to shirtsleeves in three generations" remarks on a common cycling of status: a self-made man (family) raises children who maintain and possibly expand their parents' estate, while the third generation, grown soft through wealth and privilege, dissipates it. In other words, work did not just implicate the individual and that individual's technical competence and willingness to work hard; it was a defining feature of the most important relationships in which people were engaged, whether between kin and neighbors or employers and employees.

Other aspects of life were important to those I interviewed and whose memoirs I read, particularly religious beliefs and practices. These, however, are rarely recounted except in passing. It is the world of work that seems to provide the organizing principle around which social life revolved and through which individual identities were created. In this world of work-dominated daily life, courting in particular appears as a disjunctive phase, a stage that initiates new forms of work (sewing one's trousseau, seeking distant wage labor to accumulate enough money to set up independent housekeeping), removes former work obligations (not always with the willing consent of parents), and presages the assumption of adult forms of labor. Notable in accounts of this phase, however, are not the work roles involved but the strong awareness of feelings—falling in love (and in its lesser and more ephemeral form, "being struck on")—an awareness that is rarely expressed in other circumstances. In the oral histories I and others collected, courting does not appear as a major phase. It looms large, however, in Edith Rendleman's memoirs, which suggests to me that distance in time and interviewers' interests tended to submerge this important transitional phase.

In any event, work, more than any other activity, organized and gave meaning to people's lives—work enacted in the specific location of farm, family, community, and, in the background, nation. At the same time, history is important, both the lived, relatively inarticulate history of people who grow up within a tradition, a tradition that privileges work, and the conscious history that people create as they age and attempt to create a coherent story of their past.

Not everyone subscribed to the work ethic; some people were "come-easy, go-easy," and some simply were unable to manage well. But, despite the changes wrought in this ethic by the rising importance of consumption and the easing of drudgery since World War II, hard work remains a core virtue for both women and men.

Historical Memory

Farm families in southern Illinois trace their personal histories through at least two streams: their family genealogy, and the history of the farm on which they live and through which they adopt some of the history of those who once owned the land. Most of the people with whom I have spoken and whose memoirs and interviews I have read tell history as vignettes of the past that evoke the time being spoken of; like a family photo album, which is rich in meaning to family members who use the photos to recall past events and people, its meanings are largely opaque or flat to the outsider. This difference struck me when I asked some of my students to write about an exhibit at the University museum.[3] The theme was rural churches in three southern Illinois counties and had been mounted by a local woman. She presented a sample of churches from each county. Around a photograph of each church she arranged a few photographs of members of the congregation, sometimes standing as a group outside the building, sometimes working on a new addition or participating in a baptism. She had also collected items from some of the churches—an old pew, a friendship quilt, or religious objects. At the entrance to the exhibit she said she intended to show the place of the church in the rural community. I saw the exhibit as filled with people who identified with and found identity through the buildings with which they were associated. My students, except for one archaeologist who works with historic sites in southern Illinois, saw the exhibit as flat and lifeless. They saw the photographs of the people as representing alienation from the structure, which stood as a lifeless embodiment of a flattened religion. All noted the lack of an explanatory narrative that would have communicated the meaning of the church buildings to an outside public.

Great events in history, such as world wars, the influenza epidemic of 1918, or the introduction of electricity, may appear in memoirs and oral histories, as may notable individuals and their exploits. But the less visible processes of history—formation of the Rural Electric Cooperatives through which electricity was brought to rural regions (and on whose board the individual may have served); shifts in the market for agricultural commodities, as in the sharp drop in commodity prices after World War I; the general prosperity and rise in land prices after World War II—are rarely spontaneously recounted as significant events, even when people recognize their significance when questioned. Further, it seems that for most people "history" is what happened in one's childhood and early adult life.[4] Since most of the people I interviewed were born in the 1890s to 1910s, I found it difficult to obtain good oral histories for the post–World War II period.

As a "half-native" I intuitively understood the form in which history was told, and in an attempt to gather detailed data about changes in farm life I chose a strategy of learning the histories of specific farms. Like personal biographies, histories of farms are intrinsically interesting; but they have a longer life span than individual histories, and they make it possible to see shifts in rural life that individual life cycles might mask. Farm structures tend to be maintained and converted from one use to another, so the "built landscape," as geographers term it, encodes a wealth of historical knowledge. In 1984 I studied the histories of five specific farms, creating "biographies" of these farms that, at the same time, were partial biographies of the people who lived on them. In 1990, with far more resources, I reconstructed the histories of two other farms. Much of the data for this book is drawn from these studies, and so, before presenting the larger story of how farm life in general has changed, I introduce these seven farms and the families who are connected with them.[5] Their recollections reappear throughout this book.

Seven Union County Farms

The seven farms sketched here are, in general, representative of Union County farms. They were drawn from the different ecological zones of the county, and although none of the farms is located in the eastern portion of the county, they reflect most of the county's diversity (see fig. 1.1). The farms range from those in the uplands that specialized in livestock or fruits and vegetables, to bottomland grain farms. The families who raised several generations on the land represented the different settlement streams that populated the county: eighteenth-century Lutheran and Dunkard immigrants from German principalities, English and Scots-Irish colonists from the mid-South and Pennsylvania, mid-nineteenth-century German and Czech Catholic immigrants, and Upland South whites who came after the Civil War. Most of the significant religious groups are represented: Lutheran, Baptist, Presbyterian, Methodist, and Catholic. Only the Mennonites, who settled in the Mt. Pleasant area in the 1960s, do not appear in this account.

Despite this diversity, the farms show considerable similarity at each historic period. At some time all the farms housed resident laborers both in the family home and in houses on the land. All seven farms relied on family labor, but some were more like plantations, with housing for many laborers. The farms changed in comparable ways in the course of their histories, through shifting crop mix and degree of specialization, in reliance on labor and technologies, and through family members' involvement in the larger community politically and as workers and employers. Despite considerable differences in wealth and ethnic background, the women on all the farms worked hard, although not all developed ways to earn income when their poultry and dairy markets disappeared in the 1950s. Women were instrumental in founding several of the farms, with landless men marrying into landed families, and women remained important in weaving together kindreds to maintain and advance the family fortunes. In the 1990s only two of the seven farms continued to support fully the landowning families; since the 1960s the rest have rented out part or all of their farms to neighboring farmers.

The lives of these seven families can, then, be taken as representative of the area in general. Their stories, supplemented by others, will tell the

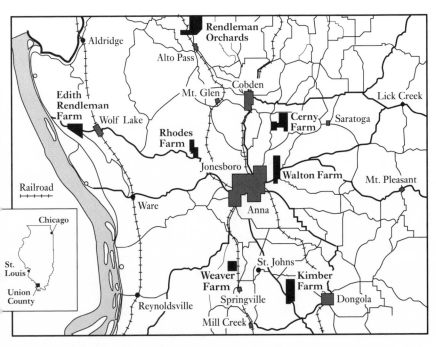

Figure 1.1. Union County, with Location of Seven Farms
Sources: Derived from Griffing 1881 and U.S. Geological Survey.
Note: Roads appear as in 1881; towns are ca. 1980.

history of how farm life has changed since the 1890s in the hills of southern Illinois.

THE WEAVER FAMILY[6]

Illinois had been a state only three years when Christopher Lyerla arrived in Union County with his family in 1821.[7] Lyerla's father was a founder of St. John's Lutheran Church in North Carolina, so it was natural that he settled close to the other members of the church, who had organized the St. John's Lutheran Church of Union County in 1817.

As with most early settlers Lyerla, who was fifty-seven years old when he arrived, brought with him several family members. Among them were his daughter, Sarah, and her husband of a year, John Weaver. Lyerla bought a quarter section from Henry and Juley Clutts, who had come earlier from the same North Carolina community. It lay astride the ridge dividing the Mill Creek and Dutch Creek Valleys and was watered by several springs. The ridge is littered with flint chips, the remains of prehistoric Indian workshops. The flint was quarried at Mill Creek and traded throughout the Mississippi Valley. The Lyerlas transmitted eighty

Aerial view of the Weaver farm. Photograph by C. William Horrell, 1984. C. William Horrell Collection, Morris Library, Southern Illinois University, Carbondale.

acres of their farm to their son-in-law in 1831. The elder Lyerla died the following year, and in 1834 Jonathan Lyerla deeded his interest in his father's real estate to his brother-in-law.

First Generation

According to oral traditions the first house sat on a knoll to the west of the later farmstead, but around 1832 John and Sarah Weaver built a log house that served as the family home for the next sixty years. This house, used later as a smokehouse and storage space, still stands. It was originally built on a ridge overlooking the juncture of two small seasonal creeks that join to flow into a branch of Mill Creek. A good spring lies just down the hill, feeding the northern branch, and probably supplied water for the house.

Many years later a springhouse was built over the spring, and the small valley became the site of the vegetable garden. It came to be called Machine Shed Hollow for the storage building in it. The log house was built in the standard style of the time: a large room downstairs with a small bedroom partitioned off at one end. Steep, narrow stairs ascend to an unfinished half-story, which was used as a bedroom and for storage of foods that needed to be kept relatively warm and dry.

The kitchen was a separate building connected by a breezeway to the house. A porch once sheltered the front of the house, and a brick chimney provided a flue for the fireplace on the eastern side of the house. Many of John and Sarah's eleven children were born in this house, and their son George and his wife, Mary (Otrich), continued to live there and raised their family within its walls.

Second Generation

The Cairo and St. Louis Narrow Gauge Railroad, later replaced by the Mobile & Ohio (later Gulf, Mobile & Ohio) was built along the eastern side of their property in the 1870s, following the route of the old Cairo-Jonesboro road. A switch was built at the cut between the Dutch Creek and Mill Creek watersheds, called Weaver Hill. This became the site of a grain storage shed, operated by one of the Weaver brothers, and a sawmill, and the trains would stop for passengers and freight. The timber that covered most of the farm in 1870 was removed (except for one portion that was never cut) and used in farm structures and sold to the sawmill.

Before George's death at age forty-five, in 1884, he built a large Victorian-style, two-story house on the ridge across the spring from his parents' house. George and Mary's son, Bruno, and his wife, Minnie (Sauerbrunn), moved into this house with Mary when they were married in 1907. Mary stayed in this house until she died in 1917, after which it housed families who worked for the Weavers. When it burned in 1927, they built a small house for Oscar "Dutch" Lingle and his family, who had been living in it and working for the Weavers.

Mary oversaw the building of a large, banked, post-and-beam horse barn in 1891. The basement of carefully cut limestone was accessible from the southern slope of the hill on which the barn was built, and the first floor was accessible by an earth and plank ramp built on the northern side. The Weavers raised livestock, wheat, and some small fruits and vegetables, including sweet potatoes, for which they built a heated, sawdust-insulated potato house.

Third Generation

In 1915 Bruno and Minnie, parents of a five-year-old son, Charles, pulled the log house back from the promontory on which it stood and built a one-story "plains style" house on the site.[8] Families who helped with the farm work continued to live in the log house, and an elderly woman who lived there for many years attached a privy to the front porch as she grew frail. In 1960, after Bruno died, Minnie added indoor plumbing to the frame house. When old age forced her to move in with Charles and his wife, Ruby (Coomes), the frame house was left vacant, and in 1980 it was torn down.

Minnie had a large chicken and egg business and tended several cows. With the money from the dairy and poultry she—like most women of her generation—was able to feed and clothe the family. She built a chicken house by converting an existing machine shed and adding a brooder house, doing the construction work herself. Bruno owned a steam engine and wheat and clover separators with which he threshed wheat and clover for farmers in the area. In the 1920s he bought his first tractor, and in 1935 Charles went in with him on a new threshing outfit, which they operated as partners. Bruno rented out much of the wheat ground, focusing on livestock and vegetables, especially sweet potatoes, in addition to a wheat-clover-corn rotation on the land they farmed themselves.

Fourth Generation

In 1922 Bruno and Minnie acquired the Barnhart farm, directly across from St. John's Church. He channelized the creek and repaired the house Jacob Barnhart had built in 1883 and used it to house tenants who worked that farm. In 1938 Charles and Ruby moved into the house. Ruby, like her mother-in-law, kept chickens and dairy cows to cover household expenses. In 1946 Charles and Ruby moved to the small house that had been built for Dutch Lingle on the home place, and Charles's sister, Cleda, and her husband, Wayne Vaughn, moved into the Barnhart house and farmed that land. Wayne terraced the hills and established a crop rotation, for which he was named "conservation farmer of the year" by the county Extension Service.

Fifth Generation

The Vaughns moved to his home farm in 1958, and the Barnhart house remained vacant until Charles and Ruby's son, George, and his new wife, Marita (Hogue), moved there in 1960. The seventy-seven-year-old house was showing its age. It had extensive termite damage, the roof and sills were in need of repair, and it required general renovation. The yellow poplar framing, however, was still intact, and over the next several years the young couple, unable to obtain a loan to improve it, remodeled the house as they lived in it.

When her husband died, Ruby Weaver moved to Anna, and her son and daughter-in-law rented out her small house. George and Marita both developed careers as teachers, he in the forestry department at Southern Illinois University and she at John A. Logan College until the late 1980s when George became chair of the forestry department at the University of Kentucky. For many years a neighbor farmed the land, except for a small beef herd that the Weavers maintained. Ruby Weaver died in 1988, George in 1993.

THE CERNY FARM[9]

The Norbert and Betty Cerny family lives in what may be the oldest frame house in Union County.[10] According to Green family traditions, it was built in 1844 by David Green. One of the first settlers in what became Union County (then Randolph County), he arrived with his parents and his uncle's family from North Carolina in 1805 when Illinois was still a territory. The Greens settled in the bottoms along Clear Creek. David's father died not long after their arrival, but the young boy was raised by his uncle and cousins, who established a ferry across the Mississippi.

A series of severe floods, beginning in 1844, drove many residents of the bottoms to higher ground. David Green was reputed to have been among the first to leave, relocating just west of Saratoga. Saratoga in 1844 was a promising mineral spa and resort. Stagecoaches passed through, and that year a post office was established in a store owned by A. Cover, just west of the village. A sawmill must have been operating nearby, for Green built a substantial house, using milled lumber for most of its construction.

The house was built on much the same design as other log houses of that period. The main part of the house was a rectangle measuring about 20 by 30 feet. This was divided into a 20-by-20-foot main room with a central front door, a 9-by-10-foot bedroom, and a small front room that also opened onto the front porch. Twenty-foot logs, their bark left on, formed the floor joists. Stairs led to the unpartitioned second story. A fireplace took up much of the end of the main room. Upstairs, five windows on the front and three windows on the back gave a great deal of light.

As was common at the time, the kitchen was separated from the house by a breezeway. The kitchen was 12 by 14 feet, with a fireplace on the far end. The main room was large enough to hold two sets in square dancing, neighbor Al Basler recalled. The joists were resilient and, when people really got dancing, the floor would roll up and down.

Coming of the Illinois Central

With the Illinois Central Railroad being built in the 1850s, Green bought land on the right-of-way and established a store and boarding house just south of what was to become Cobden, at Green's Crossing. Tradition has it that Sir Richard Cobden, for whom the railroad named the village, stayed in Green's hotel when he came to inspect the railroad for its British investors. Green bought the first lot in the village that became Cobden, then named South Pass, where he moved his store.

For the next 100 years the farm was worked by tenants. The census of 1860 shows that David Green owned 1,100 acres of land, of which only 150 acres were cleared. His farm implements and machinery were valued at only $150, while his livestock was valued at $1,600. He had eighteen horses and mules, six working oxen, thirty-one head of cattle, ten sheep, and thirty swine. The major crops were wheat and Indian corn, and he also raised some hay, Irish potatoes, orchard products, and peas and beans. The oxen suggest that he was also active in timbering or other activities that required hauling heavy loads.

David died in 1877, and his farm went to a son, Nathaniel. Like his father, Nathaniel was interested mostly in the store, and he left the farm operation to tenants. His son, Emery, was the last Green to own the grocery and farm.

The Cerny Story

About the same time David Green moved to Green's Crossing, John Cerny and his family arrived in Union County from Bohemia. They quickly bought land and established themselves, for the 1860 census indicates they were living in Hileman Precinct with a Dongola address, farming forty-nine acres valued at $400. Their farm implements and machinery were valued at only $60, while the livestock was worth $155. They had one horse, two working oxen, six head of cattle, and fifteen hogs. It appears that John had brought agricultural notions with him from the Old World, for that first census year they raised 100 pounds of hops, 50 pounds of flax, and 1 pound of flaxseed. They also raised wheat, rye, corn, oats, Irish and sweet potatoes, hay, and fruits from an orchard.

John died in 1871; his wife, Mary Magdalena, outlived him by thirty-five years, dying in 1906. In 1883 their youngest son, Jacob—the only child born in this country—married Margaret Basler. Within a few years he bought a small farm adjoining the Green farm, joining other German-speaking Catholics who established truck farms east of Cobden. From logs cut from his land and sawed at his brother's sawmill, he built an eight-room house in 1890.

Jacob specialized in large draft horses, particularly Percherons. Shortly after the turn of the century he bought the Green farm at Green's Crossing and built the large house and stock barn that in 1994 still stood as

Aerial view of the Cerny farm. Photo by C. William Horrell, 1984. C. William Horrell Collection, Morris Library, Southern Illinois University, Carbondale.

landmarks just south of the Cobden village limits. He named this farm Willow Springs Stock Farm; the home farm he named Spring Valley, a name it retained. He also raised large amounts of vegetables and put in large hot beds, which the Cernys continued to use to start their tomato plants.

When his sons married, Jacob sold Willow Springs Stock Farm and retired into town. His oldest son, John M., bought the home place and continued to operate it. John and his wife, Elizabeth (Bigler), had four

sons, Hugh, Lawrence, Norbert, and Richard. The sons, back from World War II, persuaded their father to invest in modern farm equipment, but aside from the technological changes, they continued farming much as Jacob had, concentrating on the newly developed Polled Hereford cattle, small fruits, and vegetables.

After World War II, the development of supermarkets and agricultural specialization forced small general stores out of business. Emery Green sold the store in 1946, and in 1948, approaching retirement, he sold the old home farm to his neighbor, John M. Cerny. With the enlarged acreage, John took his sons Hugh and Norbert into partnership. Hugh died in 1949, and when John died in 1956, Norbert joined with his other brothers, Lawrence and Richard, to continue farming the land as partners. The operation is one of the most diversified in the region. Polled Hereford cattle, sold as beef and as breeding stock, and tomatoes, along with hay and some grain, provide most of the farm's income.

Lawrence never married and continued to live in the original house with his mother, who died in 1993 at age 100. In 1965 Richard bought acreage and a modest house near the home farm from another branch of the Green family and in 1966 moved into it with his new wife, Jo. In 1970 Richard and Jo built a new home, visible from the recently built highway that replaced old U.S. 51. One sister, Catherine, worked at the Cobden bank, became its vice-president, and built a house on the farm; the other sister, Dorothy, left the immediate area with her husband.

Remodeling the Green House

When Norbert married Betty Nebughr in 1955, the original Green home was remodeled for the newlyweds. The kitchen was torn down, and a modern kitchen was added, with an inside entrance to the basement. The twenty-foot span across the main room proved too long for the beams to hold, and the ceiling sagged. The Cernys jacked up the floor from the basement and put a bearing wall down the middle of the main room, making separate living and dining rooms. They also added a bedroom on the northern end of the first floor and divided the upstairs into two bedrooms, covering two of the upstairs windows. The house had been without either bathrooms or closets, and they added these features upstairs and down. They landscaped and furnished the remodeled house with mementos of the past, including a cast-iron kettle, a cream separator, a dinner bell, and a millstone, found on the creek and probably from a gristmill recalled through oral traditions. Quilts and handsome antique furniture, some of it from the Catholic school in Cobden that was sold when the school closed, added to the interior of the house. Betty developed a large poultry operation, establishing an egg route that supplied friends and neighbors. Despite the fact that in the 1960s the eggs stopped covering the costs of raising the chickens, Betty continued to maintain her flock because her customers valued the eggs. As her father aged, Betty and her sisters also helped him at the drugstore he operated in Cobden, until he finally retired in the mid-1980s.

Norbert and Betty's children entered professions, and several located in the area, where they help with the farm work at peak periods. One son, Tom, bought a neighbor's farm after the neighbor died. Tom plans to build a house on it, but not to farm. The younger two of Richard and Jo's three children, Theresa and Eric, are more agriculturally inclined.

Theresa developed an herb and flower operation, and Eric experiments with a variety of horticultural techniques and vegetable varieties. In 1991 and 1993 Theresa worked as an intern on a French horticultural operation. In 1994, however, it was unclear whether or not any of the fifth generation of Union County Cernys would continue the farm operation when their parents retire. The family is active in the Catholic church, farm organizations, and school and civic activities. In 1991 the Cerny families were participants in the Smithsonian Folklife Festival, with its theme of the midwestern family farm.

THE RHODES FAMILY[11]

The Gold Rush was on when William S. "Bill" Rhodes's grandfather bought the farm on Caney Creek from the U.S. government for $1.25 an acre. By 1849 the choice lands were already claimed, so John N. Rhodes, arriving from Kentucky, bought forty acres spanning the narrow but fertile creek bottom. The log house he built at that time housed three generations of the Rhodes family. John located the house just below a good spring that, until a cistern was dug in 1899, provided the family's water.

Many of the original log structures remain. The house was built in the southern style, with the kitchen a separate room off the back of the main house. Its massive logs were whitewashed with kaolin from the clay pits not far east of the farm. Nearby a log smokehouse preserved the family meat supply. Canned food and food that needed to be kept cool were stored in the smokehouse as well.

Bill Rhodes recalled his home in the early years of this century: large cast-iron kettles sat behind the kitchen and behind that stood the chicken house, with the privy at the back of the yard area. On the northern side of the house, clotheslines defined the back of the yard. The woodpile was located here, with dry storage beside the kitchen and the house for immediate use.

Maude Kinder, Bill Rhodes's sister, recalled that neighborhood men came Sunday afternoons to play croquet. Between these games and the chickens, geese, and ducks, the grass was kept cropped and the lawn never needed mowing. A large garden for home use was laid out south of the house, between it and the barn lot. A 40-by-50-foot hotbed, in which thousands of tomato plants were started for their commercial crops, was bounded by the garden on the end closest to the house.

During the twentieth century the Rhodes farm, like many in Union County, produced large amounts of small fruits and vegetables. The 1870 census indicates that horticulture was not one of John N.'s specialties: the farm produced only $50 worth of orchard products, but 100 pounds of

Aerial view of the Rhodes farm. Photo by C. William Horrell, 1984. C. William Horrell Collection, Morris Library, Southern Illinois University, Carbondale.

butter, 70 gallons of molasses, and wheat, Indian corn, and some Irish potatoes. During the 1800s a farm needed relatively little equipment: the 1870 census indicated that the cash value of farming implements and machinery was only $20, while the value of Rhodes's livestock was $200. The livestock that year consisted of a mule, six cows (two for milking),

18   The Way It Was

seven sheep, and twelve swine. The sheep were probably kept for their wool, which would have been carded in a mill in Jonesboro and then spun and woven by Mrs. Rhodes.

Even at this early date the Rhodes farm produced sorghum, a trade that was passed on to John's sons. Bill Rhodes recalled the sorghum mill his father and uncle bought in 1908. Neighbors brought lard cans to hold the sorghum molasses, which the brothers sold for six cents a gallon.

The Second Generation

In 1896 William Thomas "W. T." Rhodes, one of John's sons, married Fannie Barnet Simpson, who lived in the then-bustling village of Mountain Glen and was the town's correspondent to the county newspaper, the Jonesboro *Gazette*.[12] W. T. kept the home place, while his twin brother bought an adjoining farm to the north.

W. T. and Fannie reared two boys and four girls, and with their help expanded the operation; they were able to send four of the six children to college. In the 1910s, with the family growing, the Rhodeses added a small bedroom on the southern end of the house, weatherboarded the house, framed in the breezeway, and added a porch on the front. The old picket fence was replaced with woven wire. During this same period the miles of split rail fences that enclosed every field were replaced with woven and barbed wire.

The first twenty years of this century were good for farmers, with agricultural prices rising to their peak during World War I. W. T., with his brothers, added to their holdings until they had put together a farm of about 300 acres. Hired hands and tenants lived in log houses left from their original owners. Just at the end of this period, in 1921, they replaced the old log barn with a frame stock barn. The ample hayloft and stalls with mangers attest to the importance of horses and mules. W. T., with his two sons and the three workmen they hired for twenty-five cents an hour, signed their names in the loft.

Construction work and other skilled labor paid well compared with agricultural labor, which during this period paid ten cents an hour for men, five cents for women and children. The standard workday was ten hours.

Horticultural products were a major cash crop. "[My father] was growing strawberries and blackberries and spinach as long as I can remember," Bill Rhodes recalled. "Vegetable growing used to be a big business. All these towns around—Cobden, Anna, Alto Pass, Jonesboro, Mountain Glen, Mill Creek, Balcom, Dongola—they had loading places everywhere you could see. Now there is very little. . . . One time when the Anna streetcar was running, they had a pickup at the Jonesboro Courthouse," Rhodes said. "You could load your vegetables on there."

The Third Generation

When W. T. died the farm was split up among the children: Bill Rhodes, Maude Kinder, Anna Rhodes, and Myrtle Boyd. Bill and his wife, Dorothy (Lingle), continued to live in the home place. After World War II Bill worked part time for the Department of Agriculture checking compliance with acreage set-asides and in the 1960s shifted from mixed vegetable and livestock farming to grains and livestock. In the 1950s they remodeled their house, pulling the original log kitchen back and adding a modern kitchen and porch to the back. Aside from adding electricity when it became available, however, they kept the house very much as it had always been. After Dorothy died, Bill moved into senior citizens' housing in Jonesboro and rented the farmland and barnlot to a neighbor who ran beef cattle on the farm.

The Fourth Generation

After Bill's death in 1986, at the age of eighty-seven, one son bought out his siblings. He added a bathroom to the house and rented it out. Small hill farms with a strip of fertile bottomland can no longer support a family, and the fourth generation has not stayed to take over the old farm.

THE RENDLEMAN FARM[13]

The house Edith Rendleman lived in until an illness in 1989 was once part of the vast holdings Jesse Ware, a lawyer, financier, and politician, accumulated in the Union County bottoms during the late 1800s. He had the house built for his tenants around 1907. The 240-acre farm is a short distance west of Wolf Lake, not far from the Running Lake crossing. During the late 1800s much of the land in the bottoms was acquired by merchants and industrialists who lived in area towns and more distant cities.

Ware was involved in a number of corporate ventures in Union County; he was associated with the Commercial Bank of St. Louis and with the construction of what became the Illinois Central Railroad through the bottoms. He was also a state senator in Illinois. Parcel by parcel, he put together an estate of thousands of acres. The village of Ware is named after him. He died in 1908, and the land passed to his children, Charles and Anna. Charles visited Wolf Lake, Edith Rendleman recounted, in a private railroad car with a staff of servants. He fixed up a small house that he used for summer visits and later built a large house on the bank of Running Lake.[14]

Edith Rendleman's father, Elijah "Lije" Bradley, was a tenant on a farm owned by Bruno Rixleben, a Jonesboro store owner. The farm was just across Running Lake from Ware's farm, by the Turner Brown crossing. Bradley came with his parents to southern Illinois in the 1880s from Kentucky, where his father had been a coal miner. At the time Ware was building up his holdings, the Bradleys were working as laborers on southern Illinois farms. They settled in the Beech Grove area, west of Alto Pass on Hutchins Creek. There, in 1894, Elijah married Sarah Penrod Grammer, widow of Hugh Grammer.

Aerial view of the Edith Rendleman farm. Photo by C. William Horrell, 1984. C. William Horrell Collection, Morris Library, Southern Illinois University, Carbondale.

Sarah had four young boys when she and Elijah were married, and she soon had another son and, in 1898, a daughter, Edith. Elijah kept moving the family further down into the bottoms, to larger and more lucrative farms, until in 1909 they moved onto the 300-acre Bruno Rixleben farm. He farmed for the Rixlebens for the next forty years, raising wheat, corn, and hogs. Sarah had a large poultry operation and milked cows, selling the cream as butter.

Edith Rendleman recalled that her mother leached lye from ashes to make soap, using cracklings from rendering lard as the base. She also used lye to make hominy from the white corn they grew, and to scrub the splintery pine flooring. Stove wood came from willows that grew on the river banks and bars. Most of their food was supplied by the farm.

There were many tramps that came by and wanted a handout, Edith recalled of her childhood. "My mother always fed them. She never turned anybody away without fixing them something to eat." The family occa-

sionally took in elderly persons who had no relatives to care for them and who, without any Social Security, had no other means of supporting themselves.

Lije, with the help of his large family, was able to develop a substantial operation, with teams of horses and mules, good equipment, and eventually a threshing outfit. He had Rixleben build houses for the hired hands who were needed to help run the large farm and, as the sons left home, kept other hands in the house.

After World War I the bottom fell out of the market for agricultural products, especially wheat, the major cash crop in the bottoms. Charles Ware was involved in other business interests and, in 1924, gave his interest in the land to his sister, Anna. She mortgaged the property, which was foreclosed in 1929. By this time Anna lived in St. Louis, and a number of investors had purchased interests in the note. According to the abstract of the deed, in 1932 Elijah Bradley purchased the farm for $12.50 an acre.

The Bradleys made some repairs on the house but maintained it as a tenant house for the family who farmed the land. They pulled the small house Charles Ware had used for a summer cottage closer to the main house and fixed it up for Elijah's sister. After she moved out, the cottage was used for tenants.

Meanwhile, in 1919 their daughter, Edith, married William Rendleman, son of the founder of the town of Wolf Lake. They continued to farm in the immediate area and had a daughter and three sons, one of whom died in infancy. In 1948 Edith lost her father, her mother, and her husband. She inherited the old Ware farm and, the next year, moved to that farm with her son Lee Roy, who with his older brother, W. P. "Bud," farmed the land.

They remodeled the house completely. Electricity had recently been brought in by the Rural Electrification Administration, and they put in modern wiring. "Electricity was a godsend to farmers," Edith recalled. "They never could have a bathroom until we got electricity." They installed plumbing, built closets, changed some interior walls and the location of the stairs, added a kitchen, and made the old kitchen into a dining room. She replaced the old safes and buffets with built-in kitchen cabinets. They finished digging out the basement, which her father had begun, put in a solid foundation, and replaced the old wooden shingles with a new roof. By the time construction was completed, the house was a fully modern home.

Edith had always been active in local civic organizations; her parents had belonged to the International Order of Odd Fellows, and she joined its women's affiliate, the Rebekahs, and the Masonic affiliate, Order of the Eastern Star. She became a charter member of the Home Bureau, helping organize it in 1949; was active in the garden club; and was involved in various other school and community activities.

When Edith and her son moved to the farm, Edith still raised chickens for market, and her sons raised cattle and pigs. Edith soon retired from her poultry operation, and by the early 1980s her sons had gotten completely out of livestock and concentrated entirely on grain crops. Modern grain storage bins replaced the old shed; they tore down one barn and converted the other to store equipment. None of Edith's grandchildren has entered farming, and during the farm crisis of the mid-1980s, most of the farms operated by younger families in the bottoms failed.

RENDLEMAN ORCHARDS[15]

Rendleman Orchards, now operated by Wayne "Ren" Rendleman Sirles and his wife, Betty, has been in the family four generations. In 1875, John Rendleman and his wife, Isobella (Keith) bought her uncle Cyrus Keith's 180-acre estate. The family moved from near John's father's farm on the Buttermilk Crossing road south of Alto Pass to the farm just south of the Union-Jackson county line.

John worked for a Chicago fruit commission house during the 1880s but did not have extensive orchards. His son, Grover, took over the farm on his father's retirement. Three large stock barns testified to his mule trading interests. "My grandfather got his start in business in mule trading and mule breaking and selling," Ren Sirles recounted. "He had at one time 167 head of mules on this farm. The most mules he ever had in harness at one time on this farm was 33 teams—66 head. He would not sell mules to the coal mines because they would go blind from working underground so long. He sold a lot of mules to the South."

The original home, still occupied by Helen Sirles, Grover's daughter, was probably built before 1875. Through the years the house was enlarged beyond the original three rooms, with a bay window added between 1887 and 1898. Later the porch was enclosed, and electric wiring and plumbing were added.

In the 1920s Grover Rendleman and his nearby neighbors ran an electric line into the local generator in Alto Pass. According to oral tradition, when Central Illinois Public Service took over the Alto Pass electric system, the farmers, with difficulty, sold the rural line to the reluctant utility.

The Rendleman house was a center of social activities. The large dining room was used to feed visitors and workers. "You always cooked big on Sunday," Helen Sirles recalled, "because you didn't know who would be there. You would be very unhappy if you didn't have a bunch of company." Helen Sirles said that years ago many people worked for room and board and received only a small wage. They slept in houses provided for them, but they ate in the main house. Mrs. Rendleman and her daughters prepared the meals from canned and fresh foods they processed on the farm. "The women would be the last ones to go to bed," Helen Sirles recalled. "Everybody else including the husbands would be in bed, and they would still be doing things, getting ready for the next morning. They would be the first ones up."

Before the orchards were planted in the 1910s, the Rendlemans raised acres of asparagus, rhubarb, and sweet potatoes. Grover took the asparagus to Du Quoin, where it was canned under his private label. Helen recounted, "Every morning we children had to go and cut two rows down and come back, before we got ready to go to school."

Grover was active in community affairs, in addition to his farming interests. His obituary said "he was instrumental in organizing the Union County Farm Bureau and had been a director in the Farmers State Bank of Alto Pass for many years." His son, James, took over the home farm and also served as director and president of the Farmers State Bank of Alto Pass and participated in other community activities, responsibilities that passed on to his nephew Ren Sirles.

Aerial view of Rendleman Orchards. Photo by C. William Horrell, 1984. C. William Horrell Collection, Morris Library, Southern Illinois University, Carbondale.

The orchard business experienced alternating booms and busts. After great prosperity during World War I, when many farmers put in orchards, farming in general went into a prolonged slump. Despite bumper crops in the early 1930s, there was no market for the produce. "People said the farmers were the fattest people yet going to the poor house," Helen quipped. "You couldn't sell things, but we always had plenty of food to eat."

Price controls established during World War II set a price of $3.96 a bushel for peaches, which helped growers get back on their feet. "After

the war we did all right till forty-eight or forty-nine when the bust came," Ren Sirles recounted. "And I mean it really busted. . . . In the late forties and into the fifties you could run from Alto to Cobden and almost to Anna and never get out of a peach orchard. It lasted for about ten years."

Grover, with his son, James, and widowed daughter, Helen, kept the orchard going. In 1962 they erected a modern packing shed and in 1971 built a large cold storage building. Other coolers, workers' housing, sheds, and storage buildings were added or made over from older structures.

Grover died in 1968, only a few feet from the bedroom in which he was born. Helen's son, Ren, joined the business and, on his Uncle James's death in 1979, incorporated the well-known farm as Rendleman Orchards, Inc. Helen continued to act as bookkeeper for the enterprise but passed on managerial responsibility to her son and daughter-in-law, Betty, and their children.

THE WALTON FARM[16]

James K. "J. K." and Serena Walton founded the Walton farm, just east of Anna, in the mid-1850s. J. K., born in Pennsylvania, worked for the Illinois Central Railroad as a road grader. He arrived in Union County in 1853 and married Serena Davie Walker in 1854. Serena Davie's family was probably the wealthiest in Union County: Her mother Anna's family, the Willards, were among the earliest settlers in Jonesboro, and Anna's brother Willis was the most prominent landowner and merchant in the area; Serena's father, Winstead Davie, was a prominent merchant and landowner, the founder of the new town of Anna, and one of the largest landholders in the county.[17] In 1855 Serena and J. K. bought 160 acres just east of Anna from Davie, adding to the farm until it contained 440 acres, 160 in Serena's name. They also bought land in the bottoms, much of it during the agricultural depression of the mid-1870s; by 1883, these holdings had reached 1,500 acres. They must have prospered during the Civil War, because not long after it ended, they imported a carpenter from Pennsylvania to build their post-and-beam barn and began building a two-story brick home, which they completed in 1869.

J. K. and Serena had seven sons and two daughters; one boy and one girl died in infancy. Some of their sons operated land their parents owned in the Mississippi bottoms; one son, Edward B. "E. B.," stayed on the home farm, inheriting it when Serena died in 1909. J. K. specialized in hay, wheat, corn, and stock, which probably included cattle and sheep, as well as draft stock and racing horses; his biographer in the 1883 county history characterized his farm as "a model farm, [which] displays in every design and improvement the good taste and judgment of its owner."[18]

The Second Generation

J. K. died in 1886, when E. B. was twenty-three years old, and E. B. operated the farm with his mother. During the 1890s they began a dairy operation, perhaps responding to new opportunities provided by a cooperative creamery in which Serena held an interest.[19] The creamery failed, but the Walton dairy continued, with daily deliveries to homes in town. The Waltons appear to have begun growing small fruits and vegetables and set out a peach orchard during this period as well. With increased labor needs they oversaw the building of three new tenant houses; five families already lived on the farm in log houses that may have pre-dated the Walton's acquisition of the farm.

E. B.'s wife, Kate Seastone, an artist, died without having borne any children. In 1906, when he was forty-three years old, E. B. married the recently divorced Louise Kroh, mother of a small son, and two years later their only child, Edward D. "Ned," was born. Louise was the daughter of a minister who was very active in political affairs. According to her granddaughter, Barbara Throgmorton, she was a cultured woman who earned enough money from her poultry operation and music lessons to buy a small farm and an automobile. She also played opera on the phonograph while she served the threshing crews their dinner. Around the turn of the century they extended an electric line from town for the main house and barn.

Throughout the nineteenth century and at least into the 1920s the Waltons always had hired hands living in the house. The men lived in an upstairs room with an outside entrance; a maid generally lived in a small downstairs room off the kitchen. In the 1930s E. B.'s adventurous brother William came home and lived with them until his death in 1936.

The Third Generation

In 1931 Ned married the daughter of an area box manufacturer, Rosemary Gunn, who was teaching in the Alto Pass school. During the depression the Waltons maintained their basic mix of dairy, strawberries, sweet potatoes, and orchard, with apples, particularly early transparent apples, replacing peaches. They sold their dairy distribution business to Anna Producers Dairy when it was organized in 1931, but they continued to provide milk and cream to the new business for a number of years, finally selling their dairy herd by the end of the decade. Rosemary did not maintain Louise's poultry operation, but she made cottage cheese that she sold to customers in town, and for a short while she worked in the shoe factory. Cash was so scarce that Rosemary recalled that once they were unable to afford a three-cent stamp. One of their tenants, Ed Brimm, remembered that one Christmas he had only $3.00 and he was unable to buy any gifts for his children. With World War II the agricultural economy revived, and the farm began to prosper once more. Labor was extremely scarce, but some of the larger growers, including the Waltons, were able to get German prisoners of war, housed in a nearby Civilian Conservation Corps (CCC) camp, to pick their crops.

After the war the migrant stream resumed for a few years, leaving Barbara Throgmorton with vivid recollections of the migrants' abject poverty. People who worked for the Waltons during that period recalled that they were unusually generous to and respectful of their help. This may be why the families who settled on the Walton farm stayed for so many years. Ed Brimm, who was born on the farm and who remained on it his entire life, estimated that over 100 children were raised on the farm.

Louise and E. B. died within a year of each other, in 1946 and 1947.

Aerial view of Walton farm. Walton Collection, Morris Library, Southern Illinois University, Carbondale.

Ned and Rosemary had two young children, Wesley, born in 1934, and Barbara, born in 1942. They tore out the apple orchard in the early 1950s and planted permanent pasture, experimenting with beef cattle and row crops. With Wesley old enough to help, Ned developed custom combining and custom hay-baling operations, and Rosemary returned to teaching in order to supplement the family's income. In 1948 they renovated the house, adding a modern kitchen.

The Fourth Generation

Wesley went on to get a doctorate in classics. Barbara earned a teaching degree, then married an Anna boy, David Diefenbach, who had become an Air Force pilot, and moved away. Ned died of a massive heart attack in 1964, and Rosemary rented the operation to a neighbor, who in 1994 still rented the cropland and some pasture land for his beef cattle. Rosemary had one of the newer tenant houses pulled close to her house and renovated, so the last remaining tenant family, Ed and Christina Brimm, could keep her company. Over the years, as Anna expanded eastward, they sold parcels of the farm that lay south of the highway. When Barbara's husband was killed in a training accident in 1971, leaving her with an infant son and recovering from breast cancer, she returned home. In 1982, when her son was old enough to help out, she began a small sheep operation, largely as an activity that she could do with her son. In 1988 her son was killed in an auto accident, but by now the sheep operation had become a major enterprise, supporting itself through sales of wool, breeding stock, custom butchering, finished hides, and other specialty items. A year and a half later Barbara remarried, to Marlin Throgmorton, and in 1992 her mother died just after her eightieth birthday, leaving Barbara the farm. Barbara is active in civic and church affairs and worked with the reorganization of the regional wool pool, a wool selling cooperative. In addition, she hosts tours of the farm for visiting groups.

THE KIMBER FARM[20]

In 1848 Elizabeth Davidson, born in Union County and twice previously married, wed Valentine Kimber, a recent arrival in Union County. Kimber was a Methodist minister and a carpenter by trade. They bought a 180-acre farm from her father, adjoining his, near the crossroads settlement of Peru (pronounced Pee'roo) on the main road between Jonesboro and Caledonia, on the Ohio River. Her grandparents, Mosias and Elizabeth Davidson, were original homesteaders; her father had been sheriff and county clerk and had held other county offices. In a county where, in 1850, only 36 percent of women (and 71 percent of men) were literate, Elizabeth's parents believed in education: in 1845, twenty-one-year-old

Elizabeth received a certificate from a Jonesboro school, and her brothers attended McKendree College at Lebanon, Illinois, founded by the Methodist Church in 1835. The Kimbers first lived in a two-room cabin and erected a large log barn, and then Valentine began building a comfortable two-story house with a large el. Across a breezeway the original log house became their kitchen and dining room. Valentine established a steam sawmill on the creek below the house and went into business cutting lumber. Elizabeth bore three girls and a boy, and the couple adopted a girl whose unmarried mother abandoned her. They took in other dependents as well: The 1860 census lists a nine-year-old boy for whom Valentine was guardian, and the 1870 census lists a sixty-seven-year-old man residing with the family.

The Second Generation

After the Civil War the Kimbers appear to have fallen on hard times and, in 1872, they sold fifty acres from their farm. Their only son, Morris, stayed at home to help his aging parents. In 1896, three years after his father's death, at the age of thirty-four he married Edna L. Avitt. She had five sons; one died in infancy and another died of influenza in 1920. Like many women of her age, Edna developed a large poultry operation. The housework was so demanding that she wrote on the back of a photograph of the house showing the summer kitchen, "This house is a woman-killer."

Morris did not maintain the lumber mill but expanded into small fruits, especially raspberries and strawberries, and sweet potatoes. He helped organize the Union County Farm Bureau in 1917 and participated in their promotion of Latham raspberries. In the mid-1920s, with his growing sons, Merrill, Paul, and Frank, to help, he built a gambrel-roofed bank barn he designed himself. Two families lived in tenant houses on the farm and helped with the crops.

The Third Generation

Merrill had no interest in the farm and left home to work on the railroad after he married. Paul married Josie Cauble in the late 1920s and built a small house just south of his parents' home. A few years later Frank married Helen Plott and rented a farm near Anna, across the road from Helen's father. Morris died in 1934, and Frank and Helen moved with their infant son, Bob, to Frank's home to help Edna. In the 1930s Frank and Helen bought an adjoining farm when the owner was unable to pay his taxes on it. The two brothers and their families, each with a son and a daughter, divided the farm, forming a loose partnership. When their brother Merrill lost his job during the depression and came home, they helped him. Merrill and his wife, Lorene, soon opened a restaurant in Dongola they called the Blue Willow, which they operated until World

Aerial view of Kimber farm. Kimber Collection, Morris Library, Southern Illinois University, Carbondale.

War II, when Merrill got a job with the Illinois Central Railroad, where he worked until he died in 1954. During this period, Edna went to live with Merrill and Lorene, where she stayed until she died in 1950.

Soon after Edna left, in the mid-1940s, her sister-in-law Florence, who had never married, became too old to adequately care for herself. Florence had supported herself by taking in boarders, ironing, and babysitting in the large house she rented in Anna, retiring to a two-room house in Jonesboro, where she lived on a meager income. Frank and Helen converted one of the front rooms into a bedroom, and Florence lived there until she died in 1953 at the age of ninety-five.

Like Morris, and like Helen's father, Frank and Helen were active in the Farm Bureau and in Farm Extension and joined the local Rural

Electric Cooperative in 1940, and Helen and her sister were among the original members of the Home Bureau when it organized in 1949. The Kimbers specialized in sweet potatoes, although they also raised strawberries, cucumbers, and other vegetables. They raised as many as 7,000 bushels on their farm and bought sweet potatoes from other farmers that they cured and packed, using a machine Frank invented to brush and polish them.[21] During World War II they faced severe labor shortages, but after the war the migrant stream briefly resumed, leaving Frank and Helen's daughter, Jacquie, with vivid impressions of the deprivation many of these migrant families experienced. With help from Helen's father, who had been very successful raising peaches during the war, Frank put in a peach orchard.

Industrial jobs soon became more attractive than farming, and the Kimbers found they could not get good help. At the same time the market for fruits and vegetables began to disappear. Curtis Smith, who had worked for the Kimbers and wanted to keep farming, recalled, "They quit growing fruits and vegetables so much and went to other stuff and so the young folks growed up, well they headed out for the city, got work." The Kimbers turned to raising beef cattle, bought a self-propelled combine, and did custom combining in the 1950s. In 1953 Paul and Josie moved to Waukegan, Illinois, where Paul worked in a factory. Helen wanted the children to go to college and desired modern conveniences, so she found a job at the Anna State Mental Hospital. They remodeled the house, putting in a modern kitchen and bathroom and a picnic table for summer eating. Jacquie recalled her father, who did not like the indoor toilet, remarking, "Times are really different. We used to shit outside and eat inside. Now we shit inside and eat outside!"

The Fourth Generation

Paul and Josie's children found urban jobs and kept only a visiting relationship with the farm, where their parents returned when they retired. Jacquie and her brother, Bob, who was partially deaf, also chose to get a university education and find nonfarm work. Jacquie married the boy who lived on the next farm and went on to become a professor at the nearby university; her husband worked for the Agricultural Stabilization and Conservation Service. Bob worked as a bank examiner and then as an auditor for the state until he retired in 1993. He bought parcels of his Uncle Paul's farm after Paul retired, and Bob, Jacquie, and Jacquie's husband, Jack, increasingly took over management of her parents' farm after her father had a heart attack in the mid-1960s. They leased the orchards to larger growers and, when the government began a conservation reserve program, they entered the farm in it. By 1990 most of the cropland was in the program, and some acreage was planted in ash trees.

These seven farms, and the people who lived and worked on them, each have their own distinctive histories. But along with the recollections of many other people and information from many sources, they tell the story of the way farm life has changed since the nineteenth century.

Goldenrod

There are roads that lure me ever

where the hills of Egypt lie—

and each breeze that passes by—

Makes the corn leaves sigh and quiver.

Where the Lord in gracious bounty

Blessed a portion of the sod—

Sowed it then with Golden Rod

And we called it Union County.

When I can no longer travel

Where the lanes of Egypt smile—

I would spend the after whiles—

Dreaming as the years unravel.

—Ben H. Smith[1]

And We Called It Union County

Eric Wolf writes that human beings create our universe through our transformation of nature, which we do through our relationships with one another—that is, in society. This highlights three dimensions of our experience: First, it focuses on our relationship with nature, how we transform it into something we use to feed, clothe, and shelter ourselves and give meaning to our lives. Second, it stresses our relationships with one another, how we organize our activities as kin, neighbor, boss, employee, and friend. Finally, because all of this occurs in time and through time, it is necessarily historical.[2] Stripped of history, our actions become arbitrary and absurd; understood as a moment in a historical process, created continuously by living, thinking, feeling, purposive human beings, seemingly irrational, even destructive activities are comprehensible. Because these activities become understandable, they are amenable to change. This chapter provides background on the physical environment—nature as it is given to us and as we have understood and transformed it—and on the history of the area leading up to the century on which the book focuses.

The Place

I am writing of two places, or one place seen from two vantage points: the specific locale in southern Illinois in which I talked with people, probed archives, and roamed the countryside, and the larger society in which this small region participates, the United States and the world. Most of my work is in Union County, Illinois, although I draw on my own life experiences in adjoining Jackson County and in the rest of southern Illinois. Southern Illinois is a discrete section of the state, called "Egypt" since at least the 1840s.[3] Geographically and culturally it is more part of the Upland South—Appalachia and the Ozarks—than of the rich prairie regions to its north. Yet politically it is part of the North, and this has shaped its particular configuration as much as its topographic and historic affinities with the mid-South.[4]

The county is bounded by the Mississippi River on the west, with a three- to five-mile floodplain between the river and a ridge of high hills and bluffs that mark the western edge of the interior uplands. Once-swampy bottomlands reach around the southern part of the county where the Mississippi joins the old Ohio floodplain. The escarpments of the Shawnee Hills rise northward, forming the watershed dividing the Mississippi and Ohio Rivers. It is cut by two small rivers, the Cache River, which flows into the Ohio on the east, and Clear Creek, whose mouth opens into the Mississippi on the west. The Big Muddy River, draining Jackson County, forms the northwestern boundary as it cuts through the bluffs and meanders across the Mississippi floodplain.

The county is underlain by limestone, creating a landscape dotted with sinkholes and springs. Natural ponds that occasionally drain overnight remind residents that the region is geologically unstable. The Shawnee Hills mark the southernmost extension of the Pleistocene glaciations, but the region was affected by them despite the absence of direct glacial action. Wide creek bottoms, where intermittent streams now flow, are relics of the torrents released by the melting glaciers. The western hills are mantled by thick deposits of rich loessial soils—windblown dusts from glacial deposits.

The climate is temperate, with mild to severe winters and hot, humid summers. Rainfall averages around 44 inches per year but can vary widely. In 1982, for example, 66.53 inches of precipitation fell, more than 20 inches above average. The Shawnee Hills, with their wide range of micro-environments, are the northernmost habitat for several plant varieties, including swamp or bald cypress and tupelo gum, and the southernmost habitat for other species.

But the landscape does not exist as something independent of human activity. Human beings have used and reworked the landscape in radically different ways at different times: The Indian peoples who populated the region made great use of the cherts that are part of the limestone formations that make up the western hills. These deposits were so important that an archaeologist wrote, "In terms of prehistoric chert exploitation, Union County, Illinois, can be called the 'Pittsburgh' of the middle Mississippi Valley."[5] Remnants of flint-knapping "workshops" litter area fields, and farmers frequently unearth stone tools as they cultivate their crops. Many people collect, display, and trade these artifacts. Aside from the interest these cherts have to collectors and archaeologists, however, these deposits have lost their economic utility. In contrast, the limestone that is presently mined and crushed and used for roads and fertilizer served no such purpose 150 or 500 years ago.

In the process of exploiting these resources, human beings radically transformed the landscape: the great oak, poplar, and hickory forests; the sugar maple groves; the vast flocks of water fowl; and the bears, wolves, panthers, and other wildlife that the first settlers found have been virtually eradicated. The first settlers carved out and fenced small fields for their crops and let their livestock roam in the unfenced woods. After construction of the Illinois Central Railroad in the 1850s linked Union County with Chicago, some 350 miles to the north, the hills were found to be well suited to fruit and vegetable production. The mild climate allowed peaches to thrive, especially on the higher ridges since freezing air of a late spring cold snap drains into the valleys, leaving the ridges relatively frost free. The deep loessial soils that erode badly under annual tillage provided a rich base for more permanent crops, while the fertile but generally narrow creek bottoms provided excellent locations for small fruits and vegetables. However, the demand for hardwood for railroads ties, mine supports, and building materials denuded the hillsides of their forests, and a strong wheat market during the 1910s encouraged wheat production, with predictable consequences for the soils. By the 1930s the hill lands were scarred with deep gullies, and large wild animals were virtually eradicated. With the exception of some bottomland swamps and a few patches of old-growth forest, the landscape had become defined and often impoverished by human activities.

Since World War II this landscape has been again transformed by changing land-use practices: Most of the remaining bottomland swamps have been drained and put into crops, while much of the hill land has been taken out of crop production. Many farms have been cut into smaller residential acreages; federal and state governments have purchased large tracts for forest; and government conservation programs have encouraged farmers to put their land in grass or other long-term cover crops. Deer, beaver, coyotes, predatory birds, and other wildlife have proliferated to the point that they now compete with farmers for their crops and livestock.

We are implicated in the construction of the landscape not only through the way we physically alter its contours and uses, but also through the meanings we find in it. Our environment is never stripped of meaning, of evocations of significance, no matter how stripped down our language. How we perceive the land determines what we will do with it. Although nature of course exists independently of us, we determine what meaning and utility we find in it. The changing significance of chert and limestone points to this difference. So do the patterns people make upon the land, the more or less permanent marks and traces they leave by the thoughtful (and careless) practices of making a living, what cultural geographers term the "built landscape." Throughout this work I have used the landscape, and particularly the buildings people built, as a repository of memory and have sought to decipher the meanings it holds and once held for the people who lived in and created it.

The Indian people we term Mississippians who lived here in the thirteenth century attached some significance to the bluffs overlooking the Mississippi bottoms; their carefully made stone graves attest to this. But they seemed to choose the bottoms to live in: These people, who created a civilization in the Mississippi Valley between A.D. 800 and A.D. 1500, built two mounds in what is now Union County. One is located where Dutch Creek cuts through the western ridge to join Clear Creek, on the banks of an old channel of the Mississippi now called Running Lake, near the modern village of Ware. The other, called Linn-Heilig, is also located near Clear Creek near the southern county line. Earlier Indian peoples chose the interior ridge tops on which to live and grow their crops. This book is not about the aboriginal inhabitants, however. They enter our story either as oral recollections of occasional hunters who traded through the area, as a fragment band that settled among the whites, as a great-great grandmother who was Cherokee or Choctaw, in the guilty recollection of the Trail of Tears of 1837–38, or as memories embodied in the stone tools and other artifacts turned up by plows and spring rains.

The early settlers saw a region with many springs and signs of fertile land, high enough to be relatively free from the malarial fevers that plagued the Mississippi Valley since at least the mid-eighteenth century.[6] They settled along the watercourses—the Cache and, especially, Clear Creek and its tributaries—following them to the center of the county where the two streams rise, and in 1818 on a high ridge built the first town and county seat, which they named Jonesboro.[7] The propensity of the

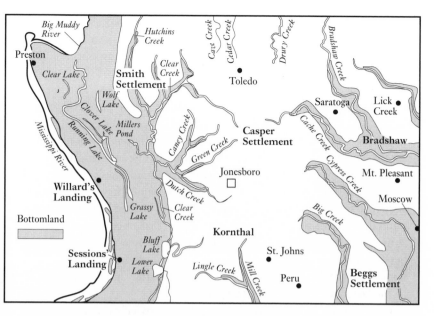

Figure 2.1. Union County in the Mid-Nineteenth Century
Source: Derived from Griffing 1881.

Mississippi to flood annually and at irregular intervals to fill the entire floodplain, along with endemic malaria (fever and ague, it was called), made the broad bottoms unattractive; only a few small settlements that served landings on the river were established during the early and mid-nineteenth century.

Other areas had greater potential. Among the earliest lands taken out from the government were tracts along Lick Creek, named for the mineral licks in the area.[8] Another mineral spring in the northeastern part of the county seemed so promising as a health resort to an early booster that he named the town he founded Saratoga, hoping to capitalize on the famous name of Saratoga Springs in New York state.[9] The earliest settlers sought land near existing trails and with year-round sources of good water (see fig. 2.1).

Nineteenth-century boosters saw great industrial potential in iron deposits on the ridge west of Cobden optimistically named Iron Mountain.[10] These deposits were never rich enough to develop, but the kaolin clays nearby became an important resource for a local pottery during the late nineteenth century and were later exported.[11] The remains of ancient marine shells that underlie much of the county have, since the late nineteenth century, been the county's most important mining resource.[12] Limestone, burned for plaster and crushed for road gravel and fertilizer, and silica, used for a wide variety of industrial purposes, have been exploited for about a century. Other dreams of mineral riches have proved as ephemeral

We Called It Union County   41

as the iron ore on Iron Mountain. Promoters have periodically prospected (unsuccessfully) for oil, hoping to replicate the successes of the oil fields just north of the Shawnee Hills, and the coalfields end just north of these hills.

In public discourse the land has had several meanings. The ones alluded to above stress its utility as an economic resource to be exploited to enrich it owners and, perhaps, to enhance the lives of the general public. Another set of meanings is embodied in the attachment of people to the piece of land on which their ancestors settled. The land and landscape encode memories that would otherwise be lost. Dead Man's Corner Field near Weaver Hill on the GM&O Railroad was named for an unidentified dead man found in a boxcar. An abandoned road marked by its deep banks reminds a native of a settlement and homes that once populated it. A spring, now drained by a culvert, triggers an elderly woman's memory of her inability, as a child, to restrain the bolting horses as the family rode home from the Anna fair, to her eternal mortification and the destruction by mud of their best sets of clothes.

In day-to-day speech, when people refer to a specific event, they often locate the event by naming all the people who lived where the event occurred. For example, Edith Rendleman, in writing about the flood of 1943 that drove them from their home, said, "We . . . stayed in a little country motel that Fannie and Dick Davie owned. That motel was on the place where the old Wolf Lake school had stood, the one that my brother Curt and Dora lived in."[13] One day when we drove past the site, she added, "That's where Geneva Wiggs lives," and recounted the rest of the site's residential history. Such memories may go back before the birth of the narrator and give a detailed genealogy of everyone who has inhabited a particular location. These are the small events and relationships that make up the fabric of daily life. But sometimes the landscape can trigger memories that reveal the deepest and most abiding schisms within society. For example, the limestone in a town's buildings embodied a memory of years past, when slavery was still within the reach of human experience. Charles Thomas recalled,

> Up above the cemetery [in Cobden] in that range of bluffs is where all the stone for the stone buildings was quarried. They had a great big husky Negro man that did the cutting and shaping of the rock. I can remember him as a child. . . . He was mammoth and strong and he had been, as a child, he had been a slave and had been beaten severely. 'Cause I remember one time he—I was just a little bitty fellow and of course probably everything looked bigger, but anyway, he took his shirt off and showed the boys his back and it was really striped from lashes. That's always of course impressed me. . . . But he cut all the stones in these stone buildings.[14]

Still another set of meanings connects the realm of land as resource for economic use with that of land as a reservoir of private memory. Whether or not an old grove forest or an old log barn will be preserved takes on political significance as people contend over whether or not to "stand in the way of progress," and over the direction of "progress." Throughout the written history of the county a tension has existed between the desire of the people to leave a bountiful legacy to future generations and to extract maximum utility and profit in the present. Part of the story of this book is the story of this tension. Sometimes the tension is visible in conflict, or at least disagreement, between different groups. More often, however, the tension exists within each individual or family group, as needs in the present conflict with the desire to care for the land and preserve a valued legacy for future generations.

Historical Background

Most of the people who populated Union County came from the southern backcountry.[15] The county was known as a Dutch settlement in its early years because most of the early settlers were German Lutherans and Dunkards (German Baptists or Brethren) who came, directly or with stops in Kentucky, Tennessee, and Alabama, from Pennsylvania and from North Carolina's Yadkin Valley. The county's name comes from a union camp meeting held in 1817 between the Dunkard preacher, George Wolf, and a Baptist minister reputedly named Jones.[16] In the 1820s most of the Dunkards appear to have become Baptists and joined the Clear Creek Church, organized in 1820, which then became the nucleus for the Clear Creek Baptist Association, which was formed in 1831. Wolf left with what remained of his flock for Adams County, Illinois, around 1826. The Lutheran settlers founded the first Lutheran church in the state in 1817.[17]

The county, although heavily German, included a number of people from other backgrounds. The eastern side of the county was initially settled by upland southerners of English and Scots-Irish ancestry, some of them Quakers. A small colony of African Americans settled in their neighborhood. A few of the southerners brought slaves; as late as 1840 four people appear on the census schedule as slaves.[18] In the 1840s a group of Austrian Lutherans colonized a fertile creek bottom in the southwestern part of the county in an area they christened Kornthal, or fruitful valley, and in mid-century, German, Swiss, and Czech Catholics, as well as a few Irish, settled west of Cobden.[19]

A southern pattern of government was established when the county was organized in 1818. Administrative and judicial functions were centralized in the county seat town, but each precinct had its justice of the peace, constable, and overseer of the poor. The county court appointed road commissioners for the many road districts, election judges in each precinct to oversee election returns, and township commissioners to administer the school lands. The court or local justices of the peace empaneled juries to inform the court or coroner on any issue of importance, such as building a mill pond that might flood neighboring land or roads, or determining a cause of death. The county court licensed taverns, ferries, and some other businesses and administered the county's business, keeping detailed records of its transactions. By the 1830s a Masonic lodge and several churches had been organized.[20] The militia exercised regularly and fought in the Black Hawk War in 1832 and the Mexican War in 1846–47.[21] Equally important, dense networks of kin, many of whom were related before coming to Union County, held the society together. People lived in settlements dominated by particular families (see fig. 2.1). Few people worked for wages, but they reciprocated in swap work and neighborly assistance. Recreation, which according to some accounts was often quite rough, tended to be organized on neighborhood lines, although many mills were also distilleries and men whiled away the time until their grain was ground by drinking and socializing. The 1840 census listed fifteen distilleries in Union County, suggesting the quantities of liquor that might have been consumed—although it should be noted that liquor was also a convenient way to convert bulky corn and fruit into a commodity more easily shipped.[22]

The dynamics of this society remain poorly described, but we do know that the commercially minded Yankees who visited the area were not impressed with its industriousness.[23] One historian wrote: "[The Yankee] deplored the survival of 'intemperance accompanied with ignorance and indolence' that dated from the earlier settlers from the south. 'One thing is certain,' declared a new arrival, 'that where New England emigrants do not venture, improvements, social, agricultural, mechanic, or scientific, rarely flourish, and seldom intrude.'"[24]

By the 1840s the pioneering period was over, and many of the families whose names still dominate the property tax rolls and telephone book had established homesteads. In the 1850s the Illinois Central Railroad was built through the center of the county, bringing with it, on its completion in 1856, a direct connection to the Chicago market and an influx of commercially minded farmers and developers. The line bypassed the old county seat town of Jonesboro, and local entrepreneurs sited a new town, Anna, just west of Jonesboro, its center being a station on the railroad. The railroad built other stations at approximately five-mile intervals: North Pass (later Makanda), just north of the county line in Jackson County; South Pass (later Cobden, named after the British free-trade liberal who was instrumental in financing the Illinois Central),[25] at the southern edge of the uplift that formed the northern boundary of the

Until a system of hard roads was built, beginning in the 1920s, railroads provided the primary form of transportation between towns. The railroad was also one of the major employers in southern Illinois. Here a crew repairs track near Cairo. Louise Ogg Collection, Morris Library, Southern Illinois University, Carbondale.

Shawnee Hills; Anna; and then Dongola, on the southern boundary. Sometime after the Civil War the unincorporated village of Balcom developed as a station and small village. About seven miles north of Makanda an ambitious Yankee businessman founded the town of Carbondale, eventually the site of Southern Illinois State Normal school, which, after World War II, became a major research university.[26]

In the 1870s a rail line was built connecting Cairo, at the confluence of the Ohio and Mississippi, with St. Louis, and five stations were estab-

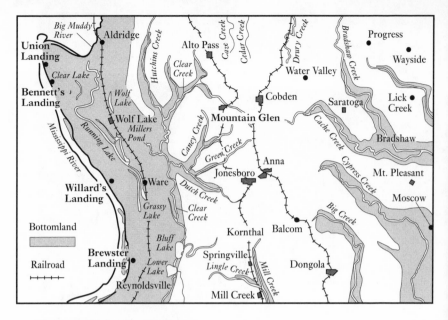

Figure 2.2. Union County in 1900
Source: Derived from Griffing 1881.

lished in Union County: Jonesboro; the incorporated villages of Mill
Creek and Alto Pass near the southern and northern boundaries of the
county, respectively; and the unincorporated villages of Mountain Glen,
near the kaolin mines southwest of Cobden, and Springville, between
Jonesboro and Mill Creek.

In the 1890s a railroad company later purchased by the Illinois Central
built a line on the eastern edge of the Mississippi bottoms. The stations of
Aldridge, near the Big Muddy crossing; Wolf Lake, at the northern end of
the county; Ware, at the juncture of the old toll road from Jonesboro to the
river landing; and Reynoldsville, at the juncture of the road leading to
Cape Girardeau, Missouri, were created along this line (see fig. 2.2).
Shortly after the turn of the century a railroad that eventually was bought
by the Missouri Pacific was built through the bottoms alongside the Illinois Central line.[27]

Older settlements sited at crossroads—Peru, Saratoga, Lick Creek, Mt.
Pleasant, Moscow, Toledo—and river landings on the Mississippi diminished in importance despite attempts by local boosters to promote them,
although most retained a general store, a school, a church, and a post office
until the 1940s.

The building of the Illinois Central Railroad through the center of the
county in the 1850s brought an influx of New England immigrants as well
as a few professionally trained Europeans. Most of these Yankees settled

Table 2.1. Population of Union County, 1820–1990

Year	Total Population	Rural Farm	Rural Nonfarm[a]	Alto Pass	Anna	Cobden	Dongola	Jonesboro	Mill Creek
1990	17,619	1,456	4,805	403	4,805	1,104	719	1,727	97
1980	16,851	1,875	10,482	369	5,408	1,210	611	1,842	97
1970	16,071	2,191	9,116	304	4,764	1,114	825	1,676	78
1960	17,645	3,441	9,924	323	4,280	918	757	1,636	102
1950	20,500	6,426	9,694	462	4,380	1,104	704	1,607	127
1940	21,528	9,989	7,447	459	4,092	1,098	638	1,521	210
1930	19,883	9,659	6,788	485	3,436	1,036	635	1,241	173
1920	20,249	17,230		500	3,019	944	660	1,090	209
1910	21,865	19,047		551	2,809	988	702	1,169	221
1900	22,610	19,992		518	2,618	1,034	681	1,130	273
1890	21,549			389	2,295	994	733	—	
1880	18,102			166	1,494	800	599	879	
1870	16,513				1,269			1,108	
1860	11,181				397			435	
1850	7,615							548	
1840	5,523								
1830	3,204								

Sources: U.S. Bureau of the Census, *Census of Population*, year as noted.

[a]Before 1990, "Rural Nonfarm" included all towns classified "rural." In 1990 the census included a category of residents outside incorporated areas.

in the new railroad towns or developed commercial farms near the rail lines. The cultural divide between the upland southerners and these new arrivals was great. Bert Casper, whose family had been among the earliest settlers and who lived in the Cobden area, recalled:

> I think in general you'll find that the culture and background of the immigrants differed. Therefore, there was a difference in the people socially, economically, and culturally. It's a natural consequence. One of the things that I've never been able to put into words is this difference. It's kind of like oil and water: they just didn't mix. There were professional people such as doctors and lawyers and wealthy people, those who owned the industries and stores. We poor whites didn't amount to much. Personally, I didn't think much of Cobden when I was growing up, because when I would go down there they would ignore me. I wasn't anybody.[28]

Although the Yankee migration was most noticeable because the northeasterners assumed positions of power and prominence, throughout the nineteenth century, upland southerners continued to migrate into the county, largely from Kentucky and Tennessee. With most agricultural land privately owned by 1870 the newcomers appear to have settled as tenants and laborers on the increasingly commercial "substantial" farms.

The area was torn by divided loyalties during the Civil War, which were intensified by the strongly Democratic county newspaper and the garrisoning of Union troops in Anna.[29] After the war the combination of tight money, unstable markets, and a rapidly changing political economy stirred the farmers to action. In 1873 Union County farmers joined farmers across the state and nation in organizing against eastern economic interests, characterized as trusts and plutocrats. The movement quickly faded, leaving in place designs for marketing cooperatives and a realignment of county politics more focused on the railroad towns than on the dispersed rural settlements. After a protracted fight, in 1891 county voters narrowly passed a law requiring livestock to be fenced. The end of this battle, fought in the name of the "poor widow" who, if she had to fence her cow, would not be able to feed and water it, or who, alternatively, was victim of neighboring livestock, marked the end of an era when it might be possible for a family to subsist on a tiny acreage with little recourse to a cash economy. It signaled the consolidation of modern notions of private property, production aimed largely at external markets, and reliance on wage labor. It also signaled increased pressure on the land as all arable acreage was settled and turned to farming or manufacturing.[30]

The story told in this book begins during this period in the late nineteenth century. Earlier times are beyond the reach of living memory and have largely been erased from the landscape. This story begins, then, with the countryside fully populated, with most farms producing for urban markets, with at least one-third of the farms operated by tenants, with a large number of laborers living as renters on substantial farms, and with a thriving timber and wood products industry. It begins with population at its peak (see table 2.1) both in towns and in the countryside; with mills turning local timber into boxes, barrels, and lumber; with the towns, newly electrified, busy on weekends; and with a streetcar shuttling between Jonesboro and Anna.

CHAPTER 3

We never wanted for anything. We
never got hungry, we never went cold,
neither did we have a lot of luxuries.

—Helen Kimber

We Never Wanted for Anything

One thread of people's historical memory recalls the relative self-sufficiency of farms and rural communities before World War II and the interdependencies of people within their communities. By at least the latter part of the nineteenth century virtually all farms in the area were commercial operations; however, they simultaneously provided most of their own subsistence needs. Although by the late nineteenth century many manufacturing processes had been separated from farms and rural communities and were returned as industrial commodities, farmers still raised and manufactured a large proportion of the materials they consumed and used in production. This made farming, even as it joined the world of industrial capitalism, very different from industry, where both workers and owners had to buy most of the items needed for their subsistence. It set a different course for the farm household, in which production and consumption remained integrated, from the urban household, where remunerative labor largely moved outside the home and the home became a site of consumption and of the activities associated with consumption and "homemaking." As we will see, this had a very different consequence for relations between property owners and their laborers and for relations between husbands, wives, and children.

Virtually everyone who grew up on Union County farms before World War II recalls that they never lacked food. "We didn't have much to buy," Maude Kinder recalled, "baking powder or something like that." A Jonesboro businessman, Cecil Norris (b. 1899), recalled, "A lady was in here; her name was Turner. I said, 'Mrs. Turner, this is fall now. What do you have put away for winter?' She looked at me and said, 'Well, about everything I'll need except for coffee, sugar, and a few things like that. We raise a little wheat and take out a little wheat; I've took it to the mill and had flour made out of it, so I've got my own flour and everything.'"[1] Ada Gurley, who was born around 1884, told a similar story: "We didn't buy much—only sugar, coffee, and rice sometimes. We raised our sweet potatoes, Irish potatoes. We raised the wheat—or the men did—to make the flour, and we raised corn to make cornmeal. We just didn't have to buy very much."[2]

Almost all families, even the poorest laborers, had a few chickens. More prosperous farmers, including many renters, had chicken flocks that yielded eggs and chickens for frying and stewing as well as eggs and live birds for sale. Most families also owned a cow or cows that gave milk for home use and butter for market. Most families also had gardens that provided vegetables in season that they also canned for winter. Sweet and white potatoes, turnips, and apples were stored in root cellars or temporary dugouts. Berries, including wild blackberries, and perishable fruits like peaches, cherries, and plums were eaten in season and preserved in sugars for the winter. Women dried some fruits and vegetables for winter use. Those families with enough ground raised hogs, which families slaughtered in late fall or winter. Occasionally a family might slaughter a steer, dividing the meat with a nearby kinsman whom they expected to reciprocate. As indicated in the above quotes, families were able to have their wheat ground into flour at mills located in the towns, and many farmers operated gristmills. Ada Gurley recalled, "At one time there was what they called a gristmill. It was over at the creek where there was plenty of water. They ground corn there. It was coarser, but it made awful good cornbread. But afterwards, they would take it to town here, have it ground, and have meal that looked like it does now. It made good cornbread."[3] Every neighborhood had at least one farmer with a sorghum mill who made sorghum molasses on consignment and sold it by the gallon.

Making soap and yeast was a normal part of a woman's household work. Families often made vinegar from home-pressed apple cider, and a number of farmers distilled liquor from their corn and fruit.[4] The hills and woods provided many medications, from sassafras to "thin the blood" in the spring, to roots and leaves for poultices and infusions, and the mineral spring at Saratoga provided a tonic that was widely used for various ailments.

There was some variation in the degree to which families provided for their own needs. Laborers may have had less access to corn and wheat—crops that demanded more acreage than the garden plot that came with the house—and so had to purchase more staples. Edith Rendleman was unable to recall any pigs on the two hill farms her family rented in the first decade of this century, although they always owned at least one milk cow, and she recalled that her mother regularly bought beef from a peddler.

If one thinks of the farm as a factory (and farm people did not), the farm supplied virtually all the food and shelter for the farm labor force. The specific social relations through which the residents of farms—family members, tenants, and laborers—produced their daily needs is described in these chapters.

The farm also provisioned most of the draft stock. The rule of thumb was that one-third of the land went to crops and pasture to feed the livestock, mostly horses and mules. Before 1891, when a law requiring livestock to be fenced was finally passed,[5] small farmers could let their animals range in unfenced woodlands and devote all their acreage to their family's subsistence and cash crops. Fencing; lumber for buildings; wood for handles, pegs, latches, and miscellaneous tools; and wood for cooking and heating also came from the farm or a nearby open range.

Hunting, fishing, and foraging were also an important part of daily life. These activities provided entertainment, cash income, and food. Pelts of fur-bearing animals; rabbits for the Chicago market; hickory nuts, walnuts, and pecans; and ginseng and other medicinal herbs were significant (although unenumerated) sources of cash. Possum, raccoon, rabbit, quail, ducks, geese, and fish supplemented farm-raised foods.

Despite the ability of farm families to provide for most of their day-to-day needs from the farm and surrounding woods and streams, they required cash to maintain their farms. By the 1880s women had ceased spinning and weaving wool and linen,[6] so they needed money for fabric and clothing. Although most families repaired their own shoes, the shoes themselves had to be bought. Substantial amounts of cash were needed for such items as wood-burning cookstoves, sewing machines, iron and steel farm equipment, harnesses, and for those with enough capital to invest, saw-, grist-, and sorghum mills and threshing machines. Landowners and people with taxable personal property also had to pay county taxes and, after 1908 when drainage districts were established in the bottoms, taxes to support the levees and ditches built by these districts.[7]

Farm families were, therefore, dependent on commercial production. This dependence, however, was highly variable. In a bad year a landowning family could subsist with only enough cash to pay taxes and the mortgage, if there was one. Maybe they could buy some ammunition for the guns, forgoing new shoes, remodeling old clothes for growing children, and paying for needed services in kind.

In this cash-poor household economy, thrift was a much-needed virtue. People recycled durable items until they lost all utility. Women repaired remade clothing until it was too ragged to use; then it was cut into quilt patches or sewn into strips for rugs. Abandoned machinery was scavenged for parts; lard cans served every conceivable use, including seating. At a session at the 1991 Smithsonian Folklife Festival on recycling on the American family farm, a woman noted, "Today we recycle because we're drowning in waste. In the past it was a way of getting every bit of use out of scarce resources."

Self-Sufficient vs. Commercial Farming

Historians and popular writers have tended, when reconstructing nineteenth-century farm life, to create a sharp duality: the self-provisioning farm versus the commercial market.[8] Agrarianism, especially urban agrarianism, tends to focus on the self-provisioning aspects of farm life and on the individualistic moral qualities of self-reliance, honesty, hard work, and skill thought to be required to maintain such a life.[9] If one looks at the landscape, at how people have built their lives into the land, this duality appears confirmed: The countryside in the early twentieth century was made up of freestanding, independent farmsteads, with perhaps a few tenant houses placed a few hundred yards from the main house, each with its own garden area. Each farm appears as an autonomous unit that either supports itself from its own products (self-sufficient) or through selling its products on the market (commercial). While most historians have recognized that most farms were to some extent both commercial and self-sufficient, the farm has generally been viewed as an individual enterprise. People's recollections, however, betray the shallowness of this characterization. While farms generally existed as legal entities operated by families that were more or less separate from other families, people recall that they were strongly dependent on their neighbors, kin, and hired hands for the necessities of daily life. Work was almost never carried out solely by members of the nuclear family; rather, households included many different people who stood, in relation to the members of the nuclear family, as kin, hired hand, or unrelated dependent. Neighbors swapped work and goods, both formally and informally.

People organized these relationships through a number of institutions. One- or two-room schoolhouses and church houses, often closely associated, created the visible site for many less formalized social interactions. Prosperous farmers who valued education and religion generally donated land for churches and schoolhouses, so they were located with little reference to crossroads or settlements. A hierarchy of denser settlements, from small crossroad hamlets consisting of a general store, post office, and a few scattered houses, to the county seat town, created a network of marketing centers accessible to virtually all farms (see fig. 2.2).

This settlement pattern emphasizes family autonomy and is congruent with the dominant ideology that stresses individual initiative and responsibility. The built landscape—the landscape inscribed by mapmakers and the landscape that archaeologists would find—divides the environment into agricultural production units or farms, sacred and educational sites separated from production, and commercial centers that, in some instances, were also industrial and governmental centers. It is largely these functions that people recall—the country school around which social life revolved, cutting across class, religious, and political lines; the rural church that defined communities of faith; and the towns that served as links to the larger world of commerce and government.

The formal landscape of roads, houses, schools, churches, settlements, and towns, however, leaves nearly invisible many of the social networks that people created to sustain themselves—networks of neighbor and kin.[10] These relationships, inscribed in the landscape, if at all, only as ephemeral footpaths linking home to home, also appear in recollections of daily life—relationships of reciprocity, of formal swap work, and charitable sharing. Making the social map still more complex, relationships of class, visible in the style and siting of houses and outbuildings, distinguish rich and poor, landlord and laborer. In addition, most farms carried out many nonagricultural manufacturing and service functions such as blacksmithing; milling lumber, corn, sorghum, and lime; sewing; and rug weaving for people in the area. Despite the tendency for these manufactures to be increasingly industrialized and centralized in urban centers, farm families persisted in small-scale manufacturing of those products that could not be more cheaply produced in factories, using an economic calculus that incorporated multiple and shifting labor demands and reciprocal obligations as well as money. When one recognizes these many and varied interdependencies, the categories developed by policymakers in the 1920s that contrast self-sufficient farms with commercial farms appear as an outsider's misperception. All farm families relied on cash to survive, even as they met many of their needs within the resources of the farm and neighborhood.

The eighth grade class at Egypt School, 1914. Merrill Kimber stands at the far left, and Frank Kimber stands to the left of the teacher, Harley Peeler, who wears a tie. Kimber Collection, Morris Library, Southern Illinois University, Carbondale.

At least fifty-six children attended Egypt School in 1914. Kimber Collection, Morris Library, Southern Illinois University, Carbondale.

Church and School

The rural schools and churches were the most obvious community institutions. By the early twentieth century virtually all children attended school at least part time, and adult members of the community attended the various activities associated with the school year—pie suppers, holiday celebrations, end-of-year ceremonies, and spelling and other bees. Oral recollections indicate schools often focused local political competition between substantial farmers as they sought seats on the school board in order to determine who would be selected to teach or who would get the contracts to build or repair the schoolhouse.

Churches similarly brought people into association with one another. Perhaps significantly, few of the people I interviewed or spoke with volunteered much information about churches, despite, for many of them, deep religious convictions.[11]

Political parties were also significant players in rural society although, even more than churches, their role is largely unrecollected and unreported. They were organized on the precinct level and generally held annual picnics for local activists; they also controlled significant patronage positions in road construction and employment at the state mental hospital in Anna.

None of these formal institutions had much to do directly with household subsistence; they were not a central focus of my research and do not occupy a large part of the subject matter of this book. Yet they were important dimensions of community life, being, if nothing else, along with Saturday marketing, election days, and the annual county fair in Anna (Thursday was the day the farmers would attend), the only regularly occurring public meeting places. Of course they were much more: The schools inculcated a discipline in thinking and behavior that prepared those students who persisted for the increasingly scientific, routinized life associated with industrial production. The churches, in addition to nourishing members' spiritual existence, served as an important arena for formulating moral standards and exercising juridical control, particularly in the nineteenth century, when other forms of social control were weaker. Bert Casper, for example, recounted that the First Presbyterian Church of Cobden in the 1870s

> felt that it was obligated to see to it that people conducted themselves in such a way that they would set a good example for their fellow man and also be rewarded for it in heaven. If a person got out of line and did something which the church disapproved of, he was called before the elders and was supposed to make restitution and work out some plan whereby the act would be overlooked, and he could go on as before.
>
> The church had trouble especially with one person who at that time was the head of the mill that later became DuBois Mill. He was accused of all kinds of unethical things. A great portion of the early notes of the sessions had to do with hearings which dealt with the conduct of this individual. The funny thing was that he wouldn't come before the session. So the session became kind of a church court. One time I think they had ten or twelve charges against him. One was that he was accused of shortchanging people who came there to buy grain. They said that he had a measuring basket with a false bottom in it. He would sell someone a half-bushel of corn, and it wouldn't be a half-bushel because of the false bottom. Of course, he denied that. Another was that he was cruel. Some of the people's pigs would get out and be running around town. He had a long metal rod with a hook on the end of it, and he would catch these pigs when he could, throw them in the boiler, and burn them up alive. It was very amusing all the things that he was accused of.
>
> Finally, he wouldn't come to answer the charges, so the board just dechurched him—excommunicated him.[12]

Nineteenth-century records of St. John's Lutheran Church and of Clear Creek Baptist Church indicate similar juridical functions.[13]

The authority of churches was limited, however, and with civil authority weak, some areas developed a reputation for being "rough." Edith Rendleman recalled the early years of the twentieth century in her memoirs of life in the Mississippi bottoms:

> Wolf Lake at that time and before had a pretty rough name. Bunk Anderson who worked for Bob Rendleman was a tough guy. So was Aud Travis supposed to be tough. They all drank and gambled a lot and it would end up in cutting somebody with a knife or a shooting. The Randle boys were tough also. They would not fight fair. . . . They shot Oscar Trainer down in the Cinderella Ballroom (or better say dance

hall) like a dog. Milas and Harrison [Randle] went to the penitentiary for . . . life. . . . They were bullies and Oscar Trainer could whip all of them at one time. So they shot him down in cold blood murder. They used to call Wolf Lake Pistol City. But it wasn't any worse than any other small place that didn't have a police officer.[14]

Relationships among Neighbors

Many other forms of social interaction and mutual responsibility were less formalized yet were central to the continuation of both individual and community life. S. Earl Thompson, for example spoke of "social customs such as concern for your neighbor and a willingness to help out in times of illness and death. When our house burned [ca. 1914], we moved over to this log house, and the neighbors started coming in immediately as soon as we got over there. Some had a quilt under each arm; some had hams and boxes full of canned fruit. But all of them brought something."[15] Clara Elder (1906–1987) similarly recalled that in the 1930s "David [her husband] had an abscessed appendix; he was in the hospital nine weeks. . . . They came over and they finished his hay and dug our potatoes and put them in the corncrib, and they canned peaches for us and put them in the basement."[16] The line between charity and neighborly generosity was thin. For example, Wayne Corzine recalled that his father had a farm outside of Dongola. There was a poor family living nearby, named "A." One winter the As had no food to eat and no money, so Wayne's dad hired Mr. A to clear a ridge on which he then put apples. Wayne's father also had no cash, so he arranged with his brother, who owned a store in Dongola, for the man to get credit for groceries. The As were spared the indignity of charity, but Mr. A was given the opportunity to provide for his family.

As with the Elders, charitable assistance was no shame when the need was patently obvious. The September 6, 1892, Jonesboro *Gazette* reported, "Mrs. Adams' cow died last Sunday morning. Mrs. Adams is a poor and hard working widow with a large family of children to support, and this was quite a severe misfortune for her, but money was easily raised during the week among our citizens to buy another cow for her." People who were born around the turn of the century frequently recalled that their fathers gave hoboes a place to stay and their mothers fed the poor and indigent. Edith Rendleman recollected that her mother (b. 1861) "never turned anyone away from her door hungry. Up until Social Security and nursing homes came in for people to have a place to stay, there were lots of tramps, hoboes, and bums coming to the door and asking for something to eat. She always fed them and helped orphan children and anyone in need. She always . . . visited the sick and went to every funeral."[17]

This ethic of generalized reciprocity pervaded exchanges between people. If someone came to visit, they would often be given some produce from the farm as they were leaving. This ethic still exists, although there are fewer venues for its expression. As I did my fieldwork, people often gave me fruits and vegetables from their farms; at the Carbondale Farmers' Market vendors give out extra portions to regular customers, both as an explicit marketing device and as a means of creating a personal relationship with customers who have moved from a status of impersonal buyer to that of friendly acquaintance.

There were (and are) subtleties in this generosity. Edith Rendleman recalled, "Aunt Minnie was greedy. She got everything off of Mom she could for nothing. When they lived in Granite City and they came down in the summer, she would tell Mom she wanted to buy two or three chickens. She would fry them before she left and then say, 'Sarah, how much do I owe you for them chickens?' Mom would say, 'Oh! Nothing.' And she never insisted on paying."[18]

A man I shall call John recalled that a distant relative I shall call Elbert gave John a bushel of peaches because of a long-standing relationship between their families. John offered to pay him, but Elbert refused. When John got home, he called another peach grower and asked how much the peaches were a bushel; then he sent Elbert a check for that amount. Elbert did not expect John to pay him and would not have held it against him had he taken the peaches as a gift. John knew, however, that if he sent the money, Elbert would think better of John's honor and integrity.

This sort of generosity blends into more or less formalized systems of what anthropologists call "balanced reciprocity"—giving with the implicit understanding that the recipient will return something of more or less equal value sometime in the future.[19] These bonds were particularly important in tying together neighbors and kin. Al Basler, for example, recalled that in his youth people cut wood for one another, making a party of this chore.[20] House and barn raisings had been largely replaced by professional builders and their crews by the early twentieth century, although a few people reported resurrecting this form of help during the Great Depression. Nonetheless, people often hired neighbor youths for this sort of work so that the money stayed within the neighborhood and in order to assure that the youths would be reliable, since not only their reputation but that of their family would be at stake. Butchering, a relatively small-scale but routine operation, remained a cooperative activity until after World War II. Bill Rhodes recalled such a relationship between his father and his father's twin brother, who lived on the adjoining farm: "We'd butcher one [cow], and Dad's twin brother, we'd give him half of it. Maybe in the first of November. Then Dad's brother would butcher one later and give him a half back. That way you had a half as long as it could be hung in the smokehouse and flies wouldn't bother it."[21] Hog butchering was even more common as a joint activity drawing neighbors together to share work and the product of their work.[22] It was a major event in the late fall, when the hogs were fat from summer eating and the weather was cold enough that the fresh meat would not spoil. Butchering was generally a community affair, with all the neighbors pitching in to help. Each family "hosted" a butchering and slaughtered several of their own hogs, "four or five, according to how large the families were," Ruby Weaver told me. Bill Rhodes recalled that they generally butchered eight to ten hogs, which lasted the rest of the year.

Several days before the slaughter, the men in the family built a platform at the edge of the house yard—near the chicken house seems to have been a favorite place, perhaps because the building provided one support for a scaffold set up at the rear of the platform from which to hang the carcasses. They leaned a barrel up at one end of the platform so that the hogs could be easily dunked in scalding water to loosen the hair.

Everyone got up extra early on the appointed day. "We'd set the kettles up," Ruby Weaver recalled. "We'd get up at three o'clock in the morning and fill the kettles and build a fire."

"Neighbors would be in there early the next morning just a little after daylight to go to butchering your hogs," Bill Rhodes recounted. "They were usually shot in the pen. When I was a kid my uncle had an old Civil War rifle, you had to load it from the end of the barrel, but later we got a .22 rifle. You'd shoot them in the head and somebody would jump in there and stick a knife in their heart to bleed them. They'd just kill one at a time and take them out and dress them and come back and get the others." Meanwhile, somebody poured the hot water into the barrel. "One fellow would test the water and it had to be just so or else it would cook them and the hair wouldn't come off," Ruby Weaver told me. "It would take several men to handle these hogs, 'cause sometimes they weighed three, four hundred pounds."

They dipped one end, then the other, then rolled the carcass onto the platform. "If they had plenty of help they'd roll the first one to the back of the platform, and the other fellows would go on scraping," Rhodes recounted. "Then these other fellows would go to dipping the other one, getting him ready." After the men scraped off all the hair, they would hang the carcass from the scaffold or a handy tree limb. "Somebody would rip him down and take the guts out and trim him there," Rhodes said. "Cut his head so he'd bleed out."

"That was when the women would clean the intestines to stuff the sausage in," Weaver recalled. "We never did use the large intestines, but some of the family would clean them and they would stuff them with the head cheese or liver sausage. But we just took the small intestines. The women would take them in a building, it was always cold, and clean them." Edith Rendleman recalled that two women took the fat off the entrails. Not everybody cleaned the intestines or used the fat along them, however. Rhodes said, "I'd have help sometimes say, 'Oh, I ain't going to fool with that. Too much work.' They'd just dump the intestines somewhere."

Meanwhile, the rest of the women were in the kitchen fixing a big dinner. Everyone helped cook, but the hostess provided the food.

After the hogs were gutted, the men "would leave them hang and drain a while," Edith Rendleman recalled. "Then they would lay one down and cut it up, different cuts for sausage and lard and ham, shoulders, heads, ears, tails, backbones and ribs and everything." "Most of the time you had a table back of the house," Rhodes said, but "if the weather was bad you'd have to move inside the house, and you'd cut them up on that table, and get the lard ready. Maybe if it was a pretty day somebody would start rendering the lard. And maybe somebody would start grinding sausage too." Sometimes the women helped cut the lard, but butchering was mainly a man's job.

Lard was generally rendered in the same large cast-iron kettles that had heated the water. Sausage was ground with a special grinder. "Sometimes they'd hook it onto the wheel of the Model T," Edith Rendleman recalled. The sausage was usually seasoned by the wife and was generally used bulk. Some people, however, stuffed the sausage into casings and smoked it. "When I was a kid, most of the time they put the sausage in cloth sacks, about 2½ inches, that they sewed," Rhodes told me. "Later on, we had a press that hooked on our sausage mill, and we got intestines for stuffing at the store."

The people who came to help generally went home with some fresh sausage, liver, backbone, and head cheese. The work of cleaning up the mess, and canning and salting down the rest of the meat, was left to the family.

Only one other activity required more formalized systems of swap work and greater coordination of labor. This was threshing wheat. Two families whose farm histories I documented owned threshing outfits. Bruno Weaver and his son, Charles, owned both a wheat thresher and a clover separator, and Edith Rendleman's father, Elijah Bradley, although a tenant farmer, also owned a threshing outfit with his son-in-law, William Rendleman. The Weavers had a threshing route in the St. John's Church area; Bradley worked the Wolf Lake area.[23]

Around the Fourth of July the thresher began his rounds, following an established route radiating from his farm. A group of farmers in a neighborhood went in together to hire the thresher and cooperated in the labor necessary.

About three weeks before the thresher was called in, the farmer cut and stacked his wheat. Oscar "Dutch" Lingle, who grew up north of Mill Creek, recalled his father using a cradle to harvest wheat. "It's got a blade longer than my arm," he told me. "And it's got fingers. You give it a big hit and pile the wheat or whatever you were cutting." When enough wheat was collected in the cradle, it was removed and bound just below the heads with a piece of straw and placed with other bundles into shocks.

It took skill and experience to be able to measure out a bundle, tuck it under your arm, deftly twist a wheat stem around the bundle, and draw it tight. Lingle described gathering these bundles together to make a shock: "Generally, you'd take one bunch in each arm, have about six bundles on each side. Then we'd pull the heads together." These were placed on the ground and another bundle was broken and placed over the stack to make a waterproof cap.

By the turn of the century, binders were widely used, but in a recently cleared field that was full of stumps, farmers still had to use the cradle. Binders cut down on the hand labor needed to cut and shock the wheat, but they required considerably more horsepower. "It took four head of horses to pull our binder," Rhodes recalled. One person drove the team or, later, the tractor, while another rode the binder to stack the bundles as they came out. Two or three men then placed the bundles into shocks. Much of this labor would be hired if there were too few family members to do the job.

"In about three weeks they would thresh it," Ruby Weaver said. "The whole neighborhood would get together. The men would bring their wagons and haul. Some of them would pitch wheat with a pitchfork off the shock and on the wagon. They hauled it in and put it in the platform of the table of the thresher, and it would thresh it." It took about twelve bundle wagons to keep the thresher working steadily, although if the wheat field was close to the thresher, fewer wagons could handle the job.

These machines took considerable skill to run and maintain, and the owner of such a rig had to find competent help. Dutch Lingle and Mike Kelly helped Bruno Weaver for a number of years. At first Lingle hauled water in the water wagon for the boiler, but as he got older, he learned to tend the engine, first helping Kelly, and then, when Kelly got too old to work, Lingle took over. The pay was good for the time, at $5 a day, since the going wage for farm labor during the early 1920s was around $1 a day.

If it rained, Lingle told me, they threw a canvas over the machinery and Weaver went home, but he and any other crew members generally stayed at the home of the farm they were working on. "Mom used to have the thresher at their house as long as two weeks if it rained a lot, and it always seemed to," Edith Rendleman recalled. "There were four to six that stayed with the thresher at night. You had to feed them and fix beds for them, and they were there to cook for even if it rained."

Threshing was a community activity. Families on a thresherman's route teamed up to haul wheat from the field to the threshing machine, while the women cooked a large meal that fed not only the workers but everyone else who could find an

Most farmers stored the wheat until spring if they were able, in order to get a better price. A grain storage house was built at the railroad switch at Weaver Hill. John Weaver, Bruno's cousin, whose farm abutted Weaver Hill, had two wagons he used for hauling wheat from the thresher to the granary. He accompanied Bruno on his runs, Lingle said, but made his own arrangements with the farmers.

Most farmers left the straw in a pile, but some farmers had it baled by

excuse to invite themselves to the dinner. This engine and thresher were probably owned and operated by Morris Kimber. Kimber Collection, Morris Library, Southern Illinois University, Carbondale.

someone who owned a baler. If the straw was to be baled, the thresher could be set up in the field, cutting down on the number of bundle wagons needed.

While the men were working in the field, the women of the neighborhood fixed a big dinner in the house where threshing was being done. "You had to furnish your own food," Ruby Weaver recalled. "We always baked a couple of hams and killed hens and had chicken and dumplings

The Waltons owned a large steam engine with which they did custom threshing. They also used it as the engine for a variety of farm tasks. Walton Collection, Morris Library, Southern Illinois University, Carbondale.

and lots of pies, 'cause some of those men could eat a whole pie. We had a great big long table that would feed about twenty men at a time in the front room."

Edith Rendleman remembered the big threshing dinners her mother and their neighbors prepared in the early years of this century: "They always killed four or five hens to make dumplings. Aunt Ett was the dumpling maker. They called them slickers. Mrs. Jones was the cake and pie maker. They made two and three kinds of pie. They would have chicken and dumplings, and maybe ham or sausage, sometimes beef, sometimes salmon cakes, all kinds of beans—green, Navy, and always Spanish beans. Corn fresh off the cob, potato salad or bean salad, slaw and potatoes. Everyone helped each other. You had lots of visitors drop in for a good dinner."

Threshing, then, was a complex mix of contract work, hired labor, swap work, and family cooperation among a group of farmers who contracted with the same thresherman. In addition, the dinners drew in townspeople, such as the banker and merchants, with whom the farm family did business, creating an arena in which business relationships could be amplified and given a personal dimension. In the early years of this century, as in the previous century, the farm was an arena for many public gatherings. Not only threshing, which had elements of a harvest festival, but funerals, weddings, and social events were held within the farm home. Despite its apparent physical autonomy and privacy, the farmstead was the location for many public events.

The dead were laid out in the home, washed and dressed by the women of the neighborhood, and neighbors brought food to supply the bereaved family and those who came to sit with them. Marriages were enacted in the home. As Edith Rendleman recalled of her wedding in 1917, "You never heard of a church wedding in those days. They were mostly justice of the peace ceremonies. It was years and years before church weddings were for common people."

The house was, therefore, in addition to being a residence, dormitory, and workshop, on occasion a ritual center. It was also a social center. Edith Rendleman, who lived in the Mississippi bottoms, recalled, "People used to have parties and square dances and invite everybody in the community. . . . At the parties you played games. At the square dances you generally had an ice cream supper with it, also soda you bought."[24] Al Basler, who lived between Cobden and Saratoga, recalled that the renters on the adjoining Green (later Cerny) farm "had a bunch of kids there and . . . just as soon as it would settle a bit, warm up of a night, get some warm nights, [he] would open it up for an ice cream supper and dance." Boys around the neighborhood provided the music. "Wasn't sophisticated players," Basler recalled. "My brother, he could play a violin. . . . Shoemakers was all musicians, the girls and the boys all played instruments."

"All of the year," Basler related, "they had dances there. Outside, inside where they had the big room . . . they could run two sets in it. When they was putting that two sets on there and playing that square picking music, that floor would wave up and down. Those logs, the timbers under [the floor], they had spring to them."[25]

Other forms of recreation within the home were more generally confined to selected neighbors and kin. Maude Rhodes Kinder recalled that her father had a croquet set in the side yard. "Old men would come in and a lot of times on Sundays they would all play croquet. . . . Just neighbors. Dad was the only one who had the croquet set. They would just play sometime in the morning or they would play in the afternoon. Mother would never have to fix the meal for them. . . . Just the men would come."[26]

These more intimate forms of entertainment persisted and, although I lack any recent accounts, probably still exist. Some men had regular pinochle groups that cycled among the members' houses, the men playing pinochle and the wife of the host providing refreshments. A few farm families were closely linked with town elites and joined them in bridge clubs; ladies' clubs met in the afternoon, and mixed clubs met in the evenings. Groups of women would also sometimes take shopping trips by train to St. Louis.

Visiting was common, although some families were noted for being particularly open. Helen Rendleman Sirles's parents, for example, not only had a large extended family but especially enjoyed company. "Sunday afternoon was just like a fair out here," family members recalled. "You would be very unhappy if you didn't have a bunch of company," Helen Sirles said. "Mother was very entertaining. A lot of people came to visit with her. . . . She wouldn't repeat anything malicious at all. She was a source of a lot of . . . good information. She had a lot of people who would ask her advice, and they would tell her things they wouldn't tell other people."[27]

Neighbors also looked after one another. According to Geraldine Stadelbacher,

> Mrs. Joram [a close neighbor] used to come over after my first one was born. She'd come over on the days that I was very busy in the house. . . . She'd take Bobby and go out—that's how good a neighbor she was—while I did a big ironing or something. . . . [Just before one of my girls was born] I wasn't feeling very good in the night and [Louise Sweitzer who lived way up there on the hill] saw the light here and the next morning, here she was. And the baby was born that morning. Now that's the kind of neighbors we had. She saw the light and she worried that something was taking place. And then you know another [day] after Norbert was born, . . . I had milk fever and I was all alone. [My husband] Leo was out in the field and . . . I was just deathly sick, and she come over, and then she sent her daughter to stay with me three or four days.

Some of these informal networks were inscribed in the landscape, visible in the earliest (1938) aerial photographs as paths leading from house to house. Geraldine Stadelbacher recalled, "We used to have a path between each house where we'd visit one another, you see, and that was entertainment more than going to town and such things."[28]

Trading among Farmers

In addition to the formal institutions of church, school, political party, and business enterprise, and the neighborhood bonds of reciprocity, farmers arranged formal trade among themselves. As Cecil Norris, for example, recounted, "There used to be a kind of a trading idea among the various farmers; if one was willing to buy corn, he would bring his wagon in with his sideboards on it, and another one would come in with a load of corn. He would raise corn, and he would sell it to the man that needed the

Picking and packing the apple and peach harvest required large amounts of seasonal labor. Women generally worked in the packing shed, while men picked fruit in the orchard. Herb Meyer's collection.

corn right on the square. I've seen many a time they would unload corn from one man to another, and they would buy their corn from each other that way."[29]

Bill Rhodes remembered selling their watermelons and vegetables: "You could just drive around with the old wagon and team, stop maybe, and some fellas would see what you got and buy some. Course most of the time you went to the store where you'd try to sell them [vegetables]." Hay was also a commodity that was needed in town and by farmers who had stock but too little land to raise enough hay. Rhodes recalled, "Old man Tweedy there, he'd cut a lot of red-top for Dad and haul it to Anna, Jonesboro, and sell it by the wagonload. And then he'd take groceries or coupons for it—most of the time you didn't get money—up into the early twenties I guess, even into the thirties."[30]

The code of honor that pervaded exchanges among neighbors carried over into these sorts of transactions. Jacquie Eddleman recalled that her father and grandfather had reputations for so overloading their baskets of peaches that the peaches overflowed. Another man recalled an incident in which a customer from town challenged his father: The apples inside the basket, she believed, were not as good as the facing apples. He, insulted,

Every small town had a flour mill. This mill was probably located in Dongola.
Kimber Collection, Morris Library, Southern Illinois University, Carbondale.

told her to check. She took them all out and found that they were all first
quality.

Towns and farms were intimately connected with one another. The
towns provided markets for farm produce, while farmers provided the
major market for town manufacturers and service providers. One woman,
before I interviewed her, got together with a friend and compiled an
inventory of the businesses she recalled operating in Cobden in the 1920s.
These included four hotels, seven groceries, three lumber companies, two
milliners, a large livery, a blacksmith, a machine shop, a harness shop, a
jewelry store, two or more barrel and box factories, two sweet potato
houses, and slaughter pens. There were a couple of inventors, a rock
quarry, a shipping association, and, for a few years in the late 1800s, a flour
mill, a fruit drying factory, and an icehouse. She recalled three doctors
and a dentist who practiced in the town. Virtually all of Cobden's enterprises either processed materials provided by local farmers, including
timber, or served farmers, or both. The other towns in the county were
comparable.

Despite the wariness with which many farmers viewed townspeople,
and the snobbery with which many townspeople viewed most farmers,
towns were major activity centers for all county residents. Saturday was
market day, and although farmers might go to town other days, particularly to ship produce, Saturday was the traditional day to trade in the
stores and with one another. The county seat was particularly important,
since virtually all legal proceedings were enacted at the courthouse. The

annual county fair, instituted in 1856 and by the turn of the century transferred to Anna, drew most county residents. Thursday was "farmers' day," and state prize money encouraged farmers to enter their best livestock and produce, and women and craftspeople to enter their best handiwork, for judging. This provided a venue in which people could show off their abilities to one another, and at the same time it was seen by educators as a means to enhance the quality of peoples' products.[31]

The proceeds from farming and the commerce and manufacturing it supported were disproportionately concentrated in the towns, as evidenced by the relatively large number of fine homes, generally Victorian in style, in the towns. Although there were many substantial homes in the countryside, and some of the larger fruit-growers built homes equal to those in town, farming remained generally less remunerative than other enterprises. With the exception of the export of agricultural and timber products and the import of manufactured items, the county's economy was largely based on its internal circulation. The hotels and the railroad, and warehouses, loading docks, and stock pens associated with it, represent the linkage of the local economy to the larger national economy. In an earlier period the river landings were equally important in shipping agricultural and forest products out of the county and bringing in goods. Drummers—salesmen and agents of Chicago produce commission houses—stayed in the hotels. A number of the commission men became friends of prominent growers with whom they did business. They would sometimes visit the growers in the fall for duck and goose hunting in the bottoms, and their homes in Chicago sometimes served as an entryway for growers' children visiting or attending school in Chicago.

This portrayal of farm life stresses the self-provisioning aspects of farm families and the ways in which their lives were enriched and their livelihood made possible by the density of their relationships with their neighbors and kin. This is the story of farm life that is recalled as "the good old days." It is a story, however, that is limited in a way that people, in their retelling of their lives, never themselves limited it. For purposes of arranging this story, I have taken apart experiences people keep together in their recollections. What has been largely stripped from the account of farm life in the early twentieth century, a time when "we never wanted for anything," is the central importance of commercial production. Wheat, of course, was grown mostly for market; but fruits and vegetables were far more important—and far more labor intensive—in Union County's agricultural economy than were livestock and grain.

The task of providing food, clothing, and shelter for one's family in the first half of the nineteenth century, when money was scarce and little was needed, had been a sizable job. As cash became ever more central to household maintenance—for cloth and equipment as well as taxes and incidentals—farm families were relieved of some work, but they were also burdened with many more responsibilities. With agricultural production ever more strongly tied to the developing industrial capitalist economy and ever more vulnerable to financial booms and busts, a new dynamism entered agriculture.

We would work overtime, ten or twelve
hours a day on a tractor, something
like that, and make a couple of dollars
extra—you thought you was doing
good. And sometimes you didn't get
that much. It would have been a job to
get by on a farm. I helped one person
for fifty cents a day threshing wheat.
That's when you had to work for a dollar a day.—Ed Brimm

Work was cheap then, by the day. You
got up and got out early and you stayed
out late, especially in the summertime.
And it was all for one price.

—Faye Smith

We Worked Can See to Can't See

People who grew up before World War II repeatedly recall the
amount and arduousness of labor required by farming. It is a source of
constant comparison in individuals' recollections. "It took so long to do
anything," John Aldridge, a retired farmer near Alto Pass, recalled in an
interview with his granddaughter:

You take making hay those days. You would mow it with a mowing
machine then. You would mow it, and when it got ready you would rake
it. Then you would go out there with forks, and generally there would
be some of the women out there doing that. You would make it into little stacks that we called shocks. There would be thirty or forty pounds
of hay in each shock. You would pile it up straight and make it nice so

73

that if it rained, it wouldn't get wet all the way through. You had to stack it up neat, so if it would come a rain, you wouldn't have to scatter it all to pieces to dry. . . .

You had a hay frame on the wagon. Somebody would be the stacker on the wagon. You would drive the team up between two shocks; the people would throw a shock up on each side of the wagon. The fellow on the wagon would place that on there and stack it. It had to be handled in the shock, and it had to be handled to be put on the wagon. The man on the wagon had to move about half of it, keeping it level so it would ride into the barn.

Then you would get to the barn with it. One man would throw it off, another man in there would throw it back, and another would throw it back farther until you got the back end of the barn full. It was handled five or six times to get it back in the barn. To get it down and feed the cattle in the wintertime was about the same.[1]

Throughout the nineteenth century, labor requirements per acre and bushel of production fell due to increased use of labor-saving technologies. According to the U.S. Department of Agriculture (USDA), corn production, using the most advanced available technologies, required thirty to thirty-five person-hours of labor per acre to produce forty bushels of corn in 1850; by 1930 that had fallen to six to eight person-hours. In 1822, using hand technologies except for a walking plow, wheat production required fifty to sixty person-hours per acre. By 1890 that had fallen to eight to ten person-hours, and by 1930 (using tractors, combines, and trucks), only three to four person-hours were needed.[2]

Southern Illinois hill farms remained relatively labor intensive due to the small scale of farms, the crop mix, and the terrain. Except in the Mississippi bottoms, Union County farming was so diversified and relatively small scale that it was generally not feasible to invest in labor-saving technologies, so labor requirements were relatively high for grain crops. Further, fruit and vegetable production, which predominated in the county, was and remains the most labor-intensive form of agricultural production. When compared with industry, agricultural labor is expensive to replace with technologies because the need for farm workers is "lumpy": Unlike industrial labor, which is not tied to natural cycles, agriculture requires bursts of intensive labor and then periods when little labor is needed. This creates needs for a seasonally available labor force that is not necessarily sustained throughout the year by the farming operation itself.[3] The need for seasonal labor was recognized as soon as commercial fruit and vegetable production was established. In 1866, for example, less than a decade after the Illinois Central Railroad was built, a correspondent to the county newspaper, signing himself "Egypt," promoted settling tenants on the land to provide the necessary seasonal labor:[4]

Workmen on the Walton farm pose for a photograph, ca. 1900. The man on top arranges the hay the other men pitch up to him. Note the split rail fence in the background. Walton Collection, Morris Library, Southern Illinois University, Carbondale.

Farmers whose farms are large are apt to overwork their families, unless they build tenant houses. Having had twenty years experience, we know this plan works well. We have ten cabins scattered over our lands. Industrious families generally stop with us several years. Married men are more steady, and we can depend on them better than on single men. . . . Where large and small fruits are grown, there should be one good team on every 40 acres of land, and one industrious family on every ten acres. The fruit sales of ten acres should annually reach $1,000, and one half of this amount will pay the labor of quite an industrious family. I presume not one half the men in this [Union] county that hire out by the day, with the assistance of their families, earn this sum annually.[5]

The lumpiness of agricultural labor needs was also ameliorated through growing a variety of crops. S. Earl Thompson, who was born around 1911, recalled,

My father, as all people living on a farm at that time, worked very hard from daylight until dark or after. We raised winter onions, skinned them and sold them in the hopes that we would have enough from them to make the first payment on the taxes. We raised rhubarb[6] and strawberries and had a small orchard of apple and peach trees. . . .

My father had a variety of crops coming on at various times of the year and some source of income, although not a great deal, scheduled throughout the growing season. Of course, the stability of the sale of butter from the milk cows kept us going during the winter.[7]

John Aldridge's childhood was similar:

> The main livelihood was truck farming. . . . On this place green onions was the first thing that come in in the spring. Then rhubarb came in; almost all farmers had a little patch of rhubarb. That was a little early money for them. Generally, that was the first money they got in the spring of the year. . . . When it come good you made enough money to pay your taxes that year. When strawberries got ripe, nobody wanted rhubarb; so it was an early crop. Along with rhubarb came asparagus, and everybody had a few acres of asparagus. They would go out, cut it every morning, bunch it, pack it, and ship it to Chicago.[8]

Some families raised daffodils—Easter flowers—which also came in in early spring, and other flowers such as Madonna lilies for Memorial Day and graduation parties. These flowers were sold in Chicago and, in the case of daffodils, to Woolworth stores throughout the Midwest.[9]

While the asparagus and rhubarb were being harvested, the ground was tilled for row crops, and plants were tended in hot beds and, as the ground warmed, planted in the fields. Then strawberries and raspberries were harvested in May. With the grain crops in the ground and the tomatoes and other horticultural specialties transplanted to the fields, the first hay was made in early June. Then it was time to cultivate the corn, cut and shock the wheat, and harvest oats. In mid-June the squash, beans, cucumbers, and tomatoes began to come ready for market, along with the early transparent apple harvest and, in late July, the peach harvest. Then it was time to harvest clover seed and make the second hay cutting. August, when the county fair was held, offered a brief period of relative respite from fieldwork. In the fall the sweet and Irish potatoes and fall apples were harvested, followed by corn. Labor demands from early May, when the strawberries began, through late September, when the apples were harvested, were intense, and all hands—men, women, and children—pitched in. During the winter months farmers took care of the livestock, cut firewood, and did other maintenance jobs. To bring in some money to supplement the women's poultry and butter income, men and boys hunted rabbits and fur-bearing animals and cut timber.

The scale of farming varied considerably. Many farmers, like the Rhodeses, the Aldridges, and the Thompsons, raised a wide range of crops and relied heavily on family labor. Other growers were more specialized: the farmers at Balcom, in a broad creek bottom south of Anna, specialized in cantaloupes and cucumbers. They formed a cooperative to bring in manure from the stockyards in St. Louis, as Cobden growers had earlier.[10] "We had several strawberry growers in the Anna area that had up

The fruits and vegetables raised in southern Illinois required large amounts of labor. Rhubarb was one of the earliest crops to come on the market. Women and children generally cut and packed the stems, while men loaded the crates. Note the apple trees in bloom. Helen Kennedy Collection, Morris Library, Southern Illinois University, Carbondale.

as high as forty acres of strawberries," Ruel Hindman recalled.[11] These operations often approached plantation conditions, as at "Berryville," also called "Thomasville," after its owner. This was a strawberry farm southwest of Jonesboro that sold strawberry plants all over the world.

Most people who lived through that period recalled vividly the long lines of wagons waiting to unload into the refrigerator car.[12] Hindman remembered when "they would load twelve or fifteen express cars of strawberries in Anna. . . . I can remember when the farmers' wagons would be lined up a half-mile each way waiting to get their turn to unload their produce—strawberries and rhubarb. They would wait their turn to unload them at the express office here in Anna. Of course, they had the same thing at Cobden and Dongola."[13]

On marketing days the workday would often extend beyond "can see to can't see": milking and preparing breakfast would begin before dawn so workers could get to the field as soon as it was light enough to see. Perishable fruits were taken to the depot in the afternoon to catch the express train to Chicago, but cream, eggs, and poultry were generally taken in after the day's work was done. Bertie Hunsaker, who farmed east of Cobden in the 1920s, recalled taking cream to market: "We worked all day, and you'd eat a bite right quick and take the cream to market. That was rest. . . . We usually stopped [at my mother's] and visited a while, and we got back home then and slept the rest of the night."[14] The stores stayed

The large southern Illinois strawberry crop used both local and migrant labor. Here women and children, neighbors of the Kimbers, take a break from picking berries to pose in good clothes for the photographer, ca. 1915. They were paid about two cents a quart for the berries. Inside the shed, from left to right, are Amy Kimber, her brother Morris and his wife, Edna, and Florence Kimber. The child in white is Frank Kimber, standing in front of his brothers Paul, Merrill, and Clark and other children. Kimber Collection, Morris Library, Southern Illinois University, Carbondale.

open equally long hours. Floyd Karraker, who owned a feed store with a cream and poultry station in Dongola, recalled,

> On Saturdays we'd buy maybe forty and fifty cases of eggs, thirty dozen cases of eggs, and we'd buy maybe fifteen or twenty ten-gallon cans of cream. And we'd buy a house full of chickens or something like that. We bought a lot of produce, but we didn't make very much on it. . . . Saturday was our big day then. The bank would stay open until four o'clock then. And we'd buy a lot of produce after four o'clock. . . . We had been over there sometimes till midnight on Saturday nights before we'd get away. We used to have a [movie] show here in town, and people would come and go to the show. And [when it would] get out, [they] would come and get their feed money.[15]

Commercial agricultural production began in earnest after the Illinois Central Railroad was built in the 1850s. As noted earlier, this linked Union County to northern, particularly Chicago, markets. The increasing importance of commercial production can be seen in sharp increases in fruit, vegetable, and wheat production and in the number of head of draft stock, particularly mules (see tables 4.1 and 4.2). Mules are a particularly

Table 4.1. Indicators of Commercial Production, 1850–1920

Year	Wheat (bu.)	Cattle (head)	Horses (head)	Mules & Asses (head)
1850	31,902	5,935	2,348	68
1860	168,530	6,290	2,605	352
1870	180,231	6,955	3,919	901
1880	371,620	6,350	3,982	1,425
1890	462,340	10,750	4,450	1,713
1900	435,210	8,489	4,904	2,236
1910	341,095	7,724	5,344	2,897
1920	247,995	7,502	4,648	3,691

Sources: U.S. Bureau of the Census, *Census of Agriculture*, year as noted.

good indicator of both commercial production and use of hired labor, as John Aldridge explained:

> While a mule is more contrary than the horse, he is tougher, and . . . you can't drive one when he's exhausted. He'll quit; you can't force him to go. Another thing is that you can't drive him into a place where he will hurt himself. It's almost impossible to get one of them to do anything to hurt themselves. They have some super judgment of danger. They were especially beneficial for men who had a lot of hired hands to drive them because a lot of times you would have a man that didn't understand a horse. He would overwork a horse because he was willing to go on. You can push a horse on until he drops dead; you can't do that to a mule. He'll just quit. . . . If a team of mules gets scared and runs away when they are hitched together, they won't straddle a tree. They both go on the same side of every tree and hole. They have a built-in instinct of self-preservation. Being tough, they will stand more labor and punishment than a horse. They are more valuable in use of farm work for energy than a horse.[16]

Most farmers, both renters and landowners, owned considerable amounts of draft stock. Bill Rhodes, whose parents operated a moderate-sized farm, recalled that they "usually had two teams. We usually had seven to eight head of stock. We kept a mare to raise the colts, and we'd usually have one or two young ones there . . . mostly mules. Kept the mare to raise them."[17] Edith Rendleman recalled that her father, who rented a 360-acre farm in the bottoms, had fifteen horses and mules.[18]

Mule raising was a commercial enterprise in its own right. Ren Sirles recalled, "My grandfather got his start in business in mule trading and

Table 4.2. Value of Orchards and Market Gardens, 1850–1990 (in dollars)

Year	Value of Orchards	Value of Market Gardens
1850	1,615	—
1860	32,894	7,784
1870	150,576	24,510
1880	37,101	136,653
1890	—	140,563
1900	34,771	305,925
1910	279,967	480,249
1920	917,494	1,167,748[a]
1925	—	—
1930	1,075,104	353,379
1934	—	27,517
1939	—	133,827
1944	1,284,949	381,230
1949	1,224,522	349,246
1954	1,006,465	281,012
1959	885,062	304,234
1964	929,912	326,311
1969	917,000	431,386
1974	1,418,000	454,000
1978	2,177,000	604,000
1982	1,935,000	622,000
1987	3,794,000	539,000

Sources: U.S. Bureau of the Census, *Census of Agriculture*, year as noted.

[a]Includes sweet and white potatoes.

mule breaking and selling. He had at one time 167 head of mules on this farm. . . . The most mules he ever had in harness at one time on this farm was 33 teams, 66 head of mules. . . . He would buy, sell, break, train, go show. . . . He would try to raise mules for tobacco mules." Ren's mother, Helen Sirles, continued, "He would not sell mules to the coal mines, because they would go blind. When they would work underground so long, they would go blind. He just didn't want that. He sold a lot of mules to the South."[19] Horses and mules were a major commodity, and in the 1930s W. H. Bishop began a horse and mule market on the outskirts of Anna, which in 1938 he turned into a horse and mule auction that was reputed to be the largest in the world.[20]

The increased use of mules is, therefore, an index to two linked phenomena: the increasing replacement of human labor with animal labor and technologies, and the increasing reliance on wage labor.

Stories of American Agricultural History

One story that has been told of American agriculture—the dominant story, in many respects—has focused on these technological developments and on the development of marketing systems.[21] It is a story that has generally omitted, or treated as unrelated, the corresponding increase in tenant and wage labor, and farm women's development of commercial agricultural enterprises that they managed and whose proceeds they controlled. The account that presents agricultural history as progressive technological development in an ever expanding market is flawed as well in presenting agricultural history as an inevitable progression from "inefficiency" to "efficiency." That story has its kernel of truth, of course: over the long sweep of time, labor has been more or less consistently replaced by technologies that have allowed fewer people to produce more goods, and farmers have become increasingly engaged in and dependent upon commodity production, mediated through ever more centralized marketing systems. However, to tell the story as one of continual progress in a single direction, while congruent with one set of historical facts, removes people from the narrative and drops periods, such as the Great Depression, when both processes were reversed as national and international markets disintegrated.

One of the key elements of making the historical account a record of people's lives, rather than of, say, agriculture as a putatively impersonal system, is that people could have (and often did) act in ways contrary to the dominant stream of history that we, looking backward, can discern. In fact, farmers were remarkably slow in adopting new technologies, even when the benefits in terms of labor savings were patently obvious.[22] Reformers and educators persistently expressed frustration at farmers' reluctance to adopt "modern" methods.

"Fruitgrower," a regular correspondent to the Jonesboro *Gazette* in 1866 and 1867, was such a reformer, aiming to educate his neighbors, whom he characterized, in the literary formulas of the day, as "Hezekiah Slovenly" and "Jim Careless" (contrasted with another neighbor, "Paul Thrift").[23] People locally recollect the distinction between the "wide-awake" farmers and the "backward" ones as between immigrant Yankees and the old settlers from the southern hills. However, the contrast was also between entrepreneurially oriented commercial farmers and the established farming community.[24]

In this period in the mid- to late nineteenth century the developing industrialization and urbanization stimulated the growth of commercial production in regions like Union County that were relatively remote from expanding urban industrial centers. The growth of urban factories created a strong and ever expanding market for agricultural products, and the construction of the railroad provided a way to get the goods to these markets. It also brought into play the inevitable tendencies toward concentration and social differentiation that are built into competitive economies: land became a valuable investment not only for speculation but also as a source of sustained wealth, made possible by a large pool of tenant and waged laborers (these relationships will be described in Chapter 6). The consequences for landowning farmers were twofold: they had to work harder in order to maintain their relative economic and social status in the community, and they had to increase the scale of their operation, which required them to rely on seasonal labor. Smaller farmers, in order to stay afloat, had to supplement their work on their own farms with seasonal labor for their neighbors. This effect can be seen in the landholdings of farmers who were active in the agrarian movements of the 1870s: immediately following the Civil War this group of "substantial farmers"—country squires—were among the largest landowners; by 1880 the absolute size of their farms had increased, but a number of very large landowners had emerged, many of them townspeople who were not involved in agrarian organizations. Because of increasing concentrations in landownership, the agrarian leaders had slipped to the lower end of the top 44 percent. This loss in status, which carried with it a loss of power to direct the course of daily life, to a new breed of self-identified capitalists was undoubtedly part of the environment that stimulated the agrarian movement that swept the region in 1873.[25] The agrarian leaders, however, generally made the transition to the new order as successful commercial farmers and businessmen, while their poorer neighbors became ever more dependent on working for them. These substantial and large farmers, often in cooperation with some town merchants, formed the core of the shipping associations and the Farmers' Mutual Benefit Association and its organizational descendants, including locals of the Farmers' Educational and Cooperative Union of America, organized in 1910, through which farmers negotiated with millers for better terms on their wheat and in other ways mobilized to protect their interests. In 1917 they organized as the Union County Farm Bureau and hired a farm adviser through the University of Illinois Cooperative Extension Service.[26]

By the late nineteenth century several strata of farmers can be distinguished. A small number of large landowners saw their farms largely as an investment and had other, nonfarm investments and enterprises. Most of these landlords did not actively work their farms but left them to renters or managers. The majority of farmers were "substantial farmers"—diversified commercial farmers who were deeply embedded in networks of neighbor and kin and who generally hired labor rather than hiring out their own labor. These farmers often had auxiliary enterprises such as grist- and sawmilling, blacksmithing, threshing, stock buying, and timber cutting and selling. This group included renters who owned their own livestock and farm equipment, like Elijah Bradley, particularly in the Mississippi bottoms. Teenaged children of these families often worked for wages in neighbor's fields.[27] Ranging below them economically were smaller farmers who were dependent to a greater or lesser extent on wage labor. The poorest farmers, like Elijah Bradley's parents and the tenants on the Walton farm, lived on rented land and worked for wages.

Significant technological innovations became available in the early years of the twentieth century, particularly electricity, tractors powered by internal combustion engines, chemical fertilizers, more productive pure-bred livestock and grain varieties, and a vaccine against hog cholera.[28] Farmers, however, were slow to adopt these new technologies. Productivity in general did not increase during the early years of the twentieth century. Cochrane observed, "The first decade of the twentieth century was a highly prosperous time for American farmers, but not because the average, or representative, farmer was greatly expanding his production. . . . In fact, the index of farm productivity, output per unit of input, actually declined in the period 1900–1910."[29] The sluggish rate of technological innovation continued through the 1910s, the period that set the parity rate for farmers for the rest of the century. Because of strong agricultural prices, returns to labor in farming during the 1910s were, for the first (and only) time, roughly congruent with industry. In the 1920s, stimulated by a sharp and sustained drop in commodity prices, farmers began to apply fertilizers and practice crop rotation more than in previous decades. Nonetheless, little labor was replaced by capital investments; neither were efficient business practices developed, as indicated by the keeping of accounts and other records.

The previous chapter, which described some of the networks of neighbor and kin through which farmers reproduced their lives, points toward a partial explanation of the slowness with which farmers adopted new technologies: not only did these relationships dampen the economic pressures toward innovation, but perhaps they actually made greater dependence on cash relationships more risky over the long term, leaving families vulnerable in ways that are not easily measured economically—in those domains of "social security," both emotional and physical. As we will see in the next chapters, farmers' decisions to adopt or not adopt new technologies were also shaped, in part, by considerations of class and power. The history of farming, therefore, cannot be told apart from the histories of the people who farmed (or quit farming), for, as the Amish so clearly demonstrate, at any point we as a society, or segments of our society as subcultures, could have done otherwise and still may.

Well, my mother and dad taught us to
work. —Helen Kimber

Neither of us thought it was a disgrace
to work. And we had to work to make a
living. . . . I never knew when I got
enough work. I worked from early
morning till late at night. . . . Seems as
though that's all anybody ever wanted
with me, was to work. And I've done
my share of it. . . . I would hate to live
my life over, I worked so hard.

—Edith Rendleman

All I Knew Was to Work

If the nineteenth-century development of commercial agriculture increased labor requirements in general, it increased most farm women's labor in particular. This did not generally lead to new or novel kinds of work for women; rather, people drew on the previous division of work between men and women as they developed new products or increased production of existing ones. Every society we know of divides activities between men and women and by age. Southern Illinois farmers were no exception. In general terms, in the families that settled Union County in the nineteenth century, women were responsible for the house, and men were responsible for the farm, although the two domains interpenetrated and called upon the labor of men, women, and children—family members, neighbors, and hired hands. Well into the twentieth century, women were generally responsible, through their direct labor and through their cash earnings, for making sure that the people housed within the home were fed, clothed, and cleaned and that their medical needs were taken care of. Men were, reciprocally, responsible for crops, draft stock, and commercial large livestock operations, if any. The house and its associated yards and outbuildings were generally under the wife's management; the barns and their associated yards and outbuildings, fields, fences, and woodlots were generally under the husband's supervision. In general, wives "helped" their husbands in the barn and field; husbands "helped" their wives in the house and its environs. Children, neighbors, and hired hands "helped" whoever gave them direction. There were many exceptions, however, for any individual could take primary responsibility for any chore: a wife could have a commercial strawberry patch; a child could have her own melon patch; a husband could bake cakes.

Several recent studies show that what was considered appropriate work for men and women varied from region to region, from group to group, and even from family to family. Kohl and Bennett proposed an "agrifamily system" as a contrast to urban families. The families they worked with in the Canadian prairies divided labor between husband and wife, with the husband having responsibility for the "enterprise" and the wife managing the household but also providing crucial labor on the farm. The "system," however, varies widely from this pattern. Osterud, who studied a region of upstate New York that in the nineteenth century specialized in dairies, found that husbands and wives frequently treated each other as partners in the dairy operation, even as they divided management of other farm tasks along gendered lines. However, in the wheat producing Great Plains and in the corn and livestock regions of Iowa, husbands and wives seem to have few areas of overlapping management: women appear to have been responsible for the household, with poultry and small dairy production, while men managed the field crops and large livestock, even though women often helped their husbands and fathers with the crops and livestock.[1]

How to interpret these differences is a matter of some debate, and the degree of difference may to some extent be an artifact of the questions asked by different scholars. Nonetheless, the growing number of detailed studies of farm families reveals significant differences in the value different families attribute to women's and men's work in agriculture and elsewhere. Some of these differences are undoubtedly related to the major commodities raised; while women are not inherently incapable of operating extensive fields or ranching, and some women have done such work, these forms of production require long periods away from the house and are not compatible with care of infants and young children. In contrast, it is possible to carry out dairying and horticultural activities in the context of other household responsibilities.[2] Ethnic and religious backgrounds also influence whether or not women in a particular agricultural community or farm family will have managerial responsibilities (or co-responsibilities) for various aspects of the farm operation, and the degree to which men will help with household tasks. Salamon discerned two different systems of husband-wife relations, those of German "yeoman" farmers and those of what she distinguished as entrepenurial Yankees. German women tended to be more involved in production than their Yankee counterparts, but their status and power within the household was more dependent on whether or not they brought land to the marriage, since German families were more concerned with transmitting land to their heirs than were Yankees.[3]

Ethnicity and crop specialty cannot fully account for different gender patterns, however. Barlett, who studied farmers in a Georgia county, also discerned two marital models, which she termed "agrarian" and "industrial." To the degree that Barlett could find any significant correlations, generation, class, wife's farming or nonfarming background, and to a lesser extent, race appeared to affect the degree to which a wife participated as a full partner. The differences Barlett perceived were also based on different underlying values than were the ethnic differences Salamon discerned: in agrarian families, wives strongly identified with the farm operation; in industrial families, wives treated the farm as their husband's job.[4] In contrast, Salamon's analysis is based on differing modes of inheritance between Germans, who are strongly oriented to transmitting the family estate to their heirs, and the more individualistic Yankees.

Gender relations among southern Illinois farmers display the wide variability that Barlett saw in Georgia, although the historical roots of this variability differ. The families that originally settled Union County and continued to predominate socially came from the Upland South, from German-speaking or Scots-Irish backgrounds. They had lived in the Appalachian mountains among the Cherokee—among whom women were the agriculturalists—for at least one or two generations before moving westward. Faragher argues that among the early settlers in Sangamon County, Illinois, who were also from the southern backcountry, women carried a great deal of the responsibility for agricultural activities.[5] They displayed much more equality of behavior in relation to men than did Yankee women and were the butt of Yankee satire, as in an 1857 lampoon by "Invisible Green." According to him, the people of the southern part of the Old Northwest were a "lazy, triflin' people." He wrote, "Them squatters' gals do all the little matters about the house . . . [and] make all the clothes of the men folks, from the natral [sic] wool. . . . They shoot like old hunters . . . [and] help the men folks in the field. . . . They do a heap of the tradin', . . . [and] they ride horses astraddle . . . and milk the cows."[6]

Before mechanical rakes replaced hand labor, women often assumed responsibility for raking the hay, while men forked it onto wagons, hauled it to the barn, and unloaded it. Here Sara Estelle "Stell" Murray rakes hay. Louise Ogg Collection, Morris Library, Southern Illinois University, Carbondale.

These brief notes do not allow us to draw a comprehensive picture of the work of southern Illinois farm women in the first half of the nineteenth century, nor do we have good data on the gender relations later immigrants from the northeastern states, Germany, Austria, and elsewhere brought with them. We know that women prepared the wool, cotton, and flax from which they spun, wove, and sewed virtually all the family's clothing. Edith Rendleman recalled that her mother, who was born in 1861, told her about carding wool for spinning when she was a child. In the 1870s widows stopped choosing spinning and weaving equipment when their husbands' estates were settled, indicating that this was no longer an important household activity.[7] By the late nineteenth century these tasks were largely replaced or lightened by purchased fabrics, home sewing machines, and ready-made clothing. By the latter part of the nineteenth century, woodstoves had lightened the labor of cooking as well.[8] Aside from these two areas of work, however, new technologies did not replace or significantly lighten women's chores. Rather, they enabled farmers to produce more for the expanding urban markets. This in turn increased demands on farm family labor, much of which fell on the housewife.

Markets for agricultural products affected farm women far differently

The family cow or cows provided milk and cream for home consumption and for sale at the local grocery or cream station. Annie Weimeyer milks a cow while Birdie Murray looks on. Louise Ogg Collection, Morris Library, Southern Illinois University, Carbondale.

than the markets for industrial products affected their urban counterparts: while urban middle-class women became consumers in the new industrial era, farm women became petty commodity producers.[9] By the turn of the century virtually all farm women who had land to do so raised poultry for meat and eggs and sold dairy products as whole cream, butter, and cottage cheese. They oversaw their children's work caring for and milking the cows and churning the cream, and they controlled the income from these products. Farm women of all classes also produced a wide variety of other products: dried apples, corn shucks for tamales,[10] flowers, and duck and goose down. Women also earned money by taking in boarders, sewing for other women, making rugs (woven and braided) on order, taking in washing, acting as midwife and/or doctor's assistant, giving music lessons, and, for young or poor women, working as farm laborers and as domestic help.

"Those women would work," Helen Sirles recalled of her childhood. "Be the last ones to go to bed. Everybody else including the husbands would be in bed, and they would still be doing things, getting ready for the next morning. They would be the first ones up [at 4:30 to 5:00 in the morning]."[11] Maude Kinder recalled, "She [my mother] always had to have breakfast. We had ham and eggs and biscuits every morning. . . . It was always fixed when us kids got up."[12]

Mary Walton Hill's recollections were similar, although her family was relatively wealthy: "[My mother] got up early, around five. She got Dad's breakfast, and we girls didn't get up until later. And she started in—she never stopped. I never saw her sit down and just lounge and not do anything. There was always so much to do—when you don't have electricity and when you don't have running water, you know."[13]

Commodity Production

Work aimed at earning a cash income and work that provided daily needs were not sharply distinguished, just as child care was not a discrete body of activities. Similarly, work that was appropriate to men and to women was, in many cases, not strongly distinguished. Nonetheless, people recalled distinctly what earned money and what did not, and what specific jobs men and women did. As Ruby Weaver related,

My mother-in-law made butter and sold butter to people, and eggs. [She had a big egg operation]. And chickens, she raised chickens. Then, she had cows. The men didn't help her do that—she did that. . . . When she made butter and cream, she had different people that she'd take to, and then she dressed chickens in later years, too, and she had regular customers for that. And then I would help her take them to town, she would take eggs to town. She had cases and she took them to the poultry house. . . . She always got around 500 baby chicks, and she'd sell the roosters—the fryers—and she'd keep the pullets. . . .

Of course we had chickens, too, and when we lived over there at St. John's Church [1938–45], we dressed chickens for people. There was a Villa Hotel down at McClure, and we dressed about thirty-five to forty a week for them, besides all the others that we would dress that I would deliver in town. I had regular people that would take two and three a week. . . .

That was what we ate on [and bought clothes on]. Everything. He [my husband] helped me, though. We'd usually dress on Friday and I'd take them on Saturday. . . .

I milked cows when we lived over there. I had a whole bunch of cows. I milked as many as fifteen cows—by hand. My dad would help me. Charles [my husband] always fed [the cows] for us, but he didn't help us milk.[14]

Children were pressed into service as soon as they were old enough. Edith Rendleman, telling of her own family in the 1920s and 1930s, recounted, "I milked [four or five] cows and ran the cream separator. . . . When [the children] got big enough, why they began milking too. Bonnie first, and when Bud got big enough, why he took over."[15]

Mrs. Rhodes sold cream, also. Her daughter Maude Kinder (born in the 1910s) said, "[My mother] would put it in these crocks and skim, hand skim it. . . . She got [a separator] later on. When she sold the butter, she would hand skim it and then churn it. We had a lot of good buttermilk. . . . If we had more than we needed, we would feed it to the hogs."[16] Her brother Bill Rhodes recalled that the children helped milk and churn the butter, which his mother sold to a store in Jonesboro.[17]

S. Earl Thompson recalled that his mother "traded butter for things we couldn't grow, such as sugar and salt. It produced some cash income, because he [the grocer] paid for the surplus in cash."[18] The sale of this butter kept them going through the winter when they had no crops to sell on the market. Only a few farmers sold fluid milk, either directly to customers or to local dairies, and these were fully commercial businesses generally run by men, although women were sometimes hired to work in the operation.[19] Rosemary Walton made and sold cottage cheese to town customers, using milk from her husband's commercial dairy.

The development of dairying was intimately connected to the development of towns and of industry. While most families had a cow or two that provided milk for home consumption, commercialization of milk and cream did not begin until the 1880s. Butter production increased until 1910 (see fig. 10.2). It was increasingly supplanted by cream until 1929, when fluid milk became the more important commodity. This corresponds to shifts in the dairy marketing system: the local market was largely for butter, while commercial creameries, most of which were located in central and northern Illinois, bought cream. After World War II, as food standards became more rigorous, dairies bought fluid milk for pasteurization and conversion into powdered milk; with increased demand and with new electric milking technologies, the scale increased significantly. This process is further analyzed in Chapter 10.

Poultry was the other classically female product (see fig. 7.2).[20] The henhouses and the brooder house, if any, were generally part of the house yard or located nearby. Some, although by no means all, families kept guinea fowl and martin houses to help ward off predators. "There had to be a martin box up over the chicken house to keep the hawks and crows from eating your chickens up," John Aldridge recalled. "Martins fight off crows, sparrows, and hawks. . . . One time I remember the martins were having a terrible fit, and we were at the dinner table. Dad and some of the older men ran out, and there was a black snake that was coiled around this pole and sitting on top of the martin box. It was just drawed up trying to get its head in the nest. That created quite an excitement then. . . . The martins were really having a fit."[21] Edith Rendleman raised chickens for eggs and sold three or four crops of fryers annually to the St. Louis market. According to her,

I would have about 200 [chickens]. I raised chickens in an incubator. I would set an incubator with about 300 eggs, . . . maybe 200. . . . [They would be from my hens] or they might have come from the neighbors if you wanted their kind of chickens. . . . And then we got so we bought baby chicks early, and I had a brooder in a chicken house. . . . [The chickens] were mine alone. My husband didn't have anything to do with the chickens, only buy the feed.

The hens were over in the henhouse and sometimes I'd have 50 to 75 hens through the winter to lay eggs. . . . [The children sometimes collected the eggs] but usually I did that myself because they done the milking. When they got old enough to milk, why they were milking, getting in the wood, water, and coal while I gathered up the eggs.

I bought our winter clothes out of chickens.

"My mother kept the table going with her eggs and milk and butter," Rendleman recalled further. Referring to a family portrait, she said, "Every one of the boys had on a suit, and I'm not sure but a necktie. And that was when I was one year old—eighty-four years ago [1899]. How she ever managed to buy a suit of clothes for all those boys, I'll never know. . . . She [sewed] mine, but she didn't the boys. But they all had on a suit. She bought a lot of things with that butter and milk and egg money."[22]

Clara Davidson ran a 1,000-hen egg operation with her brother, supplying the Union County Hospital with eggs for twenty years.

Women of all agricultural classes had commercial egg and chicken operations. Louise Walton, for example, whose parents were Anna businesspeople, "was a gracious lady and rather shy," her granddaughter Barbara Throgmorton recalled. "She saved money from giving piano lessons and selling eggs and things like that and bought a little farm. . . . I believe she also saved enough money to buy herself a car."[23]

Despite the occasional woman who was successful enough (or sufficiently subsidized by her husband) to buy land or, in the case of one woman I interviewed, build a house, most of the earnings from women's commercial operations were plowed directly back into the household, which was the housewife's primary responsibility.

Housework

Household work, apart from commercial enterprises, was a big job. Farm households were large. Not only were farm families relatively big— in 1900 the average Union County farm family included more than nine people—but they included related and unrelated dependents and, frequently, hired hands. John Aldridge recalled that "there was nearly always a hired hand or a farmhand or two that boarded with us. . . . He lived in the house, boarded with us, ate at the table with us, and had his own room. . . . Besides the family and hired help, there was nearly always one or two of the older relatives in the house—maybe a grandparent, great uncle or great aunt. There were no nursing homes for them to go, so they stayed with their relatives."[24] Orphans and unrelated indigent elderly dependents were also farmed out by the county to families, who were paid a small stipend for their care.

A home economist writing in the 1930s estimated that farm women spent an average of sixty-one hours a week on "homemaking activities" (remunerative labor and farm labor were specifically excluded from these studies).[25] About 44 percent of these sixty-one hours was spent preparing and clearing away meals; 20 percent was spent in care of the house; 10 percent, laundering; 8 to 10 percent, sewing and mending; and the rest of the time was spent in care of family members, managerial tasks, and other activities.

"Washing for a woman was an all day's job," John Aldridge commented. Ada Gurley recounted:

[My mother] washed on the washboard. I washed on them. I washed for several years after I was married before I ever had a washer. We would put us on a big iron kettle of water, heat it, and then we would wash. We would boil them, take them out, rinse them through two waters, and wring them with our fists. . . . I've washed many times 'till dinnertime, got dinner, and then finished with the big washing we had. They were all boys but [one]. I told them after the boys got any size that it looked like a shirt and overall factory whenever I would get their shirts and overalls washed and hung up.[26]

The girls often took over washing when they got old enough. "Me and this oldest sister worked together with the washing," Maude Kinder recalled. "Mother would help some but not too much. . . . [The boys] would generally help with the water."[27] Standards varied considerably from family to family, and some people rarely if ever washed work overalls, believing they lasted longer if they were not washed. People also generally had few changes of clothing, although large families and resident laborers, for whom the family provided laundry as part of the pay, created large laundries.

Ironing, like washing, passed to the girls as soon as they were old enough. According to Maude Kinder, "At first we did not have an ironing board. We had to pad the table. Course we didn't care about that old table. . . . I must have been eight or ten [when I started ironing]. Especially the flat pieces, like pillow cases, handkerchiefs, things like that. But I remember, Mother would come and inspect, and if it didn't suit her, I had to iron that over. . . . We used to wear dresses when we were twelve, fourteen, and all with them ruffles. . . . So us girls did the ironing. . . . We always used those sad irons."[28] More affluent women hired teenaged girls or poorer women to do the washing and ironing, although few people I interviewed recalled any domestic help, except during brief periods of illness or at the birth of a baby.

Sewing was another skill women were expected to have. Bert Casper recalled, "My mother was a very good seamstress, and she made our clothing. She bought very good blue denim, and she would make our overalls and shirts. I was a great big boy, perhaps twelve years old [ca. 1915] before I had ever had any store-bought clothing such as trousers."[29]

Cotton feed sacks were an important source of fabric for sewing. Women bleached the brand out of white cotton sacks, and when feed companies started using floral prints for their sacks, they made sure to get enough sacks of a particular design to make a garment.[30] As Edith Rendleman remembered, "You saved all the cotton sacks that you bought chicken feed in. . . . About 1928 and '30—somewhere along there—they had printed sacks."[31] Elizabeth Cerny recalled, "I used to laugh at my sister-in-law. . . . They used the flour sacks, . . . and she said one time it happened they didn't get all the print out of the flour sack, and they teased her so much about the prints [the brand mark] on the seat of her pants. . . . I made little dresses out of the printed flour sacks."[32]

Women's sewing also provided most of the family's bedding—ticks for straw mattresses (pulling fresh straw for the ticks was children's work) and feather beds, pillow casings to be stuffed with feathers or down, and quilts. Maude Kinder recalled that her mother quilted. "She let [the quilting frame] down on chairs, and then at night when she didn't want to quilt, she had nails and she would put it up on the ceiling."

Her mother also raised and plucked geese. "After she passed away, Dad he had some geese and he wanted me to pluck those feathers. . . . I never got used to it. Put that old head between your legs and they just fight. . . . I got mad and finally I just give up. After we had been there fifteen years. I had big white ducks. I had thirty of them. I would get them and pick them. Oh, I got the most pretty feathers. . . . I just made pillows."[33]

Not all women were good seamstresses. Ada Gurley recalled, "I never was much of a hand for a needle. . . . My daughter has done my sewing. . . . My daughter has made my clothes ever since she was fourteen years old. She taught herself. I couldn't teach her much because I didn't know much about it. I could make them so the children could wear them when they were little. But I never was much of a hand with a needle. But I was a good hand to milk cows, raise chickens, and to see after the children."[34]

Women were also primarily responsible for providing the food the family ate. This included not only cooking three meals a day and cleaning up afterward, but growing, processing, and preserving food for most of the family's needs. The housewife planted and tended a large "kitchen garden" that provided vegetables in season and for preservation for winter use. Helen Kimber remembered that "you worked out in the field all day and then canned your beans, tomatoes, and things at night."[35]

Elizabeth Cerny recalled, "I'd put up about seventy cans of peaches and maybe forty cans of berries, and I'd make apple butter and applesauce, pickles, . . . some green beans, . . . pickled peppers, a few."[36] Ruby Weaver recounted what she put up: "I used to can three and four hundred quarts of fruits and vegetables a year. . . . Well, we'd buy peaches and apples, . . . but we'd have all kinds of vegetables, . . . green beans and cucumbers, tomatoes, cabbage. I got to where I could raise cauliflower and broccoli. You just name it and we had it. . . . I had asparagus . . . and hulley beans and green beans and garden peas. After I got the freezer, I'd freeze them. . . . And sauerkraut. We made sauerkraut [and pickles]."[37]

Hog butchering, described in Chapter 3, provided much of the family's meat. The heavy work associated with butchering was largely left to the men, and canning the sausage was left to the women; but the other jobs—seasoning the sausage, salting and smoking the meat, and rendering the lard—seem to have fallen on whoever had the skill and the desire to do it. Charles Thomas recalled, "You can go around the country everywhere and think the building's on fire, smoke would be coming out of the cracks—the old smokehouse. I had an aunt who lived down in Anna. She was absolutely an expert."[38]

Farm women made soap from lye—in earlier years leached from wood ashes, in later years purchased—as well as yeast from hops and corn meal, and cottage cheese. "If we didn't make it at home, we did without," Maude Kinder said.[39]

Cooking was a major, time-consuming activity, given the size of most farm households and the amount of processing needed to turn the raw materials into food. Sunday dinners were likely to be particularly large, and many women did not go to church in order to prepare the meal. Helen Sirles recalled, "On Sundays, chicken and dumplings, 'cause many times you never knew how many was going to come home from Sunday school and church with the children. Because it was understood back in those days that Sunday—they didn't have movies and all the entertainment—you go to somebody's home. . . . Always cooked big on Sunday."[40]

All of this work was done with water that was, in most homes, carried by the bucket from the well or the spring. Maude Kinder commented, "I think when you have water like that you are stingy with it. Now, you know that bucket, you can't just use that and in fifteen minutes go and get another bucket. That had to last for a long time."[41]

The number of people who were in and out of the house and the amount of activity that occurred within it—particularly in the kitchen—in an environment in which mud or dust were ever present meant that keeping the house clean was a continuous task. It was remarkable to me, therefore, how few women commented on housecleaning as a discrete chore. Edith Rendleman, when asked about keeping the house clean, said, "It was [a big job], but we never thought anything about it. Just like emptying the ashes out of the coal stove—sometimes there would be three pans full, but you just had to [do it]. . . . They always took their boots off on the back porch."[42] Nonetheless, the quantity of work required, and the constant need to clean, especially in a house with few daughters, made Edna Kimber's comment that her ten-room house was a "woman-killer" a sentiment that was probably widely shared by women of her generation.

The quantity of domestic production, particularly the large amount of processing done over fire, was also sometimes hazardous. An item in the Jonesboro *Gazette*, February 10, 1872, from the Campground neighborhood warned women, "A few days since a childing [*sic*] belonging to Mr. Z. Carter, was severely and fatally scalded by a kettle of half finished soap falling and spilling over it while it was playing before the fire. Keep your soap kettles out of the house, women." In her memoirs Edith Rendleman recounted a similar instance in her mother's family. Al Basler recalled a similar case that had less catastrophic consequences. When his neighbor Nathaniel Green was six or seven years old [ca. 1862], he nearly lost the use of his leg:

> It was kind of a cold, rainy day. Those kids was huddled up around the cookstove. The women was a'cooking the dinner. There was a big kettle of soup or something that one of them had set on the back of the stove. To cool, I guess. But these kids had nestled around the stove and had their place there, to keep warm. He [Nathaniel Green] was down there. I don't know whether one of the women bumped the kettle or if it was one of the kids, but that [kettle] come off on those kids there. The main part of it hit him. It just scalded him. He told me that the flesh just come off and his leg drawed back like this and he couldn't straighten it out.
>
> This doctor—this woman that was doing the doctoring—she had all the men in the neighborhood that she could get, go and bring some fishworms. And they dug fishworms and made the oil out of those fishworms. And she had some other boys go out and get her some hickory sapling. She bent that [sapling] and put it behind this leg and bandaged it. And that straightened his leg out.[43]

This incident suggests other roles women played in the rural community. Doctor and midwife were important, and oral accounts of births indicate that male doctors frequently called on skillful women to assist them. Women were also schoolteachers, a job that some kept after marriage.[44] Some women were also particularly sought out for their wisdom and sound advice. Maude Kinder said of her mother, "I know whenever anyone would lose a mother, it seemed like they would come to her, because she knew. She had been raised without a mother. Her sister kept her and was so good to her, but when you lose a mother like that, you just don't know what it is to grow up and not have a mother or a father."[45]

Farm Work

Most farm women also worked on the farm in one capacity or another outside the home, as described in Chapter 4. This was particularly true on fruit and vegetable farms, where the wife was often in charge of the packing shed while the husband was in charge of the pickers. There was some variation: most people I spoke with reported women doing farm work alongside men. Ruby Weaver, for example, said, "He [my husband] and I both farmed." Her husband gave her a tractor as a birthday gift one year so they could both work in the field at the same time.[46] A man who was born around 1910 recalled that his mother preferred to handle the horses and mules to housework, and John Aldridge, as noted in Chapter 3, said that women were often involved in making hay. Helen Kimber expected and was expected to work in the horticultural fields. Finally, after she had two babies, she recalled that she "balked. I said, 'Nope, I'm not gonna pick,' but at times I would help in the shed."[47] Maude Kinder said that while her mother enjoyed fieldwork, handling the horses was "something we never did." That was left to the men and boys.[48] One man I briefly interviewed told me that "his women" did not work in the fields—including work on horticultural crops—although he hired women to do fieldwork. This attitude, although not widespread, cropped up from time to time in interviews.

Southern Illinois farmers seem to be somewhat different from farmers in more northern regions, in that women were generally expected to work in the fields as well as take care of the house. Deborah Fink writes that women in northwestern Iowa "helped" on farm tasks like haying and picking corn and, like virtually all farm women, raised poultry and managed the dairy, but that they did not consider their agricultural activities as "work."[49] Southern Illinois women, as the above quotes indicate, seem to have seen themselves as farmers who were proud of the work they did and, to use a recent term, felt "ownership" in many agricultural processes. Clara Davidson (d. 1991), a neighbor and relative to the Kimbers, made a block on a friendship quilt sewn by members of St. John's Church that bore the legend "Clara Davidson—Retired Farmer." Numerous oral accounts indicate that girls frequently took on activities that were normally boys' activities. Sometimes this was done because the family did not have any, or enough, boys to do the work;[50] at other times it seems idiosyncratic. For example, Charles Thomas recalled that Lou Rich, daughter of one of the most prominent farmers in the Cobden area, "was raised with a bunch of brothers. She hunted with them, 'coon hunting, and so forth."[51] Edith Rendleman considered herself a "tomboy" and, with some of the other girls, played team games with the boys. Nonetheless, different families had different expectations about what work women should do, which ranged from full participation in all aspects of farming, including plowing and clearing land, to, in a few instances, exclusion from all fieldwork.

While all the women I interviewed saw their adult labor as their own, some spoke of men who "drove" their wives. Edith Rendleman's uncle drank heavily and "was a mean, cruel man to his family," she recalled. "He made everybody work but himself." She wrote of the time his wife, Mag, finally had as much as she could take:

> When Dad had that field cleared known as the pasture, Uncle Richard put it in corn with a one-horse plow. In those days they just sawed a tree down leaving the stumps two or more feet high, trimming the trees with an ax and burning the limbs and letting the stumps rot out. Aunt Mag had to do the plowing with that one-horse plow and Uncle picked up the roots, etc. After she plowed all day he would make her sit up till midnight reading the Bible. So one night she got up and pretended to go to the toilet in the chicken yard, and she left him and went to her sister's.

Her parents also discouraged her interest in a young man whose father beat his mother—a predilection the young man apparently applied to his wife after he married. These stories are rarely told in the course of formal interviews, but there is no doubt that it was not uncommon for men to use violence against their wives, children, and other dependents both to make them work and to enforce their authority. Wife beating was less sanctioned than was beating of children, as indicated by Edith's aunt, who was protected and supported by all her kin, including her husband's family. A rebellious child, on the other hand, unless suffering severe neglect or excessive abuse, was expected to stay home until old enough to support him- or herself. Edith's uncle stepped over that line as well, beating "his son so badly they got the law after him." In addition, "one of his daughters ran off and got married at fourteen just to get away from him."[52]

Reformers saw the heavy work done by farm women as injurious to their health and well-being. In 1884 Jonathan Periam, in his widely used *Home and Farm Manual*, wrote,

> Woe to the man who shall mar the happiness of the home life. And how many a farmer unthinkingly does this! He amuses himself; he goes to town to buy and sell; he hires labor when there is much to do, but he habitually neglects his fellow-toiler and helpmeet in the house. At the

busy season the work heaped upon the "women folks" almost crushes the life out of them. All this is to his future infinite loss. The life of too many farmers' wives is what no man could bear, and no woman should be made to suffer. It would be a standing shame to the men of America—a disgrace to our nation—if anywhere the women should become slaves without even the slave's holidays, as brutally sacrificed to the chase for the almighty dollar, as ever victim dragged before the throne of Moloch.... Work, the wife of a farmer must, but he should make the burden as light as possible.[53]

In 1913 a survey by the USDA found women still complaining of excessive workloads.[54] Some women, like Edith Rendleman and her mother, Sarah Bradley, worked hard because of their own ambitions to supply their families with things they otherwise could not afford; in other cases, husbands drove their wives to increase their workloads.[55] Both mothers and fathers drove their children, under the threat of whippings, to work hard.

In this environment women had fewer options than men; their financial dependence on men forced those married to domineering, abusive, stingy, or philandering husbands to put up with a great deal. A strict moral code that was widely (although not universally) adhered to also kept women bound to and dependent on men. A traditional Appalachian song goes,

> Oh hard is the fortune of all womankind,
> She's always controlled, she's always confined:
> Controlled by her father until she's a wife,
> Then a slave to her husband the rest of her life.[56]

Women who did not marry had few options in rural communities and tended to leave for urban areas where they could find work, although they might return, as did Florence Kimber, to live with their relatives when they grew old.

Girls' sexuality was also closely circumscribed, in part through a sense of acute shame concerning sexuality and their body that was communicated to young girls.[57] It was not uncommon for a single girl to become pregnant, but if she did not quickly marry, she faced a life of disgrace. I was puzzled by a 1913 will I read, in which a relatively wealthy woman gave one of her daughters $1. The meaning of this deliberate exclusion from her estate became clear when I read a letter from the daughter to her mother, a brave and pathetic letter from her new home in a southern city. The baby, she said, was healthy and happy, and she knew his father would marry her as soon as he was able. Apparently he married another woman, and despite the fact that the daughter appears to have later married, her mother never forgave her. Edith told of another family in which "N" got a poor neighbor girl pregnant. N's father mortgaged his farm to get $1,000 to "get [N] out of trouble." The young man's father eventually lost the farm because N died young and N's wife refused to honor the debt.[58]

Parents therefore maintained a strong interest in their children's behavior and choice of potential mates. Edith's parents intervened in their sons' as well as their daughter's romances, discouraging marriage into families who were known to be shiftless, drunken, or otherwise undesirable, and encouraging marriage into prosperous families. The burden of respectability fell on both the father and the mother. As Edith's recollections indicate, a drunken, abusive, slothful, dishonest, or philandering father decreased his children's chances of marrying well, although philandering seemed to be tolerated if it was not too blatant. But the wife, with primary responsibility for appearances and cleanliness, also had considerable influence. Edith's mother scrimped to buy one of her sons a new suit so he could date the daughter of a prosperous farmer, rather than the poor girl he was interested in. Edith recalled a "poor, nasty family" who were infested with lice, and another family group made up of a mother, her daughters, and their illegitimate children. Children of such families were made the butt of other children's jokes and, assuming they stayed in the area, unless they worked very hard as young adults to distance themselves from their family's reputation, had little chance of marrying into more affluent or ambitious families. Class lines were permeable—a poor person like Elijah Bradley could, by dint of hard work and upright character, marry into a "substantial" family—but oral accounts and my own recollections of my childhood indicate that people were closely ranked on various status hierarchies that determined who was and who was not a desirable partner for a child of a family that valued its respectability.[59]

Despite a relatively rigid morality and set of judgment standards, there were incidents that violated the norms: a married man ran off with a "colored" woman; a girl from a respectable family ran off with a "colored" boy; apparently "good" marriages failed because of personal failings on the part of one or both partners; there were illegitimate births; and so forth. But in most cases, people who perpetrated scandals left the area— "ran off." Except for an occasional disowning, as in the case noted above, most remained members of their extended families, but not members of the community. Farm life in the early years of the century was very difficult without a husband and wife who could work together and cooperate with their neighbors; those who went too far beyond the norms that allowed marriages and neighborly interdependence to be sustained could not survive for long and tended to be transient members of the community, little remembered by people still alive.[60]

In general, women in Union County appear to have had a considerable degree of autonomy within their households. As noted above, because of their roots in the Upland South, southern Illinois farm women may have shared in farm management more than did women in some other areas of the country.[61] The particular crops grown in Union County were probably equally important in creating a basis for wives to maintain an active interest in the agricultural enterprise. As in the plains regions, few adult women plowed or did other heavy labor with the draft stock. However, Union County farmers specialized in small fruits and vegetables. These crops require a great deal of hand labor, virtually identical to that used for gardening, a job women traditionally handled. It is also a small step from managing the complex work done in a kitchen to managing a packing shed, a job women often did. An explanation based on the technological requirements of different agricultural systems fits well with Esther Boserup's observation that women tend to be associated with hoe agriculture but not with plows and draft stock.[62] The strong aversion a few farm men had to "their women" working in the vegetable fields must, however, be based in ethnic or other particular cultural foundation, for their cropping patterns were no different from their neighbors', where the housewife also enjoyed harnessing the horses and plowing.

Even after World War II, when virtually all public education and media promoted a narrowly defined domesticity for girls and women, Union County youth remained flexible in their work roles. Four-H club records show that there was a great deal of overlap in projects undertaken by both boys and girls. No girls, however, participated in corn or soybean projects, and no boys participated in clothing, food, or home beautification projects.[63] All other projects—livestock of all kinds, garden crops, agricultural engineering, shop, crafts, and landscaping—had participants of both sexes, although boys tended to predominate in livestock and crops and girls in crafts and landscaping, while poultry was evenly divided.

Child Labor

Children were integrated into the labor process as soon as they were old enough. Clara Davidson recalled that she began picking strawberries when she was five or six years old: "My daddy made me some handgears to put your quarts [of strawberries] in to carry them. And he made me a one-quart carrier because that's all I could carry."[64] Ed Brimm, whose family lived and worked on the Walton farm, recalled that one of his first jobs was carrying strawberries "for our mothers." He and the owner's son, Ned, "thought we was something big, with two quarts, and I carried them in for my mother while she picked out there."[65]

As they got older they took on greater responsibilities, graduating from stamping basket lids with the farm name and planting sweet potato slips.[66] Maude Kinder recalled,

Dad didn't have to hire any work 'cause we were workers. I must have been twelve [when I started going into the fields]. The best I can remember [first] would be the green onions. You would have to clean them and put them in bunches and put a rubber on them. Later on came the rhubarb, and of course the leaves had to [be] cut off and they had to be cleaned. . . . We did that at the edge of the field. At strawberry time, they had a shed and we picked the berries and put them in boxes and bring them into the shed. . . . We had blackberries for a few years. . . . We raised tomatoes, and you'd start them out in the hotbed and then you would have to block them out. And then you would have to set them in the field and take a hoe and put dirt around them. . . . Of course we would have a watermelon patch. That wasn't all the time, just for home use. Just like our garden.

A lot of times we [planted corn], because we didn't have a machine. . . . You would plow the ground. You would take a one-horse plow and mark that off, you mark it off this way and then you mark it off that way [making a grid], . . . and where [the furrows crossed], you drop the corn. . . . I don't remember, we must've taken a hoe and covered that. . . . About two or three [kernels], that's what we'd put in there and then when we wanted to grow beans, that's where we would plant our pole beans. . . . The stalks of the corn acted as a pole for the beans, you see.[67]

Ed Brimm's recollections were similar:

[When tomatoes] came up, oh, get about an inch and a half high, you had to transplant them so many inches apart; then when they get grown, why take them out in the fields and set them. Cucumbers the same way. Sweet potatoes, you have to bed them; that was my job, laying them things down. . . . I'd always hate to see the sweet potatoes get big enough to set; that was rough on your back. . . . My dad would spade them, and I'd have to go along and back down sticking them. . . .

It was my job every night running [the sheep] in out of the pasture—keep dogs from killing them—and shutting them up.

Most of us kids worked in the barn, we was raised up in it, girls along. . . . [The girls] had to help feed the cows. . . . Me and my brother always had to take a jaybird saw and cut wood for the night and the morning before we went to school, . . . about half a cord, a rick it was really.[68]

Helen Sirles's family raised several acres of asparagus and of rhubarb. She recalled, "Usually, parents would take smaller children and put beside them. [Children worked] from the time you were old enough to get out there just about." They were expected to cut two rows of asparagus out and back before going to school. Rhubarb was similar: "That's a cold job.

You pull rhubarb and strip it [the last week of March]. You tried to bury yourselves in the leaves for protection. . . . The men would pull it, and every so far there would be a pile, and the women [and children] would follow and trim it. And you usually had a table you took out in the field, and one or two would pack it. . . . And then they'd take one person to nail the lid on the top."[69]

The children were not always willing workers. One woman recalled that her father would take a switch to them if they were balky. Other children found other subterfuges. One girl whose parents were not too insistent on her working disappeared for long periods of time in the woods—a tactic that my brother also used on occasion. Edith Rendleman laughed as she remembered how she and her brother got around planting beans: "My mother always liked soup beans. She used to make us plant cornfield beans in the spring—me and my brother. And when the corn got about a foot high, and then we went in there with a hoe and dropped two or three seeds, made a place for it and covered it up. We'd catch Mom at the other end of the field, and we'd dig a hole and put a whole handful of beans in it so we wouldn't have to plant so much."[70]

On occasion children's size particularly fitted them for specific jobs. S. Earl Thompson, for example, remembered "as a boy being assigned the task of picking the apples out of the tops of the trees because I was lighter than any of the men who were working. One or two of them would hold the ladder and I would go up and pick the apples out of the top."[71] Girls as well as boys might take on heavy jobs, although as noted above, some families did not think that fieldwork was appropriate for girls or women. Helen Kimber, however, was encouraged to do farm work:

[We did] cleaning and mowing weeds—getting ready for the crops. My sister and I would hitch up old Patty and Prince [the work horses] to the sled. We'd go up to the orchard. We'd haul brush. You name it, we done it. . . . We didn't cook. My mother did that. That's why I never liked to cook, because she said, "If you girls work out there, I'll do all this cooking and the housework." So, it was baited nice for us. . . . But we did take the washing off of our mother and, oh, if there was extra work in the house, we always tried to do that. . . . We all cooperated.

My dad gave us, when we got a little older, he gave us a crop, melon crop or spinach crop or something like that, you know. And we worked and sold that. In fact, the year . . . Frank [her husband-to-be] and I went together, . . . May and I, my sister, had a melon crop, and she and I cleared $600. That was money![72]

Faye Smith, whose parents were tenant farmers, recalled,

Well, far back as I can remember, I'd have to carry in the wood. . . . It'd be split for the heating stove or the cookstove, and me and my brother

. . . we'd carry in the wood. . . . Clean the lamp chimneys, and [when I was like ten or eleven years old] we had seven or eight cows and I had to help milk them. . . . And then when we moved . . . out there [to another farmer's place], . . . we'd have beans to ship and sweet potatoes to set, and I was there a-hoeing and a-picking and all—milking cows morning and night; wash the separator. Whatever there was to do. Milking, wash, iron, that usually fell on me too.[73]

Maude Kinder spoke of the work she did during her childhood:

[At age six or seven] sometimes us girls had to help carry the wood, because a lot of times the boys would be [busy]. And the dishwashing was my job. I was about four or five. I had a little box that I would stand on and wash dishes. This older sister of mine, she would go to the front living room, and that's where she would work. . . . See, we had the homemade carpet . . . woven. And we had straw underneath that. That was her job to clean. Of course, we would all have to help. That was her job. But mine was to fill the lamp, fill the salt and pepper shakers. . . . [I would do the dishes every meal], but the rest was about once a week.

Her mother sewed, using a treadle sewing machine, but the girls helped her. "She would give us other jobs, and I'd do the rug or the carpeting. We'd tear up our old clothes, and then we would have to sew them in. And a lot of times if we got meanness or anything, she would say, 'Listen, you go and you begin making some rugs.' That was something we hated to do, I don't know why. . . . Sew the ends together and then roll them up in balls, getting them ready for the [woman who wove them into rugs]."[74]

Teenaged children began to assume adult jobs and often worked for wages. Ed Brimm, for example, recalled, "I had three sisters, and I think all of them worked up here [at the Walton's house] when they was in their teens, till they got married."[75]

Children sometimes did not work willingly, but in most families they learned obedience young. One woman recalled that her mother kept switches stuck in the walls of their log house so one would be handy whenever it might be needed to prod a balky child. Edith Rendleman recalled that she and her brother once got into a fight when he tried to force her to do his share of the work cutting pumpkins to feed the cows. He smeared pumpkin guts all over her face, and she ran home crying. As a consequence their father "give Leora the last whipping he ever got (he was 15 yrs old). Man, he had no mercy with that big switch. . . . Man, in those days everybody beat their kids something awful. That's why I was so scared of Dad."[76]

The lot of orphans was often even harder. Substantial farmers sometimes took in orphaned children, who then frequently were assigned the most tedious and distasteful jobs. My mother recalled a neighbor who was "raised an orphan" and, because of his precarious status, at the age of five or six was put to work pulling garlic from the wheat field.

The intimate relationship between the farm and the house meant that child care was integrated into the activities of daily life, and once a child was old enough to tag along after older siblings, "parenting" was widely shared. When women had many children, the older children began helping as soon as they were at all capable. Ada Gurley recalled, "My mother would keep that cradle sitting by the side of her bed. Maybe she would have the least baby over there right where she could get it, and maybe there would be one behind her sleeping, and one at the foot."[77] Edith Rendleman recalled that her oldest child "practically raised" her youngest, who was ten years younger. "She always took care of him and let me do the work."[78]

Farm fathers retained far more contact with their children than did most urban fathers. As Helen Kimber recalled, her mother shooed her and her sister out of the house to help her father; other women as well as men recalled spending a great deal of time tagging along after, helping, and being supervised by their fathers. For many girls, these early experiences gave them skills and sentiments that carried into their adult lives. Barbara Throgmorton remembered,

> I was on [my father's] shirttail all the time, which pleased my mom because she ran the kitchen, and she did not want me in the kitchen and I did not want to be in the kitchen. I followed him around, but when it would get bloody, he would send me to the house. If they were going to dehorn cattle, "No, no, Babe, you'd better go to the house." Or he would put me up on the front of the truck, and I would hold on to the hood ornament. See, everybody today would say, "Oh, that's so dangerous, how could you do that, you know we'd never let you do that," but I rode, and nobody thought anything about it. I sat up there on the hood of the truck and held on, and we'd drive out through the tall fescue and look for the calves, and I would spot the calves, "Here's one, Dad, here's one." But if he found a cow that was having a calf, "Babe, better get you back to the house." He would not let me in on that. He gave me an old sow, and I helped in her delivery of her pigs and took care of that, and I guess that's what got me started, and now I do all this vet work with the sheep and just right in there in the awfullest messes anybody's ever seen, but I think my dad would think, "My goodness, what is this girl doing?"[79]

Many of my own recollections of my youth involve helping my father with the sheep and pigs we raised. I helped with difficult births, raised orphan lambs, watched him shear the wool, and played in the hay while he worked. I helped him inoculate the pigs and joined the ever frustrating chase to move them from field to field, although he, like other men in the neighborhood, shooed me away when they castrated the pigs. This is a marked difference from the urban pattern that developed in the nineteenth century and formed the basis for reformers' and home economists' prescriptions about women's proper role as nurturing mother.[80]

Neighbors also had some authority over children. Al Basler laughed as he told a story about when he was five or six years old:

> Dad told me one day—he had a little tomato patch down over here— he says, "You go down and tell Mrs. Hunsaker she can come and get her canning tomatoes any time. So you just go down and tell her that; she might want to come down and pick today."
>
> So I went down there. She had this boy Dan, he was about my age. She says, "Well, that's fine, I'll just get my basket and you and Dan can go along and help me pick them."
>
> That suited us all right. We went along. When we got in the tomato patch, the first thing we done was to get us a tomato war started. He hit me with a good big juicy one. I grabbed one up and he run from me and he run for Mrs. Hunsaker. She had her apron, and he got under her apron about the time I throwed. I hit that apron and she stopped the tomato war right then.
>
> "I'm gonna get me a switch," she says, "and you're gonna stop this right here." She didn't go get her switch—we stopped. If we hadn't of stopped, we knew that she was going to get a switch. Lots of things like that went on.[81]

The story told here stresses the centrality of women's and children's work in the continuation of farm families, whether those families were farm operators (to use the current terminology) or tenant laborers. I have not told the corresponding story of women's lack of power relative to the men in their family. Yet without that side of the story the vast quantity and arduousness of women's work would not be fully comprehensible. For the fact is that most women developed market enterprises because they had to: Joan Jensen writes, of colonial Philadelphia, that women developed commercial enterprises to "loosen the bonds" of patriarchal authority.[82] In some cases, the stimulus to earn money appears not so much women's attempt to gain some autonomy from the authority of the patriarchal husband, but simply as an attempt to gain access to cash and the things cash would buy. Edith Rendleman wrote in her memoirs,

> My Dad used to go to Waltonville and buy a team of fancy mules. He would pay as much as $500.00 for them. But they never tho't a woman would like a new piece of furniture. . . . It seemed a woman never asked her husband for money. You just tried to earn it.

None of the men, even my Dad, ever gave their wife any money. . . . They never wanted to buy anything for the house. . . . I boarded school teachers, even washed for other people to get some furniture.[83]

The farm was one unified enterprise, with the husband given legal and customary authority over all members of the household. Until 1872, women could not own and manage property in their own names if they were married, and their ability to serve as guardians for their own children if their husband died was greatly restricted: for most legal purposes they were treated as minors.[84] This is probably the historical basis for the virtually total control most men retained over earnings from the part of the farm that was not associated with the household. In the early 1900s, when commodity production largely supplemented the maintenance of the overall farm operation on many farms, reciprocity between husband and wife maintained a rough balance in the relations between them. However, complaints by wives of improvident husbands, as exemplified in the Appalachian folksong about "the young man who wouldn't hoe corn," and, less frequently, stories about hostile wives, such as that of "the Devil and the farmer's wife" (who went down to hell and got sent back again), were the stuff of songs and moralistic writings. An agricultural item in the Jonesboro *Gazette* of June 3, 1867, gave a list of things a farmer should not do:

A farmer should not allow his wood-pile to be reduced down to the "shorts," merely drawing a little by piecemeal, and green at that. He must expect to encounter the sour looks of his wife and family, and perhaps be compelled (in a series of lectures) to learn that the man who provides green wood to burn in winter, has not mastered the rules of domestic economy. Nor should he employ some "botch" mason to build his chimney "upside down" so that his family will be nearly smoked out of the house, and the walls of the room become as yellow as saffron.

A farmer should not let his building look as old as the hills and go to decay, while he can easily afford the means to keep them in good repair; nor should he allow tattered clothes and old hats to be stuffed in the windows in place of glass. If he does, he need not be alarmed if he acquired the reputation of a mean man, or one who tarries long where liquor is sold by the glass.

The fact that the writer thought it necessary to instruct men in this way suggests, of course, that such behavior was not uncommon.

Direct access to cash income did not mean less work for women, but it did mean control over money, to be used as the wife determined. Edith Rendleman, for example, objected to housing hired hands in the house. She was required to cook, clean, and launder for them, for which they received less wages. She, however, did not receive the difference. After housing was built for the laborers, she took in boarders, generally school-teachers, whose payments she controlled.

Women's earnings, however, as noted above, came in small amounts and were needed for day-to-day living expenses. Women still relied on their husbands for major investments, as in expensive equipment and housing. One woman told me that her mother had persistently asked her father for a new house, and although he was agreeable, it never happened. One day, while her father was in town, her mother recruited her brother, and together they razed one wall of the house. Needless to say, she got her new house. As we will see in Chapter 11, this differential access to cash also affected the adoption rates of labor-saving technologies, particularly after World War II, when farm and household work was radically transformed.

The flexibility in gender roles, the great importance southern Illinois farm women—both landowning and tenant—had in farm production, and their long history of earning cash income through their own agricultural and cottage enterprises meant that when farming conditions changed and their ability to earn money and their contributions to the farm were diminished after World War II, farm women reacted very differently than had nineteenth-century urban women of propertied families. That story will be taken up later.

This chapter has also focused on the commonalities among most farm women. There were, however, significant differences between those women who operated, with their husbands, their own farms, and those who were laborers on other people's farms. These relationships are the subject of the next chapter.

They were all poor people. Those tenants, most of them had large families, and all they had was a roof over their heads. That's all it consisted of. You know, of course, they were good people, and you pick that type of people. If they like you, there's nothing in the world they wouldn't do for you. Absolutely nothing. But of course, a lot of them are shiftless and ignorant, but yet I liked them. —Charles Thomas

House of Plenty, House of Poor

Class and status relations in Union County around the turn of the century were complex, in part because of the complicated and varied cropping regimes practiced, and in part because of differing conceptions of and values surrounding relative wealth. It is surprising, even to young people who grew up on farms in the county, that laborers lived in their grandparents' house and that small houses dotted the farms, inhabited by tenant laborers.[1] The "family farm" myth, rooted in agrarian ideology that characterizes farming as typically done by owner-operator families with little if any supplementary labor, so dominates popular conceptions of farming that other forms of tenure and labor relations slip into invisibility.[2] We will see in later chapters that this myth, if it ever had substance, predominated, in Union County, only in the early and mid-nineteenth century and perhaps (on nonfruit and vegetable farms) during the 1950s and 1960s. Present tenure patterns are dominated by various forms of rental; large amounts of seasonal and year-round labor are required on farms that have orchards and horticultural crops and, increasingly, on farms in general. But that anticipates our narrative.

Around the turn of the century, five basic types of farm tenure and labor relations could be distinguished: (1) landlords with urban residences and businesses, (2) farm owners who hired resident and other day labor to help with the crops and other farm-based enterprises, (3) renters who often also hired resident and other day labor to help with the crops, (4) small farmers who occasionally hired day labor and themselves often worked for wages on other farms, and (5) tenants who worked as day laborers and generally farmed their own small garden plots and might or might not have owned draft stock, small livestock, and poultry. The terms *tenant* and *renter* are commonly used interchangeably to refer to all renters—to those who rented entire farms and operated them more or less independently as well as to those who rented a house and garden plot and worked as day laborers for the landowner. Additionally, some landowners broke their farms into family-sized plots and rented these units on shares, similar to the sharecropping system in the South. Another group, seasonal migrant laborers, was important for orchard and some small fruit and vegetable growers. Some of these seasonal workers, like the Bradley family, ended up settling in the area.

Farm operators varied greatly in the size of farm they operated (see table 6.1). Before 1950 one-fourth or more of the farms were smaller than 50 acres, another 30 percent were between 50 and 100 acres, while only around 1 percent were 500 acres or larger. This does not reflect land *ownership*, however, for nearly 37 percent of these farms were operated by tenants in 1900 and 1910, and the proportion of tenant-operated farms did not fall below one-fifth until 1950 (see table 6.2). One landowner frequently owned several farms, often in different parts of the county. The Waltons, for example, appeared to follow Serena Davie Walton's parents' pattern of speculative investment in land; they operated their home place and also rented out a farm in the Mississippi bottoms near Big Barn (Willard's Landing). Edith's family always rented from wealthy, absentee landlords, first in what is now the State Forest, then in the bottoms.

Rented farms tended to be somewhat larger than owner-operated farms, as indicated by the fact that only 60.3 percent of the land was operated by the 63.9 percent of farmers who were full owners in 1920, compared with the 33.1 percent of farmland that was operated by the 30.2 percent of farmers who were renters. These figures probably reflect the relatively large size of farms in the Mississippi bottoms, almost all of which were operated by renters. In 1940, bottoms farms averaged 211

Table 6.1. Number of Farms by Acreage, 1920–1987

Year	Total Farms	1–49	50–99	100–179	180–259	260–499	500–999	Over 1,000
1920	2,006	585	595	489	215	101	19	2
1925	1,996	639	551	506	198	82	18	2
1930	1,752	440	535	484	188	83	20	2
1935	1,983	566	624	511	171	93	14	4
1940	1,724	486	532	442	171	90	20	1
1945	1,683	438	482	477	169	99	16	2
1950	1,535	396	408	410	180	123	17	1
1954	1,245	279	299	324	178	140	24	1
1959	1,097	224	296	281	136	131	26	3
1964	953	172	225	237	152	127	36	4
1969	867	141	194	221	144	121	40	6
1974	804	140	189	178	111	106	69	11
1978	732	156	162	145	92	109	55	13
1982	650	138	136	142	74	91	56	13
1987	580	129	111	135	68	73	44	20

Sources: U.S. Bureau of the Census, *Census of Agriculture,* year as noted.

acres, while the upland townships averaged 109 acres per farm.[3] Further, many very small owner-operated farms in the uplands were able to persist because of available day labor in the fruit and vegetable harvests, timbering, and silica mines.

Landowners and renters used a few rules of thumb in negotiating rental agreements. Bertie Hunsaker, who began farming on her mother's upland farm, which they supplemented with forty acres of rented corn land in the Cache River bottoms, explained: "Where we owned the equipment and the animals to tend the land with, we got two-thirds. Now where the owner of the land furnished everything and the cropper just did the work, it was on a fifty-fifty basis. . . . That was just on the row [crops] 'cause it ran about the same way [with livestock]. If the landowner had the animals, you got about a fifty-fifty proposition with the increase in the livestock. But if you owned the animals, then it was two-thirds and one-third."[4] Because they rented from a family member, as did 19 percent of all tenants in 1925,[5]

You did a lot of things that you wouldn't have done if you hadn't have been on a mother's farm. And she, of course, did a lot of things for us, but it was still on that same principle that you expected to give her something because there were certain upkeeps on the farm that she had to meet even though she did have a daughter on the farm. . . . [She was responsible] for the taxes and things like that. But that was one of the

Table 6.2. Proportion of Farms by Tenure, 1900–1986

Year	Full Owner (%)	Acres	Part Owner (%)	Acres	Manager (%)	Acres	Tenant (%)	Acres
1900	62.8	—	—	—	.6	—	36.6	—
1910	62.4	—	—	—	.8	—	36.8	—
1920	64.0	60.3	4.2	4.4	1.6	2.2	30.3	33.1
1925	63.5	59.1	4.9	5.8	.6	1.8	31.1	33.3
1930	58.2	52.4	8.6	9.5	2.0	3.5	31.2	34.6
1934	50.5	49.0	13.6	12.1	1.3	2.6	34.6	36.4
1940	69.8	63.6	5.2	6.3	.6	1.5	24.4	28.7
1945	67.7	57.7	9.7	14.2	.7	1.7	21.8	26.4
1950	69.5	58.0	15.2	21.2	.1	1.2	15.2	19.5
1954	65.9	52.4	19.8	28.2	.5	1.0	13.7	18.4
1959	68.8	54.0	20.1	31.5	.6	1.9	10.5	12.6
1964	70.8	58.7	19.9	29.3	.3	.8	8.9	11.2
1969	74.7	59.6	17.4	27.9	—	—	7.8	12.5
1974	69.4	54.5	22.0	36.1	—	—	8.6	9.4
1978	66.1	50.8	24.9	39.9	—	—	9.0	9.3
1982	66.0	46.5	27.4	46.1	—	—	6.6	7.3
1987	71.0	45.6	22.0	45.3	—	—	6.9	9.1

Sources: U.S. Bureau of the Census, *Census of Agriculture,* year as noted.

reasons we went on the farm was to help take care of that land because she was land poor. My father passed away in 1919, and it left her with that 280-acre farm [we moved onto] and with a 160-acre farm east of Cobden, and some other land that eventually they let the payments on it go by default. . . . She finally got rid of it. But she was land poor when my father passed away.[6]

Landlords exercised varying degrees of managerial control over their farms. Bertie Hunsaker's father had apparently exercised oversight on their farms, which her mother was unable to continue. Landlords who owned farms in the Mississippi bottoms appear to have given little direct managerial control to their tenants. Most of the families who rented and farmed these lands themselves owned considerable property in livestock and equipment. Edith Rendleman explained, "The tenant always owned everything. All the machinery and the horses and everything. All [the landlord] did was get one-third of the profit. [The crop rotation] was left up to the tenant."[7] In these cases the landlord's primary managerial task was to locate and choose competent, ambitious renters; if he were a poor judge of the families he rented his farm to, he would do poorly, as some oral accounts suggest.

A greater degree of control was generally associated with fruit and vegetable farming. Clara Bell Miller, who lived in Cobden, recalled that they spent the winter planning what would be planted on their five farms and working with their tenants to execute these plans. John Aldridge's family, who farmed near Alto Pass, operated something akin to a plantation:

> I guess my father was what you would call a big farmer for those days. He had as many as five tenant houses on the farm. Maybe one or two of them would just be a man that worked by the day. He got around a dollar a day for his work.
>
> These tenants that lived on the farm growed truck crops, tomatoes, cucumbers, and sweet potatoes; they delivered things to ship. Dad would furnish them with a team and tools. If they used fertilizer, Dad would pay half and they would pay half. Dad would pay half of their expense of the boxes or packages to ship them in. The value of the crop was paid in rent of one-half of the product. Now if a man furnished his own set of tools and everything, Dad charged him a third. There was one man that furnished his own, but most of the men didn't. If he had five tenants and a team apiece for them, that was ten horses for them. You generally had two or three teams for you to work. So it run up to seven or eight teams; there was that many horses to feed every night and morning.[8]

The Aldridge situation, in which the tenants actually cropped specific acreages (as recommended in 1866 by the correspondent to the Jonesboro *Gazette*), appears somewhat unusual, or it may have been a more common pattern in the nineteenth century than in the twentieth. On most farms for which I have information, tenants served more as a resident wage labor force than as farmers in their own right, although they generally had small plots on which they controlled production, like crofters in Scotland or *huasipungueros* in the Andes. According to Charles Thomas, who lived on the outskirts of Cobden,

> We didn't have sharecroppers in here very much like we did in the South. Those families were paid a salary, which wasn't very much, and they always had a hard way to go. But most of the farmers, they had just about as hard a way to go as their tenants; their farms were small. . . . They [the tenants] all had their own garden and own livestock and everything, and some of them even did do a little sharecropping. Most of them worked only so much a day for so much an hour. . . . But you know, one thing through here, whenever the work closed down in the fall of the year, they didn't have any income. And they were really— hard way to go. Now a lot of farmers that had more feeling for them would carry them through the winter, but I remember lots of them didn't have any income at all in the wintertime, and it was really a big hardship.[9]

Tenants and small farmers were dependent on store credit to supply them with necessities they could not grow or make themselves. Oral accounts, as given in the previous chapter, suggest that the wife's poultry flock and, if they had a cow, her butter paid the store bill and kept the family more or less solvent through the winter. The men frequently trapped fur-bearing animals and cut timber in the winter to earn some income.

Bertie Hunsaker recalled that, when they farmed her mother's farm, "we had a tenant house. We usually kept a family there. The man and a lot of times the wife helped hoe because what I said that we raised . . . sweet potatoes and sometimes cucumbers and strawberries and other things."[10]

Hired hands also lived in the house. Edith Rendleman described their situation:

> Nearly everybody had one or two or three hired hands. Some kept them in the house. My husband kept ours in the house. I had a hired hand from one to three or four during the wheat harvest, all the time. That was a thorn in my side. I didn't like a hired hand in the house. There was no privacy with your family. . . . I always treated them nice 'cause they couldn't help it, but I didn't like to have to wash and iron and cook for somebody Sunday and all. Had no private life at all. . . .
>
> What you kept in the house was just a single man. . . . They were generally somebody you had known through the years. We had one we didn't know. And that house at Sublett had a little side room from the upstairs out on the bare roof. You could see the rafters and everything out there. . . . And they was some empty paint buckets or something that had a little paint in them, that the painter had set in there. And after he left when I went in there one day, there he had wet them buckets all full of water [urine]. . . . Believe me, I was mad.[11]

The shift from housing laborers under the family roof to providing them with separate accommodations began to occur in the 1870s, although as Edith Rendleman's account indicates, it persisted into the 1930s. The Makanda correspondent to the Jonesboro *Gazette*, February 20, 1875, wrote, "Many families have moved here from Tennessee, Kansas and elsewhere, until every house and cabin is full, and some are camping out in the woods, and yet every one seems to be engaged, and 'hands' are not plentiful, except tramps. Farmers are acquiring enough 'gumption' to hire a man and allow him to board himself, instead of encumbering his family by having every available space occupied by outsiders."

A number of the families we interviewed were part of this migration. Edith Rendleman's father, Elijah Bradley, arrived in Illinois in the mid-1870s with his father, a coal miner from Morganfield, Kentucky. At first he lived in barracks built for farm laborers in Johnson County; then he took work as a hired hand in the western hills of Union County, where he eventually married the widow of a family he had worked for. When Elijah was a young man, in the early 1890s, he worked in timber in the winter, walking six miles to cut railroad ties for fifty cents a day.[12] By this time most of the old growth forest in the uplands had been cut, but the rugged hills in the western part of the county and in the Mississippi bottoms were timbered out somewhat later.[13] The silica mines that developed in the late nineteenth century also provided jobs for poorer people who lived in the western hills (and also gave them silicosis). Some men and women found seasonal work in the box mills and limestone quarries, but most of these jobs seem to have been held by townspeople who relied completely on wage labor.

.The tenants who lived on the Walton farm were in some ways remarkable because most of them had come from the area around Woodbury, Tennessee, in the nineteenth century. Descendants of Silas "Toodle" Elkins wrote down the story of their move to Union County:

Family returned to Illinois in fall after wife and mother passed away [1895], and Father (Silas) worked for Tom Gorley at Lick Creek, Illinois. Went back to Tennessee in the spring and made a crop, coming back to Illinois again in the fall. They made several of these trips traveling in a covered wagon with all the family. When they returned the second fall season they arrived in the night and found the house still empty they moved out of in the spring. They moved back into it and in the morning Silas went up to see Mr. Gorley and told him he was ready to go back to work and that was fine with Mr. Gorley. The second fall after wife and mother died Silas was married to Lillie Vesta West Elkins and she traveled with the family. When Jadie [b. 1880] and Willie [b. 1876] got old enough to work they quit going back and forth, they stayed in Illinois. One time when Silas decided to come to Illinois he had two hogs so he killed them one night and loaded them in the wagon with the family and came to Illinois. Minnie said that they all crossed the river on the ice one time—with the wagon drove across the ice. Jadie said when they got back [to Illinois] one time Silas went to a store owned by John Kelley and asked for credit to buy soap to wash their clothes. Kelley wouldn't let him have credit so he went down to Henry Yost . . . and received credit so he traded with him from then on. Later on in years instead of him owing Yost, Mr. Yost owed him for he would sell him cream and eggs and just take due bills for them. He could buy his groceries and still have a balance due him all the time. The writer can remember seeing him carry his cream and eggs to the store. He carried a two or three gallon cream bucket in one hand and an old fashioned wooden plaited market basket on the other arm and would walk about three miles into town and three miles back. He would fill his bucket and basket with grocery supplies to carry them home. The roads were dirt and mud [and] hilly. He lived at this time at the old Charlie Hess? farm [in] a little three room red house back of the big barn. This was the later years of his life. When you'd go there most times you'd find him sitting out in the shade of the house with a cloth, a red man's handkerchief tied around his head for he had very bad head aches and later years a scabby sore place came on the side of his face above the temple which turned out to be cancer and caused his death [in 1935]. After his health got bad he bought him a big tent, made a 4–5 foot wall on the inside of the tent and put a floor in it. He put it up down on the Ed Walton farm down in the pasture, close to his Grandson's house [John West]. It was here he spent his last days.[14]

The Waltons had a reputation for being good landlords, and the number of related families who settled on their farm and stayed for many years supports oral recollections.[15] During the early years of the twentieth century the Waltons grew tobacco specifically for the use of workers on the farm, and they kept kerosene, flour, cornmeal, and other supplies for the tenants to use. It was common for landlords to maintain a store of sorts for the tenants, but most seem to have been somewhat more formalized than the Walton's, which ran more or less on the honor system. Ed Brimm, whose family were tenants on the farm, recalled E. B. (Mr. Walton) taking them to town for shoes and coats, and that he insisted that they go to school. "He was just a good old man," Ed Brimm remarked. "Well, he was just like a father to everybody, he was."[16] This kind of interest in the well-being of the tenants' children was not uncommon. David Elder recalled that their boss, Rufus Loomis, "thought you had to go to school. He made you get out and go to school."[17]

The Waltons, whose kin and social circles included many of the county's leading families, were far removed socially from their tenants. Nonetheless, the Brimm boys played as equals with E. B.'s only son, Ned, and despite the great differential in wealth and in the social circles in which the Waltons and their tenants moved, there was apparently much mutual respect and affection between them.

This sort of mutual respect appears to have been common. Ruby Weaver, for example, explained why an old log house where tenants lived was located so close to the main house on the old Weaver farm: "I heard Mrs. Weaver talk about her friend. She was real good friends with this lady and her husband [who] lived there."[18]

In many cases tenants appear to have had considerable discretion in using their landlord's land. A renter on the Walton farm, John West, provided space for his relatives: he built a one-room house for his father, Joe, on their plot of ground, and Silas "Toodle" Elkins and his wife, Vesta West Elkins, also moved onto the farm, as told in the above account.[19] By the early years of this century most of the tenants living on the Walton

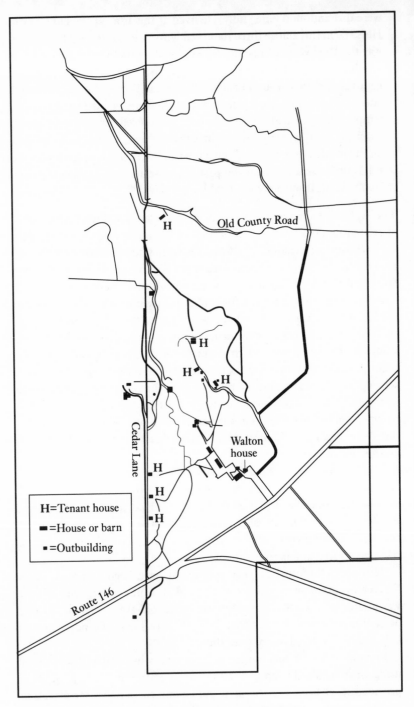

Figure 6.1. Walton Farm, with Tenant Houses and Paths
Source: Derived from aerial photo, 1938, BHF-1-88.

farm were related or became related through marriage. Their houses were spaced around the farm (see fig. 6.1); some may have dated to the 1840s, before the Waltons acquired the land. Around 1890, as E. B. expanded the farm operation by beginning a commercial dairy, he had the resident tenants build three houses along the Cedar Lane on the western boundary of the farm. The frequent visits among the tenants are visible in the footpaths that were revealed in the U.S. Geological Survey 1938 aerial photograph.

People who used tenant labor screened the families who wanted to work for them and, it appears, were careful not to compete for workers.[20] Helen Sirles's family had a number of families living on their farm. She recalled,

> We had two or three families that wanted to move from Cobden and come over here, and [we'd] always say, "Why are you leaving so-and-so?" You know, it's not a good thing just to hire somebody from someone else. And they would say—very honest—"We are tired of picking Easter flowers under ice." They would say that is the hardest and coldest work yet. They were very honest. "We don't like that kind of work."
>
> They would want to work fruit, because you wouldn't have that cold and bending over. Same way as picking strawberries—a lot of people don't want to bend over.[21]

The heavy seasonal demand for labor in strawberries and tree fruits led to a pattern of seasonal labor migration. In the late nineteenth century most of the migrants appear to have come from the surrounding territory for the strawberry harvest. At first they were welcomed, as in a note in the Jonesboro *Gazette* for April 5, 1879: "Strawberry pickers are already coming in at some of the largest growers in such numbers as to make business quite lively with our merchants, who are eagerly looking forward and daily preparing to meet the wants of all who come, in the way of dry goods and groceries."

By the 1880s, however, many people greeted them as a nuisance. The note in the Jonesboro *Gazette* Alto Pass News, and echoed in the Cobden News, for May 14, 1887, complained, "The tramp berry pickers are about as numerous as usual, and, as is always the case, are ahead of the berries and begging from house to house for something to eat."

The earliest oral recollections come from the 1920s. Witt and Mary Venerable, who were young orchardists in that decade, recalled a regular group of pickers who came from the South:

> The labor worked from year to year, and they usually came ahead of time, maybe ten days or a week. You would line up—we worked up to forty or fifty. We had cotton choppers. They would come up from the South. By that time they were laid off the cotton fields. . . . They would

come up here to work for what they called "cash money" because they didn't get cash down in the cotton fields.[22]

They would come a whole family and they would do their own cooking. It was an outing for them. They did a lot of courting. Sometimes even marriages.

You provided shelter. Anything that would keep the weather off would provide a shelter. They used oil stoves most of the time. Some of them cooked over open fires. If you didn't have a building for them to go in, they camped.

They would stay around ten days, and sometimes they would have as many as six workers in one family, and they would take a good deal of money home. Some of them would draw a little bit of money on time, but they wanted to be paid when they left out to go home. They just drew enough money to survive on. They didn't want to carry it and have to keep it. At the end of the crop, why we'd bring the money out here in buckets.

I never did pay piece work to amount to anything, because a lot of them would abuse the privilege. I mean by that that they'd bruise the fruit and everything. . . . We let them set their own pace and handle the fruit carefully and we didn't [measure] everything. They would have a common container to put them in, and it was a little more efficient in not keeping it apart.

[There were] about ten to sixteen or maybe eighteen men in what we called a field crew. They would have a foreman, somebody with a lot of experience and we thought pretty good judgment. Sometimes there was a little politics. . . . We had a [man named] Price. . . . Well, he knew a bunch down in Missouri. There was a family of four in one family of workers. He was the foreman, the father, and two brothers, twin brothers, and then he had a group that he knew down there, and they would all come, and that is what I call a little politics. We got along with him, and he got along with the people. If you help me, I help you, you know. They may have come for twelve, fifteen years. Now we provided a house for a group like that. Probably sleep three or four to a room, and some would stay in other's quarters, tents or something, but he might have overseen from twelve to twenty, depending on what we were doing. He knew how it should be done, and he as a rule saw it was done so they kept busy. You told them, if they didn't they wouldn't get to come back, and they all went pretty smooth that way.

The Venerables were relatively large growers, and Mary Venerable recalled, "I kept some of the books, and I usually paid. . . . I would call and locate the help and sometimes go and get them. I was active in the business but not in the shed. . . . Early apples I bossed the shed." The peach shed was too big an operation, with two men overseeing it, so Witt managed that part of the operation as well as the picking.[23]

Wealth and Family Size

People who lived in the first half of the twentieth century recall great disparities of wealth. Tenants lived in houses that had been abandoned by the first generation of landowners as they became able to build more substantial and comfortable houses, and new tenant housing that was built often replicated the older forms—log or frame one-story or story-and-a-half I-houses with a lean-to kitchen on the back.[24] The foundations were generally stone piers that created a space for chickens, dogs, and other animals to find shelter beneath the plank floor. Wind, snow, and often rain found many entries in the floor, walls, and roof. Water was frequently a considerable hike down a hill or across a field to a spring, and privies were often nonexistent.

Bill Rhodes told of a young widow who "lived in a little log house down in the valley. . . . She had three boys and a girl. Mother told me one time it come a rain and the house leaked so that she had to put her little girl in a bureau drawer, so she wouldn't get wet."[25]

Edith Rendleman recalled her childhood in the first years of the twentieth century:

> The old house consisted of one large living room and bedroom combined, a kitchen, and one room upstairs where the boys slept. We had 2 beds in the living room and in the summertime we had what was called mosquito bars over the beds. . . . Most every night Dad would smoke out the mosquitoes late in the evening by taking an old iron pot and putting rags in it, setting it afire enough to make a smoke, and set it in the center of the floor. That would run them out for a while and many times we all got up and took our quilts and went to the hay loft and slept on the clover hay as the mosquitoes were supposed to not like clover hay. But that didn't keep them all away as many times we battled them all night. . . . We had screen doors but no screens on the windows.
>
> Very few people had horses, cows (maybe a few chickens), screen doors or much to eat, only what we raised. We always had plenty to eat except meat. Very few people had any kind of meat except hog jowls and fat salt pork, once in a while. We didn't always have flour but we always had cornbread.
>
> . . . People I knew didn't have toilets or privy. We went to the chicken house and behind it and the men used the barn.

They moved to a larger farm in 1904, at the bottom of a hollow. The hills were dotted with shacks and, she recalled, "A man and a 12 year old girl [his daughter] lived up the . . . hollow in a tent. She used to carry milk, butter, and eggs from our house. I'll bet a tank car would not hold the milk my mother gave to people that didn't have anything."[26] People converted chicken houses, sheds, and other structures into housing. Sometimes these buildings provided temporary shelter for transient seasonal laborers, but in some cases they were occupied for several years. Al Basler recalled the conversion of a brooder house his brother had built:

[Mr. Kimbro] and his grandson come by here when we was picking strawberries. He wanted to pick strawberries, him and his grandson. . . . So, he picked berries that day, and he says, "Say, have you got a place around here where me and this boy could stay? We just like to pick so, well, we'll just stay with it till the berries are done, if you could fix us a place to sleep."

"Well, Mr. Kimbro," I said, "I tell you, I got a little house here in the woods. It's got a bedroom down there. It's got a stove in there, an oil stove that you can cook on. You look at it down there and see what you think about it." I was getting ready to take the berries into town.

He said, "We'll go look at it." I tell you something, he looked at it. When I got back, he was already moved in down there. He was tickled to death, him and that boy. . . . He was in that three or four years. . . . I hated to see them go. I've missed them. . . . After that time, we used it for people like Mr. Kimbro and that boy. They were just tickled to death to be in that little house. People I've had live in there who would help me through the summer. . . . It would be usually just a man and his wife. I don't know if there were any children in there. It's just one room.[27]

Edith Rendleman's grandfather, John Bradley, worked as a laborer for a farmer in the Hutchins Creek valley and lived in a slat double crib they boxed in. He died there in 1900 at the age of fifty-two from pneumonia.

Farm families in general tended to be large: in 1910 white rural farm women in Illinois between forty and forty-four years old had borne an average of 4.4 children each; for urban women the average was 3.3 children.[28] The aphorism "The rich have the money and the poor have the children" seems to be borne out, as wealthy families approximated urban fertility rates and tended to marry later. The Waltons are perhaps an extreme example, as E. B. and Louise married very late and had only one child. (The founding family, J. K. and Serena, although marrying late, had nine children, raising seven to adulthood.) Their tenants, in contrast, tended to marry young and have large families. This differential became apparent to me when I tried to create a meaningful generational chart of the farm. The Walton family, from founding to the present, spanned four generations (J. K. and Serena, E. B. and Louise, Ned and Rosemary, and

Around the turn of the century at least seven families lived on the Walton farm and worked as day laborers. In this photo, taken around 1910, E. B. Walton poses with some of the tenants. E. B., on the far left, is holding his son, Ned. At least four families, in addition to the Waltons, are represented in this photograph. Walton Collection, Morris Library, Southern Illinois University, Carbondale.

Barbara, born 1942, and her brother, Wesley, who does not live on the farm), while the tenant families spanned six for a comparable period. A Walton generation spanned about forty years, while the tenants' spanned about twenty. The Kimber family, although they did not have a comparable number of tenants associated with their farm, had a demographic profile similar to the Walton's.[29]

Despite laws requiring children to stay in school until they were sixteen, many children began working young. The school year was short, so they had several months off. Additionally, their parents often needed their income to help the family get by. David Elder recalled,

When I got to be sixteen I told Mr. Loomis, "I'm sixteen, I want to quit school." He said, "Naw, naw, naw." I said, "Yeah, now you can work me, or somebody else can work me." And I've been working like a slave ever since. So he said, "Well, if you feel that way, you know the farm here, and I'd rather have you here than have just somebody that don't know it." So I went to work. To help my father. Making a living then was kind of rough. . . . [The going wage was] fifteen cents an hour. A dollar and a half for ten hours. And I just earned twelve and a half cents an hour, a dollar and a quarter a day for ten hours. But then I was big for my age. My father went to Mr. Loomis, and he said, "He does work right alongside the men." "I know it," he says, "and I've been thinking about that, 'cause I ought to be giving him men's wages." So I started drawing men's wages.

Farm laborers often lived on their employer's farm and were given a small house lot for their own use. This woman probably sold eggs and poultry to supplement the family's income. This is probably one of the Walton's tenants. Walton Collection, Morris Library, Southern Illinois University, Carbondale.

When David's father died the next year, and his mother died when he was eighteen, he took over the care of his three younger siblings.[30]

Women in families without property had fewer options. They might have use of a house with a yard large enough to raise a commercial poultry operation and a large home garden, but they were paid one-half to two-thirds of a man's wages for fieldwork, and housework paid far less than fieldwork. Clara Elder recounted her mother's efforts to provide for her family: "My father was an invalid. There was fifteen years before he died that he didn't feed nor dress himself. Couldn't even stand up without someone holding him. Mother did housework for a living. . . . [We lived on] the Walter Loomis farm, and then Rufus Loomis was his brother, was over near the park [Giant City]. And Mother did her housework. . . . She'd push [the baby] over in a go-cart. . . . She'd push him over there and work, and then they decided that was too hard on her, and we moved in a house over there on that land."[31] Young, unmarried women were more likely to do housework or, like the women who lived on the Walton farm, to be the wives of resident laborers. However, few Union County farm wives were able to afford hired help on a regular basis.

Class Structure and Social Relations

As I gradually became aware of the enormous differentials of wealth between large farmers—the 15 to 20 percent of farmers who, in

1920, farmed more than 200 acres and, more significantly, the landowners who owned several farms who themselves might or might not actually farm—and those who worked for them, I wondered why there seemed to be no organized antagonisms between them. As early as 1875 workers in a soap factory in Dongola struck for higher wages,[32] although organizing by workers in Union County was sporadic until passage and Supreme Court validation of the National Labor Relations Act in 1937. However, only a few miles to the north coal miners had organized persistently and often violently since the late nineteenth century.[33] Their activities gave rise to such internationally famous individuals as Mother Jones; John L. Lewis was a regional hero.

Agrarian discontent, unlike labor struggles, did not take on a specifically class configuration. Rather, economically and socially threatened small and medium-sized landowners resisted domination by "moneyed interests" and middlemen, in the 1870s through farmers' clubs and the Grange, and later through the populist movement that was organized in southern Illinois through the Farmers' Mutual Benefit Association.[34] In the 1870s some farmers who worked the land expressed some antagonism toward "gentleman" farmers, as evidenced by an item in the September 27, 1873, issue of the Jonesboro *Gazette*. At an organizing meeting of the newly insurgent farmers' club at Roach School, Ephraim Kimmel, a substantial farmer, "pitched into the society of the county association for not being accustomed to stand in the sunshine of the harvest field. Mr. Kimmel felt no sympathy with any movement which admitted to membership men who made their living, or any considerable part, under shelter." These expressed oppositions appear to have been between country "squires" and a newly emergent entrepreneurial class of landowners. The sympathies of the squires appeared to be divided between defending the agrarian society that had developed in the early and mid-nineteenth century and embracing the new commercial capitalist order. Entrepreneurial farmers and townspeople, concentrated along the railroad line, repeatedly tried and failed to pass a law that would have required fencing livestock and laws that would have permitted taxation for improved roads.[35] Both of these were issues that affected poor, less commercially oriented farmers who depended on forest rangeland to feed and water their livestock and who had little interest in smooth farm-to-market roads. By the 1890s the issues had been settled in favor of commercial production, and poor farmers, whether they owned or rented their farms, had become part-time laborers on their more prosperous neighbors' farms. The country squires or their heirs had made the transition to being capitalist farmers in the new regime of intensive commercial production using large amounts of wage labor, and the old antagonisms had, apparently, dissolved, lingering only as a suspicion of townspeople by farmers.

This new elite developed a variety of organizations and institutions, some of which benefited the larger community and some of which created solidarity among themselves. The shipping associations have already been mentioned; along with these, progressive farming, business, and professional people formed joint stock companies to establish building and loan associations and other business ventures. The Masons had been established as early as 1822, but in the mid- to late nineteenth century various temperance and fraternal organizations sprang up. The most enduring was the International Order of Odd Fellows and its women's wing, the Rebekahs. Both the Masons and the Odd Fellows had a wide membership among substantial farmers and townspeople. Businessmen in the larger towns formed a variety of businessmen's associations to boost the community. These booster organizations tried persistently to attract industry to the county and became particularly important during economic hard times. Women's Clubs were organized in the towns in the county in the 1910s, growing out of the various women's auxiliaries and clubs that put on public entertainments and fund-raising events.[36] Alongside these public organizations, some groups formed exclusive hunting clubs, some of which were incorporated and owned land in the Mississippi bottoms. These same sets of families tended to socialize together on a more or less regular basis. The wives often had a regular weekly afternoon bridge game, took shopping trips to Cairo or St. Louis, and entertained one another in the evening as couples or family groups. In the towns, church membership was also important in defining social groups. The Yankee immigrants brought Presbyterian and Congregational religions with them, and many of the business and professional families belonged to these churches. The Catholics were treated as a stigmatized minority and were generally not active in civic affairs until the 1930s. The older churches—Baptist, Lutheran, Reformed, Christian, Cumberland Presbyterian, and Methodist—had their roots in the rural areas. In later years Pentecostal and other nondenominational churches, often characterized as fundamentalist, developed, drawing their congregations largely from poorer working people.

Farm families, particularly poor farm families, had no organizations comparable to those of the urban professional and business people. The Grange, which provided a social organization for farmers in many parts of the country, existed in Union County for less than twenty years following its enthusiastic organization in 1873–74, although it persisted for many decades in other southern Illinois counties. Many farm families belonged to the Odd Fellows and Masons, and a few, with strong kin ties to prosperous town families like the Waltons, were members of a number of town-based clubs and activities. Many farm men belonged to producer associations; by the early years of the twentieth century this was primarily the Farmers' Educational and Cooperative Union of America,[37] which had locals around the county and, somewhat later, the Farm Bureau. But most farm women belonged to no organizations and socialized through their church, the local school, and with neighbors and kin. This meant that a farm woman who married out of her natal community and had no relatives in her new home might find herself more isolated socially than a woman who was able to stay close to her natal community. She would have few avenues for creating ties with other women, although often the mother-in-law/daughter-in-law bond appeared warm and supportive. Poor farmers and laborers generally belonged to no formal organizations except perhaps a church; their often-transient status worked against their developing responsible roles within either their church or the local school.

Except during the initial period of movement agitation in the mid-1870s, farmers' groups did not organize along class lines, nor did poor tenants and laborers, who became increasingly numerous throughout the nineteenth and early twentieth centuries, organize collectively to better their conditions. I can only guess at the reasons organized conflict did not arise between relatively wealthy farmers and landowners and their poor tenants and laborers. Part of the explanation may have to do with the span of time covered. As E. P. Thompson has shown, the development of class consciousness is a lengthy and uneven process.[38] A capitalist rural economy was not consolidated in Union County until the 1890s; by 1921, only thirty years later, it was deeply and permanently undermined by the onset of a prolonged and constantly deepening depression that impoverished landowner and laborer alike. The dominant ideology that resisted capitalist relations of production in agriculture was couched in terms of land-ownership and marketing—the deeply sedimented ideology of the yeoman farm—not in terms of landowner/laborer opposition. Barnes argues that the southern populist movement of the 1880s and 1890s was not able to ignite sharecroppers, who were the majority of southern (Texas, in her study) farmers, until Macune developed the subtreasury plan that united renters and landowners in a common program. This program appears to have had little impact on southern Illinois, where the movement focused on creating cooperative shipping and purchasing organizations—the old Granger program that primarily served landowners.[39]

Structural preconditions for creating a class opposed to wealthy land-owners also appear to have been absent. The extreme variability of labor and rental arrangements meant that nonlandowners were unlikely to see themselves as a class with a common set of interests that were opposed to the interests of landowners. Many tenants were relatives of the landowners and could therefore expect to inherit the land; many other tenants achieved upward mobility through acquiring capital stock—draft animals, threshing outfits, and other farm equipment. Being landless did not nec-

Landlords and laborers often shared recreational activities. Ned Walton (third from right) and some of the young men who lived on his farm, with a large catch

essarily mean being propertyless. Many people who worked as farm laborers were also small landowners, and many renters aspired to owning their own plot of land.

Further, the relationship between employer and employee, and between landlord and tenant, tended to be highly personal and involved far more that selling labor for a wage. The Bradley children, for example,

of fish, ca. 1930. Walton Collection, Morris Library, Southern Illinois University, Carbondale.

referred to their landlord, who lived in Jonesboro, as "Grandpa Bruno."[40] Farming, unlike factory work, requires skill and a degree of commitment to the outcome. Farm owners or managers cannot exercise oversight of their laborers except in specific circumstances, as in harvesting when large numbers of people are assembled in one small space. White farm laborers had no tradition of servility, and they did not take kindly to being treated with arrogance. Edith Rendleman recalled that one of the few landowners who lived in the Wolf Lake area of the bottoms "were supposed to be rich and high above common people, all except Mr. Ren.—he was always common."[41] Renters could, and did, move to another farm if they were dissatisfied with their working conditions. Charles Thomas explained their relationship to specific farms:

> I would say that the majority of them moved around, but there were a lot of them in this area that stayed on the same farm for years and raised their families. I knew several families that the children were raised to adults before they [left]; the parents would die before they would even split up. . . . As a whole, they moved around quite a bit. . . .
>
> Over here at [Grover Rendleman's], I guess they kept their tenants longer than anybody. There's a man over there [who] was born and raised there, and whenever his parents died, he stayed and raised a family. Altogether he was there between fifty to sixty years. . . . And then he had other tenants live there a long, long time. And occasionally . . . one or two of them finally were able to buy some property off of them [the Rendlemans] and start their own farms.
>
> As a whole they would come and go, depending on their ability and, also, depended on the person they were working for. If the farmer was mean to them, another would be good to them.[42]

All of these factors undoubtedly exercised some "discipline" on the employers of labor: it limited the degree of exploitation and contempt that employers could exercise if they wanted to get reliable workers and smoothed the obvious differences in material wealth with a lubricant of respect and reciprocity.[43]

The ethic that all people have equal worth and should be treated with respect, which de Tocqueville commented on as a fundamental American trait, appears to have been widely practiced, at least in superficial relationships. Alongside these markers of equality and respect, however, a complex set of status relationships defined peoples' social standing.[44] Some of these have already been examined in terms of raising marriageable sons and daughters (see Chapter 5). Ancestry and property ownership were important aspects of a person's status; but character traits like honesty, reliability, hard work, and diplomacy could elevate a poor person, while negative traits could lower the regard in which a wellborn person was generally held. Status was not a unitary characteristic: A man generally scorned by women because of his moral character might be accorded respect by his male associates because of his political savvy and ability to cut deals; a poor person, who through his ability to tell good stories and be a charming companion might be welcome in more wealthy homes, might not be extended credit to buy a home or farm by these same people because they evaluated him as financially unreliable. Conversely, a poor person who was honest and hardworking might never be invited to join the bankers' family at their hunt club but might be unquestioningly extended credit and treated with honest respect.

With the passage of time it is difficult to resurrect what Scott terms the "hidden transcripts"—the expressions of opposition to those with power that might reveal a systematic and well-fleshed-out understanding of class opposition. The strong ideology of community harmony that Kohl found pervaded the writing of community histories, and which tends to personalize remembered conflicts and antagonisms, erases most stories and aphorisms that point to explicit, organized forms of resistance to domination, leaving only hints that must be interpreted with care.[45]

Another factor that may have mitigated against the development of an organized sense of opposition between landowners and their tenants and laborers was the relative poverty of the region. A tiny fraction of wealthy farmers lived like "city people" with the conveniences of electricity, live-in maids, and so forth. Even members of these families tended to engage in hard manual labor on their farms, although the women often hired help to do the laundry and ironing and the daughters were generally not required to do fieldwork or heavy housework. In 1930 the average value of a Union County dwelling was $971; in wealthy Tazewell County in the Illinois prairie, it was $2,561. Fruit farmers were the most prosperous, their dwellings averaging $1,856 in value.[46] Wage scales in southern Illinois were far below those of the central and northern part of the state: In 1930, according to figures in the Census of Agriculture, farm laborers in Union County averaged $1.87 a day, although oral accounts give figures closer to $1.50 a day. In contrast, farm laborers in Tazewell County averaged $2.21 a day, slightly more than the national average of $2.16. This differential corresponds to the different wage rates paid in the east north central and east south central states for common laborers on federal-aid highway projects ($.38 and $.24 per hour, respectively), reinforcing the perception that southern Illinois was more like the rest of the Upland South than it was like the northern states.[47]

It is also significant, in terms of agriculture in general, that agricultural laborers in both regions earned about half what a common laborer earned, indicating the great lag in agricultural productivity relative to industry. By the 1910s many people who had ambitions to improve their material condition were seeking off-farm employment and beginning to migrate from the region, as indicated by the drop in the county's population, particularly its rural population, after 1900 (see table 2.1). Labor mobility, as well as interfarm mobility, therefore, tended to defuse farm laborers' discontent. Edith Rendleman's siblings, all of whom were born before 1900, may be exceptional because of their parents' ambition for them, but their careers are not extremely unusual. All but one of her brothers went to college; three got jobs with the railroad, and one became a lawyer. She married the son of one of the largest landowners in the area and was the only one to stay in farming.

Finally, much of the labor force was not local. Transient labor was widely used at peak harvest periods. In the nineteenth century, people came from the surrounding counties, particularly for the strawberry harvest in May. In the first half of the twentieth century many of the labor needs continued to be supplied within the region; I recall women and girls in my neighborhood traveling the twenty or so miles from Ava to Etherton Switch to work in the packing sheds. However, at peak harvest periods more labor was required than could be supplied within the immediate region. As noted above, a migrant stream developed that was documented in the 1920s. The largely white families in this stream wintered in the Missouri Delta, working as timber cutters. In the spring they planted cotton; when it was laid by, they came across to southern Illinois to work the fruit and vegetable crops, returning to Missouri in the fall to pick cotton. One woman I interviewed, whose family was part of this migrant stream, was born in a tent in southeastern Illinois in the first decade of the twentieth century. Her family eventually settled as resident laborers in Union County, where she grew to adulthood, married another laborer, eventually bought a farm (that they sold to the government in the 1930s), and raised her family. These families, as long as they remained migratory, were so weakly tied to the region or to one another that they presented little potential for organizing jointly with local laborers.

Extralocal conditions were also undoubtedly important in the failure of farm laborers and tenants to organize against their employers and landlords. Within Illinois, Union County was somewhat anomalous due to its extensive horticultural production. It required more labor and, because of this, supported more small farms than did the more prosperous counties in the prairie regions. For example, in 1930 Union County farmers who reported farm labor said they used an average of 227.8 days of labor per farm; farmers who reported hired labor in Tazewell County, one of the richest farming counties in the state, said they used only 156.8 days of labor per farm.[48] It was anomalous even within the region: neighboring Pulaski County, which shared Union County's relative poverty but which had less fruit and vegetable production, reported an average of only 207.4 days of labor hired per farm.[49]

The only regions where farm laborers persistently attempted to organize were in the South, through the agency of the Southern Tenant Farmers' Union, and in the West, by Dust Bowl refugees. In Union County, the cropping regime appears to be too diversified, with frequent strong and long-standing personal linkages between landowners and their tenants and laborers, and too anomalous in relation to the surrounding region to have created conditions within which the families that came from a "house of poor" could have organized in opposition to those who came from a "house of plenty."

CHAPTER 7

When the depression hit, a lot of
things changed. You couldn't sell
things. You know they said the farmers
were the fattest people yet going to the
poor house. . . . We always had plenty
of food to eat.—Helen Sirles

We Were the Fattest People Ever Going to the Poor House

So far the story has been told as if the world stood still for thirty years, from 1890 to 1920. This is, of course, not true: the economy went from depression to boom; revolutionary and imperial wars accelerated; technological innovations continued, especially electricity and the internal combustion engine; national reform movements emerged—history did not stop. However, a distinctive social pattern solidified in Union County by 1890, a pattern that remained dominant through 1920. The basis of this social economy was agriculture, and its leading members were landowning businessmen who derived their wealth from the laborers who worked for wages and/or as tenants on their farms and in their businesses. In the farm's domestic economy, women maintained the farm household not only through the service and reproductive work that characterized urban homemakers, but also as producers of primary products and as paid and unpaid agricultural laborers. On larger commercial farms this freed most of the proceeds from the men's primary products to be reinvested in the farm enterprise or to be realized by the landlord as rent. Despite agriculture's profitability during this period, and even though many farms were organized as capitalist enterprises and virtually all were deeply involved in commodity markets, agriculture did not display the same dynamism in regard to productivity as did industry.[1] Reformers were concerned about the conditions of agriculture not only because of the rural poverty created by existing labor relations, but also because industrialists wanted inexpensive food to feed their growing labor force. A technologically stagnant agriculture could not expand agricultural productivity to keep pace with the urban workforce.

The relative stability of social organization did not mean that other dimensions of agriculture remained unchanged. A number of technological innovations and market forces prompted farmers to change their crop mix during these decades. As described in Chapter 5, growing urban markets enabled women to develop successful poultry and dairy enterprises. Wheat also came into heavy demand during the late nineteenth century as Europe, facing the same pressures from its industrial workforce, bought large amounts of foreign wheat.[2] Union County farmers, like farmers in the rest of the country, increased wheat production and invested in reapers, binders, and threshing machines. Elderly people I interviewed could sometimes recall harvesting wheat with scythes and sickles, but generally where reapers could not be used, in areas such as fields dotted with tree stumps. No one I talked with recalled using a flail to thresh wheat; by the 1870s threshing machines were beginning to be used. The pace of change was slow, however, and children born in the 1890s anticipated being able to continue their parents' way of life relatively unchanged.

Perhaps a farsighted economist could have foreseen the crash, when commodity, particularly wheat, prices spiraled to unprecedented heights during World War I. But there is no evidence that anyone anticipated a twenty-year depression that would change the course of American history. People interviewed recall the war years as a time when brothers went off to war and as the time of the great flu epidemic. Those who recollect unusual economic conditions remember the optimism engendered by strong, even booming, commodity prices. Of course, most of the people interviewed in the 1970s and 1980s were children or young people just beginning farming during this period, and they would not be likely to recall unusual business cycles. For them the world was beginning; they could only anticipate that it would remain as they experienced it growing up during the increasingly good years of the early twentieth century. The postwar agricultural crisis was, therefore, a great shock. Bertie Hunsaker, who began farming her mother's farm after she married, recalled,

> The bottom fell out of everything. It was all right and looked clear that farming was good in 1920, but it started down from there and the longer, the worse. . . . We stayed with it ten years. We stayed with it till 1930, and we were working from daylight to dark and never taking a vacation or thinking about anything but what we were going to do next to try to make a dollar. We'd raise a good crop of tomatoes or peaches or anything else, and the bottom would fall out of the market and you couldn't hardly give them away. . . . I taught all except 1920 and '21. I taught the rest of the years in the rural area there.[3]

Her husband, Finis, recalled one of his most serious misjudgments, made around 1924 or 1925:

> The farm had grown up. It was in pasture; it'd grown up in persimmon and sassafras sprouts. . . . Well, [we] took grubbing hoes and axes, and we went out and we cleared that farm. Me and the hired help together, . . . about three of them boys. . . . First year I bought a tractor, and we had livestock—mules and horses—and I put out a big corn crop out there. All right.
>
> There was a fellow by the name of Carl Chamness moved into our neighborhood that run a sawmill. He had a bunch of mules and horses, and he wanted to buy this corn from me, and he offered me $1.10 a bushel for this corn, which was all right at that time. Well, I refused to sell the corn. I had a bunch of shoats, about 80 or 100 pigs running around out there. I thought that I would feed that corn to those hogs and make a killing. Well, hogs at that time was a good price.
>
> I fed that corn, 3,000 bushels, to those hogs. Well, when they got to where they weighed 250 pounds, right for the market, hogs were about a cent and a half a pound. And they never did get any higher than about two and a half cents. Well, I kept on feeding them thinking that the price would get better. I fed those hogs until a lot of them weighed about 500 pounds. Looked like cattle out there in the yard.
>
> Well, my only alternative was to get rid of those hogs. So I went over to Cape Girardeau and I bought the largest sausage grinder that they said I could get—got an Enterprise sausage grinder. I had a three and a half horsepower [engine] that I used on my spray rig to spray my peaches. Well, I rigged me up a wheel and got me a belt and rigged it up to grinding sausage. Talk about grinding sausage, we ground sausage. We run it through there twice. Whole hog sausage. We'd take one of those big hogs and dress him today, tonight we'd grind him in the sausage mill, tomorrow I'd deliver him. . . . I had a sausage trade, and I just about got the price of my corn back, by doing that. After all that

work, I just about got the $1.10 a bushel for my corn. And I doubt very much that I did that. But that's the way. We'd grow these crops and bottom fell out of the market.[4]

Many people recognized a political dimension to the crisis, as illustrated in an irony-laden editorial in the June 5, 1923, Jonesboro *Gazette*: "The farmer is puzzled as to what to grow or raise to make some money. Compared to what he is required to pay for most of the things he has to buy, the prices for farm products are entirely too low. . . . But President Harding and Secretary Hoover have held out the comforting assurance that the farmers can get back at the sugar thieves, at least, by doing without sugar. Also, they might get back at some other profiteers by going without clothing, hats, and shoes."

Throughout the 1920s—as long as the booming industrial economy attracted labor from agriculture—farmers tried to increase their commercial production. County farmers, who had increased wheat production by 50 percent during the war years, responded to the collapse of the wheat market after World War I by sharply decreasing wheat acreage, from 19,930 acres in 1920 to 9,653 acres in 1925. This acreage was replaced by beef cattle and peach orchards. The number of head of cattle increased sharply, from 3,344 in 1920 to 9,177 in 1925 and 10,647 in 1930. The number of peach trees jumped from 269,697 in 1920 to 541,349 in 1930, although the proportion of farms with peach (and apple) orchards dropped, indicating that orchards were increasing in scale and that smaller growers were dropping out of the commercial market.[5]

Ruel Hindman was representative of this trend. He was just beginning farming after World War I. "I was raised in the livestock business," he recounted in 1983.

These people that had small peach and apple orchards . . . were making so much money . . . that I got the peach orchard fever. I would pick as a kid, picked out here in some of the orchards, and they were making two or three thousand dollars an acre from their peaches. I got in when everybody else got in. . . . I bought this farm here in 1923 and set it in peaches. . . . In the beginning, this area went into the peach business pretty heavy in the twenties, and over in Massac County they were going to have a million trees over there by 1930. And Union County had more peaches than Massac County. . . . In fact, almost every farm got into the fruit business.

. . . At that time the peaches all were marketed and shipped in iced cars on the railroad. . . . In 1931 I loaded twenty-one carloads off of my orchard there of number one type peaches. And [after the freight charges] they net back sixty-five cents a bushel. Can you imagine that?

Around 1917 or 1918, Hindman recalled, peaches had brought as much as $3.50 a bushel.[6]

Farmers seemed to be demoralized by the postwar collapse in commodity prices. In 1918 they had optimistically organized a Farm Bureau and hired an extension agent. According to a later farm adviser, "The Post-War period involved sudden extreme decrease in membership of the sponsoring organization [Farm Bureau] and a curtailed budget."[7] Despite the loss of membership, Farm Bureau members responded to the postwar crash by organizing producer cooperatives. In 1918 the county agricultural extension agent, Charles E. Durst, wrote in his annual report,

> The county now has shipping associations at each important shipping point in the upland sections,[8] all the fruit and vegetables being grown in that part of the country. These associations simply attend to the procuring of cars, their icing and loading, and the billing of the same to point of destination, which for Union Co. is usually Chicago. Each shipper puts his stamp on his packages and at Chicago the products are distributed to the different commission men. In other words, the shipping association simply assists in a mechanical way and makes no effort to standardize grades, to build a reputation for the sector as a whole, or to find a better market for the products. In the Adviser's opinion the very greatest opportunity exists for improvement along this line, but in view of the conservative attitude of many persons it promises to be a very stubborn problem.[9]

In 1921 the Extension Service promoted the creation of branches of the Illinois Fruit Exchange. Durst, working as a representative of the Illinois Fruit and Vegetable Department of the Illinois Agricultural Association, spent a month or two in Union County during the spring, setting up local branches in Anna, Dongola, and Makanda. Durst wrote in his 1921 annual report,

> At Dongola and Anna products, cucumbers and tomatoes, were marketed through the newly formed Exchange. At the former, Dongola, the returns for products were very satisfactory, really flattering, however at Anna they were not so. Slow and poor returns due to a glutted market on cucumbers, together with unsatisfactory means of inspection as to standardization may account for a greater part of the failure at Anna. The failure of the tomato crop in this district was another attributing factor. . . . The Makanda local did not act this year but postponed starting until the 1922 season.
>
> Our growers were expecting too much from the newly formed Exchange due in all probability to overselling the proposition at the start. The feeling among such mis-informed members is quite bitter and may reflect on the Farm Bureau which aided in establishing the Exchange. The feeling, however, among a greater part of the fruit men is very encouraging.[10]

They began plans for a cooperative packing and grading facility, and several prominent fruit growers from Union and neighboring counties toured Michigan, Ontario, and New York "to study central packing sheds used in connection with cooperative associations." A small circle of these growers sold their number-one pack under the Blue Goose brand. Blue Goose was the brand used by the American Fruit Growers, which bought several hundred acres of orchard land in the county.[11]

During the early 1920s, livestock shipping associations were formed in Dongola and Anna, and breeding associations were formed for Hereford cattle, Jersey dairy bulls, and Duroc-Jersey hogs. These organizations foundered as they failed to accumulate necessary capital or to sufficiently educate their members, but the larger farmers and fruit growers began to develop a more scientific and businesslike approach to their vocations, even as smaller farmers were cast back on their meager farm- and family-based resources.

The 1930s

As the depression deepened and industrial workers were laid off, smaller farmers began to suffer. Clara and David Elder did not make it through the depression as farmers. They had met on a farm where they and their parents worked as day laborers; they married and bought a 240-acre farm in the early 1920s. David got a job at a milling company in St. Louis, but when they began laying off their workers, he came back to the farm. "It's a good thing we was down on the farm when the depression hit," David recalled, "because at least we had plenty to eat." But the farm did not provide much income. "We'd just work all day and not make one penny," he said. "The poor guy didn't make it and the rich guy did make it, because he waited until he could get something for his stuff. But the guy like I was, . . . we farmed ten years and that was during the depression. We'd work all day long and ship up to Chicago and it wouldn't pay for the freight."

Clara continued: "At one time we shipped 110 boxes [of asparagus. The boxes cost ten cents apiece.] One time we got a due bill back from Chicago wanting us to send them nine cents to finish paying the [shipping] charges. . . . I didn't pay it."

Finally they developed a truck route in Carbondale, the largest town in the area. Clara recounted: "We raised everything then. David and the oldest boy would go into town and sell it, and when they got back home, why me and the kids would have another load nearly ready, and they'd help us finish it and then start with it the next day. . . . We even had chickens, frying chickens, cabbage, and beans."

David continued: "If you've got everything, you know, asparagus, beans and cabbage and tomatoes and just everything, you know, they ask, 'You got any of these?' And you say, 'Yup,' and they say, 'Well, I'll take some of them.' And you can sell to almost everybody if you had the right things. And that's what we tried to do. We raised an awful big truck patch. We had everything."

Clara went on: "Then we started in raising a lot of hogs. Day we had a big bunch ready to put on the market, . . . they took the cholera. And we lost every one of them."

At another time in the 1930s, David recounted, "I took a load, all I could stick in a wagon, sideboards on it, you know, and then a lid on top of it, and I put the hogs in it as long as I could get one in it. I took them down to Anna and got three and a half cents a pound for them. My whole load brought me $45. A whole load of hogs. . . . We tried everything. Cream's a nickel a pound, eggs a nickel a dozen."

According to Clara, they would "take a five-gallon can of cream and get back a dollar and a half."

They finally gave up the farm and bought a small place nearby. David explained: "The government bought the place. I was already of a notion of quitting, and I told them, well, I didn't much want to rent it to somebody else, I just wanted to get rid of it. Back then the government was paying $6 an acre. . . . So the whole 240 acres [were] planted in pine trees."

Clara recalled, "We sawed [the house] apart—I say we, David did. We sawed this thing apart and moved it over here, believe it or not, on a wagon and on a truck. First we moved the smokehouse and the milkhouse, which were built together, and set them right out there. And we lived there from March to November. And then they put up these four rooms here, two downstairs and two upstairs. And they had to put that up with main strength and awfulness."

David continued: "You know years ago they used to have house raisings. So we come up with the idea of a house raising. Oh, it just tickled the old people around the country to death. They never did have one for years, and they wanted to come over. So we had a big dinner out here. Our neighbors come in." "There was forty here one day," Clara remembered.[12]

Farm families were thrown back on their own resources. During the 1930s the farm population increased: between 1929 and 1934 the number of farms increased by 12 percent. The number of very small farms proliferated (see table 6.1), and even this may represent an undercount. Oral reports indicate that some relatively wealthy landowners allowed people to live in vacant houses on their land essentially rent-free and to use part of it for their own subsistence production, even if they did not need the family's labor. Even more significant than the proliferation of small farms,

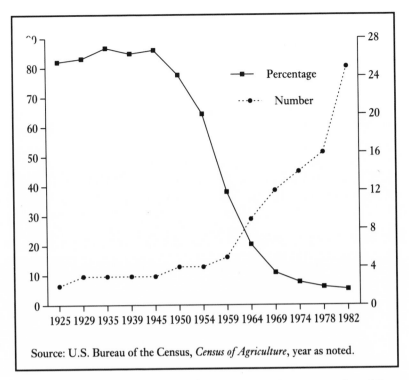

Source: U.S. Bureau of the Census, *Census of Agriculture*, year as noted.

Figure 7.1. Percentage of Farms with Dairy Cows, and Average Number of Cows per Farm, 1925–1982

the number of farms with cows and poultry increased, although the average number of cows per farm remained at three (see figs. 7.1 and 7.2).

Many men hunted in order to supplement their income. Ed Brimm, who lived on the Walton farm with his wife and young children, recalled that he would bag "anything I could catch . . . skunk, possum, or anything you could. And you stretch them and you might make twenty-five, thirty dollars. [I'd] sell them to get my kids Christmas presents." One year, he recalled, when Christmas came, they only had $3, so the children had no presents.[13]

The Karrakers, who owned a poultry and cream station in Dongola, and Robert Basler, who owned a store in Cobden, recalled buying rabbits from farmers for ten or fifteen cents each to ship to the Chicago market. As Floyd Karraker related, "Sometimes those rabbits would be pretty strong by the time they got to Chicago. We'd keep them maybe as long as a week, and they were pretty old by the time we got them. I don't know how the people up there [in Chicago] ate them, but I guess they did. We'd ship twenty, twenty-five bushels of rabbits at a time up there. We'd have big piles of them waiting to be shipped." Karraker recalled one lot that warmed while in transit. "I hadn't heard [from my broker] in a while, so I

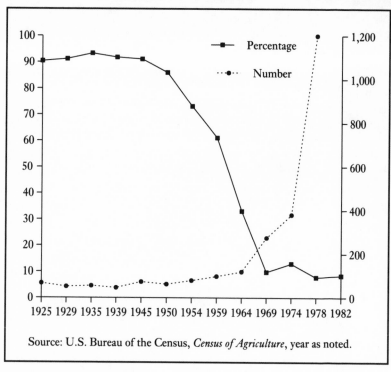

Source: U.S. Bureau of the Census, *Census of Agriculture*, year as noted.

Figure 7.2. Percentage of Farms with Chickens, and Average Number of Chickens per Farm, 1925–1982

contacted him and asked him if he had received the rabbits. I got a letter back from him that said, 'Yes, I received the rabbits and I've been trying to sell them. But when they came in,' he said, 'the odor. Oh, oh.' "[14]

Timbering also provided supplementary income. According to Leonard, timber prices were high during the 1920s, supporting at one time as many as thirty-two sawmills in the county. The 1929 crash virtually wiped out the timber market. In the 1920s, timbering regularly employed 500 people, and many others cut cordwood off their lots in winter; by 1940, fewer than 100 people worked in timber. According to Leonard, "As soon as crops were gathered the hired men were put to work cutting wood and the farmer had an income from his wood of from fifty to five hundred or more dollars. Since this form of occupation has practically disappeared in the county, many farmers do not employ labor during the winter months."[15]

Kaolin and silica deposits in the Clear Creek drainage in the western hills also provided work for laborers, but fortunes rose and fell with national demand. During World War I the kaolin pits west of Cobden, once important in local pottery manufacturing, were briefly revitalized.

Silica, dug from small mines, appears to have virtually lost its markets as earnings from minerals fell from $180,000 in 1930 to $54,000 in 1931.[16]

Many farm families during the depression were probably accurately characterized as self-sufficient simply because they were so impoverished that they were able to buy very little. This was not the self-sufficiency of the early nineteenth century, however, when existing technologies and systems of distribution might allow a farming family, living among other similar families, to supply virtually all their food, clothing, shelter, and other necessities from the land, needing cash only for a few tools and condiments, and when the state representative, as well as the poorest squatter, might wear a homespun suit. By the 1930s, in order to participate in the larger society a family had to purchase many of their needs or have them supplied through charity if they lacked the money. Some people resorted to stealing. Ada Kinder recalled, "There were several people you had to watch. A lot of people who lived on farms and butchered their own meat had their food stolen."[17]

Finis Hunsaker noted, "At that time, we would go downtown and tell who the rich people were and who the poor people were by the way they were dressed. You could tell. Whether they had something, or whether they were very poor. . . . After the WPA came in, the Works Projects Administration came in, people dressed more graciously."[18] George Parks recalled a teacher who taught at Ellis School. "She saw children bringing lunch boxes when they didn't have anything in them but a cold biscuit and a cold boiled potato."[19]

As national markets disintegrated, Union County farmers were thrown back increasingly on local markets, and the region, lacking the manufacturing base to multiply the wealth of the raw materials provided by the region's farms, mines, and forests, sank into acute poverty. The Anna Chamber of Commerce formed an industrial committee that tried to attract industry to the area. In the 1920s they persuaded a garment factory to locate in Anna, but it did not last long. A woman who had grown up on the Walton's farm and was used to working hard in the apple-packing shed got a job in this factory and recalled that dust was so thick in the air that she soon quit, although her sister stayed on. In 1931 the Industrial Committee was more successful; it renovated and expanded the former garment factory building and attracted International Shoe Company to the town. That factory, under different ownership, operated for sixty-one years, closing in December 1992. In 1939 Vulcan Heel Corporation opened a wood heel factory nearby.[20] During World War II the factory turned to making gloves and boot collars for the military; after the war, in 1945, International Shoe took over the operation from Vulcan. In the 1920s the Atlas Powder Company located on Wolf Lake, north of the village. No other outside industry was attracted to the county, and virtually all of the local businesses, except agriculture, remained oriented to local markets.

The collapse of agricultural markets therefore affected all other businesses in the county. Ruel Hindman, who began farming in the early 1920s, recalled,

> About the time the fruit [trees I had planted] came to bearing, the depression hit. I had borrowed money to buy the farm and the trees, so I was pretty badly in debt when the banks closed. The bank I was doing business with, the old First National Bank of Anna, never did reopen. . . .
>
> The bank closed because it didn't have enough assets. . . . They sent in a bank receiver, and he stayed here for about three years trying to collect all the notes and so forth that he could. A great number of borrowers were never able to pay any of their obligations to the bank.
>
> At the time it closed I owed them quite a bit of money. But I was one of the fortunate ones: I had my own orchard in production, and I had an orchard leased. In 1934 I had one of the few early apple crops there was in the Midwest. Why? I don't know, but I just didn't happen to get frozen out. I got an almost unheard of price from my early apple crop. They brought as high as $3.50 a bushel. I made some money, so I made a deal with the bank and paid them off in 1934. I was one of the few borrowers, I think, that was able to meet their obligations. If it hadn't been for that, I couldn't have done it. I happened to have an apple crop and got a good price for the apples right there in the depths of the depression.[21]

Many of the more prosperous farmers were impoverished by the depression. Rosemary Walton recalled a time when they could not scrape together three cents for a stamp, and the Hunsakers, children of prosperous families—Bertie's parents owned three farms when her father died—were forced out of farming. Her mother, "land poor," lost some of her land because she could not pay the taxes on it, and she sold the rest when she was able.[22] When, in 1938, the Cobden Lions Club organized a peach festival with a peach queen, the girl who was elected queen—Delores Flamm, the daughter of one of the largest growers in the area—had to wear a borrowed dress and was crowned with a paper crown. Townspeople were also affected. George Parks recalled, "People who had had money suddenly found that they didn't have an income. Their securities weren't yielding any proceeds, or they didn't get any dividend checks from things that they owned. People that might have been on the top level were suddenly found to be without money or income."[23] The Wares, for example, had long depended on rents from their extensive landholdings. When proceeds dropped in the 1920s, Anna Ware mortgaged her share of the estate and eventually lost it, enabling Elijah Bradley to buy the farm to which his daughter, Edith, retired.[24] Charles Thomas, who opened a restaurant in Cobden in the late 1920s, recalled, "It got so bad that . . . they were days when a customer was just almost a stranger, and of course you can't last very long at that. Whenever Prohibition was repealed, of course, they brought beer into town real quick. . . . I was going to have to either sell it or sell out." Since Thomas was pro-temperance, he quit the restaurant, first leasing and later selling it to a tavernkeeper.[25]

The Hunsakers quit farming and in 1930 moved to Cobden. Like many people with some resources, they maintained the older ethic of neighborhood reciprocity. Finis recounted:

> I bought a garage and filling station off of a fellow, and we moved to Cobden, and we were in the garage and filling station business there for five years. We took all the money we had, had a sale, sold off our livestock and everything, brought what little we had right here out of it, came here and put it in an old garage and filling station. . . . When I quit, I had $11,000 on my books, and I don't think we collected $10.00 of it ever. . . . These people would come in there with a long face, and maybe had a load of fruit on their truck. They just had to have a tire, just got to have a tire. All right, old bighearted Fin would sell it to them on credit. Put it on the books. It's still there on the books. . . . So I was a poor businessman.[26]

Helen Sirles recalled finding shoeboxes of notes that had never been paid when her father died.

A great leveling was beginning to occur. The impoverishment of the elites during the depression decades reversed a trend, visible at least since the Civil War, of increasing class divisions within agriculture and between farmers and town-based merchants and manufacturers. Despite the general impoverishment, however, the old order could have been reestablished had events in the larger political economy not further undercut the ability of local businessmen and growers to influence the direction of change. That story is told in Chapter 9.

Despite the general immiseration of the 1930s, some dimensions of life were enriched. Clara Elder asserted,

> There was a lot of good things come from that. There was a lot of community life, and families got together and enjoyed themselves and children. Why, our kids wasn't running all over the country of a night. They'd get the guitar and get out in the yard, if it was pretty, and they'd play and sing; and if it was bad, they'd play the piano and sing in the house. . . . When I say "the good old days," David and one of our son-in-laws says, "There wasn't anything good about it." And I say, "There was too. People thought more of each other, and if anyone needed anything, there was always a dozen here."[27]

CHAPTER 8

God bless Franklin D. Roosevelt for
giving farmers the privilege of living
like city people. . . . I will always love
Franklin D. Roosevelt 'cause he gave
the farmers electricity.

—Edith Rendleman

God Bless Franklin Roosevelt

The New Deal was a watershed in Union County, as it was in the rest of the country. Most people in the county had been hostile to government intervention and taxation. The democracy that the county voted for election after election was the democracy of Andrew Jackson and the Civil War. It promoted states' rights and a weak and small federal government. The New Deal, which the majority of Union County voters supported through their elected representatives, created a rupture with this tradition in two ways: it greatly expanded the amount of government investment in areas traditionally funded by government, such as roads and schools, and it created many new institutions that made government a full partner in regulating and operating the economy.

During the nineteenth century, counties and smaller units of government—townships and road, school, and drainage districts—had primary responsibility for raising funds for roads, schools, charity, and other aspects of local civil administration. The federal government reserved one square mile in every township for schools in newly surveyed areas, and in Illinois the state government assessed a small tax that was apportioned to the counties for their unrestricted use. Beginning in 1923 state funds came with specific mandates, such as requiring contributions to a teacher pension fund.[1] The New Deal did not alter these procedures; only after World War II was state school-funding used to encourage school consolidation.

Government had a long history of promoting transportation with government-supported canal projects and, later, large grants of public lands to railroad companies to help underwrite railroad construction. However, until 1915 virtually all road building was left to counties and private road companies. Union County had three private roads at the turn of the century: a toll road that began at Clear Creek and ran to the landing at Big Barn, operated by Jonesboro businessmen; a toll road linking that road with Jonesboro; and a gravel road operated by a joint-stock cooperative that linked Anna and Dongola (and that never met expenses).[2] The rest of the roads were built and maintained by the county and various road districts and relied heavily on labor volunteered by residents along the roads. Except where creek gravels were handy, roads were generally dirt, graded more or less skillfully so the water would drain rather than gully the tracks. Over the years these roads washed down so that the crests of hills are often cut far below ground level. People often used seasonal creek beds as roads, and most creeks were forded rather than bridged. Common law decreed that a track that was regularly used as a road became a public thoroughfare, so landowners were careful to regulate traffic across their property. I recall that people who lived behind us sometimes used a track across our farm when the dirt road going back to their farms was impassable. My father was careful to keep a closed gate across the gap linking our farm track to the road so that no one could claim it as a public road.

In 1915 the state of Illinois began to intervene vigorously in road building, adding state aid for roads. In the 1920s Illinois governor Len Small initiated an ambitious road-building program that "got Illinois out of the mud." The highway now known as Old Route 51 (originally Route 2) was completed during 1923 and 1924. It more or less paralleled the Illinois Central Railroad tracks through Union County, winding on a deliberately scenic route through the hills. Floyd Karraker recalled working on a section of the road between Anna and Dongola for the excellent wages of twenty-five cents an hour. In order to pay for improved roads, the state passed a motor fuel tax in 1927, with one-third of the income going to counties to supplement county road taxes.[3]

Nearly ten years passed before more roads were paved in the county. What is now Route 3 through the bottoms was paved from Ware south in 1931 and from the northern county line to Ware in 1932. In 1933 the road that is now Route 146 was paved, replacing the old toll roads to the bottoms. Six more years passed before the Black Diamond Trail—now Route 127—was blacktopped, and it was not completed until after World War II.[4]

Union Countians generally approved of state support for schools and roads, although people who felt the impact locally might quarrel with specific requirements the money entailed. Other forms of social investment, however, were actively opposed or deplored by many, even as a majority seem to have welcomed the funds infused into the local economy.

In 1930 the county voted 2,730 to 1,027 against funding a statewide system of conservation and forest preserves and recreation grounds.[5] Despite this vote, the previous year the Department of Conservation had purchased 3,228 acres for the Union State Forest, which eventually expanded to over 5,000 acres, 120 of which became a state tree nursery.[6] In 1928 Giant City State Park was created on the Union-Jackson County line.[7]

Despite persistent votes that gave the county a very conservative cast, including a narrow vote against repealing the Eighteenth Amendment, which established Prohibition, and a substantial vote against allowing women to serve on juries, the voters strongly supported Kent Keller for the U.S. Congress in 1930.[8] Keller became a strong New Dealer who obtained a large number of government projects for southern Illinois, including one of the largest man-made lakes in Illinois, Crab Orchard Lake (begun in 1935 or 1936 and filled at the beginning of the winter of 1939–40), which opponents of the New Deal christened "Kent Keller's Frog Pond."

Politics had always been important in many families, with partisan loyalties going back to the Civil War and with many judicial and county-level decisions influenced by family and partisan considerations. However, with the exception of the state mental hospital in Anna,[9] crises like World War I, and some state support for road building and schools, government above the level of the county had little direct impact on most people's daily lives before the 1930s. After that time government became an integral part of daily life. People in the community served on governing and advisory boards of the many New Deal programs; town and county governments sought grants from various federal agencies; and the federal government, or local governments with federal money, hired large numbers of people. The integration of government into the fabric of daily life became so pervasive and institutionalized that people I interviewed rarely recollected the radical transformation this involved. Only by reading accounts written during the period is it possible to get a sense that many people strongly resisted the new order; most young people (that is, people still alive in the 1980s) welcomed the new programs because they provided jobs and a lifestyle that was closer to that of urban people. The WPA (Works Progress Administration) and other programs gave people work and raised the price of labor. The Jonesboro *Gazette* editorialized July 23, 1938:

> Times are better for Union County people. . . . When the Gazette man came to this county about five years ago, married and single men were being paid at the rate of 50 to 75 cents per day (without board and room) and the average time was for about three days, only, per week. Much of the time there was no work for anyone. In addition to those handicaps, laborers were often required to work a distance of from 3 to 6 miles, and this distance was also the rule when employed on "work relief jobs." Now, that has been changed.
>
> Just now, boys not over 12 and 14 years of age are receiving as much as $1.50 per day.
>
> With the WPA work, bean picking, berry, asparagus, tomato, apple, wheat and melon seasons, there should be no idle laborers in Southern Illinois.

A few stories suggest the divisiveness these programs engendered. One woman recalled that a young man whose family had long been strong Republicans went to a Democratic convention or meeting and came back a converted New Dealer. The woman who told me the story, herself a lifelong Republican, implied that his conversion may have been stimulated by the job he could get if he became a Democrat. Another woman recalled that her husband hated the WPA because, he claimed, he could not get men to pick fruit for him because the government paid them to loaf. Another man told me that he got a WPA job because his father had political pull; but, he assured me, he qualified anyway. Finis Hunsaker, who became a paymaster for the WPA after the Hunsakers moved from their farm into Cobden, recalled a fight over whether or not to seek a federal grant for a housing project:

> You take, for instance, I was very active at that time in the American Legion. And I was going to get a project to build a new legion [nursing] home, closer over here. And there was a fellow who was very much opposed to WPA—he was kind of a politician, you know, and he just fought it like everything. There were some of these guys that agreed with him, and so we didn't get it over. Otherwise, we would have built a project of houses, many over there, and a big community center. That's what I was working for. But this guy got a few of his friends on an opposing party, so they raised hay in Columbia about it, so we just forgot it.[10]

Many people were at best deeply ambivalent about the government programs, which they saw as a form of charity. Many more prosperous people, whose words were committed to paper, believed that anyone who wanted to work could generally find shelter that, if they were thrifty, they could make livable, and that they could feed themselves, while neighborly charity would take care of clothing and emergency needs. Leonard quotes a county commissioner who was in office in 1930 and who was therefore involved in providing relief orders for paupers. "We thought we met the needs adequately and there did not seem to be any complaint about the assistance given," he observed. Leonard summarized the prevailing attitudes, as she interpreted them: "It was only unusually lazy people who did not avail themselves of . . . opportunities [to glean their neighbors' fields], and these people were so criticized by their neighbors that many people accepted the gifts to avoid having a reputation of being lazy." Leonard's observations on the changes in the following decade are worth quoting at length, for despite her attempt to speak in a dispassionate voice, she clearly reflects the attitude of people who generally disapproved of New Deal programs:

[A drastic change] has taken place during the last ten years when our public assistance has increased from $14,450 in 1930 to $629,470.37 in 1938 in spite of the fact that a large factory employing 500 people was opened up during that period. This $629,470.37 does not include large amounts of money that have been loaned to the farmers and home-builders, it represents only the amount of money that was given outright to the people of the county who said they were unable to earn a livelihood for themselves and would have to be supported by the government.

One drastic change that has taken place since 1930 is the fact that the citizens who do not need help have taken the attitude that the government should help the poor and [that] the individual citizen need no longer give the attention he formerly gave to his tenant, his neighbor or his poor relative. A second drastic change that has taken place is that the poor person no longer feels that he is being helped but demands support as a civil right. Most recipients of WPA jobs do not consider this a form of relief and demand that their political friends use their influence to obtain this type of job for them.

There is not room here to enumerate instances where citizens who consider themselves honorable have abused the privilege of being aided by the government by demanding help when they might be able to devise ways to help themselves. This is not true alone of Union County but of most of the counties in the whole United States. Since the appropriation for this assistance comes from the federal and state governments mainly, all needs are estimated at a maximum rather than minimum extent so that by the time all estimates are totalled it makes a tremendous amount of money necessary to meet the estimated needs.[11]

Leonard noted that the county board established to administer relief funds differed with "experts" on the county's need: "In contrast to [the opinion of the members of the local Illinois Emergency Relief Commission committee,] in the opinion of economists who study the problem at large and in measuring the standard of living [in] Union County find that it is lower than most counties in Illinois. Therefore it was their constant advice to give more assistance to make the standard of living comparable to other counties."[12] It is clear, however, that the county relief commission did not speak for all people in the county, even all relatively affluent and "honorable" people, whom Leonard accused of abusing the programs.

The "drastic change" in people's attitudes toward government subsidies can be seen as the result of two processes. First, the old order had increasingly differentiated poor from rich and industry from agriculture. These inequities had grown steadily since the Civil War and were causing strains both in Union County, where young people desired more urban standards of living, and in the nation at large, where a growing labor movement demanded redistribution of wealth and reorganization of industrial relations. These strains were exacerbated by the depression and were tolerated locally only because people saw no alternatives, and because the mediations of kinship, neighborliness, and patronage made it possible for individual families to survive, if meagerly. The second factor, originated in the larger social movements of the time, was the New Deal, which provided options. The alternatives provided by New Deal programs promised immediate material benefits, both to the severely impoverished and to many members of the middle and upper classes, whose wealth had been undermined by the depression. Only the relatively privileged could maintain the belief that the old way of doing things—helping poor tenants, neighbors, and kin—was still viable.

George Parks, an Anna druggist and banker, recollected the initiation of New Deal programs:

The thing which gave immediate work in Union County and everywhere, was the enactment of the Works Progress Administration (WPA). This did much toward the building of country roads [and] the development of a system of private benefits from the construction of new outdoor privies for the farm dwellers whose facilities had deteriorated much through the years. The work on schoolgrounds and playgrounds and public parks was a part of this enterprise, as was the erosion control program for the farms. Our farmers were in dire circumstances as far as their established mortgage loans[,] and the Federal Agricultural Adjustment Act set up emergency farm mortgages which provided a relief from the pressures of existing obligations which many farmers had and which were unable to be met.

The merchants were mildly receptive to the NRIA [*sic*], which set up certain standards and enlisted an honor system of adaptation to these work standards and quality standards. In addition to all of this there was a farm credit program set up whereby farmers could obtain government monies at a moderate loan interest rate for the improvement of their farms and the putting out of crops. The biggest assistance that the county here received immediately was the Federal Emergency Relief Act which enhanced the operation of the state relief program[,] and a system of relief for the hungry and the needy was put into action, and promptly.[13]

The New Deal made government money available for public utilities, such as sewer systems and waterworks, under the CWA (Civil Works Administration). In Anna, with some stimulus from the county farm adviser, E. A. Bierbaum,[14] the businessmen and city government cooperated with the CWA to build the Anna City Market, and the city made sure it would be successful by passing an ordinance that prohibited house-to-house peddling. The People's Fruit and Vegetable Shippers Association of Cobden, in contrast, raised funds from their own membership and from voluntary donations to build a similar market in 1935.[15] As Fin Hunsaker's reminiscence about the town's refusal to seek funds for a housing project attests, the village of Cobden was quite divided on whether or not to take New Deal money for improvement projects. After some disagreement, however, the Cobden village government contracted with the WPA to build a waterworks and, four years later, the village installed a sewer system. These projects seemed to energize many of the business families, who had been unable to organize and sustain a businessman's organization, for in 1938 the Lions Club was formed to promote civic improvements. They began the Peach Festival to raise money toward a fire engine for the volunteer fire department; in the 1990s the festival continues in the tradition of small-town community fairs.[16]

The government also began buying land for a national forest, approved in 1933. Although sales were voluntary, many people later harbored some resentment toward the Forest Service because landowners sold at extremely low prices at a time when they desperately needed money or were threatened with losing their land for back taxes. Many Union County farmers, including David and Clara Elder, who farmed in the north central part of the county, sold their farms to the Forest Service. In the eastern part of the state, at Dixon Springs, the University of Illinois began an extensive experiment station to develop and promote farming practices appropriate to the southern Illinois hills. In 1936 the Forest Service bought the site of the historic Lincoln–Douglas debate in Jonesboro for the headquarters office of the local Shawnee district.[17]

Several CCC camps were located in the area, mostly in the newly established (1933) Shawnee National Forest and state parks and forests, including a camp in the Union County State Forest and in Lake Hills. Camp occupants in Giant City State Park developed trails, created stone retaining walls, and built a stone lodge and cabins. Men from the camp at the state forest east of Wolf Lake undertook reforestation projects, built roads, reclaimed seriously eroded land, and fought forest fires. In cooperation with the state forest, they began a tree nursery that continues to the present.[18]

The new bureaucracies often overlooked local bodies, such as road districts, and therefore ran into jurisdictional problems. As he did with other New Deal programs, E. A. Bierbaum, the farm adviser, ran interference. He reported that he gave the WPA "assistance in calling the farmers of communities together to discuss their road problems and [having] them designate a committeeman to serve on a county committee to assist in better understanding of WPA road projects, and the committee to help as an advisory and contact committee to help iron out differences and have work proceed. Later a county-wide project was developed to complete the road plan of the county." The WPA operated gravel pits, selling gravel at cost to local road districts.[19]

Electricity and all-weather roads were probably the most important projects that changed the lives of farm people, although at first gravel appeared as a mixed blessing. Horses and mules had difficulty walking long distances on gravel, and during the war gasoline and tires were expensive and scarce. Tires frequently wore out, and automobiles were in general less reliable and more expensive than horses and mules. Despite the mud that sometimes made roads impassable, few people commented to me or other interviewers about getting gravel roads. This contrasted with recollections about getting electricity, which many farmers, and particularly farm women, welcomed enthusiastically. Edith Rendleman has said many times, "Thank God for Franklin D. Roosevelt, because he brought us electricity." She lived in a house with electricity before the REA (Rural Electric Association) was established in 1935, because, with prodding from her and her father, her husband had rented a farm that had an electric generator. This relieved her of the heavy work of pumping and hauling water, but the voltage was inadequate for electric irons or for strong interior lighting. It did, however, operate a pump, allowing her to have a motor-operated washing machine.

In contrast to funding for urban infrastructure like the market and waterworks, which some people saw as boondoggles, there seems to have been little controversy surrounding the establishment of the REA, although the cooperative had some difficulty attracting members and some people objected to the projected costs of construction.[20] A history of the Southern Illinois Electric Cooperative recounts the problem:

> Back in 1938 and 1939, most rural people had only a vague idea of what it meant to have electricity. . . .
>
> An early leader in the rural electrification project [explained], "To many people, electricity was a cord hanging from the ceiling with a light bulb dangling from one end. They couldn't foresee a day when they would be using 15 or 20 electric appliances in their homes and probably as many in their barns."
>
> When these objectors were told the Cooperative would require at least two electrical outlets in the kitchen and one in each room many refused to sign a membership application. They complained they would never use all of the outlets.
>
> "Who ever heard of putting electric lights in the bedrooms?" one irate woman inquired. "We can carry a kerosene lamp to our bedrooms and cut down on the cost of electricity."
>
> There were many farmers in the area farming relatively small tracts of land—40 to 80 acres in size. These were truck farmers, producing big crops of vegetables for unremitting labor in the fields. The returns were small, however. When a farmer who had worked 12 to 15 hours doing "stoop labor" to harvest tomatoes, peppers and the like was asked to pay $5 to join the Cooperative and told he must pay the minimum of $3.00 monthly, he naturally rebelled.[21]

Despite these initial objections, in 1938 the farm adviser reported that the organizing committee had secured 344 patrons on 117 miles of line within Union County, and that with adjoining counties 1,014 patrons on 360 miles of line had been secured.[22] By February 1939 most of the necessary easements for the first lines and a federal loan had been obtained, and in May 1940 the first lights were turned on. As with many New Deal programs, especially those in rural areas, the REA was democratically organized. Everyone who got power from the cooperative had to become a member; the coop was run by a board elected by the members, and most of the administrative staff and contractors came from the immediate area. Much of the actual administration, however, was in the hands of technical experts, so the range of policymaking left to farmer board members was relatively small. Nonetheless, initially the board members were very active, recruiting support in the communities, helping gain easements through farms, and so forth.

Gaining easements was not always easy: I spoke with a woman who was not interested in using electricity and who steadfastly refused to let the line come through her property. She was determined to make them pay as much as she could get for the easement. Such tactics, although not common, were not unusual: I heard several stories of people who refused easements for local road relocation projects. Holding out for more money became more common (and more socially approved) after World War II when the government sought to condemn land by right of eminent domain for development projects, particularly freeways and lakes.

The Kimbers helped organize the Southern Illinois Electric Cooperative and were fortunate enough to get electricity before the war stopped construction. Jacquie Kimber Eddleman, who was born in 1936, recalled what it meant to get power:

> I barely remember the night that we had lights. Daddy was coming in from the potato house in town—he packed sweet potatoes out there in the winter. And I remember that the big deal was to get all the lights in the house on as he came up the road. That's one of the very earliest recollections that I have. I barely remember having to use kerosene lamps. I know a lot of grade school friends that I had, we'd swap off staying all night with each other. There were a lot of those people who got electric lights long after we did, and so one of the big deals for them was to get to come here where we had electric lights. And one of the big deals for me was to go over to their house, for we always had to clean the kerosene lamps.

Soon after, with credit from the Electric Home and Farm Authority, they bought an electric refrigerator, stove, washer, and pump from a store in Dongola.[23] Edith Rendleman had a similar recollection:[24]

> They got the line up to our place in 1942, but Mom and Dad didn't get electricity until after the war ended. That was a wonderful day in our life when we got electricity. [My sons] Bud and Lee were in the field working when they came and turned the electricity on. They didn't know we had lights, and they came in from the field at noon, and we said something about having lights. They said, "Yeah, I bet you got lights." I said, "Well, turn them on," and they liked to flipped when the light came on. Oh, it was a wonderful day. We could have a bathtub, a bathroom. And it helped the farmer so much and all his work.

The New Deal also invented a large number of programs oriented specifically at agriculture as an economic sector.[25] Farmers, through their organizations and representatives in Congress, had long sought special protections from government, but largely in the area of data collection, technical assistance, education, and regulation. A series of laws, beginning with the Morrill Land-Grant College Act of 1862 and including the Hatch Act of 1887 that established agricultural experiment stations and the Smith-Lever Act of 1914 that established agricultural extension, provided agricultural education. Throughout the nineteenth and early twentieth centuries the USDA expanded the kind of data it collected, as reflected in the Census of Agriculture, which after 1920 was taken every five years rather than every ten, and in a variety of other special reports. In 1922 the USDA had established the Bureau of Agricultural Economics.

In the 1910s, urban reformers associated with the Progressive movement became concerned about the rising price of food and about the working and living conditions of the immigrants who were filling up the slums of the eastern and northern industrial cities. Some of these progressives organized themselves as the Country Life Commission and formed a sometimes uneasy alliance with farmers and the group of congressmen who came to be known as the Farm Bloc, to try to bring modern standards of living and of doing business to rural areas.[26] In the first two decades of the century they passed a series of reforms designed to guarantee healthy foods for consumers. This legislation provided the laws and, with the establishment of the Food and Drug Administration in 1927, the agency to regulate the quality of food products marketed. They also believed that without adequate credit, farmers, who unlike corporations could not tap large amounts of capital, would not be able to invest in new technologies. In 1916 Congress passed the Federal Farm Loan Act that established twelve Farm Land banks, one in each Federal Reserve district,[27] and in 1923 the Agricultural Credits Act established a Federal Intermediate Credit Bank, also in each Federal Reserve district. The Farm Bloc also passed the Capper-Volstead Act, which exempted farmer cooperatives from antitrust regulation, and fought for a variety of other programs and, especially, tariffs to protect U.S. agricultural products.

When Roosevelt and his advisers developed programs to help agriculture, therefore, there were already a large number of precedents to draw on. Between 1933 and 1936 most of the institutional and programmatic foundations of current agricultural policies were established. In 1933 the Agricultural Adjustment Act, the first "omnibus farm bill," established the Agricultural Adjustment Administration (AAA), which sought to coordinate various agricultural programs. It was, however, invalidated (as was the National Recovery Administration) by the Supreme Court in 1936. Congress then passed the Soil Conservation and Domestic Allotment Act to operate those parts of the adjustment program the court left intact. Other legislation was more successful: The Soil Erosion Service (later the Soil Conservation Service) undertook ambitious programs to stem the serious erosion problems throughout the country. The Farm Credit Administration consolidated the Land Banks and the Intermediate Credit Banks and in 1934 added crop production loans. The Commodity Credit Corporation gave farmers loans on their harvested crops so that they could hold them off the market, and the loan rate functioned as a floor below which commodity prices would not fall, acting as a "buyer of last resort." Congress addressed the problem of overproduction (which by the 1930s was more a problem of underconsumption) by distributing the commodities they acquired under the Commodity Credit Corporation to needy people through the Surplus Relief Corporation. In 1934, 1935, and 1936 Congress passed several acts to provide production controls and establish marketing agreements and orders on various crops. In 1934 the Federal Emergency Relief Administration began a rural rehabilitation program, and in 1935 the Resettlement Administration, later renamed the Farm Security Administration (FSA), helped tenants buy land and establish cooperative enterprises. When it was disbanded in 1946, its lending programs were taken over by the newly organized Farmers' Home Administration, which served as "lender of last resort" for low-income farmers and rural people who wanted to build new homes. The REA was also established in 1935, and the Child Nutrition Act was passed that established school breakfast and lunch programs.

As with the REA, the WPA, and the CWA, E. A. Bierbaum, the county farm adviser, played a crucial role in linking the new federal bureaucracies to local actors. In 1940 he summarized the work of the Farm Bureau, which at that time was the governing board of the Agricultural Extension Service. It coordinated the New Deal programs, the County Agricultural Conservation Association, the FSA, the local credit associations affiliated with the Farm Credit Administration, and the Forestry Service, and it coordinated these programs with the county school nursing service, the county superintendent of schools, business and civic organizations, and the county bankers' association. Unlike areas in which farmers specialized in major agricultural commodities like cotton, wheat, and corn, the acreage set-aside programs that aimed to reduce agricultural overproduction did not have a great impact on Union County farmers. Soil conservation programs had far greater impact on the small, highly diversified hill farmers that dominated the county's agricultural economy. Bierbaum began to promote vigorously soil conservation in 1936 and reported that he had set up Agricultural Conservation Associations in seven communities with twenty-one leaders and 1,150 farmers cooperating. "Those not cooperating represented in large part small farms with acreage not large," he wrote. The first goal of the associations was to plant "five acres of alfalfa on every farm."[28] The Kimbers were active cooperators, and Helen's father, H. A. Plott, had been a longtime member of the Farm Bureau. When Frank and Helen moved to Frank's home place when his father died in 1934, he soon began to work with the county farm adviser. A 1936 conservation plan Bierbaum and Frank Kimber mapped out shows thirty-seven plots on their 123-acre farm; the largest, planted in lespedeza, was 17.3 acres.

The following year the association sponsored a number of demonstration projects, including use of fertilizers, terracing, crop selection, keeping farm accounts, and making farm surveys.[29] By 1939 Bierbaum reported, "Of the 1,954 farms in the county, 1,538 (representing 85 percent of the cropland) were cooperating in the AAA program. However, 209 of the 1,538 performed *no* soil building or soil conserving practices."[30]

By the 1930s much of the soil in the county had degraded from years of overuse. As early as 1918 the farm adviser reported four portable limestone crushers in the county, and in 1928 the adviser reported that limestone use had risen from an estimated 200 tons in 1919 to 10,000 tons in 1928, and that sweet clover and other legumes were being used as a cover crop in orchards and disked in. George Weaver, however, reported that his father did not use lime until probably the late 1940s, and that the pH was so high in some fields that they would not even raise a crop of clover.[31] In 1940 Bierbaum reported a sharp increase in limestone use because of an AAA grant that supported the development of a new quarry "under the supervision and ownership of Geo. E. Dillow."[32] As with other programs, government investment in conservation practices was interrupted by World War II.

The War

By the late 1930s the economy was slowly improving. As Europe armed, world trade rebounded, rippling back to Union County, where the kaolin clay deposits south of Mountain Glen, which had been mined during World War I, were reactivated. When the Japanese bombed Pearl Harbor December 7, 1941, the nation went on a war footing. For the next several years the war was a major focus of life. The newspapers were full of stories related to the war. There were articles about Union County boys in the military; announcements about the availability of rationed goods, like sugar and tires; appeals for scrap metal, rubber, and other materials (including, in 1944, a campaign for milkweed pods to be used in making life jackets); and campaigns to sell war bonds. Despite its poverty, Union County consistently overshot its quota of war bonds. A Union County man developed a war bond promotion, auctioning off a pig named "King Neptune," that between 1942 and the end of the war in 1946 raised $19 million statewide. King Neptune was buried along a Union County highway, and in 1990 a memorial was erected at a rest stop on the interstate that passes through the county.[33]

The war also tightened the labor market. The Federal Reemployment Service, established in 1937, helped coordinate growers' labor needs.[34] In 1941, Bierbaum devoted much of his annual report to the labor situation. He wrote, "The rapid re-employment of young men in industry, leaving the county, and others entering the armed services, makes the farmers more dependent on migrant and other help during peak labor seasons."[35]

A number of New Deal agencies—the WPA, the Illinois Employment Service, and the Labor Division of the FSA—undertook a survey of labor conditions and needs. The Farm Bureau through the Extension Service disagreed with an FSA proposal to build camps for migrant workers near Anna, Cobden, and Alto Pass, and instead proposed to operate a tent rental service so that growers could place tents on their farms. They also helped provide toilet facilities and better drinking water, bathing, and washing facilities.[36]

In July 1942, the Anna *Gazette Democrat* appealed for help with the peach crop: "Ask everyone to help with peach crop: shortage of labor is worry to county growers," read one headline. The war continued to drain labor from agriculture, from both the migrant stream and the county. By January 1944, 1,327 Union County men were in the military.[37] In 1943 the U.S. Employment Service established offices at the Cobden and Anna markets and at the farm adviser's office to refer migrant labor, and the Extension Service and the employment service recruited labor from neighboring counties. That year 650 farmers used the service. In 1945, at the request of a Farm Bureau committee, the government brought in Jamaicans to help with the crop and allowed farmers to use German officers who, as prisoners of war, were housed in what had been a Colored CCC camp in Pomona, in Jackson County.[38] The War Food Administration leased the camp in the Union County State Forest for the Jamaicans and helped coordinate groceries for them.[39] The heavy demands the war made on the male labor force led to heavy recruitment of women, although not as peach and apple pickers. In 1944 the shoe factory advertised for women to work "day and night shifts in essential war work"; the following year they advertised, "150 women and some men are needed immediately for essential war work in making boot collars for combat boots." It was a seller's market for labor, and the plant offered "full time work; no experience necessary; group insurance; pay while learning; vacation with pay; unusually pleasant working conditions."[40] Even before the war, garment and shoe manufacturers generally hired more women than men, and the shoe factory—and the garment factory it replaced—had been employing women like the young women who grew up as tenants on the Walton farm (see Chapter 10). The war effort, however, expanded production and drew ever more women off farms and out of homes and into relatively well-paid jobs.

The war drove up prices for farm products; in 1943 the newspaper headlined, "Peaches sell for more than $8 a bushel. Beans on rampage Monday sell for $5.50." The following year the Office of Price Administration placed ceilings on produce prices, which brought organized protests from peach growers. A number of civic groups, including the Cobden Lions Club, with support from the FSA, organized a cooperative of 250 farmers, the Jackson County and Union County Purchasing and Marketing Associations, to build a tomato cannery, called the Egyptian Plant, to provide tomatoes to the military. It did not continue operating after the war, facing stiff competition from other canneries within easy trucking distance.[41]

Under the direction of the county superintendent of schools, and with government support in 1944, a cannery for home canning was set up in Jonesboro.[42]

Newspaper accounts give an impression of feverish economic activity. "Peach fever" struck farmers again as prices rose, and they set out thousands of new trees. Despite the labor shortage, farmers planted acres in green beans, tomatoes, and other crops. A story in the Cobden *Review*, July 14, 1944, gives some idea of the way these crops were marketed:

> The person who visits the market early in the morning will see one of the reasons why Cobden is known throughout the country as an outstanding produce shipping center. Arriving from every direction are all sorts of conveyances—large trucks, small trucks, farm pickups, trailers, big passenger cars.
>
> Trucks, all loaded to capacity with tomatoes, cucumbers, beans, in fact every sort of product that the good land around Cobden produces. People milling about, checkers, commission men, warehouse employees and truck drivers, all intent on one purpose—getting the produce to the city markets; and this activity continues throughout the day and far into the night. . . .
>
> Growers say that the peach crop as a whole will be the largest since 1931. Both basket manufacturing plants, H. A. DuBois and Sons, and the Lawrence plant, have been working to capacity for some months to get packages ready for the bumper crop both here and in other states.

The systems set up to administer New Deal and wartime programs also served well for local emergencies. In 1943 the Mississippi River overran its banks in one of the worst floods in its history. On Sunday, May 23, the levee broke, forcing evacuation of the entire bottoms. E. A. Bierbaum, alerted that the levee was nearly breached, activated the network of local farm leaders. Bierbaum reported, "I phoned four leaders in Alto Pass, four leaders in Cobden, two leaders in Dongola. I asked these leaders in each case to call all farmers on all rural phone lines and have them, with their trucks (tanks filled with gas) to report to me immediately at Ware, to evacuate the bottoms. I then called a farmer key man on each rural line of the Anna exchange and had him call all farmers on his line and asked them to report likewise." About 125 farmers arrived with trucks, and they

In the great flood of 1943, the levee broke just behind the house in which Edith Rendleman's parents lived, on the banks of Running Lake. The water nearly covered the chicken house and reached the top of the windows of the house. Edith Rendleman Collection, Morris Library, Southern Illinois University, Carbondale.

quickly began to evacuate livestock and household goods. Using the same system, Bierbaum coordinated pasture space with farmers who lived in the hills. The army and coast guard barges completed the evacuation in the following days, and the AAA, the CCC, federal loan agencies, and the USDA War Board helped provide relief and restore the buildings and farms after the waters receded. Bierbaum reported, "The farmers in the area returned to their farms and made a surprising comeback, spurred on by the thought that every pound produced was needed in the war effort. Corn and fresh vegetables were planted for market. The fall of 1943 saw about normal wheat and barley acreage seeded and a large acreage of alfalfa reseeded."

God Bless Franklin Roosevelt   159

The flooded area had included, in Union County, 181 farms and about 250 farm families. Over 39,000 acres were under water, more than half farmland. Nearly 18,000 acres of crops were destroyed. Due to the tight coordination of the various agencies, none of the estimated 2,400 cattle, 9,200 hogs, or 300 sheep were reported lost.[43]

The levee broke the following year, although the flood was not so high. In 1945, as part of one of the government's many flood control and land reclamation projects, a large levee, "approximately four times the size of the present levee" and with a roadway on top of it, was built.[44]

The county had mobilized six years earlier as well, when the Ohio and lower Mississippi flooded in 1937.[45] Through the WPA, the Army Engineers, and the Red Cross, Union Countians mobilized to help maintain levees and resettle refugees.[46] A camp for white refugees was established in Anna, and one for African Americans was set up near Wolf Lake.

During the twelve years between the beginning of the New Deal and the end of World War II a sea change occurred in the country and in the county. For the first time, government became a full partner in the economy. A myriad of government agencies assumed many of the responsibilities of regulating and providing services for businesses and individuals—what economists call the "externalities" of business accounting. Before this period, families, with occasional emergency help from the county, provided the "social safety net" for people who lost their jobs, got sick, or were injured. Whether or not a person could find work was considered important only to his or her family, or to tenderhearted individuals who might provide private charity. Those seeking jobs were left to the vagaries of rumor and well-placed connections to find work. People had no guarantees that money they placed in banks or invested would be secure, and their financial security in old age depended on their savings and their families. Although reforms of the Granger, Populist, and Progressive movements had placed some regulations—antitrust, consumer protection, and so forth—on business, the New Deal extended the principle that government should regulate and coordinate business to the benefit of the larger society.[47] The principle that the federal government had the primary responsibility to provide infrastructure in the form of good roads, flood control, sewer and water supplies, and electric and telephone systems also enormously expanded the historic role of government in providing such services. These changes were particularly important for farmers. Conservation programs, crop allotments, the "ever-normal granary," and a variety of credit programs that were created or extended through the New Deal, along with government reclamation and flood control projects and rural electrification, fundamentally altered the bases on which farmers made decisions, and created an economic environment that, after the war, encouraged them to expand and invest in expensive technologies and high-yield crop and livestock varieties. The New Deal programs and the wartime labor shortages also drew farm women into community organizations and off-farm work.

When World War II ended, then, although the countryside looked much as it had in 1933, a new social economy was in place.

You can trace the change from the
labor-intensive work to work that one
man could handle with one or two
hands.—Barbara Walton Throgmorton

Labor Got So Tight

The new order, that on hindsight appears to have been firmly instituted by the end of World War II, did not appear so solid in 1946. The people who had primary responsibility for guiding their families and the county's political and social direction had grown up during the first, prosperous decades of the century. Many of them appear to have expected to reconstruct that social order as the nation returned to "normalcy." Had Union County been the nation, perhaps the merchants, small manufacturers, and substantial farmers would have been able to eliminate most of the New Deal programs and reestablish the now fundamentally disturbed social relations. However, the county was tightly integrated into a nation that, with the end of the war, had emerged as the dominant political and economic player on the world's stage. In this radically reconfigured social economy, voices that had been marginal to the old order gained strength, and new voices emerged. Perhaps as important, people who experienced the depression and the war as children saw the world with eyes that were significantly different from their parents'. They never knew the relative stability and security that their parents—if they were from property-owning families—had grown up with. Young people born as the farm economy collapsed after World War I fought in World War II and came home with a range of experiences that opened them to the opportunities offered by its victorious end.

Initially, rural and urban Union Countians anticipated continued prosperity. Wartime price controls continued for a short while, but strong consumer demand and the end of the emergency led to the lifting of many ceilings, while the government retained floors under many agricultural commodities. The July 12, 1946, Anna *Gazette Democrat* headlined, "Beans jump to $6 when ceiling is taken off. Big run of all produce at Anna Municipal Market." The story said, "The ceiling had been $2.70 at the first of the season but had been lowered to $2.50 before it was taken off. More than a thousand bushels a day are coming into the market at the present time."

Peach growers also did well. Under the headline "Big peach crop will not satisfy great demand," the August 16, 1946, *Gazette Democrat* stated: "A bumper crop this year is still not sufficient to meet great demand for the fine quality peaches and truckers from all states are lined up to take the daily output and refrigerator cars are going out on every freight train from Anna, Cobden and Alto Pass. All of the first grade peaches are selling for the ceiling price of $3.64 a bushel and were it not for the ceiling it is hard to estimate how much they would be selling for."

Postwar prosperity did not immediately touch everyone. As factories oriented to manufacturing war material closed and the military demobilized, thousands were cast out of work. Many poor people were thrown into the migrant stream. For the farmers who raised orchards and market gardens, it appeared as if their labor shortages were over. The Extension Service continued to help coordinate this labor, and Bierbaum arranged to purchase surplus army equipment for the growers, including tents, cots, and mattresses.[1] Jacquie Kimber Eddleman and Barbara Walton Throgmorton were children during this period, but unlike their parents, they no longer took rural poverty for granted. Barbara recalled:

In high school when I studied *Grapes of Wrath* I thought, "I know what these people look like because I saw them when they came to our farm." I saw the poverty that was there. I remember a lady we called "Milk"; she was so thin and old beyond her years. I understand that now, looking back. But she had a little baby and she—they were here for,

Helen Kimber's father, Harvey Plott, carrying green beans to market. Around 1946 Helen's sister, Elaine, with her husband and his brother, and the brother's wife, the daughter of Edith Rendleman, raised a large field of green beans in the Mississippi bottoms. They were unable to find enough labor to harvest all the beans and had to leave some of the field unpicked. Kimber Collection, Morris Library, Southern Illinois University, Carbondale.

what, two or three weeks during strawberry harvest. They were back on the back of the farm living on the ridge back here, and she would come up what I call the old dusty road out here and would stand outside my parents' bedroom window and say, "Milk, milk." And, of course, they would give her whatever. My dad was also a very soft touch in lots of ways for these people 'cause he felt for them. But those faces are embedded in my memory, and those were hard times.[2]

Jacquie's recollection was equally vivid:

I remember one morning in particular. Daddy was . . . picking cucumbers, and I remember a family in specific, driving in here real early in the morning. We were having breakfast. Dad got up from the table and went out to see what they wanted, and they were looking for work. They had a whole car full of little children, and they'd stopped down here on the corner and had picked some cucumbers out of a neighbor's field, and they were having—the babies in the back were eating cucumbers for breakfast. Of course, Dad came back in here, and he said, "Mama, could you find enough food, could you fix some food for these people?" Mother said yes, and she got up, and she fried meat and made gravy and biscuits, and they fed them. And then I think Dad gave them a job that day. But I don't think that lasted very long. I don't remember that family being here very long.[3]

People of their parents' generation whom I interviewed offered comparable vignettes of the painful poverty of some migrant laborers, but they
seemed to treat their condition as a fact of nature. A woman, born in the
1890s, told me of a legless man who pulled himself through their strawberry patch on a board. To her he was an object of pity, but he did not
seem to disturb her moral universe as similar pitiable people seemed to
disturb Barbara and Jacquie. Acute poverty was no longer a private matter, to be ameliorated by neighbors, employers, and kin; it had become a
problem that society as a whole should address through its social policies.

As industry retooled from military to civilian goods, the factories provided work for thousands of the people who had been migrant workers.
Those who remained in the migrant stream appeared to be less reliable, as
Barbara recalls: "Some of the people that came didn't have very much
integrity. They lived in one of those little houses. We went over there
[after they'd left], and they had hitched up their old car to the posts of the
porch and pulled the posts off the porch and used it for firewood. So that
was the end of those houses. . . . And, then, we kinda got out of the
strawberries."[4]

Helen Kimber attributed her husband's heart attack in the mid-1960s
to his difficulties finding reliable labor:

The last peach crop we had—Frank had beautiful fruit, great, big
peaches. And the orchard boss come in and he said, "Frank, I can't get
these boys to pick these peaches; they're sitting on top of the ladders."
Frank went out there and give them a pep talk I guess. He said, "There
sat one boy, he was sitting there on the ladder picking leaves off of the
trees and watching them float down to the ground." And at the same
time, he was on Frank's payroll. Now such stunts as that—I think that
that is what gave my husband that heart attack.[5]

Local farm laborers, tenants, and young people also left in large numbers for the Los Angeles area and the industrial zone in Michigan, Indiana, and northern Illinois (see fig. 9.1 for the changing age distribution in
the county's farm population). A Union County Club met for a few years
during the 1950s in the Los Angeles area, replicating a common pattern of
retaining regional ties. The outmigration was so dramatic that people
often quipped, "Our greatest export is our young people." Small-town
festivals, many of which had started during the depression to boost morale
and promote an area product became homecomings for the people who
had left and increasingly became linked to school class reunions.

In the 1930s the Kimbers had needed to expand, since the two brothers
and their families were trying to make a living from the parental farm.
Frank and Helen bought an adjoining 160-acre farm when the owner was
unable to pay the taxes on it, and they rented the house to a family named

During the depression, town leaders in many small towns created homecomings and other festivals to help mobilize community support for self-improvement. This float was in a parade in Dongola in the 1940s. Dongola *Tri-County Record* Collection, Morris Library, Southern Illinois University, Carbondale.

Earnhart, who helped the Kimbers with their operation. Jacquie Kimber Eddleman recalled their son, her classmate Harold Earnhart:

> When all of us graduated from high school [in 1954], Jack [Eddleman, Jacquie's future husband] and I and Harold were all in the same class. When we graduated, I went to college and twisted Jack's arm until he went to college. Harold Earnhart, strangely enough, went to northern Indiana—Gary, Indiana, where Jack's father [Harry] was temporarily working on construction.
>
> Harold knew that he wasn't gonna farm anymore. This farming is for the birds. He wanted to go someplace where he could make some money, so he went where Harry Eddleman was in northern Indiana, and he went to work. He lived with Harry for a while. Harold started a construction career, if you will, right there, and he's still working up there. Years into that decision then [in the mid-1960s] he talked his mother and father into moving up there. He told his dad, he said, "I can get you a job on construction," . . . and so he did.[6]

Nonfarm wages also rose locally. A man who grew up near Alto Pass recalled that two of the local growers competed for his labor. One would ask him how much the other was paying him and raise the rate, and then the other would come back with a counteroffer. One of his relatives worked for a charcoal company in Jackson County, and they paid better than any grower; so when they had an opening, he went to work making charcoal.

The women who attended McClure school, west of Anna, developed a strong bond during their school years. They continued to meet monthly throughout their lives. This photo was taken in 1946 in Jonesboro. The women pictured are Agnes Powlis, Honnie Rousmier, Mary Smith, Nellie Douglas, Mrs. Horrell and her son Bruce, Nellie Doughler, Serena Seavie Sims, Seva Keller, Ethel Dodd, and Wickie Brookhouser. Thelma DeGamore Collection, Morris Library, Southern Illinois University, Carbondale.

Because of the coalfields north of the Shawnee Hills, southern Illinois had a strong union tradition, and unlike in the South, area garment and shoe factories as well as retail sales and all the crafts were unionized.

People in the area had very mixed feelings about the high wages that nonfarm employers were paying. Most families had at least one and often several close members working in unionized jobs, and they were glad to see their children and siblings prosper. Many farmers, both husbands and wives, worked off the farm in unionized jobs and valued the job protection and relatively high wages unions provided. However, strong unions not only raised their own labor costs, but they interfered with their markets. Teamsters and other handlers in Chicago who transported the produce from the train to the markets established work rules that often hindered the quick transfer of fragile fruits and vegetables, and some growers attributed the decline of the South Water Street and other urban produce markets to these unions.

Other developments, less directly visible to small producers, played a larger role in undermining Union County's fruit and vegetable markets. After the war, supermarkets, an innovation in food marketing invented

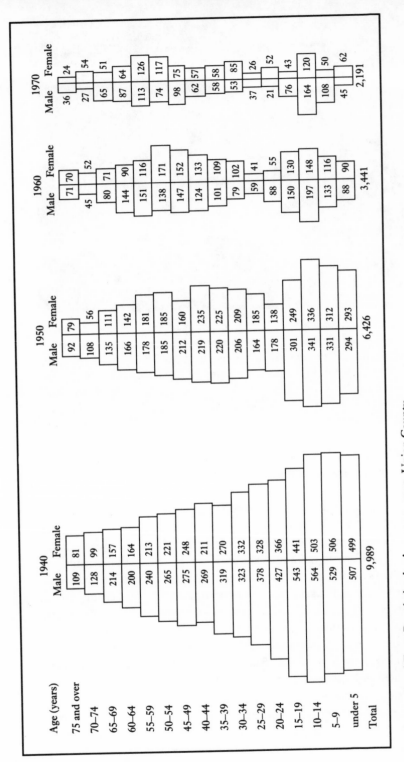

Figure 9.1. Rural Farm Population by Age, 1940–1970, Union County
Source: U.S. Bureau of the Census, *Census of Population*, year as noted.

In the 1950s, farm children shared big cars and fancy proms with their suburban counterparts. Jacquie Kimber and Jack Eddleman pose before the prom. They later married and settled on his family's farm, which adjoined her family's farm. Kimber Collection, Morris Library, Southern Illinois University, Carbondale.

around 1930, expanded. By 1953 supermarket sales accounted for nearly half of all grocery sales.[7] These supermarkets, served or operated by large wholesale operations, radically changed the nature of produce marketing. Formerly, Union County growers shipped their fruits and vegetables to brokers in the markets on South Water, Randolph, and South State Streets in Chicago or to other cities or sold them directly to buyers who came to the loading docks and farms with trucks. The Illinois Fruit-growers Exchange, a statewide cooperative affiliated with the Illinois Agricultural Association, a branch of the Illinois Farm Bureau, also operated from the Anna and Cobden markets, selling relatively small lots of fruits and vegetables.[8] While these types of marketing continued, they served less and less of the fresh produce market. The large wholesalers who owned or supplied the growing supermarket chains wanted predictable quantities and qualities of produce, which small producers could not supply. Growers came to rely increasingly on brokers who could contact outlets throughout the country.

In 1954 the farm adviser, Sture Pierson, reported that twenty vegetable growers organized the Little Egypt Growers' Cooperative.[9] Ruel Hindman, who had leased his orchard and was working as a marketing specialist for the Illinois Department of Agriculture, recalled the venture:

When I went to work for the state in 1953 . . . there was no vegetable coops in the whole area. The vegetable business was a big business in this area at the time, and everybody washed their cucumbers in the creek or in a tub and packed them and did their own marketing at the market. Well, I saw, being on the South Water Market in Chicago and places like those, [that] cucumbers that had been sized and packed, sold. One of the projects I started as a marketing specialist was to organize these cucumber growers, and since I wasn't using my shed over here (I had leased my orchards), we laid a water line to it and put in a washer and waxer for cucumbers and peppers. . . . Practically all of the cucumbers that were sold out of this area went through this shed or one at Cobden or two or three individuals. . . . [At Dongola the] Osmans had trucks and shipped to Chicago. So they put their own machinery and equipment in, and they did the work for the growers and charged them a nominal fee per bushel, and then they sold it.

It improved the vegetable business a great deal because they had a uniform pack and everybody's cucumbers went through the machines and the same graders graded them. And of course, there was a lot of dissatisfaction among some growers. They thought they graded them too close or they threw out some that should have been left in. . . . [The coop] lasted about ten years. . . . Finally the coop broke up, . . . and two or three members had bought the equipment.[10]

Tomato growers in Cobden formed a similar cooperative. This coop also had problems because some growers graded their vegetables in the field while others brought them in with a large number of culls, which raised the packing price for all members and brought conflicts about grading standards. Eventually, as the number of growers and members shrank, they went to a system in which each grower's produce was kept intact and packed and sold under that grower's name. Members were billed individually for their own lots, rather than pooling grading and packing costs among all members. In 1993 the Cernys, who were among the heaviest users of the facilities, bought out the other stockholders.

The network of limited-access superhighways that was built after the war as part of the national defense program also helped undermine midwestern market gardeners. Fruit and vegetable growers in the West, particularly California and Arizona, could produce fruits and vegetables on a large scale for these centralized suppliers. These growers had access to inexpensive water supplied by federal water projects built during the depression, to cheap Mexican bracero labor, and to flat land that, because of its dryness, did not harbor as many plant diseases and pests as did the humid Midwest.[11] High-speed freeways made it possible to ship mass-produced western produce quickly and cheaply to eastern markets in refrigerated trucks.

New, capital-intensive methods of production also became important during this period. The new technologies created unforeseen ecological problems. Farmers and farm advisers who were concerned with good stewardship of land had been concerned with the physical degradation of the soil for some time. The Extension Service had promoted lime production and crop rotations including legumes, and government programs instituted in the 1930s aggressively combated soil erosion. After World War II a wide array of agricultural chemicals became available for pest control and fertilization. The pesticides appeared as "magic bullets" that would free farmers from the scourge of hard-to-control pests. Growers had long used arsenate of lead and other sprays to control insect pests, but the new insecticides were far more powerful. DDT promised an end to the insect pests that plagued fruit and vegetable growers and that lowered the quality and quantity of the harvest. Ruel Hindman recalled,

When I was in the business, we had a tremendous amount of trouble with coddling moth in apples and oriental fruit flies in the peaches. DDT came along. I had my orchard, [and] I offered $10 for anybody who could find a wormy apple in the whole crop. DDT absolutely cleaned everything up. There was nothing. About the third year that I was using DDT, one morning I went over here and the orchard looked like it had been sprayed with copper. Mites, those mites that work underneath the leaves. DDT had killed all the parasites that lived on the mites and kept them controlled. And DDT wouldn't kill the mites. We had to use miticides. It's a constant fight. . . . Finally, they outlawed DDT.

In fact, that's one reason I went out of the orchard business. I got draggy and felt bad, and my blood pressure was down to eighty over fifty, and I almost had to carry a switch to keep me going. I went to St. Louis and went through the clinic up there, and about the third doctor that checked me said, "What kind of chemicals you been working in? You work in a chemical plant?" I said, "No, I'm just a cheap farmer, down in southern Illinois." He said, "What kind of farming?" I said, "Well, I got orchards." He said, "DDT, you ever used any of that?" I said, "A carload." I said, "I've eaten several pounds. But it's not supposed to be poison to humans." And he said, "Well, that's what you think. That's what the label says, but there's people, one now and then that it affects their nerves. And it affects their blood pressure. In your case, it's going to kill you if you don't get out of it. My advice is for you to get completely away from these spray dopes and stuff." That's when I went to work for the state. I got a job with the state, and I leased my orchards, and it took me about three years to get that out of my system.[12]

The full extent of the damage done to the environment by DDT and other powerful pesticides did not become apparent for many years. Dangers to human health and to the food chain caused by chemicals used to poison insects were revealed by DDT, and the USDA assumed greater regulatory controls in relation to these poisons. The problem of groundwater contamination, largely from nitrate fertilizers and herbicides, became apparent in the 1980s. Also, the dangers of antibiotic resistant strains of disease organisms due to widespread use of antibiotics in animal feeds became evident. In the 1970s and 1980s use of agricultural chemicals became a highly contested issue among farmers, environmentalists, health providers, and consumers.[13]

At the same time that new chemicals were rendering the production process more risky to farmers' health, the new technologies required greater access to capital. Tractors and all the associated equipment replaced mules and horses; hydraulic spray gear replaced hand–operated sprayers; and fruit growers needed cooling and packing equipment for efficiency and to maintain the quality of their fruit. Farmers needed short-term capital to buy new crop varieties, fertilizers, pesticides, and herbicides. The various governmental credit agencies and plentiful private credit allowed farmers to make the investments in land, equipment, and annual production supplies required by the new capital-intensive methods.[14]

During the post–World War II decades, then, a linked set of factors reworked national fruit and vegetable production. Agricultural labor became scarce and expensive, due to the booming industrial economy; mass marketers demanded large and predictable lots of first quality produce; the government provided inexpensive irrigation water to western growers, who were able to transport their produce nationwide on a new network of interstate highways; and expensive technologies and chemicals became necessary for high-quality production. The conjuncture of these processes drove most Union County growers out of the produce market and gave those growers who remained the credit necessary to expand their operations (see figs. 9.1 and 9.2). Ren Sirles, owner of one of the few peach orchards to persist into the 1990s, recalled,

> After the war we did all right till '48 and '49 was when the bust came, and I mean it really busted. You could run from Alto to Cobden and never get out of peach orchard. I remember that when I was a kid. . . .

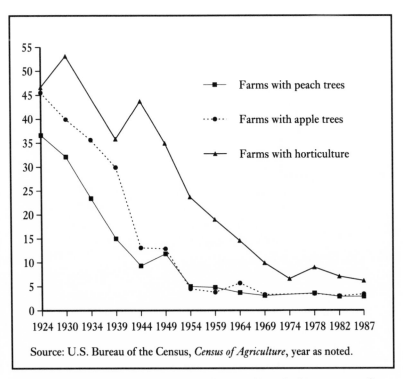

Figure 9.2. Percentage of Farms with Orchards and Horticulture, 1924–1987

All back up towards Bald Knob was in peaches. The Fount James place, and the Sitter and Angell place, and the Page place up on Bald Knob had peaches, and Carlos Norton's out there had peaches. You could go from here to Alto to Cobden and almost to Anna and never run out of a peach orchard in the late forties and early fifties. Well, even into the mid-fifties. It lasted for about ten years in there. It just went to pot.[15]

The statistics on peach production conform to this recollection. In 1925, 731 farms, or nearly 37 percent of all farms, had peach orchards. By 1954 only 62 farms, or 5 percent, still raised peaches for market. Farms raising apples showed a similar decline, from 45.5 percent in 1925 to 4.5 percent in 1954. Despite the precipitous decline in the number of farms with peach and apple orchards and in the total number of trees, those farms that continued to specialize in orchard crops greatly increased their scale: the average number of peach trees per farm rose from 571 in 1925 to 2,073 in 1954; the average number of apple trees per farm rose from 487 in 1925 to 1,233 in 1954 and continued to climb.

Vegetable growers were able to retain markets for somewhat longer, perhaps because the fresh vegetable markets continued to supply local "mom and pop" groceries and restaurants, but they did not show a similar increase in scale. As the number of farms raising vegetables for the market declined, those farmers who continued to raise market gardens did not significantly increase their acreage: in 1925 the 46 percent of farms with market gardens averaged three acres of vegetables per farm. By 1954 only 23 percent of farms raised vegetables, and they continued to average only three acres per farm. Those who persisted into the 1960s increased in scale somewhat: in 1964 the 14 percent of farms raising vegetables averaged seven acres each, and in 1969, when only 9 percent of farms persisted, the average acreage increased to thirteen—not what could be considered large operations.

Those growers who remained continued to search for ways to remain economically viable. In 1957 the network of market gardeners who had organized the cucumber and tomato packing cooperatives organized the Southern Illinois Vegetable and Small Fruit Growers Association, largely as an educational and promotional organization.[16] It does not appear to have persisted, and the county's few remaining market gardeners did not form any more organizations, although they did continue to participate in field demonstrations, field days sponsored by the Dixon Springs Experiment Station, and the annual fruit growers' school sponsored by the Southern Illinois Horticultural Society.

The fruit growers continued to organize. In 1962 Charles Glover, the farm adviser, reported, "There has been considerable interest in the building of storage facilities for fruit in the area and the State Department of Markets has taken an active interest, but to date no construction has started. Two large privately owned packing sheds were built in the county during the year. Several growers have new type grading and packing equipment."[17] The Illinois Fruitgrowers Exchange, which had a large facility in Carbondale that adjoined the Farm Bureau's Prairie Farm dairy processing building, pursued the idea and in 1963 purchased an option on land north of Cobden.[18] Their building, when completed, provided packing, brokerage and shipping services, and cold storage, and they also sold chemicals and other supplies to growers. The largest growers continued to provide their own packing and cold storage and worked through private brokerage services. In the mid-1980s a private partnership bought out the cooperative, and in 1992 Rose Farms, a large-scale horticultural enterprise begun in the late 1980s, purchased the facility, operating it as Heartland Harvest. They no longer supplied farm chemicals but continued to provide brokerage, shipping, and storage for some area growers.

In 1966, as Great Society programs were implemented, the same group of orchardists who had organized the Fruitgrowers Exchange facility organized the Union-Jackson Farm Labor Association to build housing for migrant laborers. With a loan and rent subsidies from Farmers' Home Administration (FmHA) they built thirty-six cinderblock units, with room for future expansion, just north of the Fruitgrowers Exchange. In the early 1980s the growers defaulted on the loan from FmHA, and the camp was nearly closed. A group of volunteers, working through the Illinois Migrant Council, took over the association and, with a grant from FmHA, assumed operation of the camp. Initially most of the migrants were poor whites and African Americans, but Mexicans soon began coming to the area as well. By 1980 the Illinois Job Service, which operated a placement agency in the migrant camp, estimated that 80 percent of the 1,000 farm workers in the Jackson and Union County area were Spanish speaking. By the late 1980s the migrant population had become almost entirely Mexican and Mexican American.[19]

During this same period, with technical and financial assistance from the Small Business Administration, the growers formed a corporation to operate a fruit processing plant, South Pass Products. Opening in 1970, the plant processed apples and, for a few years, peaches that did not meet the increasingly rigorous appearance standards of the fresh market. The plant froze apples for pie fillings, selling to major food processors like Con-Agra, Sara Lee, and Pet. Because of their sustained and relatively successful efforts to supply many of their technical, capital, labor, and marketing needs cooperatively, a number of intermediate level growers, who could not afford the large investments required to remain competitive on national markets, were able to stay in the orchard business.

After the war, farmers found they also needed expensive new technologies for their other crops. Hybrid seed corn replaced open-pollinated corn, so farmers could no longer raise their own seed corn but had to buy it from dealers. Frances Karraker, who operated a feed store in Dongola, told about the introduction of hybrid corn:

I can well remember the man who bought the first bushel [of hybrid seed corn] from us [in the 1940s]. His name was Mr. Oliver. We had just been a few weeks before at the meeting of the company [Funk's], and that was one thing that they stressed: "Warn the customer not to save any seed from this corn to plant next year. Be sure to warn them, because they might not get anything out of it, and then again they might." So I remember telling Mr. Oliver this. I went over it three or four times. "Now don't rely on that for seed next year. It may make a pretty ear but," I said, "I know that people save their corn. They go and pick out the prettiest ear in the crib for seed." So he came in the next fall, no, during the summer when it's growing he comes in. He says, "Well, they might tell you not to, but," he says, "I'm sure going to save me some seed." He says, "That's the prettiest corn I ever saw." . . . He says, "I'm going to bring some in and show it." He brought us some samples, and the ears were beautiful. . . . He'd shucked it back, and they were perfect. He said, "Now they can't tell me. They're wanting to sell hybrid seed corn," he said. . . . Well, the next spring he came in and he was talking about farming and I said to him, "Have you put any corn out yet? Have you seeded your corn?" He said, "No, but I have it shelled out, I'm ready." I said, "Don't depend on it altogether." I said, "Put more out besides that. Reid's Yellow Dent," I said. . . . Well at the end it ended up, he came in, he said, "I want you to warn everybody. Be sure and warn them," he said. "I've got sixteen acres of corn out and I won't get one wagon bed full of nubbins." He said, "It was the most beautiful stuff growing that I ever saw but I didn't make anything." He said, "I'll sure remember this." And he said, "You tell anybody that don't believe what you're telling them, you tell them to call me and talk to me." They soon learned that they couldn't save their hybrid seed corn; it wasn't to be done.[20]

Karraker recalled that a bushel of the open pollinated Reid's Yellow Dent seed corn cost about $3 a bushel, while hybrid seed corn was around $16 or $20.

With all the factors of production and marketing systems shifting dramatically in the postwar years, farmers scrambled to find a crop mix that would allow them to stay in business. Barbara Walton Throgmorton recalled,

My father changed the [operation]. He got rid of this labor-intensive work, the apples and the strawberries, and he went into permanent pasture on a lot of the area and began to build up his beef cow herd. When he died in 1964 he had a fairly good-sized herd built. He did a little bit of grain cropping and such, but not a great deal, just enough to have a cash crop. He also . . . was, I believe, one of the first people in the county, maybe the area, to have a self-propelled combine. He bought two of those . . . somewhere between 1952, '3, '4, '55, somewhere in there, and did custom combining. He had two John Deere self-propelled combines, and he and my brother did a lot of custom combining down in the bottoms as well as around up here in the hills. He did custom hay-baling for people; he had a hay-baler. . . . He began to try to bring in some income from off the farm by doing farm work, custom work elsewhere, and then at the same time was building his cow herd. He tried to have real good Hereford beef stock here and brought a bull from Gunnison, Colorado; it was a very fine registered Hereford. . . . But things—they went—you can trace the change from the labor-intensive work to work that one man could handle with one or two hands. It's becoming even more so today; you see that with the big round bales being made instead of the small square bales.[21]

In the nineteenth century the number of mules was an indicator of the extent of commercial production; in the mid-twentieth century they

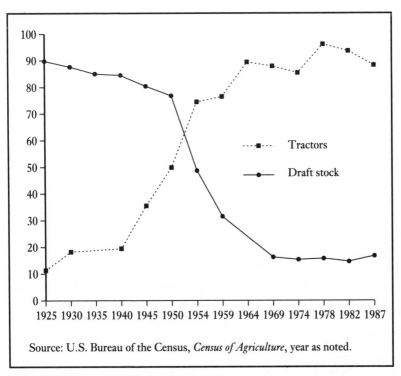

Source: U.S. Bureau of the Census, *Census of Agriculture*, year as noted.

Figure 9.3. Percentage of Farms with Draft Stock and Tractors, 1925–1987

became the opposite as commercial farmers invested in tractors, self-propelled combines, and other motor-driven vehicles and implements (see fig. 9.3). Farmers did not give up their horses and mules immediately as tractors became available, and many poor southern Illinois farmers could not afford the expense of a tractor. In 1950, 40 percent of farmers reported owning both tractors and draft stock; four years later 36 percent of farmers still reported both draft stock and a tractor or tractors. In 1950 only 9 percent owned only a tractor, 39 percent owned only horses or mules, and 12 percent owned no draft stock or tractors. Only four years later, in 1954, 74 percent of farmers reporting owned tractors. By this time, most farms that needed work done by tractors or draft animals had invested in tractors: only 12 percent of farms owned draft stock but no tractor. The shift to motor-driven power had been decisively made: nearly 39 percent had only a tractor. By 1959 virtually all farms that needed them owned tractors: 934 farms, or more than 81 percent, owned 1,684 tractors, and only 363 farms—a little more than half the number in 1954—reported horses or mules.[22]

In one decade Union County farmers crossed a watershed in agricultural production. For the first time in history the majority of the power needed by farmers to break the ground, plant the crop, and harvest it came not from the land on which the crops were grown, but from equipment and fuel bought on the market. It may be this fact, more than any other, that spelled the demise of diversified farming in hill regions. Under the old regime acreage in pasture and hay was productive and at the same time provided cover against erosion. Large-scale tilling equipment could not be used on hilly terrain, raising the cost of production for farmers who tried to compete in row crops but, more importantly, opening land to erosion.

Different farmers shifted their production regimes in different ways. The Waltons abandoned their small fruits and vegetables, as well as their dairy, and shifted to beef cattle and custom combining. The Kimbers continued to raise small fruits and vegetables, especially sweet potatoes, well into the 1950s, but they increased in scale and in labor-saving technologies and added beef cattle. Jacquie Eddleman recalled,

> Dad learned about sweet potato setters and so forth . . . through one of his farm organizations, I guess. In other places they were using machines to [plant sweet potatoes]. Dad's crops got bigger all the time. They kept making more property available for those crops. And as we got more territory to cover, we had to figure out more efficient ways to plant and to hoe, and so forth. I don't even know what year it was, but Dad had a sweet potato setter made. We never could use that thing though for the peppers. The peppers still had to be set by hand, as long as I was working in it.[23]

The Kimbers invested in a tractor during the depression, in 1936 or 1937. Helen Kimber recalled, "The boys went in debt for a tractor. And that was a big deal, I tell you. That saved a lot of horsepower."[24] Around the late 1940s, Helen recalled, they started raising Black Angus beef cattle. "When labor and all got so tight and everything, they tried that."[25] In 1965, after Frank had a heart attack and could no longer farm, they leased the orchards to a larger grower, one of the few who persisted into the 1990s.

Like the Kimbers, the Cernys continued to raise produce, particularly tomatoes, but with three brothers and their families farming in partnership, they bought more land and expanded their cattle operation. Their father and grandfather had been stock men, their grandfather raising Percheron horses on his stock farm near Cobden, and their father pioneering Polled Hereford cattle on the home farm. The Alto Pass Rendlemans, with their mule business displaced by tractors, expanded orchard production and became one of the largest peach and apple growers in the region.

The Union County hills were not well suited to the new production regimes that required ever larger equipment that could cover large areas of ground with little labor. For those upland farmers who could not

The Kimbers specialized in sweet potatoes, expanding their operation after World War II as the need for cash increased. Frank Kimber displays some freshly dug sweet potatoes. Kimber Collection, Morris Library, Southern Illinois University, Carbondale.

expand into orchards, the Extension Service promoted livestock production and pasturage. The upland farms described in the Introduction were representative of county trends: the number of beef cattle climbed steadily after the war, as did the size of herds on farms that raised beef cattle. The number of head per farm rose from an average of seven in 1940 to twenty-six in 1964 and continued to increase through 1974, although the percentage of farms raising cattle steadily declined from a high of 89 percent in 1935 to around 60 percent after 1969.

Beef cattle markets became increasingly centralized, a process that accelerated in the 1970s and 1980s.[26] Ruel Hindman, whose father had raised Black Angus cattle and was himself a cattle trader, became familiar

Farm Extension actively promoted new agricultural practices. Here a group of Farm Bureau members observes a demonstration swine herd on one of their neighbor's farms. Kimber Collection, Morris Library, Southern Illinois University, Carbondale.

with regional cattle markets when he worked as a marketing specialist for the state in the 1950s and early 1960s. He described the system in 1983:

> I set up this market news reporting service [with a federal man] that reports on the livestock auctions. At that time we had eighty-seven livestock auctions in the state of Illinois. But now there's a lot less because operators—quite a few of them have had trouble getting the volume of stock necessary to pay expenses of the operation, and so quite a few of them have gone out of business. . . . They have [a livestock auction] at Murphysboro and one at Goreville, one at Fruitland [Missouri] and one at Sikeston [Missouri]. They used to have one at Vienna [Illinois] and one at Charleston [Missouri], but they've gone out of business. . . .
>
> The whole marketing picture has changed since, I'd say, the forties. At that time all the livestock practically went to the big cities. Chicago was the biggest market in the United States, I guess. Then Omaha and Kansas City and St. Louis, and the packers all had branches—Armour, Swift, and Morrell—all had huge operations in these cities. Since that time, those big companies had so much labor problems that they have scattered out their operations in the smaller towns and they have quite a few of them in the South and in the East. And the whole marketing picture has changed. The livestock isn't shipped to those big centers

any more. . . . I'd say a big percent of the hog producers sell to a local buying station now and [to] order buyers.[27]

Farmers in the Mississippi bottoms responded somewhat differently after the war. The flat, fertile bottomland allowed farmers to compete with the prairies and the irrigated West in soybeans, grain sorghum (milo), and to a lesser extent, winter wheat and corn production. As Edith Rendleman's sons established their own operations after the war, they initially raised some beef cattle, but like most bottoms farmers they soon quit. The number of farms with beef cattle fell from fifty (44 percent of all bottoms farms) in 1955 to fourteen (15 percent of all bottoms farms) in 1965.[28] The proportion of farms with hogs also declined sharply. Lee Roy attempted a confinement hog operation, but his sewage disposal system was inadequate and he had to abandon it after a few years. During the 1960s and 1970s, with government assistance, farmers in the bottoms cleared, drained, and leveled hundreds of acres of swampy land. Like several other bottoms farmers Lee Roy developed a goose hunting club that catered to hunters from outside the region and made use of the swampy lands that could not be drained.

The levee built after the 1943 and 1944 floods made the area relatively safe from floods, although a major flood in 1973 threatened the levees and kept water that collected behind the barriers from draining. Although the levees held, much of the bottoms were flooded. The Mississippi's channel gradually filled the basin between the levees, raising the water level so that land behind the levees became increasingly susceptible to seepage. High water during several springs in the early 1980s prevented planting and damaged crops.

Large numbers of farmers left farming (see fig. 9.4). Some, like the Kimber's neighbor, lost their farm during the depression for taxes or were foreclosed by banks when they could not meet their mortgage payments. Had the postwar economy not rebounded, however, these people might have remained in farming as tenants or as landless laborers. Instead, as we have seen, many left the farm for off-farm work and, in the decades following the war, the number of farms fell precipitously. Because of the particular crops raised in the upland regions, and because the hills were not suitable to extensive row-crop cultivation, proportionately more Union County farmers left farming and left the area than farmers in most other regions of the state; nonetheless, the sharp drop in rural farm population was a national phenomenon.[29]

Conclusion

As people recall the period, the adoption of new technologies takes on a quality of inevitability. Only when one looks at alternative groups,

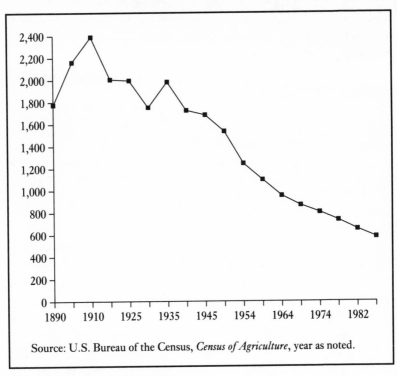

Figure 9.4. Number of Farms, 1890–1987

like the Amish in the United States or farmers in different western European countries, does it become apparent that the particular course taken by U.S. agriculture was the result of specific economic and governmental policies. On the ground—in the lives of specific farm families—the changes that occurred in the larger economy, the policy decisions that shaped the course of rural life, were generally perceived as happening *to* them. The changes had the same unavoidable force as a tornado or a drought or a flood, to which people had to accommodate no matter what their preferences. Despite the active and organized intervention of local people, families who wanted to retain a more agrarian community life found it increasingly impossible to do so, and bit by bit, they accommodated themselves to the new environment.

Despite the relatively opaque way that people I spoke with understood the political processes of the period, there were circles of policymakers who worked hard to map out the direction of the postwar economy. It is striking, from the vantage point of the 1990s, to read documents like the series of reports by the Committee for Economic Development (CED) concerning agriculture. The CED was an early "think tank" made up of "leading businessmen" whose aim was "to help stimulate private enterprise to plan realistically for business expansion and greater employment after the war."[30] Throughout postwar decades they helped shape U.S. economic and social policy. They can be read as being extraordinarily prescient about the course of the economy in the postwar period, or one can recall that the people who wrote those documents either had their hands on the levers of political and economic power or had the ears of those who did. Despite many fundamental disagreements, a broad consensus concerning agriculture developed among policymaking elites. They all believed that agriculture should replicate industrial models that had proven so successful for manufacturing, in order to bring agricultural productivity into line with industry and provide farmers an income commensurate with their investments of capital, labor, and management skills. This contrasted with many western European countries and Japan, which understood agriculture as a form of production qualitatively different from industry and which saw keeping large numbers of farmers on the land as vital to their national security. In 1945, for example, the CED wrote a lengthy prescription for agriculture. It stated bluntly that farm income could not rise unless a great deal of labor left agriculture and those farms that remained adopted capital-intensive technologies. Unlike most New Deal reformers who believed government should directly intervene in the economy to promote social equity, the CED argued that the economic forces of supply and demand were the best regulator of the economy, including what crops farmers raised. It believed that government policies should be used only to even out excessive price fluctuations and risk; to enhance the quality of rural labor through educational and health programs (that would, if their policies were implemented, migrate to other sectors that required higher skills); to encourage capital investment in rural areas, both as credit to agriculture and for rural industries; and to promote soil conservation. If the rest of the economy was strong and growing, the CED economists believed, issues of social justice and political unrest would become irrelevant.

Even though many New Deal progressives differed with postwar economic planners on such fundamental issues, in practical terms they often agreed. Both agreed that science and efficient technical and business practices should undergird farming, so both encouraged technical innovation and the credit and educational infrastructures that made it possible. Both saw the migration from farms to industry as desirable, since it would leave fewer people to share the total farm income. New Dealers, who were concerned with issues of social equity, could therefore support both low consumer prices and adequate farm income, policies that often conflict with one another in development programs.

The technological transformation of American agriculture is the story that historians, social scientists, and policymakers tell most frequently about farm life. It is generally told as if the increasing amount of products one farmer can raise from each acre of land is an unalloyed benefit to society. Some critics, especially since the 1970s, have questioned whether this system, with its high energy inputs and heavy use of environmentally damaging chemicals, can be sustained over the long term. But dominant stories are as significant in what they leave out as in what they highlight. This dominant story of the history of American agriculture rarely includes the impact of these changes on rural communities and, until the past decade, has never addressed the way members of farm families have fundamentally reorganized their relationships with one another. The rest of this book tells the story of these changing relationships, within farm families and in rural communities.

Well, farming was—we didn't have any help, couldn't make anything. Bob and Jacq was going to college, and it was either I work or we sell the farm, or I don't know what we would have done. Frank didn't want me to do it. He said, "I don't want you to do that." But I said, "I'm going to." And that's another time when I made up my mind. . . . I said, "Let's give them [Bob and Jacq] an education. Nobody can take the education away from them, but they can the farm." And I said, "To the heck with the farm."

—Helen Kimber

It Was Either I Work or We Sell the Farm

Before World War II a farm could not persist without a woman to carry out the female half of the labor and to help with the overall work of the farm. Chapter 5 described women's many and varied tasks: they generally bore and cared for a large number of children; they managed the labor of these children within the household; they processed most of the food for the family, other dependents, and resident laborers; they made most of the family's clothing; they boarded farm laborers and other paying lodgers; they helped in the fields and barnyard; and they earned money by raising agricultural products and by selling their labor as farm workers. Within the family the husband was legally the "boss," but in practice, relations between husband and wife ranged from the husband driving his wife with verbal and physical abuse to virtual equality, with mutual consultation and consideration in all important family decisions. Children were incorporated as productive workers as soon as they were physically able to handle tasks, and they were generally expected, under threat of punishment, to carry heavy workloads. Most farm women, no matter what their relationship with their husband, provided most household needs from their poultry, dairy, and other earnings. All this changed after World War II.

For at least three decades urban-based reformers, such as people involved in the Country Life Movement and in home economics, created around the turn of the century, promoted the "cult of domesticity" to rural families. During the Victorian period, as the United States industrialized and urban families lost their home-based manufacturing, a revolutionary new notion of femininity developed. This new definition of women's role built on the earlier division of labor, in which women's work was largely located in the home and men's work more frequently took them out of the home, and on English family law, which gave husbands legal dominion over their household and excluded adult women from an independent relationship with government and the courts and did not allow them to own property. It also drew on and merged two elite views of proper wifely behavior: the southern cavalier tradition, in which a man's status was validated by his ability to maintain his wife and daughters in decorative leisure and, conversely, the wife's duty was to enhance her husband's status; and the more utilitarian Yankee, Puritan tradition, which gave mothers particular care for their family's moral and physical well-being. These older traditions formed the basis for nineteenth-century agrarian prescriptions of female domesticity in which women's subordinate status as wives was coupled with praise of their virtuous and thrifty productivity.

The feminine role that developed in the industrializing North, from these merged traditions, was that of "homemaker"—a sentimentalized, desexualized Mother whose identity centered on domesticity, piety, purity, and submissiveness. According to this ideal the home was separated from the world of commerce and public production; it was a center of family consumption; the home was a "haven in a heartless world." Women met the larger economy not as producers but as consumers.[1]

By the turn of the century the new definition of femininity jelled into the Home Economics movement, which was part of the larger Progressive movement that sought to reform and modernize American society. The Progressives believed in a theory of social evolution that was exemplified by an increasing division of labor and that would lead inevitably to a better life, and they modeled that better life on their own urban middle-class experience. The work of these Progressives was most strongly carried to women by the new discipline, domestic science or home economics. Science and its practical application through efficiency became their watchwords. Accordingly, most home economists saw farm women, with their many and varied roles, as "backward."[2]

These ideas began to percolate into rural communities in Illinois in the first decade of the twentieth century, as the first generation of home economists graduated from the pioneering program in household science established by Isabel Bevier at the University of Illinois in 1900. In 1911 home economist Anna Lois Barbre, at an Illinois Farmers' Institute Short Course in Agriculture at Eastern Illinois State Normal School in Charleston, expressed the dominant notion: "Agriculture . . . provides the means whereby food, clothing, and shelter for men are obtained. . . . Household science . . . adapts these things to the needs of the family." Because they believed so strongly that homemaking was a girl's "natural destiny and her God-given right," in which man was the producer and woman the spender, they could not see that farm women were agricultural producers in their own right.[3]

Until this time agricultural educators had included women as experts and men as moral educators in the Farmers' Institute programs. For example, in 1910 Kate Maxey delivered an address to the assembled farmers called "Illinois and the Poultry Interest: What Ought to be Done; Large Profit in the Business," and another woman spoke on the production of clean milk. Men addressed the institute on subjects such as the moral climate of the home, health, household sanitation, and children's education—topics that would later be relegated to women. After 1911 farm women no longer addressed the institute; their role had been assumed by home economics experts.[4]

As we have seen, farm women were not greatly affected by these changes. They continued to produce for the market and to carry out widely varied tasks in a manner that the reformers saw as inefficient. This was partly because farm families lacked the capital to invest in modern conveniences, although wealthier families (or those in which women had more influence) did increase their labor-saving equipment during the 1920s and 1930s.[5] Helen Kimber and Edith Rendleman, for example, had kerosene stoves before electricity came to their homes, and Edith Rendleman insisted on renting a farm that had an electric generator to relieve her of the work of pumping and hauling water and to help with the laundry. The Waltons and the Alto Pass Rendlemans had electricity early in the century, as they were close enough to town and influential enough in the community to get a line run from the town's electric plants to their farms. But even these relatively affluent families did not adopt urban patterns of domesticity. Their homes retained their multiple functions as workshop, warehouse, mess hall, dormitory, recreation center, infirmary, and funeral parlor for the farm and the people who worked on it, and women's and children's hard work was approvingly contrasted with urban idleness.

It would take the postwar economic transformation to create the conditions in which the home economists' prescriptions could become possible. The idea that women's primary role was homemaker and consumer, rather than someone who earned income, profoundly shaped farm policies.[6] These policies assumed that the husband was the farmer and that the wife should find her work solely in the home in the care of the children and husband. As the farm economy shifted, increasing the scale of production, no policymakers, including the farm press, gave any thought to the consequences that losing poultry and dairy income would have on the farm wife.

Farm women were most affected by the change in poultry and dairy production and marketing systems. The previous chapter documented the impact of changing technologies and marketing systems on Union County's fruit and vegetable farmers; similar changes occurred in those products women traditionally produced. Deborah Fink has documented in detail the way that the vertical integration of poultry production, with its large-scale contract laying and fryer operations, undermined women's commercial poultry flocks. In the 1950s a few major farm suppliers, like Ralston-Purina, pioneered new production technologies based on industrial models. They marketed these technologies through contracts with farmers, who carried out the actual production.[7] At the same time that large-scale operations were able to produce poultry products more cheaply than could smaller farm flocks, health regulations made it increasingly difficult for small-scale producers and marketers to have their eggs and fryers inspected. They also faced the same problems as small-scale fruit and vegetable producers who tried to sell to the increasingly concentrated marketing systems, dominated by chain supermarkets.[8]

In the early years of this century virtually all farms raised chickens, most sold eggs, and a large proportion sold chickens for meat (see fig. 10.1). Like other changes in the organization of farm production, the shift toward industrialized production occurred during the late 1950s; however, the decline in the number of home flocks shows up as early as the 1950 census. By 1955 only a fifth of Union County farms sold chickens for meat, and by 1959 fewer than a third of farms reported selling eggs. In 1956 the farm adviser, Charles Glover, reported he had held a meeting with the Illinois State Division of Marketing to explain the new egg law. He wrote, "Most of the eggs in the county are still sold as unclassified. A large number of farmers are producing eggs for hatcheries and seem to be well satisfied." Six years later he wrote, "Poultry and egg production is in the hands of a few large producers."[9] Only a few women continued to raise eggs, either for home use or for sale. By the 1970s almost all women who raised chickens had begun as commercial producers, when their major source of income came from the poultry flock. Like Fink, I found that

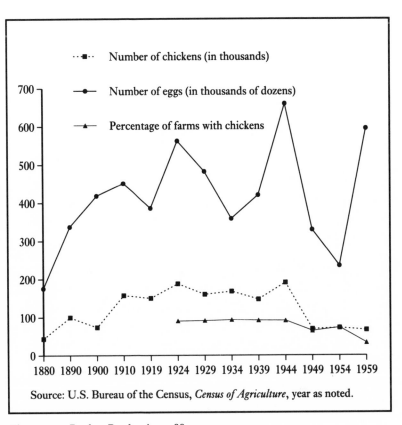

Figure 10.1. Poultry Production, 1880–1959

many women were reluctant to relinquish their flocks because they provided their only source of cash income.[10] Several women I interviewed in the 1980s laughed ruefully as they said their husbands repeatedly showed them that their poultry flocks cost the farm money, since their husbands bought the feed. However, they had customers who looked forward to getting their eggs, and they were reluctant to give up what had become, in effect, a hobby that provided some disposable income.

Women lost their dairy income as well. With the advent of electricity, farmers could buy electric milking machines. If a farm invested in the new equipment, a larger herd was needed to pay for it, and men began to take over the dairy operations. At the same time the market for cream decreased as dairy processors bought fluid milk that they then separated (see fig. 10.2). In 1931 the Waltons, who operated a commercial dairy using their own herd, began contracting with the two-year-old Producers Dairy to pasteurize and deliver their milk. This dairy expanded, buying up four small local dairies like the Waltons', and with government contracts for the state hospital and the Civilian Conservation Corps camps, they became the primary supplier of pasteurized milk in the Anna area. During

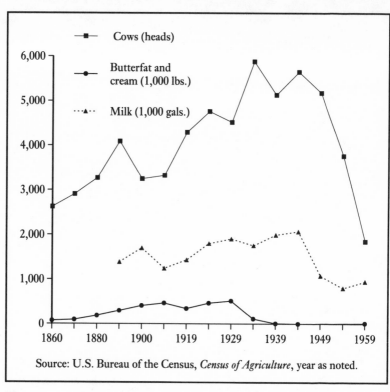

Source: U.S. Bureau of the Census, *Census of Agriculture*, year as noted.

Figure 10.2. Dairy Production, 1860–1959

the 1950s the regional dairy market became increasingly concentrated as a series of price wars drove out the financially weaker dairies or those, like the Anna Producers Dairy, who did not seek to expand into the regional market.

Before the war more than eight of ten Union County farms reported having at least one milk cow, and more than half reported selling dairy products; by 1959 only a little more than a third still had cows. Many of these cows provided milk only for home use as only 11 percent of farms sold butterfat and 13 percent sold whole milk. By 1964 very few commercial dairy cow operations existed, and with the county quite far from urban centers and on the periphery of the St. Louis milk shed, the number continued to decline.

The loss of markets for these agricultural products placed enormous strains on household budgets, since women's sales had virtually provisioned the family. At the same time, as we have seen, the horticultural crops men traditionally managed were also being squeezed out of commercial markets, and farm prices in general sagged. In 1949 the median income of all U.S. families was $3,073. Farm families, if they relied only on farm income, were generally worse off (see table 10.1). Although all

Table 10.1. Per-Farm Net Income, 1950–1987 (in dollars)

Year	Union County[a]	Illinois	United States
1950	1,925[a]	3,369	2,273
1954	2,321	2,851	2,383
1959	970	3,479	2,806
1964	3,676	4,470	3,533
1969	1,423	6,302	4,874
1974	4,045	16,845	10,345
1976	–	16,249	8,861
1979	9,007	16,578	11,015
1982	6,931	11,633	10,372
1987	8,327	19,495	21,545

Sources: U.S. and Illinois: USDA 1985, Table 8, pp. 88–89; for 1987, USDA 1988a, 1988b. Union County: U.S. Bureau of the Census, *Census of Agriculture,* year as noted.

[a]Net farm income for Union County was estimated by subtracting value of per-farm expenditures from value of farm products sold.

[b]Data were for the year preceding the census year.

Illinois farms did relatively well, Union County farms earned an average of $1,925, only 63 percent of the national family income. They continued to lag behind both national and state farm income; in 1959 Union County farms earned an average of only $970.[11]

Union County farmers, like most farmers, were caught in the proverbial "cost/price squeeze." Dependent on glutted and increasingly centralized commodity markets, carrying heavy debt loads to buy the new technologies that would allow them to enter those markets, and wanting the consumer items the postwar period made available, farm women felt their loss of income acutely. Faced with such meager earnings, if a farm were to survive, income had to found elsewhere.

Most landless farmers simply left farming, accelerating a long-standing process. Virtually all the Walton's tenants, for example, found jobs in town. The Tucker sisters, Agnes and Sybil, who had helped Rosemary with her housework and worked in the packing shed during the summer apple harvest, abandoned farm labor and found jobs at the shoe factory. In 1933 Sybil married a neighbor boy who also worked at the shoe factory, and they bought a small farm outside of town. Except for a six-month period when she quit to farm full time, she worked at the shoe factory for twenty-nine years until she retired.[12] Agnes also went to work in the shoe factory after a short stint at the garment factory. Like her sister, she worked at the shoe factory until retirement. Her husband, Elbert Cash, who grew up with her on the Walton farm, was working in a furniture store in Anna when they got married in 1925. He later worked for the government on a surveying project and then got a job with the city of Anna, and they bought a house in town.

By the mid-1950s large numbers of farm operating families had at least one member working off the farm. The 1955 home adviser, Eugenia Marquart, wrote, "More and more members [of the Home Bureau] are obtaining employment outside the home. This is necessary because of unfavorable farming conditions."[13] The farm adviser wrote a thumbnail sketch of "a farm family in extension." The Walter Miller family, he wrote, farmed 150 acres west of Dongola. They had a small dairy herd, general farm crops, and sometimes put out a small acreage in vegetables. They had a plan with the Soil Conservation District and were enrolled in the farm and home improvement program, partly because their house had recently burned. Mrs. Miller, he reported, was a Home Bureau and 4-H Club leader and worked full time with the Southern Illinois Electric Coop; Mr. Miller was on the Farm Bureau Board and the Union County Extension Council and worked winters for the Union County Cooperative Locker Company.[14]

Helen Kimber and Rosemary Walton both sought off-farm work. Rosemary had briefly worked at the shoe factory during the 1930s. That, however, was a stopgap. In the 1950s she went back to teaching, the job she held when Ned started courting her. Helen Kimber, who had only three years of high school because that was all that was available in Balcom when she was growing up, also decided to get a job. She found one at the Anna State Mental Hospital. She recalled, "I went to work in '54. When I went in up there I said, 'No way am I going to stay at this thing,' because I never worked away from home. And a lady they put me in the ward with, she said, 'Now, Helen, settle down. When you get that first paycheck you'll come back after another.' So I worked there twenty years."[15]

When women began working off the farm, a substantial reorganization of family life was required. Barbara Walton Throgmorton recalled that when her mother "started teaching . . . about 1954 or '55 . . . at that point, then, the canning and that sort of stuff kind of came to an end 'cause there just wasn't time for it."[16] Many husbands were not keen on their wives working. As Helen Kimber said, she went to work despite her husband's disapproval. Ned Walton also liked having his wife at home to eat lunch with and consult with during the day. Rosemary recalled, "When I got started teaching, he . . . fixed the evening meal. . . . He didn't much like my teaching school, but I went ahead and taught. . . . He liked having me home. He didn't like my being gone all day. But I knew I had to do it, and I knew it had to be done."[17]

Other women developed home-based businesses to replace their poultry and dairy enterprises. Ruby Weaver, who farmed with her husband, Charles, had dressed chickens for a McClure hotel and other customers and milked as many as fifteen cows by hand, as well as operating a tractor and helping in the fields. Their first investment after marrying in 1938 was a tractor. Thirty years later, several years after Charles joined her sewing business, he bought her a 2510 John Deere tractor for her birthday so she could plow corn. Like most women of her generation, she stated, "All I knew to do was work." She recalled, "While [our son] George went to college [around 1958], I worked at the shoe factory. . . . I worked seven years, three years after he got through college. Then I quit. I was helping him [my husband] farm and working at the factory, too. So I was quite a busy person. So I started sewing and thought I'd make a little money at sewing. Then I got so busy sewing I'd help him farm during the daytime and I'd sew till midnight every night." One day her son called and wanted them to come down to Knoxville where he was working on his Ph.D. and living with his wife and new child.

> I said, "I don't know whether I can or not. I've got a lot of sewing to do." I said, "I'll talk to your daddy in the morning." He'd already gone to bed. So I asked him the next morning. He said, "You want to go?" And I said, "You know I do. But I don't know if I can or not because I had some cheerleading outfits to make." He said, and this was the biggest mistake he ever made in his life, I guess, he said, "What can I do to help?" That was the day he got started and he never got through. . . . That was on Sunday afternoon that he asked me that and from there until Thursday we made those cheerleading outfits plus some other garments. I think we made thirteen garments. And got up Thursday morning and went to Knoxville.

Charles helped her the rest of his life, fitting and cutting patterns while Ruby sewed.[18]

These sorts of partnerships were rare. It was far more common for husbands and wives to seek separate jobs off the farm. In 1940 only 9.3 percent of farm women were listed as in the labor force (see table 10.2 and fig. 10.3).[19] As we have seen, this did not accurately enumerate the women who worked on their farms, but it does indicate the number who worked off the farm for wages. By 1950 the census listed 12.7 percent of Union County farm women in the labor force, although it did count fifteen women agricultural wage workers and twenty-four unpaid family workers. By 1960 more than one-fourth of all farm women were employed, most off the farm, and the proportion continued to increase although, because the number of farms dropped, the actual number of farm women counted as in the labor force held relatively steady at around 225, except for a jump in 1950 (266) and 1960 (306).

Table 10.2. Employment of Union County Farm Men and Women, 1940–1980

	1940 N	1940 (%)	1950 N	1950 (%)	1960 N	1960 (%)	1970 N	1970 (%)	1980 N	1980 (%)
Rural farm population of working age[a]										
Males	3,807		2,427		1,421		794		697	
Females	3,292		2,215		1,332		830		655	
Rural farm population in labor force										
Males	2,999	(79)	1,940	(80)	1,116	(79)	670	(84)	511	(73)
Females	306	(9)	282	(13)	326	(25)	243	(29)	235	(36)
Occupations of rural farm females in labor force										
Professional workers[b,c]	35		36		27		36		55	
Farmers and farm managers	11		22		22		17		23	
Proprietors, managers, and officials, except farm[d]	2		6		5		5			
Clerical, sales, and kindred workers[e]	24		39		36		67		86	
Craftsmen, foremen, and kindred workers[f,g]	1		1		4				7	
Operatives and kindred workers[h]	61		54		107		61		11	
Domestic service workers[d,i]	39		13		4		0			
Service workers, except domestics[j]	19		33		66		33		36	
Farm laborers (wage workers) and farm foremen[k]	3		15		11		5		5	
Farm laborers, unpaid family workers[d]	9		24		15		0			
Laborers, except farm[d,l]	15		0		5		2			
Occupation not reported[d,g]	9		0		4					
Occupations of rural farm males in labor force										
Professional workers[b,c]	31		17		33		16		21	
Farmers and farm managers	1,365		1,184		467		248		165	
Proprietors, managers, and officials, except farm[d]	34		27		16		25			
Clerical, sales, and kindred workers[e]	26		31		35		43		28	
Craftsmen, foremen, and kindred workers[f]	64		115		78		59		82	

Table 10.2 *Continued*

	1940		1950		1960		1970		1980	
	N	(%)	N	(%)	N	(%)	N	(%)	N	(%)
Operatives and kindred workers[h]	85		98		121		63		57	
Domestic service workers[d,g,i]	0		3		0					
Service workers, except domestics[m]	24		27		41		44		40	
Farm laborers (wage workers) and farm foremen[k]	428		183		149		70		59	
Farm laborers, unpaid family workers[d]	222		117		42		8			
Laborers, except farm[d,l]	94		72		55		47			
Occupation not reported[d,g]	29		37		15					

Sources: U.S. Bureau of the Census 1943a:558, 1953:13–197, 1964:15–452, 1970:15–820, 1982:15–845.

[a]Employable age varies. In 1930, age break is fifteen years and older; in 1940, 1950, and 1960, fourteen years; in 1970 and 1980, sixteen years.

[b]Includes "Semiprofessional workers" from 1940 census.

[c]1960 census lists "Professional, Techn'l, & kindred wkrs."

[d]1980 census does not include this category.

[e]1950–70 censuses list "Clerical and kindred workers" and "Sales" in separate categories. They are combined here. 1980 census lists "Technical, sales, and administrative support occupations, . . . including clerical."

[f]1980 census lists category as "Precision production, craft, and repair occupations."

[g]1970 census does not include this category.

[h]1980 census lists category as "Operators, fabricators, and laborers."

[i]1950 and subsequent censuses list category as "Private household workers."

[j]1950 and subsequent censuses list category as "Service workers, except private household."

[k]1980 census lists category as "Farm occupations, except managerial."

[l]1970 census lists category as "Other blue-collar workers."

[m]1970 census lists category as "Service workers, including private household."

At the same time the kinds of jobs held by women changed. In 1940 17 percent of employed women were domestics; by 1970 no one held that position. In contrast, the number of women who, like Helen Kimber, worked as service workers and in clerical, sales, and similar positions climbed from 19 percent in 1940 to one-third in 1960 and 44 percent in 1970. By 1980 more than half (55 percent) of all employed women in the county held these sorts of jobs. The importance of the shoe factory, the largest manufacturer in the immediate area, is indicated by the relatively large number of farm women who, like the Tucker sisters, worked as "operatives and

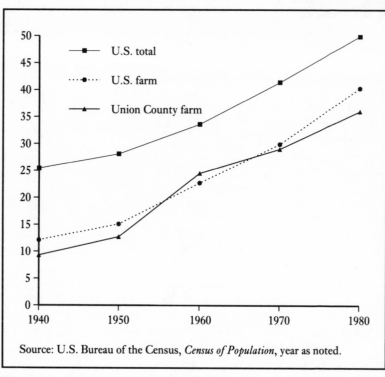

Source: U.S. Bureau of the Census, *Census of Population*, year as noted.

Figure 10.3. Percentage of Women in the Labor Force, U.S. Total, U.S. Farm, and Union County Farm, 1940–1980

kindred workers"—27 percent in 1940 and 35 percent in 1960. A significant number of farm women, like Rosemary Walton, also worked as professionals. The proportion (although not the number) of women holding professional jobs dropped from 15 percent in 1940 to a low of 9 percent in 1960. Then, as younger, better-educated farm women entered the labor market and as Great Society programs that provided professional services expanded, the proportion rebounded; in 1980 more than one-fourth of employed farm women held professional jobs. Despite their classification as "professional," these jobs generally did not pay well. Teachers' salaries rose after consolidation but consistently paid well below urban teaching salaries and well below comparable jobs held by men. Social work also increased dramatically during the postwar period, and although carrying a professional status and requiring advanced college degrees, it pays poorly compared with professional jobs traditionally held by men.

At the same time, large numbers of farm men found off-farm jobs. In 1940 only 33 percent of farm men who were counted in the labor force held or were looking for nonagricultural jobs; by 1970 more than half were in the nonfarm labor force and were, therefore, part-time farmers. This off-farm work allowed Union County farm families to earn incomes that

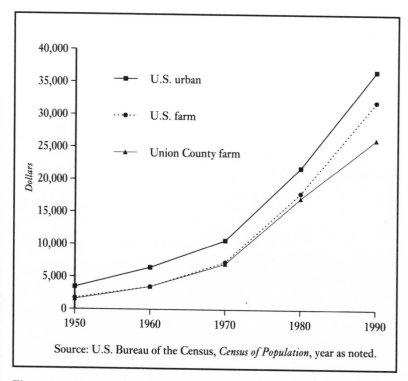

Source: U.S. Bureau of the Census, *Census of Population*, year as noted.

Figure 10.4. Median White Family Income, U.S. Urban, U.S. Farm, and Union County Farm, 1950–1990

were comparable to all U.S. farm families, despite the comparative disadvantage of their terrain and traditional crops. Like other farm families, however, most Union County farm families earned significantly less than their urban counterparts (see fig. 10.4), both because of low wage scales in rural areas and because of low net farm incomes. Despite these relatively low earnings, off-farm income allowed some families to keep farming.[20]

By the 1960s, as women lost their work in agricultural production, the division of labor on most farms appeared to be, on the surface, what the home economists prescribed and the farm press recommended. Women did little actual agricultural production, and what they did do was as assistant to their husband who was the "farmer." Only a few women like Ruby Weaver continued to work as full partners with their husbands in a somewhat traditional division of labor. The home lost most of its productive activities and became a center of consumption in which women applied home decoration skills and nurtured the increasingly small family. Like the urban middle-class home of a century earlier, most manufacturing and processing functions carried out by housewives were industrialized. Their agricultural products, largely poultry and dairy but also small fruits and vegetables, were centralized in industrial or relatively large-scale operations. Their food processing was largely supplanted by industrial food processors who could can or freeze food nearly as cheaply as women could do it in their home, and in any event, as women got off-farm work, they no longer had the time to raise a garden and put up quantities of food. At the same time, farms required fewer hands, and perhaps as a direct result, women stopped bearing large numbers of children. In 1910, Illinois farm women gave birth to an average of 4.4 children each; by 1940, with the effects of the twenty-year depression fully visible, they bore an average of only 3 children each. This rebounded slightly after the war, but then fell again; in 1980, the only year for which county data are available, Union County farm women reported an average of only 2 children, below the state average of 2.9 for farm women and 2.6 for urban women.[21] Although a number of people I interviewed had 8 to 10 siblings, almost none had more than 3 children of their own, and some had no children.

Despite these factors—greater money income, fewer children, fewer manufacturing and other productive operations carried out within the household—farm women did not in general adopt the full range of attributes associated with the cult of domesticity. Most notably, they continued to identify themselves as people who worked and sought ways to earn money, rather than becoming solely "consumers." Like urban women who, despite the florescence after World War II of what Betty Friedan termed the feminine mystique, continued to work outside the home in large numbers, farm women probably looked for paid employment because the farm would not support them and because they wanted the new consumer goods available only with money.[22] Some, like Helen Kimber and Ruby Weaver, began working off the farm to help put their children through college. But I also believe that for many farm women, working was a core part of their identity. It was important to their sense of self-worth, of contributing to the family, to have an independent source of income. When they could no longer earn money from their traditional products, they did the only thing they could think of—find a job. A few, like Ruby Weaver who had particular skills, invented home-based businesses—custom sewing, hair dressing, baking and catering, and so forth— to replace their domestic agricultural production.

The postwar period, then, saw women develop an unprecedented, new relationship to the farms on which they lived and to their families. Structurally, it looked much more like the relationship of urban women to their husbands and families than like the relationships of prewar farm families. But there was a wrinkle: not isolated in the private domestic sphere, carving out a "haven in a heartless world," farm women entered that "heartless world" as wage workers, maintaining their identities as full contributors to their family's well-being, even as their old mode of working was eliminated by the new order.

CHAPTER 11

Mother did not hang onto the old relics and the antiques and so forth. . . .
This [dining room] table, I saved it.
She was going to put a chrome legged
dinette set in here. Everybody else had
one, and she liked it, and it would wash
off easier, and you can keep it cleaner,
and so forth. But by that time I had realized we had an antique on our hands
here, and I personally saved the table.
—Jacquie Kimber Eddleman

We Used to Eat Inside and Shit Outside; Now We Eat Outside and Shit Inside

The change signaled by farm women seeking off-farm work and farm families investing in expensive farm technologies was profound. In the language of the period, farmers were "modernizing"; "progress" was lifting them out of "backwardness and poverty."[1] This language did not accurately represent the change that occurred during this period, since farm men and women had become deeply dependent on national and international markets and, in Union County, on wage labor for their livelihood. Farm life at the turn of the century was thoroughly modern in the sense that Union County farmers depended on the larger social econ-omy for their livelihood, and that the people who lived in urban centers relied on farmers' products for their own survival. Their life was in no way a relic of a bygone era.

Despite their misrepresentations, the turn-of-the-century and subsequent reformers were not totally wrong. Rural life *was* different from urban life. The nostalgia with which people now look back on the farm life of a century ago reflects an intuitive sense that something has radically changed. Since at least the middle of the nineteenth century, social philosophers have tried to pin down the difference they perceived between earlier ways of living and those of the "modern" period. Sir Henry Maine pointed to the shift in how people were evaluated—from being judged according to their inherited status based on kinship and class to being judged as autonomous individuals who freely made contracts with other individuals. Ferdinand Tönnies wrote about the shift from community (Gemeinschaft) to society (Gesellschaft)—a shift in scale that had broader implications—and Karl Marx saw the change as involving the conversion of labor into a commodity and its separation from ownership of productive property. Weber focused on what he termed rationalization, which he saw as a more or less progressive process. In recent years French philosopher Michel Foucault attempted to focus more tightly the shift so many social analysts have pointed to. He argues that the new order that came to be called "modernity" rested on a profound reorganization in the way people experienced daily life. The ways we understand time, space, and movement changed so that we "naturally" attribute a monetary value to our time and to the things we make; we separate work from leisure and public from private space; we assume that scientific methods fully explain natural phenomena; and so forth. The key elements in this shift were the division of space, time, and movement into discrete functional units—minutes to cut up the seamless experience of time, monetary units (dollars) as a measure for everything of value, and gestures to recompose in precision drills and assembly lines. Once divided into functionally identical units, these elements could then be assembled in progressively more efficient combinations, like students arrayed in the classroom under one professor rather than working as apprentices with a master craftsman. These identical units could then be arranged in hierarchical series, such as an assembly line in a factory or the managerial structure of that factory, in ways that vastly increased both productive capacity and social control. These basic approaches to nature and to social life made possible science and industry as we know it, and, Foucault argues, they are historically unique.[2]

With a unity of production processes within the farm household, and with many of its needs supplied from the farm, turn-of-the-century family life appeared much more like that of the colonial period than of the industrialized cities. Farm families resisted scientific approaches to understanding nature; they resisted the kinds of efficiency prescribed by time-motion managers who used Henry Ford's factories as their model; and they did not place a high value on what came to be known as consumerism.[3] In this sense most early twentieth-century farm families appeared "premodern" to turn-of-the-century reformers.

These "inefficiencies" were mapped in the way houses were designed. Farmhouses, like colonial houses, had few if any special-purpose rooms. Poorer houses often had only three rooms: a main room, a kitchen, and perhaps a small bedroom for the parents. Edith Rendleman described the first house she recalled living in: "It was a three-room house. It had a large living room—big, wide logs, twelve inches wide—and it had a built-on kitchen. A room upstairs as big as the living room downstairs and a porch with no roof, just the bottom boards. . . . [There were] three beds upstairs." The family consisted of six sons, herself (the only daughter), her father's two sisters and one brother, and her parents. The boys slept upstairs; she and her aunts slept downstairs with her parents. The third room was the kitchen lean-to.[4]

The Rhodeses' story-and-a-half log house was built in the style common to smaller farmers in the mid-nineteenth century (see fig. 11.1). The sills rested on rock piers, leaving an open crawl space underneath the house. A rectangular "pen," with central doors and a small bedroom walled off at one end of the ground floor, formed the main living quarters. The unpartitioned upstairs housed the unmarried men and boys and provided storage for flour, sweet potatoes, and other foods that needed a warm, dry storage space, while the parents slept in the downstairs bedroom and the girls slept in the main room. The kitchen was a detached log structure with a fireplace at one end that was later replaced by a wood-burning cookstove. A log smokehouse stood nearby. Because it was cool, the smokehouse also provided storage for other foods; other farms used springhouses and other forms of water cooling.

With the prosperity of the early years of the century the Rhodeses added a bedroom for the girls, walled in the breezeway between the kitchen and the house, and added a front porch (fig. 11.2).

Most Union County houses built before 1920 were what Kniffen termed I-houses, because they were so common in Iowa, Indiana, and Illinois.[5] These houses are typically one room deep; rectangular, with one or two front doorways opening into the main room or rooms; and one and a half or two stories tall, with a chimney or chimneys at the gable end(s) or in the middle. The kitchen is usually a lean-to or an ell added to the back of the building, although in southern regions it was frequently a free-standing room separate from the main house. By mid-century more affluent families, like the Kimbers and the Waltons, built houses on a similar exterior plan but with a central hall housing stairs to the second floor, flanked by two large parlors (fig. 11.3). Some houses, like the Green house, had two front entrances, one leading into a small parlor (fig. 11.4) or, alternatively, with each front door opening into identical large square

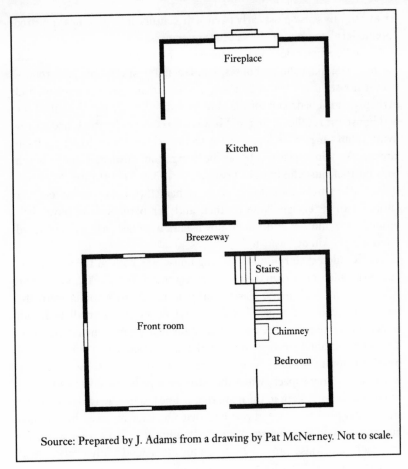

Source: Prepared by J. Adams from a drawing by Pat McNerney. Not to scale.

Figure 11.1. Rhodes House, 1850–1900s

rooms.[6] Absentee landowners often built story-and-a-half or two-story I-houses for their tenants; these houses were indistinguishable from most houses built by farm owners. They built small cottages, usually single-pen structures like the one Edith first lived in, for their laborers.

By the 1880s some families had begun to build houses in a simplified Victorian style. The houses the Weavers built in 1884 and 1915 were Victorian in style; the home George and Marita remodeled near St. John's Church, built in 1883, was a two-story Victorian, as was the house on the farm the Kimbers bought in the 1930s. These Victorian-style houses were generally simplified versions of the genre. They afforded more privacy in the sense that children often had bedrooms they shared with same-sex siblings, and rooms often had more specific functions than they did in the I-houses. However, they generally did not have the "nooks and crannies" in which people could create private moments; their porches were work

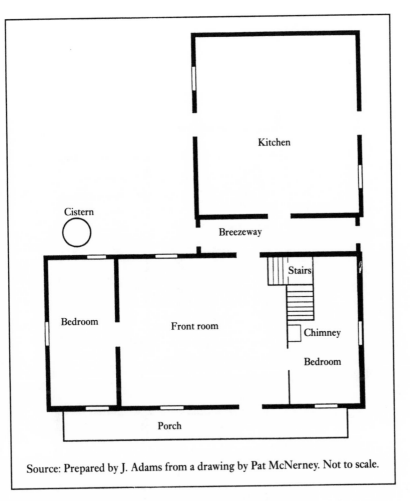

Source: Prepared by J. Adams from a drawing by Pat McNerney. Not to scale.

Figure 11.2. Rhodes House, ca. 1920–1950s

spaces, not verandas oriented toward leisurely recreation. The wife's convenience was frequently ignored as well. In the Weaver cottage, for example, the cistern was located in the front of the house, so water had to be carried through the front room (or outside around the house) to the kitchen.

The only common nineteenth-century house styles that were not represented in the seven farms studied were double-pen houses, in which the main body of the house was made of two identically sized rooms, each entered by its own door; and dog-trot houses, in which the two pens were separated by a breezeway. A few double-pen houses, but no intact dog-trot houses, remain in the county. A few prosperous farmers also built what are locally termed four-square houses, a type more commonly found in central Illinois.

Early and mid-twentieth-century reformers believed that evolutionary

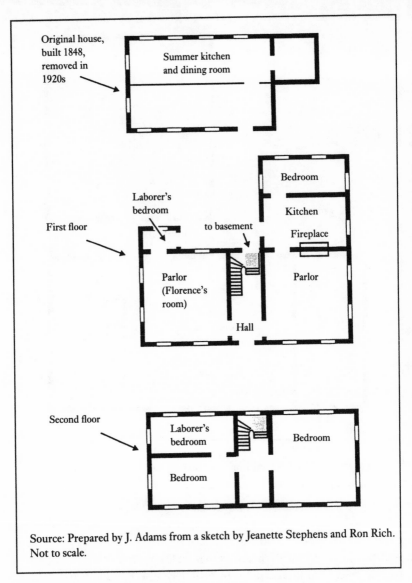

Figure 11.3. Kimber House, 1858–1940s

progress moved in one, inevitable, unfolding direction. Therefore, they believed, people such as farmers who participated in industrial society but did not live like the urban middle and professional classes were "backward." According to the ideology of unilinear progressive development, farmers were not modern; their lives reflected a bygone era. As I have argued above, this was a fundamental misapprehension: farm people in 1920 were no more like their eighteenth-century ancestors than were urban people.

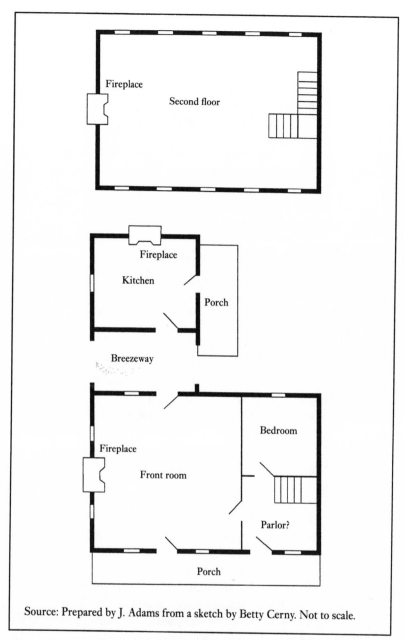

Fireplace

Second floor

Fireplace

Kitchen

Porch

Breezeway

Bedroom

Fireplace

Front room

Parlor?

Porch

Source: Prepared by J. Adams from a sketch by Betty Cerny. Not to scale.

Figure 11.4. Green/Cerny House, 1844–1950s

But these beliefs were not neutral. Because national elites believed that there was only one path to modernity, they understood relations of power as temporal relations. For example, they tended to see poor farmers and tenants who, because of their poverty and relative powerlessness, lived in old, unremodeled houses or houses built on the same plan as earlier houses as "old-fashioned." This despite the fact that, because of their poverty and lack of property, these poor farmers and laborers might be more dependent on wage work and on buying their food and clothing than were more prosperous farmers. The rhetoric of "progress" could mask the relationships through which poverty was institutionalized and maintained.[7]

These early twentieth-century progressive reformers, like those active in the Country Life movement, generally saw farmers as "backward" and needing "lifting up." Southern Illinois, like Appalachia and the Ozarks, was doubly seen as a region of relics, mired in poverty because of its backward nature. It was "the Other Illinois"—Other not only in the sense that its poverty contrasted with the industrial and prairie regions to the north, but in the sense that it stood as a mysterious Other to the defining urban elites who studied it. Outside observers were struck by the region's character, which, like Appalachia, was "picturesque" and at the same time impoverished. Much of the specific character of the region was a result of its poverty, which in turn was based on the unequal economic relationship agriculture had (and continues to have) with the nation as a sector of the national economy, and to the specific class relations within farming communities. Because they are apparent to the casual viewer, and because so much of daily life occurs within their relatively enduring bounds, houses provided one of the symbolic forms for judging "levels of development." By these measures, southern Illinois, along with the rest of the Upland South, fell far behind.

Before World War II only slightly more than half of Union County farmhouses were owner occupied. These figures do not distinguish between homes in which the renter operated the farm, which were frequently houses that were comparable to modest owner-occupied homes, and those occupied by laborers, whose houses tended to be small and poorly maintained. Some indication of the number of these houses is gleaned from the 1945 Census of Agriculture. In 1945 there were 806 more farmhouses than there were farms reporting houses (1,665 farms reporting 2,471 dwellings), indicating that almost one-third of farmhouses were occupied by resident laborers who worked for the owning or renting farm operator (see table 6.2 for proportions of owner- and tenant-operated farms).[8] That year half of these houses were listed as unoccupied, probably because so many farm laborers had left the farm for war industries or had entered the military.

Many renters and poor farmers lived in houses much like the one Edith Rendleman lived in as a young child, or like the Rhodes house before it was remodeled in the 1910s. A 1930 study of farm housing found that in what the study termed the "Appalachian-Ozark Highland section," of which Union County is a part, "almost 50 per cent of the houses . . . have single rooms used for [sleeping and living] purposes. In other sections, dual-purpose rooms are much less prevalent. . . . The small houses . . . commonly have a kitchen and dining-room combined. This is especially true in the Cotton Belt and in the Appalachian-Ozark Highland regions, where a large proportion of the houses are small."[9]

There was also a significant difference in the number of people per house and the degree of crowding between owner-occupied and tenant-occupied homes. Among farm families in 1940, owners had an average of 3.27 people per dwelling, while tenants, whose houses tended to be smaller, averaged 4.06 people per dwelling.

Rural housing was also much more dilapidated than urban housing. According to the 1940 Census of Population, less than 6 percent of the housing in Anna needed major repairs; in contrast, 57 percent of rural farm housing needed major repairs. Slightly less than 3 percent of the rental housing was vacant; of those houses, more than 65 percent needed major repairs. Reflecting both the poverty of the area and the quality of housing stock, reported rents for rural farmhouses were among the lowest in the state, averaging $6.21 a month (median $5.51).[10]

The traditional house styles that, with some modifications, dominated the countryside for a century suddenly became obsolete in the 1950s. Women attribute the change to a number of innovations: electricity that brought electric lights, stoves, and running water; linoleum that made floors easy to care for; laundromats and electric washing machines that replaced washtubs for laundry; locker plants that custom butchered and froze pigs and beef, replacing community butchering and smoking; and all-weather roads and automobiles that made it easy to run to town any day of the week. The availability of these technologies, however, did not *cause* farmers to adopt the new living patterns; these technologies only made them *possible*. The Amish, for example, never adopted modern conveniences, and many Union County families were slow to remodel. The Kimbers, for example, initially only ran lines in the house for the lights and outlets without making more substantial alterations. Farmers were slow to build bathrooms with flush toilets and to bring in hot and cold running water.

Several factors account for both the adoption of these new technologies and the relatively slow rate of adoption. One major factor was financial. Farm families had limited resources and initially invested more heavily in new farm technologies instead of their own homes or their rental units

Five generations of Brimms have lived on the Walton farm. In this photograph, taken in the 1950s, Bill and Frances Brimm sit in their home on the Cedar Lane on the Walton farm, with their son Jess. Bill helped build the house when a youth, around 1890. Note that, although electricity was widely available after World War II, the Brimm house is still illuminated by a kerosene lamp. Their son Ed's house, which was next to Bill and Frances's, was wired for electricity in 1954. Jess Brimm Collection, Morris Library, Southern Illinois University, Carbondale.

(see table 11.1). For example, in 1950 half of farms reporting owned tractors; although nearly three-quarters reported owning an electric washing machine, only a quarter had running water inside the house. As late as 1960 only slightly more than half of all farmhouses had indoor toilets and only slightly more had hot and cold running water. Some of the differential in investment in farm and home is due to the large number of tenant dwellings in the county, since many tenant houses were not wired for electricity even when it became available. Many of these tenant houses were more or less rapidly abandoned as people found town- or city-based work and moved to new housing in town or migrated out of the area. Increasingly, families used mobile homes (house trailers) as rental units, to house newlyweds, or as retirement homes as married children with their families took over the large farmhouse.

While farm owners were more likely to improve their own houses rather than their rental units, farm-owning men, with their control of the farm's investment income, often put a higher priority on farm mechanization than they did on home improvements. Since the husband's side of the farm was increasingly the farm's primary income source, as returns from poultry and dairy products decreased, wives could also see the economic logic in improving agricultural production before investing in their home. They did not always, however, share their husbands' priorities. As in

Table 11.1. Rural Farm and Home Equipment, 1940–1970

	1940		1945		1950		1954		1959		1964		1970	
	N	(%)	N	(%)	N	(%)	N	(%)	N	(%)	N	(%)	N	(%)
Total farms	1,724		1,683		1,535		1,196		1,149		953		867	
Total dwelling units	2,469				1,866				733				766	
Electricity[a]	266	(15.4)	532	(31.6)	1,256	(81.8)	1,135	(94.9)						
Running water inside	101	(3.8)			476	(25.5)			733	(63.9)			766	(91.2)
Flush toilet inside	78	(2.9)			266	(14.3)			537	(46.8)			703	(83.7)
Home freezer[b]					105	(6.8)	275	(23.0)	572	(49.8)	618	(64.8)		
Milking machine (farms w/ dairy)[b]					85	(7.1)	100	(12.5)	65	(14.8)	52	(26.7)	169	(19.5)
Grain combines, farms[c]					190	(12.4)	231	(19.3)	217	(18.9)	234	(30.8)	174	
Number of combines					190		246		228		274			
Tractors, farms	335	(19.4)	598	(35.5)	766	(49.9)	891	(74.5)	879	(76.5)	852	(89.4)	762	(87.9)
Number of tractors	359		671		933		1,282		1,373		1,467		1,420	
Automobiles, farms	1,063	(61.7)	1,061	(63.0)	961	(62.6)	701	(58.6)	826	(71.9)	747	(78.4)	641	(73.9)
Number of autos	1,203		1,188		1,083		801		917		944		768	
Motortrucks, farms	304	(17.6)	436	(25.9)	676	(44.0)	636	(53.2)	774	(67.4)	671	(70.4)	680	(78.4)
Number of trucks	335		470		754		691		897		843		879	

Sources: Data on electricity, milking machines, grain combines, tractors, automobiles, and motortrucks from U.S. Bureau of the Census, *Census of Agriculture,* for relevant year. Percentages are proportion of farms. Data on running water and flush toilets from U.S. Bureau of the Census, *Census of Housing,* for relevant year. Percentages are proportion of total farm dwelling units.

Note: After 1964 the Census of Agriculture listed no household items.

[a] Category not included for 1959, 1964, 1970.
[b] Category not included for 1940, 1945, 1970.
[c] Category not included for 1940, 1945.

earlier years, women sometimes resorted to direct action in order to get home improvements. One woman, whose husband kept buying large earthmoving equipment for his contracting operation, threatened to divorce him unless he built her a new house.

This was a matter of investment priorities, but there are also indications that men and women sometimes differed in their notions of sanitation. In several of the houses I surveyed, wives added indoor bathrooms after their husbands died. Many men (but not, apparently, women) resisted bringing toilets into the house; it violated their notions of sanitation. The Rhodeses never added an indoor toilet, and Frank Kimber initially refused to use their toilet after it was installed and kept using the WPA-installed privy as long as he lived. Jacquie Kimber recalled her father saying, after they installed the toilet and, around the same time, set up a picnic table outside the newly remodeled kitchen, "This whole wide world is topsy turvy. We used to shit outside and eat inside. Now we eat outside and shit inside." Jacquie recalled, "It was shortly after that I got a snapshot of him using the inside toilet. It was in the summertime, and he'd come in from the field to go to the bathroom, and I knew we'd made a convert!"[11]

Some older women also resisted innovating. The adult daughters of our neighbors, for example, persuaded their mother to buy an electric stove, but she insisted on keeping her wood-burning cookstove, as she understood how to judge its temperature and cooking time.

The widespread home remodeling that occurred in the 1950s and 1960s reflected a fundamental shift in the way farm people organized their relationship to the world, an unprecedented, rapid disjuncture with the past. By the 1950s and 1960s virtually all farmers, both men and women, had worked under the strict time regimes of the military or a waged job; they marketed most of their products and purchased most of their inputs; and, with income taxes and Social Security, they adopted, in their personal lives if not in terms of their farm operation, nationally dominant modes of calculating value. Increasing numbers of farmers had gone to college, at first with the GI bill and then as part of the expectation that a college education would provide them the grounding they needed to function in the larger society. Most farmers, particularly the families who came to adulthood in the 1930s and 1940s, adopted the categorization of experience—of time, space, and bodily routines—that Foucault identifies as central to modernity.

This shift was made concrete in the 1950s and 1960s as most farmers who remained on the land renovated their homes or built new houses using FmHA plans or other purchased house plans (see figs. 11.5 and 11.6). The new or renovated houses provided separate bedrooms for parents and for same-sex children; generally a relatively small, all-electric kitchen was installed; a dining room was created;[12] closets were built; and

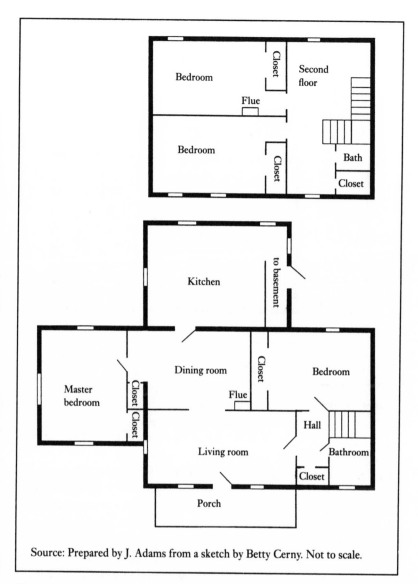

Figure 11.5. Cerny House, 1950s–Present

full and half baths were added. The Cernys, who started housekeeping after Norbert returned from service in World War II, divided the large main room into a living room and a dining room, added a master bedroom, pulled off the old summer kitchen and built a new kitchen wing with built-in cabinets, built new interior stairs to the basement, divided the upstairs into two bedrooms and a bathroom, and built closets throughout the house.

Edith Rendleman, who had aspired to modern standards since her

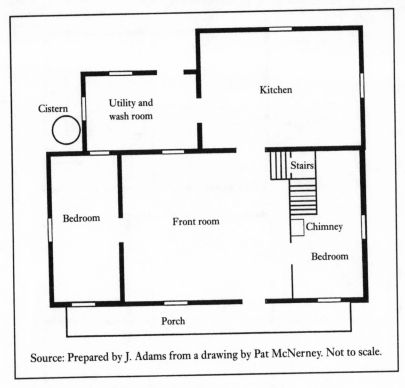

Source: Prepared by J. Adams from a drawing by Pat McNerney. Not to scale.

Figure 11.6. Rhodes House, 1950s–1980s

youth and who had attended college at Southern Illinois State Normal, was among the first to remodel her home, which she inherited when her father died in 1949. The house had been built for tenants who originally operated the farm, and her father had already begun to renovate it. She had a basement dug out, tore out the stairs and built a wider staircase to the second floor, remodeled the kitchen, divided the living room to make a dining room, and finished the upstairs.

The Weavers did not fundamentally remodel their house, which had been built in 1927 to a very modest modern design when the Victorian home burned down, although they did add an electric kitchen and bathroom and, like the Kimbers, made some alterations in first-floor rooms to house elderly relatives. The Kimbers and the Waltons both changed the kitchen areas. The Kimbers' original summer kitchen had been torn down in the 1910s or early 1920s, and the kitchen was moved into a portion of the ell at the back of the house. In the 1940s they tore out the walls between a hired hand's bedroom, a small workroom, and the kitchen and made the space into a large kitchen with built-in cabinets, and a full bathroom (see fig. 11.7). The Waltons also reworked the kitchen area.

By the mid-1960s most farmhouses had been transformed from gener-

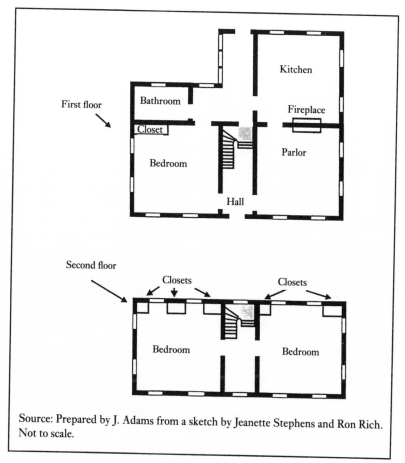

First floor

Bathroom

Closet

Bedroom

Hall

Kitchen

Fireplace

Parlor

Second floor

Closets

Closets

Bedroom

Bedroom

Source: Prepared by J. Adams from a sketch by Jeanette Stephens and Ron Rich. Not to scale.

Figure 11.7. Kimber House, 1940s

alized structures to more specialized, efficiency-oriented homes in which consumption, rather than production, predominated. The new farm home, like its urban and suburban counterpart, created a private domain separated from work, although, because of its physical proximity to the farm, it still remained more open to neighbors and kin and to the exigencies of farm work than most suburban homes.[13]

The farm home was not the only structure of daily life that changed. As we have seen, most Union County farms that persisted came to rely almost entirely on family labor. Except for the few remaining orchards that employed a few year-round workers and hired large numbers of migrant laborers seasonally, the Union County agricultural labor system was radically simplified or, perhaps more accurately, was replaced by industrially produced equipment and supplies. The changes in agricultural and household structure affected far more than farming families.

We Used to Eat Inside   213

During the postwar period the fundamental bases of social life shifted and assumed a new configuration.

Changes in Community Life

The building blocks for the new order were first instituted during the New Deal. Government expanded enormously and took on a redistributive function it had never had before. With unprecedented investments in infrastructure—roads, schools, health care, water and sewer systems, housing, national forests, and prisons—jobs opened up. Rosemary Walton got a job teaching school; Helen Kimber was hired by the state mental hospital. Some of the former tenants on the Walton farm found jobs at the shoe factory, but others were employed by the city as city services expanded. The nearby state university, Southern Illinois University, expanded rapidly, changing from a teachers' college to a major comprehensive university. An increasing proportion of college-age children attended the university, and a significant number found employment there. Jacquie Eddleman taught in the home economics department; George Weaver, after a period teaching in the public schools, taught in the agriculture department; and Marita Weaver taught at John A. Logan Community College. Virtually all the maintenance, clerical, and secretarial staff at Southern Illinois University at Carbondale came from the surrounding area and included many Union County residents.

New agencies proliferated, providing a large number of jobs. Bill Rhodes, for example, got a part-time job with the Agricultural Stabilization and Conservation Service checking compliance with acreage set-asides. Jack Eddleman, who married Helen and Frank Kimber's daughter, Jacquie, got a job in the conservation service office when he graduated from the university, and the Kimbers' son, Robert, worked first as a bank examiner and then as an auditor for the state.

Without people being fully aware of it, the economy shifted from dependence on agriculture and manufacturing to heavy reliance on government services.

At the same time local businessmen found their businesses undermined by the same processes that were impoverishing the area's agriculture. The small towns, which had served as market centers for the surrounding rural hinterland, were being bypassed. Village dairy and poultry stations lost their markets as the fluid milk market expanded. The new all-weather roads allowed consumers to drive to the larger towns, where chain supermarkets and variety stores undersold the small-town grocers and general stores. In the mid-1960s the construction of Interstate 57 through the eastern side of the county and the rerouting of U.S. Route 51 so that it bypassed Cobden and Anna drained commerce from the county's towns.

Al Basler, who worked in Green's general store in Cobden, recalled, of the late 1950s, "The business had just gone to the chain stores and bigger places. . . . Cobden looks like a ghost town now. You can see these changes; after they changed, you can see them coming."[14]

For a period the structural shifts were masked by World War II and by the rise in personal income. In 1939 the county's personal income was estimated at $7,269,000; by 1947 it had risen to $18,215,000. This translated into increased retail sales, which benefited local businesses.[15] As late as 1953 an economic development study stated, "As yet there has been relatively little impact of state and federal organizations outside of the U.S. Forest Service, the Illinois Highway Commission, the relief agencies, and the armed forces."[16] By 1960, however, only 17.8 percent of the county's labor force was employed in agriculture and 26.3 percent in manufacturing, construction, and mines and quarries, while 23 percent was employed in jobs largely funded directly by government.[17] By 1969, the earliest year for which we have data, fully 36 percent of personal income came from the government, either through direct employment (20 percent) or through transfer payments, largely Social Security and military pensions (16 percent). In contrast, less than 5 percent of personal income came from agriculture and 15 percent from manufacturing (see fig. 12.1).

These figures indicate not only a shift in the kinds of jobs people had, but also a shift in how people's worth and status were evaluated. Sennett and Cobb, in their book *The Hidden Injuries of Class*, write of the conflict working in a white-collar job aroused in men from working-class backgrounds: On one hand, the job held, by national standards, high status and pay relative to their parents' factory jobs; on the other hand, men raised in working-class families valued "real" work—work that challenged one physically as well as intellectually. "Pencil pushing" was not "honest labor."[18] Had a comparable study been done in Union County in the 1960s, I suspect the researchers would have found similar ambivalence on the part of farming and working people concerning the white-collar jobs in which they and/or their children found employment.

Some people who came from families that had traditionally been owners of businesses and worked as professionals were also ambivalent about the numbers of people who could claim equal status with them as managerial and professional jobs proliferated. At the same time that the number of people who could potentially claim membership in elite circles increased, the foundations of social status shifted, and larger farmers, businesspeople, and professionals lost real power. Before World War II, store owners provided most of the market outlets for smaller farmers and supplied most of their needs. In the process, they provided a great deal of credit to carry people through periods when they had little cash income. Similarly, larger farmers and local manufacturers, such as owners of box and basket factories, employed relatively large numbers of people, both year-round and seasonally. In the early years of the century virtually every village in Union County had a fruit box and basket mill; by 1950 only four remained: The Fruit Growers Package Co., Jonesboro; Arlie Woodard and Son, Dongola; Lawrence Box and Basket Co., Cobden; and H. A. DuBois and Sons, Cobden.[19] In the next decade all of these factories closed, unable to compete with cardboard and plastic packing materials.

As we have seen, after World War II most laborers left agriculture for larger industries, small manufacturers lost their markets, and local merchants and middlemen lost out to centralized marketers.[20] At the same time, large industries and government agencies became major employers. In 1980 the only private employers with more than 100 employees were the International Shoe Company (bought by Florsheim); Atlas Powder Plant (bought by Trojan Company, a division of International Minerals and Chemical Corporation, and, in 1982, closed temporarily and reopened as a nonunion plant by Ensign-Bickford Co.) at Wolf Lake; locally owned Lewis Brothers Bakery; Transcraft Corp., manufacturers of over-the-road flatbed trailers; and Anna Quarries, mining limestone.[21] Increasingly, people who had once run independent businesses became managers in these large organizations. These new positions, although conferring influence, did not embody the same degree of power to affect their neighbor's lives as had their previous positions. Those locally owned companies that survived, particularly Lewis Brothers Bakery, Transcraft, and Anna Quarries, expanded and developed more levels of managerial control, and small-scale businesses no longer had the same economic or social influence they had had in earlier years. There was, in effect, a general leveling of the class structure: people who had been poor and who relied on their richer neighbors for work and credit gained a degree of economic security through steady jobs, many of which were relatively prestigious, while people who had held power lost their autonomy to managerial elites located elsewhere in the country.

At the same time that the structure of people's working lives was fundamentally reoriented, the structures of community life were undermined. As we have seen, people left farms in large numbers, leaving the countryside relatively depopulated. At the same time that the informal networks of rural life were becoming frayed, one of the pillars of rural communities, the rural school, was displaced. Rural schools were far more than places to give children the basics of reading, writing, and arithmetic. They provided the only formal institution that included all members of a rural region, no matter what their class or religion. Only African American families were excluded from the social life that centered around the schools, and by the twentieth century only one small rural black community, south of Makanda at Toppington, and a larger African American community in

Helen Plott (Kimber) attended a two-year high school in the hamlet of Balcom and played on a winning basketball team in 1923–24. She is the third girl from the left. Kimber Collection, Morris Library, Southern Illinois University, Carbondale.

and close to Cobden (with its own school and church), existed in the county. By the 1950s all African American schools had too few pupils to be sustained, and the remaining black students went to the Cobden school. The school boards were the site of local political participation, and the buildings were used for many community functions.

In the late 1940s and early 1950s a number of forces converged to promote school consolidation.[22] Probably most important, the state legislature, seeking to improve the quality of education through consolidating school districts, changed state school aid formulas so that very small schools could no longer receive state aid. At the same time, the legislature promoted the formation of unit districts (kindergarten through twelfth grade) by allowing them to levy lower property taxes than the former elementary and high school districts and still receive state aid. Declining birthrates and rural out-migration therefore doomed many schools. The number of rural children between five and fourteen dropped from 4,271 in 1930 to 3,021 in 1940, to 2,719 in 1950, and to 1,780 in 1960, a decline of nearly 2,500 school-age children in three decades.[23] In other words, the number of school-age children had dropped by 36 percent between 1930 and 1950, and it continued to decrease rapidly. The decade spanning 1950–60 saw another 35 percent decline in the number of children between five and fourteen. However, many communities fought hard to

We Used to Eat Inside   217

A potluck supper, ca. 1950, at Oak Ridge School, which the author attended in 1949–50. Lillian Adams Collection, Morris Library, Southern Illinois University, Carbondale.

retain their schools, consolidating with neighboring districts rather than with larger town schools. Between 1948 and 1951 eight schools merged with neighboring districts, and these in turn sometimes merged, as in the schools in the northeastern part of the county, which in 1952 finally managed to create the only rural elementary district that survived into the 1990s. The largest wave of school consolidations occurred between 1948 and 1952; by 1959 virtually all rural schools had joined larger, mostly town-based districts.

The Farm Bureau and the Home Bureau were key players in the change. Initially, as shown in Chapter 8, E. A. Bierbaum, the farm extension agent, acted as the broker among the diverse New Deal programs in the county.

The Home Bureau and, individually, its members were active in civic affairs. They were involved in bringing public health care to the county, through a tuberculosis testing program and through working for a public health department.[24] Home Bureau members generally promoted school consolidation and improving education, although the organization took no stand on consolidation and some members actively resisted the issue.

The Home Bureau started late in Union County; it was not organized until 1947–48. Most of the charter members knew each other through participation in the Eastern Star and Rebekahs, but the Home Bureau was a different sort of organization. The sororal orders, like their fraternal counterparts, provided an arena in which stable, and generally more prosperous, members of the community could socialize across religious, ethnic, and other divisions. The Home Bureau was explicitly oriented to education and social and economic development. Although it could be characterized as an elite organization, it reached broadly into rural society. Five hundred sixty-five women were invited to attend the original planning meeting in 1947, approximately one-third of farm women between twenty and sixty years old,[25] although only seventy-five attended. No detailed membership records exist, but oral accounts indicate that, during the 1950s, most members were young and many women joined only for a few years, dropping out as their life situation changed or because of dissatisfaction with the program. With over 200 paid members (and more local, non-dues-paying participants) throughout the 1950s, probably at least half of younger farm women were involved in the Home Bureau at some point. A core of women were active throughout their lives. Many women attended Home Bureau demonstration programs, carried out at the local level, to obtain technical information about the new equipment and resources suddenly available to them. However, these programs also transmitted national norms of home decoration, clothing styles, etiquette, child-rearing practices, nutritional standards, and food preparation practices. The first year the county committee undertook a wide variety of projects: eight lessons dealt with clothing construction and care; five with cooking; five with household design, upholstering, and landscaping; four with etiquette and personal development; two with health; three with crafts; one with legal advice; and one with recreation. Although the number of projects undertaken in subsequent years was far more limited, the range and proportion of projects was representative of those undertaken throughout the 1950s and 1960s.[26]

Many women experienced a gap between what the Home Bureau offered and their own needs, particularly their economic needs. Although Home Bureau programs, like the farm press of the period, stressed thrift and provided helpful tips for cooking nutritious meals cheaply and remodeling out-of-style or worn-out clothing (for example, how to reverse shirt collars to extend the life of a shirt), its program was based in home economics, which adhered closely to the "doctrine of separate spheres," which defined men as producers outside the home and women as consumers and homemakers. Homemaking, according to home economics, did not include earning money. Home economists, who trained the home extension agents and established the range of projects offered, therefore did not consider remunerative activities part of their program and failed to incorporate farm women's traditional income-earning enterprises into their programs. They provided no advice for starting up farm-based businesses, never mentioned the changing economics of poultry and dairy production, and therefore never addressed a key part of farm women's lives—the provisioning of their households. Farm women, with no tradition of political organizing or advocacy for their needs, do not appear to have tried to reform the Home Bureau's agenda. Instead, women, like Helen Kimber, simply dropped out of the organization when they decided to go to work.

Looking back from the 1990s it appears that Home Extension missed an opportunity to innovate in ways that, in the 1980s and 1990s, seem crucial to maintaining family life. Had home economists recognized farm women as income earners, they might have developed programs to help women set up home-based businesses to replace poultry and dairy, as Farm Extension helped farm men change their cropping patterns. They might have promoted community-based child care and other supporting services for women who worked off the farm, or they might have worked with Farm Extension to redefine gender roles and bring wives and daughters into farm production as partners. But no one during that period seems to have understood the implications of the changes that were happening within the organization of farming and within rural communities, as women lost their sources of livelihood, rural communities shrank, and support networks were shredded. Rather, the dominant urban (and increasingly in the 1950s, suburban) model of the isolated nuclear family with an income-producing husband and a homemaking wife was accepted as the norm, even if it was not practiced by many families.

Despite their silence on changing women's domestic lives, Home Bureau and other "modernizing" groups and individuals often did attempt to help retain a sense of community life in rural areas. Home and Farm Extension were themselves community-building organizations, as they involved farm men and women in demonstration projects, countywide events, and, for the young people, 4-H clubs with their many and varied local and countywide projects and programs and a regional summer camp. Other attempts were more idiosyncratic. Edith Rendleman recalled organizing a square-dancing group that met in an abandoned local schoolhouse, and similar attempts occurred elsewhere. Some were more successful than others. Edith was disappointed because not many people around Wolf Lake were interested in the group, so it was made up largely of people from around the county whom she knew through membership in the Order of the Eastern Star and the Rebekahs. Unlike the dance parties held in people's homes during the early years of the century, they used recorded music and few children attended. Nonetheless, it was an attempt to reconstruct communities on new terms as the old forms disintegrated.

The radical changes in community life, with their attendant status shifts, were negotiated in small and unremarkable ways in people's daily lives. They were worked out as well in public arenas, particularly local festivals. I studied the history of one festival, the Cobden Peach Festival, for its fiftieth anniversary, and discovered that the queen contest revealed the shift quite dramatically.[27]

The Cobden Peach Festival

In 1938 a number of Cobden businessmen, professionals, ministers, and a few farmers organized a Lions Club. The organization bridged some historic divisions between German Catholics and the governing Protestants, of whom the Presbyterians were the leading element. It also, for the first time, included some farmers in what was basically a businessman's organization. Many of the founders had been active in bringing the WPA-built waterworks to the village in 1935 and in installing a public sewage system in 1939.[28] The Lions took on the project of raising funds for a volunteer fire department and, in order to do so, put on the first Peach Festival. It was explicitly designed to boost the county's premier product, peaches. They designed a one-day celebration with food donated by member businesses, games, and a queen contest, and they recruited members of the Cobden Women's Club (many of whom were their wives) to help cook and organize the queen contest.[29] The Lions initially had no plans to found a community institution, but more than half a century later the festival has become a key activity in the life of village residents.

The first queen, Delores Flamm, was the daughter of a major German Catholic grower. Electing queens for various pageants and festivities was a common fund-raising and booster technique; as was common in the area, people bought votes, and the girl with the most votes won. Only girls who had the backing of people (or, gossip has it, sometimes parents or other patrons) with enough money to buy a lot of votes had a chance of winning. The Flamms, although relatively large growers, were not wealthy. At the fiftieth anniversary celebration Delores Flamm Osbourne recalled that she wore a borrowed wedding dress with the train basted up in back to make it floor length, and that they drove to town in the farm truck for the festival. When she was crowned queen, she was robed in a cape with cotton batting for ermine, made by Mrs. Ira Casper, the jeweler's wife, and was crowned with a paper crown. In later years the queen was crowned with a tiara made and donated by the jeweler.

Girls from leading families vied for the crown; in 1945 twenty-five girls ran, requiring two eliminations. Many of the winners during the first two decades were members of the Presbyterian church, reflecting the key role that congregation played in village affairs. In a sense, the queen contest served as a "coming out" event for the young ladies of the leading families, with young boys and girls from these families acting as crown and flower bearers.

This pattern began to break down in the early 1950s when, according to some recollections, some parents who were not members of Cobden "society" asked to have their young children serve as attendants. After considerable discussion the Lions decided in 1952 to adopt national beauty queen standards for judging entrants in the queen contest. This opened the contest to girls who could not expect to be able to win a popularity contest based on purchased votes. Some people characterized the change in contest rules as an attempt to democratize the proceedings. There are indications that the change was not completely smooth. In 1952 and 1953 the number of entrants remained high; but no queen was elected in 1954, and only a small number entered the following year.

In 1956 the Cobden Village Board agreed to participate in a project sponsored by the new department of community development at Southern Illinois University. Anticipating the War on Poverty of the 1960s, community development aimed to modernize "depressed areas" through economic and social development activities.[30] The organizers recruited participants from all existing community organizations for a community council, which then developed a series of committees that surveyed the community's resources, wrote a history of the village, and tried to develop projects to improve the community.[31] The organizers persuaded the Lions to open sponsorship of the festival to other organizations, and they expanded the festivities to two days. The collaboration did not persist after the first year, and except for formal participation by the Women's Club (which had always participated informally), the Lions resumed primary sponsorship of the festival.

The community development project resulted in the village's decision in 1958 to build a medical clinic, and a variety of fund-raising activities were held. For a number of years virtually all the festival's proceeds went to the clinic, a focus that raised some conflicts within the Lions Club because some members began to favor supporting other projects.[32] In 1964, after five years of donating all earnings to the clinic, they funded building a trophy room in the high school in memory of Tom Crowell, a star on the Cobden basketball team who had drowned the previous summer.

The crosscurrents of change can be seen in the festival itself. Stimulated by the community development project, C. Joe Thomas organized a minstrel show, its cast drawn from local youths, which played for ten years until the civil rights movement (brought home by violent confrontations in nearby Cairo) made the organizers aware of the negative racial stereotypes they had unwittingly acted out. The Lions, who had generally hired a band or other entertainment, decided in 1962 not to hire entertainment so that more proceeds could go to the community. The previous year they had contracted with a small regional carnival to provide rides for the program, a practice that continued. In 1963, perhaps in recognition of shifting status relations, they initiated a dunking booth in which the public was invited to try to dunk prominent Cobden men. In 1966 it was called "Dunk the Mayor, Deposit the Banker, and Immerse the Preacher." In 1968 the game was retitled "Dunk the Monkey," and the privilege of being dunked was open to the general public, perhaps indicating that the shift from a relatively rigidly class-stratified community to a more homogeneous one had been completed.[33]

These crosscurrents continued to affect the queen contest. In 1961, Lions leadership prevailed on the festival planners to reinstitute voting on the queen and to open the competition to contestants throughout the county. The attempt was not successful; although six girls entered that year, only two girls entered the contest each subsequent year that purchased votes determined who would be queen. "Everyone knew who would win," a participant explained to me when I asked why so few girls entered during those years. Additionally, the attempt to include non-Cobden girls in the contest aroused strong negative feelings, so that the Lions abandoned that attempt.[34] Finally in 1965, the same year funds were donated to a project other than the clinic, the contest was firmly committed to abiding by national beauty queen rules, and ten girls entered; subsequently the contest never drew fewer than four entries.

Although recollections of the first half of that decade focus on personalities and specific policy disputes, the conflicts internal to the Lions Club can be seen to have been embedded in far deeper structural transformations. By 1965 the tensions were resolved, and new forms were finally institutionalized. For the first time Cobden businesses sponsored contestants, a practice that continued into the 1990s. When the festival began in 1938, the organizers hoped to boost the area, promoting its agricultural products and encouraging industries to locate in the village. Three decades later, with businesses undermined, not by an international depression but by a restructuring of American enterprise, they sought to provide visibility to individual businesses who were losing out to larger vendors.

In 1973, with local businesses closing, the queen contest was successfully opened to girls throughout the county. It became common for girls to enter both the Peach Festival and the Union County Fair queen contests, and people who identified Cobden as their hometown hoped their candidate would win. The significance of the event had shifted, however, from being a contest between different Cobden girls—and by extension their families and factions—to a contest between Cobden and other towns. The village had shifted from being the center of reference for people's social life to being only one node among many which, in the case of the queen contest, included all of Union County.

Conclusion

During the two decades following World War II, rural life in Union County changed dramatically. The entire structure and organization of daily life shifted. At the beginning of the period farms required large amounts of labor, and stable patterns of landlord-tenant-laborer interaction had been established. People's lives tended to be defined, in radiating areas, by farm, school district and church, village, and county. Larger growers and stock dealers developed independent relations with urban brokers, but the webs of social and economic interdependence were largely local. Towns were market centers that relied on a relatively clearly defined "hinterland." Town-based merchants and, in some cases, farmer cooperatives acted as brokers with the regional and national economy, and most town manufacturers, such as box-makers, used local products to create goods that were, in turn, sold locally. The economy was not insular; the shocks of the post–World War I collapse of the international wheat and other agricultural commodities markets undermined the prosperity of the area, and the Great Depression left it largely immiserated. But the structures of daily life did not change much, despite being materially impoverished.

The New Deal, and its consolidation in the modified welfare state after World War II, reorganized social life. The most visible changes were technological: electricity, all-weather roads, internal combustion engines, hybrid seeds, chemical fertilizers, pesticides and herbicides, and radio and, in the 1950s, television. Also much discussed at the time was the demographic shift as young people by the droves, and many mature people as well, left rural areas to seek urban employment. People were also acutely aware of the shift in educational standards and actively engaged in setting and contesting educational policies; far more young people completed high school and attended college. Less visible, and surely less discussed directly, although the stuff of gossip, the class structure was dismembered as farm laborers and poorer farmers left for factory and other urban jobs, and local elites lost status and power to distant corporate and government bureaucracies. The Cold War rhetoric of anticommunism celebrated individualism and made it difficult to discuss the structural shifts that were occurring; the ideology of female domesticity made it virtually impossible to discuss what was happening to the home life of farm women. Finally, the general national prosperity, which increased steadily throughout the 1950s and 1960s, interrupted only briefly by cyclical recessions, made the difficulties farmers were facing largely invisible to policy setters. This would become even more pronounced after 1964, when the Voting Rights Act forced redistricting on the basis of population and farm regions lost a great deal of power in the U.S. Congress. Farming, as a family lifestyle, had been largely incorporated into national urban forms, while national policy increasingly treated agriculture simply as one branch of industry, refusing to recognize it as a unique form of production.

Well, we retired, and we bought this place two years before we retired and came back here. . . . I was raised just a mile north of here. And it was good to come back here. You know a few people. If you're away for thirty-three years—we were away—there are a lot of changes, but there are a few of the old-timers still around.—Austin Halterman

When They Retired, They Came Back Home

By the mid-1960s a new social order had been largely consolidated, at least on the level of social structure. The upheavals of the late 1960s and early 1970s, although generally relatively remote from people's daily lives, affected what might be called the "ethos" or norms of people who lived in Union County. Some counterculture groups bought land in the county in the late 1960s, and older residents were often bemused by their communal living or by women who appeared to be married retaining their birth name. The ethic of neighborliness, however, was strong, and most young newcomers developed good relationships with their close neighbors.[1] Despite the fact that no strong movement existed in the county, the civil rights, antiwar, and counterculture movements existed nearby.

226

In the 1960s, Cairo, the old river town at the confluence of the Mississippi and the Ohio, had an active civil rights movement that initially, in 1962, attempted to integrate the swimming pool. This soon evolved into armed conflict between some whites, organized into a group known as the United Concerned Citizens' Association and militant blacks. The dispute simmered for years, occasionally erupting into violence.[2] This conflict stimulated the abandonment of the Cobden Peach Festival's minstrel show. In Carbondale some African Americans who identified with the Black Panther Party engaged in a shootout with the police in November 1970. By itself, this incident might have blown over, but by the late 1960s students at Southern Illinois University were as involved in the antiwar and counterculture movements as students anywhere in the country. The first small-scale demonstrations were held in 1965; these grew to massive riots in the early 1970s. On May 12, 1970, the president closed the university to quell the disturbances. People tell stories of the bizarre costumes students wore during this period, and twenty years later many people in the area still avoid Carbondale and are afraid to go through the town at night. Some Union County families were directly affected as their children rebelled and joined communes; one family told of a relative who committed suicide when her daughter became a hippie. For the most part, however, hippies and rioters were not directly involved in the daily lives of Union Countians.

They were more generally affected by the Vietnam War, in which many Union County youths served. I have not probed people's attitudes toward the war, and the newspaper during this period was muted in its coverage. It listed the young men in service and casualties but otherwise was generally silent. The very silence surrounding the issue speaks to the deep discomfort it aroused in the region. During this period marijuana and, to some extent, other drugs became relatively widespread. Beginning in the early 1980s the newspapers carried stories about major marijuana hauls in August and September. I was told that the subtext, and the outcome, of the 1982 sheriff's race involved marijuana. In February 1984 a federal task force arrested a number of Union County residents, including some farmers whose families went back several generations, for growing and manufacturing marijuana. Rumors flew thick and fast that virtually everyone of any status in the county was involved in the trade, resulting in a public denial in the county newspaper.[3] One woman commented to me, "If everyone who people said had been arrested had been, there wouldn't have been any business done in Anna that week," and according the newspaper, the courthouse would have been closed as well.

By the late 1980s drug enforcement efforts seemed to have quelled, although not obliterated, commercial marijuana growing. Clearings in the national forest, acres of relatively untended farmland, and deserted islands in the Mississippi River continued to make attractive sites for marijuana patches, which were, however, sought out more assiduously by the Drug Enforcement Agency. Commercial growers also often earned the enmity of their unwitting host farmers. I was told stories by farmers from around southern Illinois whose children were warned away from a back corner of a cornfield by gun-wielding men, or of running across booby-trapped marijuana plots in their fields. One farmer thought his pigs were poisoned in revenge by a man whose marijuana he had unwittingly mowed down as he cleared an overgrown field. Such farmers were likely to report marijuana growing on their land to drug enforcement authorities, and as enforcement efforts increased, farmers were less likely to turn a blind eye to an unobtrusive patch they happened to stumble across, since they might be accused of growing it themselves.

In addition to the widespread production of and trade in marijuana, which in many respects was not dissimilar from the moonshining that was common during Prohibition, I detected a general cultural shift in the region when I returned in 1982. I rented an office in a government agency building in Anna for my field research and was therefore part of the informal discussions that took place among the staff. Most of the staff were women, and when the male managers were gone, discussions often took on the tone of a consciousness-raising group as women complained about the failure of their husbands to help with household chores and child care, berated their (absent) bosses for their lack of respect, and tried to come to terms with their multiple roles as mothers, wives, daughters, and workers. I was also struck by the language, which contained many "four-letter words." When I was a child, I had been scolded by teachers for saying "darn" as an expletive, and bitch referred only to a female dog.

I also found a shift in standards accorded sexuality. In the late 1970s I was employed to do a household survey in the greater Carbondale area. Many of the people I called freely gave the names of all residents, which included many opposite-sex roommates. In the early 1960s, when I was a student in Carbondale, only bohemian artists and theater people lived unmarried with people of the opposite sex, and they did so with great discretion. By the end of the 1980s it was possible for a southern Illinois man to be elected to a county office despite the fact that he openly lived with a woman who was not his wife (they later married).

By 1970 only 13.6 percent of county residents were farmers, as compared with almost 20 percent a decade earlier. Between 1970 and 1980 the number of people living in Union County increased by a modest 780, the first rise since the 1930s, when people came home after losing their urban jobs. Most of the new residents lived in rural areas, but it did not indicate a revitalization of farming: the rural farm population fell by 316 people (see table 2.1). Many of the remaining farms were very small. The 1969 agricultural census recorded 141 farms under 50 acres and 194 between 50 and 99 acres, out of 867 farms (see table 6.1). During the next decades, a significant proportion of farms continued to be too small to support a family.

A growing proportion of farmland was not worked by its owners. Unlike in earlier decades, this land was generally rented to landowning neighbors, who depended on rented land to expand their operations (see part owners in table 6.2).[4] The landowners who supplied rental land fall into three categories: retired farmers, "ex-urbanites" who bought farmland in order to have a rural lifestyle but whose primary source of income is elsewhere, and heirs who may live on the family farm but do not farm most of it. Unlike in the richer prairie regions, few heirs who leave the region retain farmland as an income-producing investment.

Many farm children who became adults during the 1950s and found local off-farm jobs retained a working interest in their family's farm but rented much of the acreage to neighbors. Jacquie Eddleman and Bob Kimber, for example, both acquired college educations but continued to live on or near the home farm. When their father's health failed, they rented the orchard to an area grower, but the family continued to farm the rest of the acreage. George and Marita Weaver rented most of George's natal farm to a neighbor, retaining only some pastureland on which they raised a small herd of beef cattle. Rosemary Walton rented the farm to a neighbor, Leon Dillow, when her husband died, and when Dillow retired, his son picked up the lease. Meanwhile, Barb began a small sheep operation in order to give her son meaningful work and as part of a larger vision of contributing to the region. She recounted,

> I've always wanted to do something to promote this county. I've been dedicated to Union County and to southern Illinois all my life, and I continue to be dedicated to this area. . . . I saw that . . . a lot of our farmers in the area, as people did all over the United States, answered the call to plant fence row to fence row years ago, and we planted areas that should never have been broken into cultivation in this . . . hill-country up here. Now down in the bottomlands, . . . that's a different matter.
>
> I wanted to show people that . . . sheep had a place in southern Illinois agriculture. They blend with cattle, they compliment each other in their grazing practices, and sheep do not destroy the land any more than anything else will. They destroy it if you leave them in one place too long. Cattle will do the same thing; horses are terrible on grazing. It just requires management. I wanted to . . . show that they did have a place here in being restored to southern Illinois. I don't know, I've had a lot of great dreams for this.[5]

The large number of small farms and the growing proportion of rented farmland also point to the growing ex-urbanite phenomenon. This trend, picked up by analysts of rural life in the 1970s, had its roots in the "back to the land" movement that grew out of the counterculture.[6] Many young couples, largely professionals—in southern Illinois, people connected with the university or working in government agencies—sought a rural lifestyle. Sometimes developers subdivided farms, and retired farmers, like Rosemary Walton, sometimes sold part of their land for house or commercial lots. A considerable number of these ex-urbanites bought small farms and rented most of their land to a neighboring farmer.

The proliferation of small farms also correlates with the aging nature of the population. Many people who had left the area for urban employment returned when they retired. With Social Security and other pensions, they could live much more comfortably in southern Illinois than they could in a city. Many people still had strong family and affective ties to the region and enjoyed farming and rural living. A number of the growers who sell at the Carbondale Farmers' Market, a producers' cooperative that has a weekly public retail market, are people who retired to their natal communities and supplement their retirement income with fruit and vegetable production. In 1983 Austin Halterman recalled, "We decided we needed something to do besides just sit under a shade tree. So, we knew of the Farmers' Market getting started in July, either eight or nine years ago.[7] We went up and took some potted plants and flowers and a little produce up in August. Then we just kept it up, and we thought if we were going to go, we might as well take enough along to make it worth your while."[8] Other retirees raise enough cattle to be classified as a farm for tax purposes and because they enjoy the work and the extra income.

The area became attractive for retirees largely because of Great Society programs. The Cobden medical clinic was a precursor of these programs, bringing modern medical facilities to a rural village that had previously been served only by general practitioners with few supports. This program, although at the time funded solely with private funds, was in several ways prototypical of many later government-funded programs. It was organized as a locally based nonprofit corporation that eventually applied for federal and state grants to cover expenses. Most of these grants, which were mandated on the federal level, required state and sometimes local matches, creating partnerships between federal, state, and local governments and private nonprofit corporations. In 1978 Rural Health, Inc., and Medicaid and Medicare programs made it possible for private companies such as Tip of Illinois and other home health services to be organized to provide low-cost services for elderly people with limited mobility. Federal revenue sharing, begun under President Nixon, provided funds for ambulance and other services for rural areas, including senior citizens' centers with low-cost lunches, Meals on Wheels that delivered midday meals to elderly shut-ins, and other services for the elderly. Federal housing money, made available to county housing authorities through the Department of Housing and Urban Development, built 268 units of senior housing, including both single-story developments and a highrise in downtown Anna, as well as other units of low-income housing. Unlike in urban areas, where most low-income housing was concentrated in high-rise apartment buildings, the Union County Housing Authority built small-scale, single-story apartments in residential neighborhoods. The only high-rise was a project for senior citizens in downtown Anna. After his wife died, Bill Rhodes's family persuaded him to move into an apartment in the senior housing in Jonesboro. Jess and Maple Brimm, who had been tenants on the Walton farm but left for urban jobs, lived in a county low-income housing development in Anna.

These and other government programs pumped money into the local economy: In 1984, the Illinois Legislative Council found that southern Illinois generally got more back from the state than it paid in taxes. Johnson County, with its low tax base and state prison, received $9.49 for every $.90 in taxes paid; Union County, with the state mental hospital and state forest and game refuge, got back $3.24 for every $.90 in taxes.[9]

Social Security and other pensions, largely earned elsewhere, also pumped in a considerable amount of money. In 1983 fully 22.2 percent of Union County residents received Social Security, and that year government transfer payments, the bulk of which are Social Security and military pensions, accounted for 26.2 percent of total personal income.[10] This had risen from 15.6 percent of personal income in 1969 (see fig. 12.1).

Federal and state money was important in other ways as well. Governments directly hired many workers, particularly in educational facilities, prisons, the state mental hospital, road construction and maintenance, and the various state and federal forests, parks, and game preserves. In 1969 direct government employment accounted for nearly 27 percent of personal income, a proportion that rose to a high of 31.3 percent in 1986, then declined to 30 percent in 1990. These figures do not include the substantial amounts of money that enter the area through state and federal contracts with private corporations and therefore show up in the statistics as private contributions. These range from school contracts with private bus services to educational funds channeled through private nonprofit corporations like the agency that operates the migrant Head Start program.

When other sources of government income, particularly Social Security and other government pensions, are added to direct employment, in 1969 government accounted for 35.5 percent of the personal income of Union County residents; this percentage rose to 41.5 in 1990. In contrast,

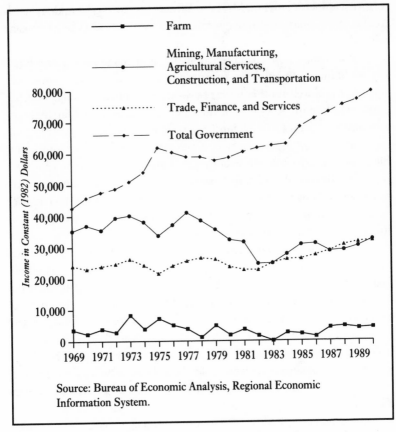

Figure 12.1. Inflation-Adjusted Income by Source, Union County, 1969–1990

for the state of Illinois as a whole, in 1969 the proportion of income from government employment was only 11.7 percent; when Social Security and other government income was included, it accounted for only 17.3 percent of total personal income. In 1990, 12.4 percent of Illinois residents' earned income came from government, and government funds supplied 22.4 percent of total personal income.

Much of the relative prosperity Union County has experienced has been a direct and an indirect result of the redistribution of wealth on a national and state level. Government redistribution has taken a number of forms. Politicians who want to decrease government spending, and people who feel their taxes are too high, focus on direct and indirect "welfare" payments that improve the quality of life for individuals through providing medical care, income support, and so forth, and on direct subsidies such as those that go to farmers for crop set-asides and deficiency payments. But social investments that allow the rest of the economy to function form a much greater part of government redistribution. These include investments in transportation, particularly roads, river channels, and locks and dams on rivers; investments in flood control through levees and drainage projects; construction of lakes and maintenance of forests; support for education at all levels; investments in water and sewage projects; and direct payments for conservation structures. Social investmemt also includes military spending, which is important in the nation as a whole but has had no direct importance to the area's economy, except during World War II, when a munitions plant was built on Crab Orchard Lake, and through military pensions. The government also significantly shapes private investment decisions through a large number of regulatory and investment interventions. These range from insured bank accounts that help stabilize banking and credit to incentives for industries to locate in disadvantaged areas (such as credit, and tax and labor subsidies) and government-operated or -mandated retirement and insurance programs.

The amount of money coming into the area through government in the form of pensions directly received by retirees, federal and state grants and contracts for social and other privately supplied services, and direct employment by government bodies helped fuel an economic recovery in the 1970s, the only decade during which the county's population increased. Figure 12.1 graphically indicates that income from services, trade, farming, and manufacturing declined or was flat through most of the 1970s, while income from government employment and transfer payments rose steadily. After a sharp recession in the early 1980s, the economy recovered modestly, although income from government employment did not recover until the second half of the decade. Only income from transfer payments, largely Social Security, showed sustained growth. These figures correspond directly to findings by Richard Kurin in 1984, who looked at scales of economic development in southern Illinois. This study found that, since 1960, all of the smaller southern Illinois towns have lost retail trade outlets, drugstores, physicians (general practitioners), elementary and secondary schools, farm supply stores, and restaurants, gas stations, and other services. Union County lost 20 percent of its businesses between 1960 and 1980.[11] Since the number of establishments was already declining by 1960, this represented the continuation of a trend that had begun considerably earlier.

In the 1970s the undermining of local private businesses was ameliorated by two trends. First, high-speed highways allowed people to travel farther to work, taking advantage of manufacturing and service jobs located in other areas, largely Cape Girardeau in Missouri and areas north of Union County in Illinois. It is not unusual for people to travel fifty to seventy-five miles to their jobs. The second factor, which I have dealt with here, has been the expansion of government investments and transfer payments, which multiply throughout the economy, supporting many of the services in the surrounding region. The money people receive through government redistributions, therefore, has contributed significantly to the stability of personal income derived from trade and services, as charted in figure 12.1.

Decline in the 1980s

When I began my fieldwork in 1982, I saw many signs of evident prosperity. After twenty years away from southern Illinois, I was struck by a number of visual features. There was little mud around the houses. Driveways were graveled or paved, concrete walkways led up to the doors, and virtually all farmhouses had broad, well-tended lawns. The houses were well kept and roomy. House trailers had replaced the tar-paper shacks that once dotted the hillsides. Although some trailers, particularly those that housed laborers in some orchards, were shabby, most appeared well kept. All the rural roads were either graveled or blacktopped, and most were in good repair. The towns' residential areas also looked relatively prosperous, although (with the exception of Anna) their downtown areas were gutted, with many boarded-up storefronts. The village of Alto Pass, in particular, was curiously open through the middle; the railroad that had brought the town into being was now out of business and the tracks had been removed. In the small towns, antique and junk shops replaced the once-busy stores, as if, no longer able to produce anything the nation wanted, people had only their history left to sell.

This superficial prosperity masked a growing economic crisis. The late 1970s and early 1980s were marked by spiraling inflation, as petrodollars flooded world financial markets. International lending agencies, including transnational banks, transgovernmental lending bodies like the World Bank and the International Monetary Fund, and individual governments through credits for purchase of specific commodities made massive loans to Third World countries. Much of this money was used for immediate consumption, including agricultural products. U.S. farmers therefore experienced an unprecedented market for their agricultural commodities.[12] With agricultural prices rising and banks eager to loan money, land prices spiraled upward. Although land prices were consistently higher than farmers' ability to cover mortgage payments out of current earnings, the expectation of continued inflation of commodity and land values made land purchases reasonable. At least that is what all agricultural economists told prospective buyers (see fig. 12.2).

By the late 1970s, the generation of young men who had fought in Vietnam and returned to farm were at the age when they should have been building up their estates. Most had gone to college on the GI bill and, even more than their parents, tended to follow the advice given by experts.

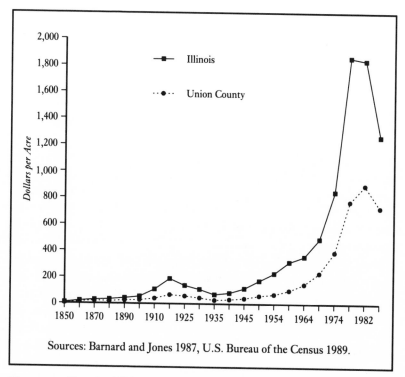

Figure 12.2. Farmland Value, Illinois and Union County, 1850–1987

Agricultural economists, like other business economists, promoted indebtedness as a virtue. While farmers had traditionally seen debt as a necessary evil, to be kept as low as possible and paid off as soon as possible, the "go-go" economics of the period after the oil embargo encouraged farmers to leverage their assets as much as possible. At the same time, double-digit inflation made double-digit interest rates cheap at the time loans were secured.[13]

These policies had particular impact in the Mississippi bottoms, where the flat, fertile land allowed farmers to specialize in row crops and use the largest, most labor-saving technologies. A number of younger farmers (and a few older ones) followed expert advice and expanded their landholdings and equipment through leveraging their inherited assets. Rising land values also brought more land on the market as some retiring farmers decided to sell rather than rent their land. In the hills, ex-urbanites were willing to pay higher prices for land to be used as residences than neighboring farms could afford for the same land to be put in crops. By the end of the 1970s, inflation had been spiraling upward for so long that even conservative farmers began to believe that if they wanted to buy land, they should do so.

In 1980 the bubble burst. Grain farmers were particularly stung by

President Carter's canceling of a grain deal with the Soviet Union, which led to a temporary market crash. However, the structural changes implemented by the next administration had more far-reaching effects. When Ronald Reagan was elected president, he instituted an array of fiscal and other policies that reined in inflation and enormously strengthened the U.S. dollar on international markets. First, he tightened the money supply, driving up the prime interest rate, which reached 20 percent in 1980. Suddenly the credit tap, which had been wide open, slowed to a trickle. In 1981 President Reagan pushed through a major tax cut that, in addition to providing a small amount of relief to individual taxpayers, drastically decreased taxes for corporations and for many wealthy individuals. At the same time, he raised military spending to a record high during peacetime. Since fewer tax dollars were available to finance this military buildup, the federal government borrowed billions of dollars by selling bonds bearing high interest rates. The United States government became the best investment in the world. Capital from all over the world flowed into this country as loans to the U.S. Treasury. The high demand for dollars to invest in U.S. bonds contributed to the soaring value of the dollar on world markets. The strong dollar meant that U.S. commodities cost more in foreign currencies. In addition to pricing American industrial and farm goods out of world markets, this helped push real interest rates ever higher, catching farmers in the worst cost-price squeeze in history.[14]

At the same time, Third World debt repayments precipitated fiscal crises in those countries. The International Monetary Fund required debt-ridden countries to implement strong austerity measures so that they would have the "hard currencies" to repay their loans. This had two results: first, these countries were unable to continue buying as many U.S. products as they had in the 1970s, and second, they increased their attempts to sell their own products, including agricultural commodities that directly compete with U.S. commodities, on world markets.[15]

The monetarist, "supply-side" fiscal and tax policies instituted by the Reagan administration and by Federal Reserve chairman Paul Volcker intersected with the inevitable business cycle to spark a recession in the early 1980s and a rash of factory closings in the northeastern United States—the "rust belt." The full effects of the farm crisis were felt somewhat later, as the rest of the economy recovered and real estate, high technology, and financial sectors entered a period of enormous expansion that masked underlying dislocations, such as those in agriculture and in the traditional manufacturing sectors.

In southern Illinois the structural aspects of the farm crisis were initially masked by several years of unusual weather. In 1983, for example, the first three months of the year were unusually dry and mild, but April, May, and June were exceptionally wet and cool, making it difficult to get crops in the ground. On July 4 the last significant rains fell, and the remainder of the summer was extremely hot and dry. The thermometer registered over 90°F for forty-six days in a row, with ten days over 100°. No significant rain fell until late September. In October and November, rains were far above normal, keeping farmers from harvesting those crops that survived the summer's drought and heat. Nineteen eighty-four was similar, with a cool, wet spring followed by a dry summer and an exceptionally wet autumn. The early spring rains caused the Mississippi River to rise, and although the levees held, water seeped behind them, submerging farmland that had not been under water since the flood of 1973. Flooding also drowned croplands in 1985. In addition to the disasters visited on grain farmers in the bottoms, winters in both 1981–82 and 1984–85 were unusually severe, wiping out the peach crops, and cold snaps in 1983 and 1984 sharply reduced the peach and apple crops.[16] It was as if the business cycle, government policy, and the weather had conspired to undermine the ability of southern Illinois farmers to stay in business.

Responding to the crisis, the FmHA made emergency loans to farmers who suffered crop losses or who lived in areas where agricultural credit became excessively tight. Barlett documents the excessive generosity of the FmHA, whereby the agency virtually forced more money on farmers than many wanted and tied these large loans to changes in their production practices.[17] These large emergency loans were virtually impossible to repay; in 1986 more than 75 percent of FmHA's total loan portfolio was nonperforming or delinquent, most of it concentrated in the emergency loan categories.[18] Some Union County farmers, particularly those in the bottoms who had suffered repeated flooding in the early 1980s, were forced into bankruptcy and/or out of business during this period.

The number of farms fell from 650 to 580 between 1982 and 1987, a decrease of approximately 11 percent. Since relatively few Union County farmers relied on farming for their primary occupation, it is probably more significant that the number of part-owners fell by 28 percent.[19] This reflects two phenomena. First, many landowners put their land into the Conservation Reserve Program and did not rent to farmers. Like the Kimbers, seventy-four Union County farmers placed land in the program; the average number of acres per farm was ninety-eight. The number of farmers who diverted their crops under the acreage adjustment program jumped from 30 in 1982 to 124 in 1987, idling an average of thirty-eight acres per farm.[20]

Second, as the number of farms decreased, the proportion of remaining farmers who supported themselves from farming declined, from 50 percent in 1982 to 47 percent in 1987. Total land in farms fell by more than 8,000 acres between 1982 and 1986, and harvested cropland fell by nearly

Table 12.1. Union County Farm Operators, by Age, 1987 and 1982

Year	<45		45–54		55–64		>64		Average Age
	N	(%)	N	(%)	N	(%)	N	(%)	
1987	163	(28.1)	151	(26.0)	123	(21.1)	143	(24.7)	53.6
1982	245	(36.6)	128	(19.1)	135	(20.2)	142	(21.2)	50.9

Source: U.S. Bureau of the Census, *1987 Census of Agriculture,* Table 10.

15,700 acres or 21 percent; only full tenants slightly increased acreage harvested.[21] The number of farmers who raised hogs fell by nearly half, from 108 to 61; the proportion selling dairy products fell by 42 percent. Only the proportion of farms raising cattle remained relatively constant, reflecting the low maintenance requirements of beef cattle, which makes them attractive to part-time as well as full-time farmers. They are, in addition, well adapted to the county's hilly terrain.

Few young people chose to enter farming, and farmers in their thirties appear to have been most liable to failure, as this was the age group that had incurred the heaviest debt loads. Whereas in 1982 nearly 37 percent of farmers were under forty-five, in 1987 only 28 percent were that young. The proportion in their middle years rose by nearly 7 percent, and those over sixty-five who still operated their own farms increased by 3.5 percent (see table 12.1).

These figures do not disclose the destruction to personal lives entailed in the farm crisis. During 1986 and 1987 I worked with a public interest group that dealt directly with the farm crisis. Like similar groups throughout the Midwest, it operated a hotline, served as advocate for individual farmers, and worked for farm policies that would permit medium-sized farmers to operate their land in a sustainable manner. The crisis was multigenerational and affected entire communities. Since the crisis was in many ways a debt crisis (even though many debt-free farmers also felt the pinch of falling commodity prices), many older farmers, forgetting that they had been helped by low-interest loans and a nearly constant appreciation of asset values, criticized heavily indebted younger farmers. While some farmers who faced financial ruin had been high-rollers and wheeler-dealers (qualities promoted by many lenders and experts), the majority were hard-working families whose worst management mistake, as Judith Heffernan observed, was to be born at the wrong time. Many parents had signed notes for their children to help them get started in farming, so when the children were unable to meet mortgage payments, the parents' farms were put at risk. In such circumstances the defaulting children generally felt enormous guilt, whether or not the parents accused them of inadequate performance. In other cases, where a number of heirs had shares in the estate, with one person farming and paying rent to the others, as receipts fell, nonfarming heirs sometimes felt shortchanged. I learned of a case in a more northern county in which a cousin-in-law accused the struggling farmer of misappropriation of assets as well as mismanagement and stirred up such sentiment against the farmer that their church was nearly split over the issue. The pressures on all farmers were so great that a woman in western Illinois reported that, only a few hours after her husband had a serious heart attack, a neighbor came to see if she would sell him her farm. "The neighbors picked the bones," she said bitterly. In Union County as elsewhere, divorce, heart attack, and demoralization resulted from the crisis.

By 1985 it was widely recognized that farm failures were the result of problems in the economic system, and not individual shortcomings. Debates concerning the direction of agriculture revolved specifically around different goals for national agricultural policy. The dominant voices, coming from the administration, from much of the media, and from most farm economists in land grant universities, argued that the United States needed fewer farmers and recommended programs that would continue to ease farmers out. A loose coalition of dissident farm groups such as the American Agricultural Movement, the National Farmers' Organization, and the Farmers Union; rural advocacy groups like the Illinois South Project, the Center for Rural Affairs, Prairie Fire, and the Minnesota Farm Unity Coalition; church groups like the Catholic Rural Life, peace and justice commissions of different denominations, and the National Council of Churches; and some environmental groups sought legislation that would keep large numbers of medium-sized farmers in business, encourage sustainable and conservation research and on-farm practices, discourage concentrations of land, and promote hunger-reducing programs in the United States and abroad. As in the 1950s, the combination of severe financial stress coincided with renewed concerns about soil erosion and degradation of water quality, resulting in long-term set-asides subsidized by the federal government. In the 1950s it was called the Soil Bank; in the 1980s, the Conservation Reserve Program. Additionally, the government instituted various debt-relief programs to help ameliorate individual debt problems (arguably because banks with large numbers of agricultural loans were experiencing high rates of failure, not because individual farmers were being bankrupted). By 1987 the overall debt/asset ratio, the figure that became the key index of the depth of the farm crisis, had begun to fall. This was not because the farm economy had recovered significantly—farm assets continued to decline in value—but because farm foreclosures and bankruptcies had begun to wring the debt out of the system. In Illinois, farm assets, which had reached their peak value in 1980 at $77,792 million, fell to $37,709 million in 1986, rebounding slightly the following year. Debt peaked in 1981 at $10,936 million and declined to $7,366 million by 1987. In 1985, the year the farm crisis hit the front pages of the newspapers, the overall debt/asset ratio for all Illinois farms stood at 21.8, up from 14.9 in 1981.[22] This was not because farmers were incurring more debt; rather, it reflected the drop in asset values, so that debt appeared as a larger proportion of total assets.

In ways that appear comparable to the 1920s, the agricultural depression of the 1980s seemed to foreshadow a more general, global economic crisis. Until 1992 Union County manufacturing was not directly affected by the flight of manufacturing to poor nations. In December 1992 two factories announced their closing. Lewis Brothers Bakery, founded in Anna in 1925, and Florsheim Shoes, established in 1931 by International Shoe Company, both closed their doors at the end of the year. The Florsheim plant, one of the few shoe factories that remained in the United States, closed with rumors that it was opening a factory in India. Its closing left more than 300 people out of work. The week after the announcement of the shoe factory's closing, the other major manufacturing plant in Anna, the Bunny Bread bakery owned by Lewis Brothers Bakery, Inc., announced it would close, throwing 125 people out of work.[23] That left only two substantial manufacturers in the county: Transcraft, which in 1980 had 190 employees, and Ensign-Bickford, Inc., manufacturer of explosives. This plant, operated by International Minerals and Chemical Corp., Trojan division, employed more than 100 people in the early 1980s but closed in 1982. It changed hands and reopened with a small crew. In 1988 EBCo. bought it and, by 1992, it employed 240 people.[24]

In 1993 the state of Illinois selected a site just south of the Union County line for a new super maximum security prison. Economic development committees mobilized to promote the region, and virtually everyone expressed elation that the area was selected, since it meant short-term construction jobs and long-term, relatively well-paid jobs at the prison and providing various support services. The other major economic development programs of the late 1980s and 1990s were tourism and riverboat gambling. Despite welcoming the jobs such services bring, many people expressed considerable discomfort at seeing an economy that had been based on agricultural and industrial production becoming dependent on prisons, gambling, and tourism.

As the federal government withdrew revenue sharing and scaled back other federal contributions to social investments and welfare, and as the region's economy sagged under the general decline in wages, the further automation of the coalfields and a decline in demand for coal, unemployment and poverty increased in southern Illinois as it did throughout the country, even as the general level of economic activity increased.

240   They Came Back Home

The erosion during the 1980s of manufacturing, farm, and direct government income indicated in figure 12.1 is reflected in increasingly high unemployment rates. Throughout the 1950s and 1960s, county unemployment rates averaged between 4.4 and 6 percent. In 1974 the unemployment rate was 6.7 percent; it rose steadily to 20.1 percent in the depths of the recession in 1983 and continued to average above 13 percent the rest of the decade.[25]

Poverty rates have long been relatively high, both in the region and in the county. In 1979 11.5 percent of families fell below the poverty level, and 16.3 percent fell below 125 percent of poverty. Nearly 40 percent (39.1) of Union County families had less than 200 percent of a poverty level income. Median family income was $15,740; the mean family income was $19,218. In 1990, a Voices for Illinois Children report showed that nearly one-fourth of Union County children lived in poverty, a figure that was comparable to other southern Illinois counties.[26]

The general ratcheting down of federal dollars available to the state and local governments placed most local governments in a state of continual crisis. All levels of government had to tighten their belts. Local school districts struggled to stay off the state's financial watch list by cutting programs, increasing class sizes, and resisting teacher union pressures to increase salaries; ambulance services persisted in part due to dedicated paramedical staff who worked for periods when paychecks did not arrive; rural health programs were cut, including loss of obstetric and pediatric care for a number of southern Illinois counties; and social support agencies had to fight for enough money to stay afloat. Meetings of local elected officials tended to be primarily concerned with making sure the governmental unit stayed within its shrinking budgetary guidelines, even as state and federal mandates sometimes seemed to make it impossible for them to meet all their obligations.

The decades following the end of World War II were a time of rising expectations that carried people through the difficult transition from an agricultural, rural-oriented to an industrial, urban-oriented social economy. In this new social economy citizens gave government increasing responsibility for maintaining the social fabric through regulation, investment, and redistribution. The post-Vietnam decades, in contrast, have been a time of shrinking expectations. It is difficult to see how long-poor rural regions, with their legacies of reliance on extractive industries, will fit into the post-Fordist regime of flexible accumulation in a globalized economy. There has been a profound shift in the world economy since the early 1970s, as financial markets have become fully internationalized. This has sharply reduced the power of national, state, and local governments and nationally based organizations like labor unions to regulate the economy. If labor unions demand good wages and benefits and safe working conditions, and if communities demand responsible environmental controls, manufacturers can easily move their plants to countries with cheap labor, no taxes for benefits, and weak environmental laws. Since at least the 1950s, with the development of the Area Redevelopment Administration, states and communities have competed fiercely with one another for industries, giving tax abatements and providing free sewage, water, roads, job training, and so forth. This process has now become international, and it is creating a structural crisis in all the "developed" industrial nations as investors move relatively low-skill manufacturing jobs and many financial transactions "off-shore."[27]

The Republican administrations of the 1980s were committed to cutting back the degree to which government invested, regulated, and redistributed wealth, and so they generally approved of and encouraged the worldwide transformation that began in the mid-1970s. It remains to be seen if government will significantly intervene to reestablish the modified welfare state created by the New Deal, or whether a new, global system will be required to bring a secure and relatively affluent standard of living to poor regions like southern Illinois.

When I say "the good old days," David
and one of our son-in-laws says,
"There wasn't anything good about
it." And I say, "There was too. People
thought more of each other, and if anyone needed anything, there was always
a dozen here."—Clara Elder

What Good Old Days?

The story I have told in this book has had two predominant
themes: the overall transformation of agriculture from a system of production that relied heavily on relationships with neighbors and kin to a
highly mechanized, individualized form of production; and the relationships among family members within the farm operation. Woven through
this story have been two other dimensions of rural life: the tension between profits and good land stewardship, and the changing role of government in daily life. Although changes that occurred in agricultural
production and in farm family organization are intimately connected—as
intimate as the family that forms the core of southern Illinois farming—
they have to some extent been subject to different historic processes.

Farmers have increasingly accepted an industrial model of organization. With it, capitalist principles of reckoning value increasingly undergird their decision-making processes. This industrial model fits relatively easily into the prior system of agricultural production that was oriented to commodity production and used greater or lesser amounts of wage labor. In contrast, nationally dominant norms for female behavior developed in a context of urban industrial development and prescribed for women a domain of private domesticity. This was directly contrary to farm women's historic role in agricultural production: although women generally had responsibility for the household, the pre–World War II farm household itself was fully engaged in processes of agricultural production. Farm women not only maintained the farm labor force, but they also raised agricultural commodities that provided most of the money for the household. They served not only as an extra "hand" during peak labor periods but, particularly on farms that specialized in orchards and market gardens, frequently managed the packing shed and other important parts of the operation. Poor farm women often joined their husbands and children as day laborers in the fields, as well as adding to the family's income by raising poultry or through other cottage industries. Given the way gender roles developed as farming became increasingly commercial, there appears to be no necessary connection between the development of industrial technologies and the development of privatized definitions of femininity. Despite their intimate connections, gender relations and economic relations are subject to different, although mutually influential, determinants. The two arenas of domestic life—farm and household—merge when seen in the context of the larger community. If the adoption of highly mechanized, chemical-dependent, profit-oriented forms of agricultural production did not necessarily force women out of farming, it is hard to imagine these technologies and goals coexisting with a strong network of reciprocal, nonmonetized neighborhood relationships.[1]

This book has tried to tell a story about the history of farm life in a poor rural region in such a way that various alternative paths into the future become imaginable. I discern at least one alternative path in this century that the combination of policy decisions by powerful economic and political entities and the cloudiness of local vision precluded: In the period of transition—the two decades from the New Deal through the mid-1950s—people in the area attempted to build strong community organizations to replace those that were becoming centralized and to bring technological improvements to farms while strengthening family cooperation. In many communities families tried to recast the rural schoolhouse, which had lost its function through consolidation, as a community center. They formed producer cooperatives to try to market their products in the face of growing market centralization. They developed community festivals, organized the Home Bureau, developed county public health departments and community medical clinics, joined in community development projects sponsored by the neighboring university, and assiduously boosted the area, trying to attract industries so that people who lost their jobs in agriculture due to mechanization could find other work locally. Alongside this community activism farm women and men sought off-farm work to supplement their increasingly inadequate income from farming. At the same time, Union County farmers worked hard to reclaim eroded and degraded farmland, making full use of government programs to build conservation structures like grass waterways and farm ponds.

During this period one can glimpse a vision of a rural society closer to that propounded in our agrarian past and most recently articulated by many New Deal activists: In this vision agriculture and industry are closely interconnected and small in scale. The institutions of government and community life are closely integrated with daily life and economic activities. Farmers act as stewards for the land over which they have temporary dominion. In Union County, women were important activists in trying to achieve such a transformation. Through the Home Bureau and other organizations they promoted such modernizing improvements as public health and the development of community centers. Many worked for school consolidation, seen as a way to improve educational levels, while others were equally active in trying to maintain rural schools in order to maintain the vitality of the rural communities in which they lived. Women worked with the men of their communities on community festivals. They sought off-farm work and intensified their home-based production in attempts to keep their farms afloat. They helped promote cooperatives and other agricultural improvements. Their names appeared increasingly in the public record, not only within their sex-segregated organizations but as board members and officers of civic and governmental organizations, although their influence was manifested more frequently in less formal venues.

At the same time many people who had worked as farm laborers also sought to retain an agrarian base, linked with neighbors and kin. A few bought farms when low-interest loans made it possible. Many others, like their farm-owning counterparts, found off-farm jobs in the area. These jobs became available as government spending and industry expanded. Farm workers also sought to participate in organizations that had previously been more exclusively the domain of the more affluent. For a brief period in the 1940s and 1950s some people were able to envision a process of economic development that would enable the people of southern Illinois communities to share the benefits of new technologies while simultaneously enriching the quality of community and family life and broadening the numbers of people who had access to democratic forms of government and civic participation.

A number of processes, however, undercut this possibility. Probably most important, the thrust of the national economy was toward increased centralization. Government policy toward agriculture had always been contradictory, holding up the icon of the family farm while simultaneously treating it as one industry among many. There are many reasons to believe that agriculture cannot function on the same economic logic as does industry. Its reliance on natural processes precludes significantly speeding up production time, and associated with this are high fixed capital costs. However, industrial models have prevailed at the level of policy. Policymakers have tended to see the replacement of labor by machinery and chemicals as an unqualified good that decreases the costs of food and fiber through increased efficiencies. The primary aim of most agricultural adjustment policies has been, therefore, to decrease the number of farmers and to ease the pain of those forced out. Further, government price supports are inevitably capitalized back into the price of land, and because landowning farmers can spread the cost of new acreage over the entire farm, they can pay more than landless farmers. This makes it difficult for young families to buy land unless social controls are put on the price and transfer of land, as is done in some western European countries. In the United States, however, governmental controls on the right to dispose of privately held property have been strenuously fought, particularly by farmers. Sonya Salamon's work demonstrates that those communities that circumvent the larger land market through strong family- and religious-based bonds have been better able to retain their integrity as communities than have those in which farmers are fully committed to an entrepreneurial ethic, but government regulation of land markets has never been part of American political discourse. Without such regulations, however, whether instituted through local community conventions or through direct government intervention, government interventions in other phases of the production process through price support programs will serve only as a short-term fix.

Farmers have generally held views as contradictory as those of policymakers. For the most part farmers after World War II, particularly larger growers as well as younger farmers who got a college education through the GI bill, accepted the siren call of technological development. Given the increased yields possible with new hybrid varieties, fertilizers, and conservation practices; the absence of any other model for increasing yields (such as those developed in the 1920s and being promoted now under the rubric of "sustainable agriculture"); and the declining market price of agricultural commodities, following expert advice appeared to be the only reasonable choice for people who wished to stay in farming. Once they were inside that system of production, however, the logic increasingly drove them to get bigger, increase capital investment, and specialize in a very few crops—processes that undercut their desire to retain a viable rural community, since it meant that fewer and fewer people could make a living from farming. While many farmers were slow and often reluctant to adopt the new technologies and while some found ways to modify the most individualizing tendencies of the new order, younger farmers who did not modernize failed.[2]

Simultaneously, some large processing firms began to invest in those areas of agricultural production that were least tied to natural, long-term production cycles. Vertical integration, a concept developed by big businesses in the 1950s, involved industrialized poultry production, both for eggs and for fryers. In later decades they extended this process to hogs and feeder cattle.[3] Additionally, as markets centralized, horticulture in southern Illinois, with its variable weather and vulnerability to plant diseases and infestations, was increasingly unable to compete with operations in California, Texas, and Florida, with their long growing seasons and irrigation agriculture. Gudeman and Rivera suggest that, in an economy in which capitalist relations of production and exchange predominate, only those producers who cannot make a profit will continue to exist outside these relationships—in what they term a "house" model of economy.[4] Once farmers committed themselves to national standards of production, those in geographically unfavored regions like the southern Illinois hills doomed themselves to relative poverty and failure, or to growing large enough to compete with more favorably located enterprises. Only a few "niche" crops, such as high-quality vegetables for the regional fresh vegetable market and high-quality breeding stock could remain relatively profitable for smaller-scale producers.

Such a commitment was not an individual one. As the Amish and the Hutterites (and, to a lesser extent, some of the ethnic communities studied by Salamon) demonstrate, farm families required a supportive community to allow alternative forms of production to survive.[5] The same processes that undermined small-scale, diversified farming undercut small-town businesses. Small-scale manufacturing could not compete with large-scale, and increasingly transnationalized, industries. The process that began in the nineteenth century with the replacement of home-manufactured cloth by eastern fabric mills appeared in the mid-twentieth century in the replacement of wood packing materials with cardboard from distant mills and in the late twentieth-century transfer of most industrial manufacturing, like the shoe and garment factories that moved to rural areas in the 1920s and 1930s, to Third World countries. Small-town merchants lost their role as bulking agents, transferring farm products to urban markets and reciprocally selling manufactured goods to farmers. Chain stores could offer wider selections for cheaper prices, and high-speed highways and all-weather rural roads made these more distant shopping centers accessible. The small towns of the area lost their economic center through the compounded processes of decreased population, loss of the manufacturing and marketing of agricultural products, and increased consumer mobility. Development committees were unable to attract industrial enterprises that would hire large numbers of displaced farmers. In the 1950s and 1960s, faced with local unemployment or poverty-level incomes from farming and as farm laborers, many families and young people left the area for jobs in the booming industrial areas in the North and West.

The previous social order also constrained people's imaginations, occluding locally generated alternatives.[6] Pre–World War II society in Union County was governed largely by a network of business, professional, and farming families. These families were often interrelated through marriage and, although not forming an "aristocracy," were conscious of their status and maintained it through membership in various more or less exclusive economic and civic organizations. The depression impoverished these families, and as the economy recovered after the war, many of their members, particularly the young, left the region. Even though many of the remaining families recovered their prosperity, they did not recover their prior influence, which was undermined by the proliferation of government agencies and centralized economic organizations. These new kinds of jobs provided vehicles for upward mobility for poorer people; the 1950s saw a general leveling of the county's class structure.

The social activism seen in the 1950s, in which women were often key players, grew out of complicated motivations: The elites saw their well-being identified with the well-being of the larger community, but their imagination was guided by their historical experience of governing, in which they were accorded power based in part on their ability to organize important dimensions of the economy. After the war they lost this ability, and with it much of the status that differentiated them from other elements of the society. We have seen how this transformation played out in the way the queen contest was organized in the Cobden Peach Festival. With no strong alternative models offered from outside the area, people were unable to imagine a fundamentally different way of organizing social life that might provide the desired affluence with a concomitant democratization of and widened participation in the economy and society.

Union Countians were unable to anticipate the consequences of their choice to generally, if conservatively, follow expert advice and dominant models of development. Nor were they able to anticipate the direction of industrial and commercial development in the larger society that would impoverish local businesses. As Al Basler, who farmed and worked most of his adult life in a grocery and feed store in town said, "After you see it, you knew you could see it coming."[7]

The other element of this story, women's roles, took a somewhat different course. Despite women's important participation in agricultural production, southern Illinois social life was quite strongly patriarchal, if not so strongly as in some other farming regions. In the early years of this century women, particularly farm women, held few public offices and rarely appeared in the public record. Some did serve on local school boards, and they were active in their churches and in the women's auxiliaries of the Masons and the International Order of Odd Fellows. These organizations, as well as family status, were bases for influence and provided the social networks through which women began to take on more public roles such as in the Home Bureau.

In the case of Union County women, national norms became far less locally hegemonic than had norms associated with agricultural production. Even as they accepted many of the modernizing conveniences and social standards, farm women maintained an active identity as household providers and workers. It is possible that women would have remained primary producers had agricultural experts (and lenders) recognized their traditional roles on the farm and not assumed that their "natural" role was that of consuming homemaker.

However, women's branches of agriculture, poultry and dairy, were among the first to be industrialized. With increasing capital requirements and decreasing access to increasingly regulated and centralized markets, women lost their ability to sell their cream, eggs, and poultry. Farm women had never been active in producer organizations like the Farm Bureau and its predecessors,[8] and they developed no organized response to their loss of livelihood. It is possible to imagine that, had the Home Bureau/Home Extension not developed from urban-based home economics/domestic science programs, they would have helped farm women organize as producers; but the land grant home extension programs were firmly wedded from their inception to the doctrine of separate spheres and lacked the conceptual tools with which to conceive of women as other than domestic workers. In addition, farm women lost their traditional sources of income at the same time that a powerful national movement idealized the "feminine mystique" of the privatized homemaker, denying any public visibility for women who earned income, either in the home or outside it. It is not surprising, therefore, that instead of organizing to create new ways of maintaining their role as farmers, farm women who were young enough to do so responded to their loss of livelihood, and to the precariousness of their farm's income, by finding off-farm jobs and/ or developing other home-based enterprises. At the same time, their role as "helper" to their husband increased.

This failure of imagination was due not only to the power of national norms and leadership but to contradictory tendencies within the lives of farm women. Women from the wealthier families, even though they had generally worked harder than their urban counterparts (who were often their sisters and cousins), believed women should behave as "ladies," and many had a strong commitment to their status within rural society—a status that was being eroded. They tended not to identify themselves with their work as much as did women in "middling" and poorer farm families. Since they formed much of the county and in some cases local leadership of women's organizations, they tended to reinforce the message of domesticity given by home economists and the national media, and to shape women's public participation in terms of women's nurturing roles in health, education, and social enrichment. Despite the fact that women's entry into the formal labor force had far-reaching repercussions on the organization of farm and community life, the decision to work off the farm was never cast as an issue of social importance but was left as a private matter for individuals and families. Not until the women's movement of the 1970s and 1980s did these personal issues become defined as political.

Under the triple processes of the adoption of modern technologies, the elimination of women's traditional agricultural production, and women's entry into the labor force, the rural home, as a site of family life, came to look very much like its urban counterpart in both appearance and function. Except for bookkeeping (in southern Illinois generally done by the husband), in many cases the farm home was as distantly related to the farm enterprise as an urban home was to the family's workplaces. There is some irony in experts' rediscovery of farm wives in the farm crisis of the 1980s. Many farm advisers have encouraged women to reintegrate their work with the farm, this time through the idiom of partnerships. Their prototypical role is to maintain the account books and handle some aspects of marketing and other records that have become increasingly complex and important parts of farm operations.[9] I have found few southern Illinois women who have assumed these jobs, although such partnerships appear to be increasingly common in the corn belt. Had women been viewed from the beginning as partners on the farm, and their labor valued as highly as their husbands', it is possible to imagine that a movement to retain diversified agriculture might have emerged and injected a new set of issues into farm policy debates. This issue was never raised, either in Union County or in the nation at large; while a great deal of controversy developed around the fate of small farms, half of the adult farming population was simply not visible on the agricultural agenda.

There appear to be particular periods when the common people, if they have sufficient vision and solidarity, might change the course of history. The period following the Civil War, when the institutions of corporate capitalism were established, appears to have been one such period. The period following World War II, when New Deal programs provided a basis for democratizing community life, appears to have been another. In both cases, the trend to centralization and bureaucratization won out over popular alternatives, in part because these forms of organization seemed to offer greater material prosperity and personal security than any perceived alternative.[10] We may now, at the end of the twentieth century, be in another such period. The globalized economy, the environmental crisis, and, in the United States, a general decline in living standards, indicate that we are now in another period when the bases for organizing social life are in flux.

People's attempts to model the future on their remembered past—remembered as a set of practices as much as consciously articulated ideas and prescriptions—can be seen as an undertow to the forward current of "progress." It has often been perceived this way by modernizers: extension adviser Bierbaum often commented on farmers' "conservatism" that made them resist new ways of doing things. This way of understanding many people's reactions to expert advice must, however, be seen as a more or less reasoned response to a contested future, not as a stubborn or ignorant resistance to a natural process. Although progress often appears in popular representations as inevitable—"You can't stand in the way of Progress"—it becomes conflated with the accurate observation that change is inherent in the ordering of the universe. Progress, unlike change, is directional and implies the working out of a project, a complex goal. Union Countians did not resist change: the historical record shows that people actively positioned themselves in relation to changes they experienced and that they tried, with the material, cultural, and individual tools at hand, to fashion satisfying lives. They did not, however, necessarily agree with the direction that changes were taking. The history I have learned shows that people, as individuals, families, and groups, intervened to shape those changes in ways that better suited their (generally inchoate and inarticulate) projects. If people were unable to create alternatives that would have led to a more satisfying future—that would decrease the intense nostalgia so many feel—it is because of at least three factors. The first is a lack of vision concerning the future: the area's culture does not provide intellectual tools with which to clarify ideals and dreams of what the future could look like. Second, there are few public arenas in which people can discuss their visions and ways to implement them. Newspapers, which in the nineteenth century were often filled with political debate, in the twentieth century only marginally provide a venue for such dialogue. Churches and political parties, the two other major institutions through which people come together, only rarely promote such discussions. Third, southern Illinois is marginalized within the national society. The progress people experience is the result of policy decisions in centers of power far removed from—and not concerned with—this area. Without a powerful counterideology, such as that which binds religious groups like the Amish and the Hutterites, or a powerful organization such as the United Mine Workers provided for the miners to the north of the county, the diversity that necessarily comprises an open region like southern Illinois renders the desires of its residents relatively invisible.

As I have spoken with many people over the past decade, researching this book, teaching, and working politically for change, I have heard a number of themes that should inform us as we move into the future: Everyone old enough to remember "the old days" would not go back. Everyone recalls the great disparities in wealth and poverty; the drudgery of most people's lives, and the misery that often accompanied poverty. They recall the daily inconveniences of mud roads, the absence of good medical care, and the whippings through which children's work was coerced. Some women recall the way men drove "their" women, and men's stinginess regarding investments in the household and family. People I spoke with welcomed the arrival of electricity and the many conveniences it made possible. They are glad Social Security, pensions, Medicare, and home health care make it possible for people to retire and live comfortably; they like to travel. Living in small towns and rural areas, most people who have relatively secure jobs or retirement incomes feel comfortable in their communities, like knowing many of the people they meet daily, and enjoy the scenery that surrounds them.

At the same time, however, most people feel a profound unease about our present time. They miss the closeness that came from relying on neighbors and kin, from singing and dancing together. Over and over people commented that they did not know their neighbors, something that would have been unthinkable a half-century ago. They fear for their children, too many of whom die from drinking and driving, get pregnant (or get their girlfriend pregnant) while still in school, and are as tempted as any children anywhere by drugs. They grieve that their children must leave the area to find a good job. They generally dislike the traffic and congestion of our cities and fear urban crime. Like most white Americans, they hold contradictory sentiments about race, and the Mexican migrants who pick the fruits and vegetables feel the sting of discrimination. Many people I spoke with are fearful of the chemicals on which they rely to farm and are anxious about the environment, despite the fact that southern Illinois, unlike much of the rest of the country, has regenerated, thanks to the national forest and the idling of much of its farmland. They are ambivalent about U.S. relations with the rest of the world, sharing the nation's unease with "the new world order."

Many people work hard to sustain community organizations, holding down full-time jobs and then volunteering in their churches, civic organizations, and other forms of community service. Even in this rural area, which to city dwellers seems slow paced, people who try to maintain some degree of community involvement feel overworked, that the pace of life is too fast to handle easily. Although people generally grant others authority over them in the realm of work, they subscribe to an ethic of equality and of mutual respect. They remain ambivalent about "expertise," although most people I have spoken with seem willing to grant experts far more authority than would have been common a generation or two ago. They generally believe in hard work but think that the larger society must make it possible for people to find jobs. This has been an area that has voted Democratic since before the Civil War and from which many progressive congressmen—and with the election of Carol Moseley Braun to the Senate in 1992, congresswoman—have been elected.

These values and sentiments do not easily translate into a program for change. Nonetheless, they point in the direction of some commonalities. This book is not intended to present a program for the next century; rather, through a retrospective look at this century, through telling a particular story, I hope to help frame and shape programs we may invent. I hope to inform our imaginations so that we can envision a society that allows us to re-create the best attributes of our past while retaining the best attributes of the present and remaining flexible for future transformations.

Preface

1. Social scientists, especially anthropologists and those associated with "cultural studies," have made the issue of the relationship between analyst and object of analysis a central problem of how we create social knowledge. See, for example, Clifford 1988; Haraway 1988; Harrison 1991; Hartsock 1987, 1989–90; Kirschner 1987; M. Rosaldo 1980; R. Rosaldo 1989. On the problem of how a scholar situates herself in relation to a community with which she identifies, see P. H. Collins 1990.

2. Adams 1986, 1992a, 1992b.

3. Adams 1987a, 1987b, 1988, 1991–92, 1993, 1994.

4. Adams 1990, Adams with Travelstead 1987.

5. Adams 1988.

6. Woodbury is southeast of Nashville, near Murfreesboro. It is the county seat of Cannon County.

7. For a comprehensive bibliography, see Hoshiko 1983. For memoirs, see Caraway 1986; Harris [1991]; Kennedy 1910; Adams, ed., 1995; R. Rendleman [1959]; N. M. Taylor 1975. For atlases, see Bauman 1899, Griffing 1881, Ogle 1908, Warner and Beers 1876.

Chapter 1

1. See Fink 1986.

2. Bourdieu 1977.

3. I gave this exercise as part of a final exam in Anthropology 400D, Anthropology Theory and Method, spring 1992. Kohl (1988) studied how women's roles were reconstructed in locally written histories in the Great Plains region.

4. Telling history is in part necessarily mythmaking; a personal history is the mythic narrative of one's life, an explanation of how one arrived at the present. In religion, origins—eschatological events—provide the energy that gives coherence to all subsequent events. Through continual reenactment, as in Passover or the Mass or the continual dramatic retelling of the events of the Gods at the beginning of time, people tap into that energy and use it to revitalize and orient the present. Perhaps because childhood is an individual's beginning time, it has the same significance in personal history. This is when "the twig is bent," creating the form for all future development, and so the events of this period are most keenly recalled and recollected to make one's life meaningful. Perhaps this is an element of nostalgia: The rapid pace of change has created ruptures between those childhood experiences and the present; attempts to reconnect with that past time as a living presence fail, leaving only the mask of sentiment, a veil between one's present and past lives.

5. Accounts of the Rhodes, Cerny, Weaver, Sirles, and Rendleman farms appeared in the "Today" section (p. 1) of the *Southern Illinoisan*, May 23, June 6, May 9, June 13, and May 30, 1984, respectively. The Walton and Kimber farms have been analyzed at greater length in Adams et al. 1990. Data on these farms came from interviews and family-held documents as well as the Union County Census of Population and Census

of Agriculture manuscript schedules, 1860, 1870, and 1880; genealogists' compilations, including Dexter [1987], Doty n.d., Hunsaker and Haws 1957, Webb 1983; other documents, including Boatman 1966, Clear Creek Baptist Association 1988, Cobden Historical Committee [1955], Condon 1987 [1871], DuBois 1927, Eller 1987, Illinois Central Railroad 1867, Karraker 1947, McMahan 1988, Miller 1976, Parks 1983, Perrin 1883, E. Rendleman n.d., F. L. Rendleman 1973, Rowe 1940, G. W. Smith 1912, Smoot and Rife 1980, Venerable 1974; atlases, including Griffing 1881, Ogle 1908, and Warner and Beers 1876; and plat books and aerial photographs.

6. Interviews used in this reconstruction include Lingle 1984, G. Weaver 1984, R. Weaver 1984.

7. "Lyerla" is spelled in a wide variety of ways: nineteenth-century and early twentieth-century spellings include Leyerele, Leyerle, Leyerley, Leyerlie, Leyerly, Leyrle, Leyrley, Lyerle, Lyerley, Lyerlie, and Lyerly. The 1994 Union County area telephone book has only Lyerla, while the Salisbury, N.C., area telephone book lists only Lyerly.

8. Gottfried and Jennings 1988:190–91.

9. Interviews used in this reconstruction include Basler 1984; Cerny 1976, 1984.

10. Other standing houses include log structures that may be even older. Geraldine Stadelbacher recalled that a neighbor told of an oral tradition concerning an Indian who came through and "stood in the doorway" of the log section of the house she moved into in the early 1910s. The log house may well go back to the 1830s, when Indian people still hunted throughout the area.

11. Interviews used in this reconstruction include M. Kinder 1984; Rhodes 1984a, 1984b, 1984c.

12. Some Union Countians migrated to Nebraska. In 1894 W. T. Rhodes's fiance, Fannie Simpson, and a friend, Ollie Davis, visited W. T.'s relative (sister?) Clara Rhodes Whitacre in Kearney. See Jonesboro *Gazette*, September 25, 1894, "Mountain Glen News." See also ibid., November 17, 1894.

13. Interviews used for this reconstruction include E. Rendleman 1984a, 1984b.

14. Union County Clerk's Office, Union County Corporate Records, Book 1, pp. 17–21, 186–88; Perrin 1883:311.

15. Interviews used in this reconstruction include Sirles and Sirles 1984. Edith Rendleman's husband's family and Ren Sirles's family are distantly related: Robert Rendleman's father was Jacob; John Rendleman's father was Henry; Henry and Jacob were brothers. Therefore, the father of William, Edith's husband, and the father of Helen, Ren's mother, were cousins.

16. Interviews used for this reconstruction include Brimm 1990a, 1990b; Hill 1990; Throgmorton 1990; Walton 1990; Wilson and Cash 1990.

17. Perrin (1883:B89–90) gives a biographical sketch of J. K. Walton. Perrin (1883:292–94) gives a biographical sketch of Willis Willard (brother to Anna) and the Willard family and on pp. B90–91 gives sketches of the Willard family and of Charles M. and Walter H. Willard.

18. Ibid., p. B90.

19. The Jonesboro *Gazette* covered the development and demise of this creamery: see March 13, April 30, May 7, July 2, July 16, 1887; March 23, 1889. See also Union County Clerk's Office, Union County Corporate Records, Book 1, pp. 159–63.

20. Interviews used to help reconstruct this history include Davidson 1990, Eddleman 1990, H. Kimber 1990, R. Kimber 1990, Smith and Smith 1990, Taylor 1990.

21. The Kimber operation was featured in the Illinois Rural Electrification *Bulletin*, vol. 7, no. 10, October 1942.

Chapter 2

1. Ben Smith (b. September 27, 1887), called Union County's Bobby Burns by Russell Lord (1937), was a foreman at a strawberry farm west of Jonesboro. He wrote a column in the weekly Jonesboro *Gazette*, and his poems were published in the farm press.

2. See Wolf 1982.

3. "Egypt" apparently was applied as an epithet by Yankees, despite a number of less invidious reasons that have been given for the name. The Cairo *Weekly Times* (January 9, 1856) picked up an item from the *Democratic Press*:

> Particularly were new facts brought to light [since the building of the Central Railroad] respecting the middle and southern portion of the State which hitherto had been as a sealed book to immigrants seeking a western home by way of the Lake and other northern routes. Yankee enterprise had but rarely planted itself in this portion of the State. It was ignominiously designated "Egypt," and but very few from the Northern and Eastern States could be induced to explore the country and judge from personal inspection of the truth or falsity of the current statements respecting it. The day of this humiliation has passed forever from Southern Illinois. It continues to be styled "Egypt," indeed, but the designation is no longer a reproach. The name has become honorable—suggestive of fruitfulness and plenty.

Bonnell (Saline County Historical Society 1947:15) dates the name to 1821, while Brush (1944:73) attributes it to people in northern Illinois "going down to Egypt" for seed grain after they lost their crops to frost in 1833. Others note the early Egyptian references, especially the settlement in the American Bottom named Goshen (hence the Goshen Road, laid out in 1808 from the salines near Shawneetown on the Ohio to the Goshen Settlement [Saline County Historical Society 1947:228]) and the naming of Cairo at the confluence of the Ohio and Mississippi Rivers in 1818. Some early travelers were struck by the similarities between the Egyptian Nile and the Mississippi, with the massive pyramids in the American Bottom and St. Louis area, and the annual rise and fall of the river (e.g., Flagg 1838: 1:131, 161–62; 2:215).

4. The geographic description given here is provided in greater detail in Adams 1987b. See also Canouts et al. 1984; Hall 1940; Harris et al. 1977; Lopinot 1984; McNerney 1978; Prigge 1973; University of Illinois, College of Agriculture 1967; U.S. Department of Agriculture, Soil Conservation Service 1979; and Voigt and Mohlenbrock 1964. Perrin 1883 and Warner and Beers 1876 give hopeful accounts of the mineral potential nineteenth-century boosters saw in the county. Archaeological accounts of the prehistory of the area include Bauxar 1978, Canouts et al. 1984, Fowler and Hall 1978, Speilbauer 1976, and McNerney 1978.

5. May 1984:71.

6. See Ackernecht 1945, Rawlings 1927.

7. The origin of the town's name is unclear. The Baptist minister who joined with the Dunkard minister in a union camp meeting that gave the county its name was reputed to have been named Jones, but Parks (1983:123) believes that the Jones for whom the town was named was a physician who lived for a time in the county and then moved northward.

8. Perrin 1883:419, Illinois State Archives original land entries.

9. Perrin 1883:234–35.

10. Warner and Beers 1876:205.

11. Perrin 1883:230–31.

12. Lentz 1927:103, Layer 1965, Southern Five Regional Planning and Development Commission [1982].

13. Adams, ed., 1995: chap. 10.

14. Thomas interview, 1982b:7.

15. For background on the settling of Illinois, see Boggess 1908, Buck 1917, Clayton 1970, Newton 1974, Otto and Anderson 1982, Power 1953, Price 1969, Rohrbough 1978.

16. A pamphlet published by the Illinois Secretary of State's office, "Origin and Evolution of Illinois Counties" (1993), attributes the county's name to the federal union of the American states (p. 63), but Perrin (1883:286–87) gives a more persuasive account, describing the county seal adopted in 1850 that depicts two men, one representing George Wolf and the other a Baptist minister named Jones, who held a joint, or union, meeting in the southeastern portion of the county. This explanation of the county's name is given in Clayton 1970:34.

17. For the history of George Wolf, see Eller 1987; for the history of the Clear Creek Baptist Association, see Dexter 1993, Eller 1987, McMahan 1988; for the history of the Lutherans, see Boatman 1966, E. D. Elbert 1985.

18. On the African American community, see Perrin 1883:428. The Census of Population listed 26 free blacks in Union County. In Illinois, the 1840 census listed 331 slaves; there were 747 in 1830 and 917 in 1820. Slavery was not finally eliminated (at least as enumerated in the census) until 1850. In 1824 there were 24 slaves enumerated in Union County and only 17 free blacks.

19. This was part of the same migration that settled much of the mid-Mississippi Valley, but the Union County Germans, despite supporting a parochial school in Cobden until the 1950s, remained a minority community, unlike in many areas closer to St. Louis. See, e.g., Coggeshall 1984. See also Salamon 1992 for an in-depth study of German farming communities in the black and gray prairie regions of Illinois.

20. For details of these developments, see Perrin 1883:361. Parks (1983:129) says that Union Lodge #10 was chartered in 1822 and rechartered in 1824.

21. Perrin 1883:326.

22. Jonesboro *Gazette*, May 26, 1894. An item concerning a late spring freeze in 1849 observed, "Most of the fruits grown then were chiefly for the juice they contained and the various stillhouses on the spring branches were given a rest that year."

23. This use of the term *Yankee* is somewhat different from that used by Salamon (1992): She uses the term as a gloss for contemporary farmers of old American stock, which would include Scots-Irish and Germans who settled the southern backcountry in the eighteenth century, as well as the English who settled New England. However, since the old Americans who settled central Illinois, where her study was done, largely

came from the Northeast and not the Upland South, empirically we are speaking about the same people. See Kofoid 1906.

24. Cole 1919:14.

25. On the naming of Cobden, see DuBois 1927.

26. Carbondale's founder, Daniel Brush, was instrumental in founding Carbondale College, with Presbyterian sponsorship, in 1856. Based on the existence of this school (renamed Southern Illinois College, sponsored by the Christian denomination in 1866) and added financial commitments by the town and the county, the town bid for and was selected as the site of Southern Illinois Normal University in 1869. The school actually began classes in 1874 and in 1943 achieved university status, changing its name to Southern Illinois University in 1947. For histories of Southern Illinois University at Carbondale, see Brush 1944, Lentz 1955, Plochman [1957]; also see Illinois Sesquicentennial Commission 1969:101–3.

27. For a more detailed account of these railroads, see Adams 1987b:63–66. Gates 1934 gives the most complete account of the building of the Illinois Central Railroad. A more local (and less reliable) perspective is given in Perrin 1883 and Lansden 1976 [1910]. On creating settled society in frontier communities in Illinois, see D. H. Doyle 1978, Faragher 1986. See also Kulikoff 1989 for a review of the debate concerning the "transition to capitalism" in rural America, and Laurie 1989 on the transformation of artisans into industrial workers.

28. Casper interview, 1975:19.

29. See Carter 1983a, 1983b; Kennedy 1910; Simon 1969. See also Gray 1942, Klement 1960.

30. These changes are detailed in Adams 1992a, Adams 1992b.

Chapter 3

1. Norris interview, 1976:29.

2. Gurley interview, 1975:8.

3. Ibid.

4. When my parents bought our farm in Jackson County in 1941, neighbors located the remains of a still that had operated at a year-round spring on the farm. Charles Thomas recalled stumbling across a still when he and a friend were exploring the woods east of Cobden, and in Parks [1980] (p. 127) Thomas tells about a still the Rich family operated in the nineteenth century.

5. Proponents of a fencing law had been trying since 1872 to require fencing livestock. This was an issue that pitted small against large farmers and poor subsistence against affluent commercial farmers (Adams 1992b, Hahn 1983, Kirby 1987).

6. As late as the 1880s a few women submitted homespun and woven yardage to the county fair. See Debbie Tayes, database on Union County Fair prizes; Jonesboro *Gazette*.

7. For details of these drainage districts, see record books on the Clear Creek Drainage District (organized 1908) and Preston Drainage District (organized 1912), Union County Circuit Clerk's Office.

8. See, e.g., Nobles 1988, Dorst 1991.

9. See, e.g., Danbom 1979, esp. pp. 24–31; Berry 1977. The "pastoral ideal" is a

deeply rooted part of our culture, stemming from a profound ambivalence regarding industrialization. See, e.g., L. Marx 1964.

10. See, e.g., E. M. Matthews 1965, Stephenson 1968. On changing family structure, see Hareven 1976, 1990; on the importance of kin networks, see Stack 1974.

11. This is equally true of the interviews done in 1976 by students at Shawnee Community College. Their interviews were even more open-ended than mine were, and a number were done by close relatives of those being interviewed; yet few recollections of religious and political life were generated.

12. Casper interview, 1975:32.

13. Boatman 1966:8, Dexter 1993.

14. Adams, ed., 1995: chap. 7. See also Jonesboro *Gazette*, April 2, 1925.

15. Thompson interview, 1976:27.

16. Elder and Elder interview 1983:17.

17. Adams, ed., 1995: chap. 1.

18. Ibid., chap. 7.

19. See Mauss 1954; also Chayanov 1966.

20. Basler interview, 1984:1.

21. Rhodes interview, 1984c:28.

22. An earlier version of this account appeared in *Monday's Pub*, May 21, 1984, p. 8. The account comes from interviews with Ruby Weaver (1984:18–19), Bill Rhodes (1984c:28–31), and Edith Rendleman (1984b:13).

23. This account first appeared in *Monday's Pub*, May 14, 1984, p. 3. It appears here slightly edited. Sources for this account include Lingle interview, 1984:24–25; R. Weaver interview, 1984:16–17; Adams, ed., 1995: chap. 4; telephone conversation with Oscar "Dutch" Lingle, April 6, 1984.

24. Adams, ed., 1995: chap. 7. On funerals, see chap. 3; weddings, chap. 8.

25. Basler interview, 1984:14–17.

26. M. Kinder interview, 1984:19.

27. Sirles and Sirles interview, 1984:20.

28. Stadelbacher interview, 1983:13, 4.

29. Norris interview, 1976:7.

30. Rhodes interview, 1984c:8, 9.

31. On county fairs, see Illinois State Agricultural Society 1858, Neely 1967 [1935].

Chapter 4

1. Aldridge interview, 1976:18–19.

2. M. S. Smith 1980:10, 15, 32, 54. It is important to stress that these represent labor requirements utilizing "state-of-the-art" technologies; these technologies were generally slow to be widely adopted by farmers in general (see, e.g., R. V. Scott 1970, Cochrane 1979).

3. Herbst 1976:4–5. See also Mann and Dickinson 1978 and Pfeffer 1983, who refer to this lumpiness as a disjuncture between production and labor time. This makes technologies relatively expensive, since they are used during a rather short period of time each year. The issue has been hotly debated regarding whether or not, in a predominantly capitalist economy, agriculture will show the same development processes as manufacturing. See, e.g., Banaji 1980, Chayanov 1966, Lehman 1986, and Mann and Dickinson 1978 for three different answers to this question.

4. Eric Wolf (1957) has shown how the members of "closed corporate communities" in Latin America during the colonial period came to serve the same function as haciendas increased the production of agricultural commodities.

5. Jonesboro *Gazette*, November 24, 1866.

6. Al Basler (interview, 1984:19) described the onset of a rhubarb blight that virtually ended commercial rhubarb production:

> We had a pretty patch out there, a couple of acres . . . by the hot bed. And some kind of disease got into that rhubarb. . . . We'd go down over the hill and look at that rhubarb patch, and [it] looked like it was standing up all right in the morning; and maybe at noon when we come up here, it would be a spot out there where six or eight hills were just wilted down. . . . We never did find anything that we thought was killing that rhubarb. Just a disease. Pretty near everybody had rhubarb.

Dating Basler's account from his birth in 1901, the blight probably occurred around 1915–16: "I was just big enough that I hated to see it go there. That was where we made our spring money. Fourteen or fifteen years old, I guess."

7. Thompson interview, 1976:7.

8. Aldridge interview, 1976:23.

9. Austin Halterman's family grew Madonna lilies (Halterman and Halterman interview, 1983:39). Arilla Spiller raised forty acres of daffodils; she sometimes bought flowers from neighboring women and packed them with hers. Her brother also had forty acres of daffodils, as did a woman near Dongola (Spiller interview, 1983). Old fields of daffodils still exist.

10. See, e.g., Jonesboro *Gazette*, June 16, 1888; November 29, December 20, 1890.

11. Hindman interview, 1975:8.

12. A handwritten note in the *History of Cobden* (Cobden Historical Committee [1955]:14) says that in 1866 Parker Earle invented refrigerator boxes to keep strawberries cool, and people recount that this box is in the Illinois Central Railroad museum. Perrin (1883:345) reports that refrigerator cars were used for the first time in 1880 and that cooling houses were built in Cobden and Anna in 1881, with similar houses being built in 1883 at other shipping points.

13. Hindman interview, 1975:6–7.

14. B. Hunsaker interview, 1983a:5.

15. Floyd Karraker interview, 1983:31; see also the interview with Cecil Norris (1976:26).

16. Aldridge interview, 1976:13–14.

17. Rhodes interview, 1984c:11.

18. Rendleman interview, 1984b:8.

19. Sirles and Sirles interview, 1984:15.

20. Anna Centennial Committee 1954:267.

21. See, e.g., Cochrane 1979, U.S. Department of Agriculture 1940, Schertz et al. 1979.

22. See, e.g., Danbom 1979, Hayter 1968, R. V. Scott 1970.

23. Jonesboro *Gazette*, December 8, 1866, "Walk and Talk on the Farm."

24. For more on this period, see Adams 1992b.

25. On the agrarian movements, see Adams 1986, 1992b; Perrin 1883:142.

26. On the farmers' union, see Smoot and Rife 1980:50, Hunsaker interview,

1983:29–30. For histories of the Farm Bureau and agricultural extension, see Kile 1948, True 1928; on the Farmers' Mutual Benefit Association, see R. V. Scott 1958, 1962.

27. Harriet Friedmann (1978) showed that, in the wheat-growing Great Plains, "extra" sons provided the needed supplementary labor for area farms. While this was true in Union County, labor demands were heavier and called into being a discrete class of agricultural laborers.

28. Cochrane 1979:108–9.

29. Ibid., p. 109–10.

Chapter 5

1. For studies of these regions, see Osterud 1991; Fink 1986, 1992; Kohl 1976; Barlett 1993; Bennett and Kohl 1982.

2. Those who correlate different gender roles with commodities raised and farm structure include Buttel and Gillespie 1984, Coughenour and Swanson 1983, Tigges and Rosenfeld 1987. See also Sachs 1983:29–34, Bokemeier and Garkovich 1987, regarding research on decision making in farm households.

3. See Salamon 1992, esp. chap. 5, for an elegant discussion of the debates in the literature regarding women's relative roles on American farms. See also Salamon 1987, 1985, 1980; Salamon and Davis-Brown 1988, Salamon and O'Reilly 1979.

4. See Barlett 1993: chap. 6.

5. Faragher 1986:101.

6. Invisible Green 1857.

7. Rich 1993:144.

8. Ronald Rich's analysis of a 10 percent sample of nineteenth-century Union County estate inventories recorded in the Union County Court House shows that stoves were rarely present before the 1850s; by the 1860s 85 percent of the estates inventoried had stoves (Rich, personal communication).

9. A large, prescriptive literature testifies to the increasing definition of middle-class (i.e., "respectable") women as consumers. See, for example, Balderston 1936, Beecher 1970 [1841], Beecher and Stowe 1975 [1869], Bevier 1907, Bevier and Usher 1906, Bruere and Bruere 1912, Frederick 1919, Gilbreth 1927, Parloa 1910 [1898], Pattison 1915, Reid 1934, Richards 1908. Despite these prescriptions, many middle-class women found ways to earn income within the domestic sphere by taking in boarders and by developing home-based enterprises. They also, along with poorer women, entered wage labor markets (see Tilly and Scott 1987 [1978] concerning France and England, Matthaei 1982 and Ryan 1981 on the United States). On farm women's roles, see the collections edited by Groneman and Norton (1987) and Haney and Knowles (1988). See also Adams 1988, 1993; Bennett and Kohl 1982; Bush 1982, 1987; Fink 1986, 1992; Friedberger 1988; Jellison 1993; Jensen 1986, 1980; Jensen and Osterud 1993; Joyce 1983; Keating and Munro 1988; Lerner 1969; Osterud 1987; Rosenfeld 1985; Sachs 1983. On the history of women's work roles in the United States in general, see Bloch 1978; Cott 1977; Cowan 1983, 1974; Degler 1980; Friedan 1963; Matthaei 1982; G. Matthews 1987; Sklar 1973; Strasser 1982; Welter 1966; G. Wright 1981; Zaretsky 1986. For discussions on petty commodity production, see Collins 1990; Friedmann 1978, 1980; Goodman and Redclift 1981. The interested

reader can find the citations to the debate around conceptualizing petty commodity production, largely in the *Journal of Peasant Studies*, in the late 1970s and early 1980s, in these works.

10. On dried apples, see, e.g., Jonesboro *Gazette*, September 24, 1870; September 4, 1875. An advertisement in a 1927 booster publication (Lentz 1927:106) illustrates the Allen Tamale Machine, with the message, "This Company pays the farmers of Southern Illinois $20,000 annually for corn shucks. Wholesalers and Retailers of Hot Tamales, Tamale Machines and Corn Shucks. The largest industry of its kind in the world and still growing. . . . Jonesboro, Illinois."

11. Sirles and Sirles interview, 1984:21.

12. M. Kinder interview, 1984:12.

13. Hill interview, 1990:36.

14. R. Weaver interview, 1984:4.

15. Rendleman interview, 1984b:6.

16. M. Kinder interview, 1984:13–14.

17. Rhodes interview, 1984c:18.

18. Thompson interview, 1976:7.

19. On dairies, see Perrin 1883:169–70, Anna Centennial Committee 1954:382–83. The Walton farm, which we documented in 1990, operated a commercial dairy from around 1890 until the 1950s. Resident laborers did most of the work, the men feeding and milking the cows, the women washing the equipment and separating and bottling the milk.

20. Deborah Fink's (1986) study of poultry in Iowa is the most complete and detailed analysis available and is largely applicable to southern Illinois. She comments (p. 136) on the pejorative symbolic meanings attached to chickens that marked raising them as inappropriate for men. However, a number of men I interviewed recalled that they or a male relative tried raising chickens, in no case successfully.

21. Aldridge interview, 1976:4.

22. Rendleman interview, 1984b:16–17, 31.

23. Throgmorton interview, 1990:23, 25.

24. Aldridge interview, 1976:2–3.

25. Reid 1934:82.

26. Aldridge interview, 1976:2; Gurley interview, 1975:7.

27. M. Kinder interview, 1984:2–3.

28. Ibid., p. 18. Before the development of gas and electric irons, heavy irons made of cast iron were heated on the stove. Sad irons generally had a detachable handle and weighed from five to nine pounds (see Israel 1968:100).

29. Casper interview, 1975:4.

30. The Smithsonian Institution mounted an exhibit of these sacks. See Lu Ann Jones, "From Feedbags to Fashion" (paper presented at Symposium on Rural/Farm Women in Historical Perspective, the Fourth Conference of Rural/Farm Women in Agriculture, University of California, Davis, June 26–28, 1992).

31. Rendleman interview, 1984b:15.

32. Cerny interview, 1984:29.

33. M. Kinder interview, 1984:27.

34. Gurley interview, 1975:19.

35. H. Kimber interview, 1990:19.

36. Cerny interview, 1984:12.

37. R. Weaver interview, 1984:2–3.

38. Thomas interview, 1982a:13–14.

39. M. Kinder interview, 1984:17.

40. Sirles and Sirles interview, 1984:16.

41. M. Kinder interview, 1984:2.

42. Rendleman interview, 1984b:7.

43. Basler interview, 1984:1.

44. See, e.g., Cerny interview, 1976:14; Rhodes interview, 1984c:31; Aldridge interview, 1976:8.

45. M. Kinder interview, 1984:21.

46. R. Weaver interview, 1984:16.

47. H. Kimber interview, 1990:19.

48. M. Kinder interview, 1984:12.

49. Fink 1986:34–35.

50. M. C. Wright 1993.

51. Unrecorded interview with Charles Thomas, August 16, 1983.

52. Adams, ed., 1995: chap. 7.

53. Periam 1984 [1884]:36.

54. U.S. Department of Agriculture 1915; see also Atkeson 1924, Bowers 1974, Ward 1920.

55. Jones (1988:20) writes about southern white men "driving" their wives.

56. Traditional song. Jean Ritchie sings another version of these words on Elektra ELK-125 (1954): "Oh hard is my fortune and hard is my fate / Controlled by my mother so early and late. / And when I get married just to end all the strife / Controlled by a man for the rest of my life."

57. In her memoirs Edith Rendleman details the silence around sexuality (Adams, ed., 1995: chap. 5), and similar silence existed around childbirth and menstruation. She also writes about how her parents used shame to keep her away from boys when she was a young adolescent. Mary Venerable (1974) writes of the shame associated with being "immodest" in a dress. My mother recalls that some of the elderly women in our neighborhood (in the 1940s) called boars "he pigs" and bulls "cow brutes," but neither Edith Rendleman nor other older women I talked with recalls such terms. Men did not talk of animals' sexual body parts around women.

58. Adams, ed., 1995: chap. 3.

59. On the importance of a strict moral code, see Joyce 1983; also see Fink 1992.

60. Edith Rendleman's memoirs (Adams, ed., 1995) provide an unvarnished view of these relationships and indicate both the flexibility and the boundaries of these norms, at least as her family worked them out. There are indications that some communities, such as the strongly German one in which the disowned daughter lived, were more rigid.

61. Control over property is a crucial dimension of social power. I do not have systematic data on property control; however, my impression is that probably as many as a third of financially able farmers in the late nineteenth century established daughters as well as sons on farms. Many of these women were powerful actors in their own right in their communities, even if they seldom if ever held public office. Of the seven farms studied, two were established by couples who settled on the wife's parents' land

(Waltons and Kimbers), and Rendleman Orchards is operated by a couple who inherited it from the husband's mother and her brother, the mother retaining a lifetime interest in it. Some women, like both Serena and Louise Walton, bought property in their own right. Salamon (1992:40–43) notes the tendency for American families to have a matrilineal emphasis, despite the patrilineal ideology of most farm families. For a detailed study of nineteenth-century inheritance processes in Union County as they concern women, see Rich 1993.

62. See Boserup 1970.

63. Union County Agricultural Extension Service, 4-H Club records. While women were only loosely tied to specific gender roles and could cross the lines relatively easily if the situation required their help, men rarely crossed over into housework. Finis Hunsaker was unusual. "I do a lot of the cooking myself," he told me in an interview July 15, 1983. "I don't think it's a disgrace for anybody to learn something about cooking. I can go in there and bake you just as nice a cake as you can get anywhere. I can bake pies. I can put on a roast. I can do anything that's supposed to be required in cooking. I cooked in the army, I baked bread for the army. And made cakes and cooked. These women cooks around here—I make cakes for them." Rosemary Walton also reported that her husband began fixing dinner after she returned to teaching in the 1950s.

64. Davidson interview, 1990:3.

65. Brimm interview, 1990a:26–28.

66. On lids, see Eddleman interview, 1990:28; on sweet potato slips, see Brimm interview, 1990a:7; see also M. Kinder interview, 1984:9.

67. M. Kinder interview, 1984:9, 11.

68. Brimm interview, 1990a:11, 15, 16–17.

69. Sirles and Sirles interview, 1984:1, 11, 21.

70. Rendleman interview, 1984b:9.

71. Thompson interview, 1976:16.

72. H. Kimber interview, 1990:38.

73. Smith and Smith interview, 1990:86.

74. M. Kinder interview, 1984:1, 3–4.

75. Brimm interview, 1990a:18.

76. Rendleman n.d. [1976]:35.

77. Gurley interview, 1975:6.

78. Rendleman interview, 1984a:30.

79. Throgmorton interview, 1990:18.

80. See also Salamon 1992:50–55.

81. Basler interview, 1984:3.

82. Jensen 1986.

83. Rendleman n.d. [1976]:36, 74; see also Adams, ed., 1995: chap. 7.

84. See Rich 1993:176–79.

Chapter 6

1. See, e.g., Aldridge interview, 1976.

2. See, for critiques of agrarian ideology, Vogeler 1981, Fink 1992.

3. Illinois Department of Agriculture, tax assessments by township, 1940. I com-

piled detailed crop production records from the county tax assessor, who enumerated the county by township, for the years 1940, 1945, 1950, 1955, 1960, 1965, 1970, 1975, and 1979. These enumerations stopped in 1979. See Adams 1987b:354–67 for tabulations.

4. B. Hunsaker interview, 1983a:6–7. Customary share rents varied according to quality of land and crop. The 1919 *Farm Knowledge* manual (Seymour 1919:73–74) details a variety of rental systems, including the "fourth system" used in cotton cropping, where the cropper furnishes all equipment and seed and the owner receives one-fourth of the crop; the "third system," in which the landlord receives one-third of the grain and which is "very common throughout the United States except in the regions of very high land values in the north-central states"; and the "two-fifths" and "half" systems generally used in the corn belt, depending on the productivity of the land. In the grain regions of Minnesota, Kansas, Nebraska, and the Dakotas and the wheat regions of the Pacific Coast it was conventional for the landlord to furnish the seed and get half the crop. Rental agreements varied in relation to use of farm buildings, pastures, hay fields, woodlots, livestock, and so forth.

5. U.S. Bureau of the Census 1927:503, County Table 1.

6. B. Hunsaker interview, 1983a:7.

7. Rendleman interview, 1984b:8–9.

8. Miller interview, 1982; Aldridge interview, 1976:3, 8.

9. Thomas interview, 1982a:21–22.

10. B. Hunsaker interview, 1983a:11.

11. Rendleman interview, 1984a:24–25.

12. Adams, ed., 1995: chap. 1.

13. The 1881 *Atlas of Union County* (Griffing 1881) shows several sawmills and box factories at the eastern edge of the bottoms; by the 1890s this timber had played out, as indicated by the distance Elijah Bradley, who lived where one of the sawmills had been in 1881, walked to cut timber. Bertie Hunsaker, who taught at Cauble school in 1917–18, up the creek from Bradley, told me that the people who lived up the hollows cut timber in the winter (B. Hunsaker field notes, 1983).

14. I have edited the longhand text, which consistently abbreviated Tennessee (Tenn.), Illinois (Ill.), and some other words.

15. Since the people who could give us oral information would have been children or not yet born during much of the period being discussed, their recollections could be varnished with the gloss of childhood memories; the indirect evidence of long-term residence by related kin on this farm is therefore important in supporting these childhood memories.

16. Brimm interview, 1990b:21.

17. Elder and Elder interview, 1983:11.

18. R. Weaver interview, 1984:10.

19. Toodle Elkins's daughter, Minnie, was John's mother; Elkins's second wife, Lillie Vesta West, was John's aunt—the sister of his father, Joe.

20. Later, as the labor market tightened, open competition for good laborers did occur.

21. Sirles and Sirles interview, 1984:21.

22. A study conducted by the U.S. Census Bureau (Truesdell 1926) followed this

population, concentrating on their lives in the Missouri swamplands as timber and cotton hands.

23. Venerable and Venerable interview, 1983:15–16, 22–23.

24. People recall houses with dog-trots separating two rooms, a common form of log construction. I have found none still standing and no accounts of any being built in the late nineteenth to early twentieth centuries. Saddle-bag and double-pen houses—houses in which two front entrances open to two generally equal-sized front rooms (or a large front room and a small "courting parlor" with stairs and a small bedroom behind it), like the I-house—continued to be built in frame as well as log construction, as one- and two-story structures and as tenant and propertied housing. All of these house forms often had detached summer kitchens or lean-to or attached kitchen wings.

25. Rhodes interview, 1984c:10.

26. Rendleman n.d. [1976]:1, 5–6, 14, 23.

27. Basler interview, 1984:11.

28. U.S. Bureau of the Census 1943a:146–47, Table 32; see also U.S. Bureau of the Census 1943b and Adams 1987b:187 for detailed table of fertility rates.

29. These cases can only give anecdotal support of the aphorism about the poor having the children. They suggest a larger study that is beyond the scope of this work, to systematically test family size and generational change between substantial farmers and landless farmers.

30. Elder and Elder interview, 1983:11.

31. Ibid., p. 10.

32. Jonesboro *Gazette*, February 6, 1875.

33. These coalfield struggles are the stuff of a number of scholarly and popular books, including Angle 1952.

34. See Buck 1910, 1913; R. V. Scott 1962. For a detailed study of this movement in Union County, and relevant bibliography, see Adams 1992a, 1986. Some Union Countians organized a shipping association as early as 1844, but it did not persist into the post–Civil War period (Jonesboro *Gazette*, April 30, 1887).

35. For extended studies of these periods, see Adams 1986, 1992a, 1992b.

36. On the importance of Women's Clubs in creating a new culture of femininity, see Blair 1980, A. F. Scott 1991, Thomas 1992.

37. F. Hunsaker interview, 1983:30.

38. Thompson 1963.

39. Barnes 1984; see also Adams 1986, Howe 1986, R. V. Scott 1962.

40. Rendleman n.d. [1976]:32.

41. Ibid., p. 34.

42. Thomas interview, 1982a:22.

43. Brenner (1985), in his analysis of feudal Europe, argues that the relative political power of different class sectors determined historical developments.

44. For studies of status relationships in somewhat comparable communities, see West 1945, Bennett with Kohl and Binion 1982, E. M. Matthews 1965. For a subtle study of how class and status relations were maintained on a colonial Virginia plantation, see Isaac 1985.

45. J. C. Scott 1990, Kohl 1988.

46. These figures were derived by eliminating "abnormal farms" from the tabulation and dividing the value of all dwellings listed in the 1930 Census of Agriculture, County Table II, by the number of farms listed in County Table I (U.S. Bureau of the Census 1932a).

47. U.S. Bureau of the Census 1932a: County Table XXI; U.S. Department of Agriculture 1936:1152, Table 9; 1934:751, Table 521.

48. These data are probably even more divergent than census figures indicate: Few Union County farmers kept records, while Tazewell County farmers were far better record keepers; this suggests that the Tazewell County figures approximate actual labor hired, while Union County labor is probably significantly undercounted.

49. U.S. Bureau of the Census 1932a: County Table XXXI.

Chapter 7

1. Cochrane 1979, Danbom 1979.

2. For a history of the grain trade, see Morgan 1979.

3. B. Hunsaker interview, 1983a:7–8.

4. F. Hunsaker interview, 1983:12.

5. Union County Agricultural Extension Service, Annual Report, appended summary, 1939; U.S. Bureau of the Census 1922a, 1927, 1932a; see Adams 1987b:372–73, Tables 23, 24, 25.

6. Hindman interview, 1983:7.

7. Union County Agricultural Extension Service, Annual Report, appended summary, 1939.

8. These associations had been organized in previous decades, as an outgrowth of the Granger movement and, later, under the auspices of the Farmers' Mutual Benefit Association and its successors. See Adams 1987b:386–89 for tabulation of all known farmers' organizations.

9. Union County Agricultural Extension Service, Annual Report, 1918.

10. Ibid., 1921.

11. American Fruit Growers failed and sold out to Metzler, who then sold out to Eckert's Orchard, a regional orchard family.

12. Elder and Elder interview, 1983:14–17.

13. Brimm interview, 1990a:6–8.

14. Floyd Karraker interview, 1983:25–26.

15. Leonard [1942]:95.

16. Layer 1965:246. Silica continues to be mined in the extreme southern part of Union County and in Alexander County.

17. A. Kinder interview, 1975:10.

18. F. Hunsaker interview, 1983:12.

19. Parks interview, 1975:12.

20. See reproduction of Anna *Gazette Democrat* column in Parks 1983:841.

21. Hindman interview, 1975:24.

22. Throgmorton interview, 1990:28, B. Hunsaker interview, 1983a:7.

23. Parks interview, 1975:11.

24. Abstract of deed, Lee Roy Rendleman farm.

25. Thomas interview, 1982a:24.

26. F. Hunsaker interview, 1983:15.

27. Elder and Elder interview, 1983:17.

Chapter 8

1. Weaver 1944:24.

2. Union County Clerk's Office, Union County Corporate Records, Book 1, entries dated 1884, 1890, 1891; on its lack of profitability, see Jonesboro *Gazette*, Anna Local News, January 26, 1889, January 18, 1890.

3. Leonard [1942]:121, Howard 1972:490. The state experimented with various building materials; this section was built of brick supplied by a paving brick company in Murphysboro, Ill.

4. See Jonesboro *Gazette*, August 11, 1933; February 3, 1939.

5. State of Illinois 1930:845.

6. Illinois Department of Conservation, Cultural Resource Study dated January 26, 1990, memorandum in author's possession.

7. State of Illinois 1927–28:484.

8. Ibid., 1930:853, 849, 863. Keller was from my hometown of Ava. Illinois Route 151 linking the town with Route 3 in the bottoms was—and still is—called the Kent Keller Highway.

9. The state mental hospital was chartered in 1869 as the Illinois Southern Hospital for the Insane, later called Southern Illinois Asylum for the Insane. In 1904 its name was changed to Anna State Hospital, and in 1975 it was changed again to Anna Mental Health and Development Center. In 1988 it was renamed the Clyde L. Choate Mental Health and Development Center in honor of longtime state representative Clyde Choate (*Southern Illinoisan*, June 18, 1988, researched by Judy Travelstead). When I was growing up, a common jest to someone who was acting foolish was "You belong in Anna."

10. F. Hunsaker interview, 1983:9.

11. Leonard [1942]:114–15.

12. Ibid., p. 117.

13. Parks 1983:796. NRIA is probably a typographical error for the NIRA, the National Industrial Recovery Act, which established the National Recovery Administration (NRA). The Supreme Court declared the NIRA unconstitutional in 1935.

14. Union County Agricultural Extension Service, Annual Report 1933. Bierbaum was farm adviser from 1929 through 1949; only Charles Glover, who served from July 1955 through 1971, served nearly as many years as Bierbaum.

15. On the Anna market, see Parks interview, 1982. See also Leonard [1942]:92. These markets served as outlets for the Illinois Fruitgrowers Exchange, which in 1935 established its headquarters in Carbondale and sold produce under the Illini brand (Illinois Agricultural Association, Annual Report 1935:55–59).

16. See Chapter 11 for an account of the festival and the way it documented the changes that occurred in the county after World War II.

17. For an account of the history of the Dixon Springs station, see Kammlade et al. 1976. For a history of the Shawnee National Forest, see Soady 1965. See also Parks 1983:843.

18. Leonard [1942]:99. The 1992 state budget crisis threatened the nursery and the

entire state forest operation, but it survived. In 1942 the Forest Service reintroduced deer, which had been hunted to extinction (Anna *Gazette Democrat*, October 22, 1942).

19. Union County Agricultural Extension Service, Annual Report 1937:20; Leonard [1942]:122.

20. Union County Agricultural Extension Service, Annual Report 1936.

21. Anon. [1967]:220. This same publication lists the directors from its formation in 1938 through the 1966 term. It includes Frank Kimber (1938–46) and Edith's husband, W. J. Rendleman (1943–48). Frank Kimber was one of the initial organizers.

22. Union County Agricultural Extension Service, Annual Report 1938:1–2; 1939:7.

23. Eddleman interview, 1990:14. Data about Frank Kimber's membership in the coop and their equipment purchase are from documents in the family collection, copies in author's collection. The equipment purchase document is undated; the form was last revised 10-1-1939, so I guess it predated the war.

24. Adams, ed., 1995: chap. 10.

25. For an overview of federal price support programs, see Rasmussen and Baker 1979; see also *Agricultural History* 1990, which deals with the history of the USDA.

26. See Danbom 1979, Bowers 1974; on the Farm Bloc, see McConnell 1953, Nye 1959, Tweeten 1970.

27. The Federal Reserve was organized in 1913.

28. Union County Agricultural Extension Service, Annual Report 1940:4–5; 1936.

29. Ibid., 1938:11.

30. Ibid., 1939:9.

31. G. Weaver interview, 1984:16.

32. Union County Agricultural Extension Service, Annual Report 1940:1, 9.

33. Anna *Gazette Democrat*, June 6, 1940; March 1, 1934. On war bonds, see, for example, January 13, July 27, 1944; January 11, 1945.

34. Union County Agricultural Extension Service, Annual Report 1937:20.

35. Ibid., 1940:5.

36. Ibid., 1941:9–12.

37. Anna *Gazette Democrat*, July 9, 1942; January 13, 1944.

38. Union County Agricultural Extension Service, Annual Report 1943:11, 1945:5; Anna *Gazette Democrat*, May 31, 1945. The Civilian Conservation Corps was segregated, as was the military during the war. One of the few conservation corps camps for African Americans was located in an isolated area in the western hills of Jackson County (Kay Ripplemeyer, personal communication). A number of growers I interviewed recalled using the German POWs.

39. Union County Agricultural Extension Service, Annual Report 1945:6.

40. Anna *Gazette Democrat*, February 17, 1944; March 1, 1945; see also February 1, 1945.

41. Ibid., June 18, 1943; July 20, 1944; see also June 22, 1945. On the cannery, see July 22, 1943.

42. Ibid., August 2, 1945.

43. Union County Agricultural Extension Service, Annual Report 1943. For a personal account, see Adams, ed., 1995: chap. 10.

44. Anna *Gazette Democrat*, June 7, 1945.

45. This was the flood dramatized in the classic documentary *The River*. The flood gave added stimulus to the Tennessee Valley Authority flood control projects, authorized in 1933.

46. Parks 1983:802.

47. My father came to southern Illinois from the Chicago area with one of these agencies, the Illinois Department of Labor, Division of Unemployment Compensation, which shared an office in Murphysboro with the Employment Service. He periodically set up a temporary office in Cobden to take claims for unemployment compensation, and the Employment Service operated a seasonal placement office for farm workers at the Cobden market.

Chapter 9

1. Union County Agricultural Extension Service, Annual Report 1946:5.
2. Throgmorton interview, 1990:15.
3. Eddleman interview, 1990:12.
4. Throgmorton interview, 1990:15.
5. H. Kimber interview, 1990:8.
6. Eddleman interview, 1990:20.
7. Zimmerman 1955:16, 58, 138. See also Paul and Manley 1970.
8. Illinois Agricultural Association, Annual Report 1940:53, 1935:58.
9. Union County Agricultural Extension Service, Annual Report 1954:7.
10. Hindman interview, 1983:38–40.
11. See McWilliams 1969 [1939], Goldschmidt 1978 [1947].
12. Hindman interview, 1983:42–43.
13. On the debates over chemical inputs, see Carson 1987 [1962], Phipps et al. 1986, Thurow 1991, Comstock 1991, Krebs 1992. These debates did not become part of "conventional" discourse until the late 1980s: the crises facing agriculture were posed purely in economic terms until the environmental and sustainable agriculture movements gained enough strength in the 1980s to begin seriously proposing legislation regulating agricultural practices. Biotechnology issues became important in the 1980s. See Fowler and Mooney 1990, J. Doyle 1985. For an example of a comprehensive work that deals with agricultural technologies only in terms of farm economics, see Schertz 1979.
14. On the growth of physical capital in agriculture, see Tostlebe 1957. See also Cochrane 1979.
15. Sirles and Sirles interview, 1984:17.
16. Union County Clerk's Office, Union County Corporate Records, Book 5, 1957; Union County Agricultural Extension Service, Annual Report 1957.
17. Union County Agricultural Extension Service, Annual Report 1962:4.
18. Ibid., 1963:8.
19. Orso, cited in Kalmar 1983:62. For information on the Mexican farm workers, see Chavira-Prado 1992, 1988, 1987; Kalmar 1983; Brooks 1960; O'Boyle 1978.
20. Frances Karraker interview, 1983:11.
21. Throgmorton interview, 1990:16.
22. See U.S. Bureau of the Census 1952: County Table 3; 1956: County Table 5; 1961: County Table 6.

23. Eddleman interview, 1990:17.

24. H. Kimber interview, 1990:10.

25. Ibid., p. 15.

26. See Marion and NC 117 Committee 1986:127.

27. Hindman interview, 1983:13–15, 23–24. The 1993–94 telephone book listed three auctions in the area: Goreville, Jackson County, and Vienna. It also listed four livestock dealers or order buyers, including Interstate Livestock Producers Association, a cooperative with four branches in the region; Heinold Hog Market, with two regional branches; Douglas Livestock in Goreville; and Doc Manus Livestock in Anna. On concentration in marketing, see overviews presented in *Yearbook of Agriculture*, published annually by the U.S. Department of Agriculture. See also Marion and the NC 117 Committee 1986, Krebs 1992.

28. Township data from 1940 through 1979 are compiled in Adams 1987b:354–67 and are given in graphic form on pp. 106–15. Compiled from tax assessments, copies in Illinois Department of Agriculture.

29. See Johnson 1985.

30. Committee for Economic Development [1945]. See also Committee for Economic Development 1956, 1957, [1962]. For an analysis of a key policy debate that cemented the CED perspective, see Hadwiger and Talbot 1965. See also Tweeten 1970, Hightower 1973, Havens 1986.

Chapter 10

1. My discussion necessarily collapses the complexities of a century's history into a schematic presentation. For a discussion on the Progressive movement, see Danbom 1979; on the southern cavalier tradition, see Taylor 1961; on the New England tradition, see Sklar 1973. On the development of the doctrine of separate spheres, see Basch 1983; Bloch 1978; Cott 1977, 1978; Cowan 1983; Degler 1980; Elbert 1988; Hartmann 1981; Kessler-Harris 1982; Matthaei 1982; G. Matthews 1987; Ryan 1982; Welter 1966; Zaretsky 1986. For the relationship between urban bourgeois and agrarian norms, see Adams 1994, 1993; Sachs 1983; Babbitt 1993; Jellison 1993. For the consequences of this ideological transformation on census statistics (and struggles over them), see Folbre 1991. On agrarian constructions of femininity, see Fink 1992 for a somewhat different interpretation.

2. The strongest thrust of these reformers' zeal was toward immigrant women who lived in unsanitary, overcrowded tenements and worked long hours, along with their children, in dangerous factories and sweatshops for extremely low wages. They tended to use the same vocabularies to describe farm women as they did immigrant women, despite the extremely different histories and structural relationships of the two groups to the larger society (see Elbert 1988). See also Adams 1991–92, Briskin 1980, J. Smith 1990. Marjorie East (1980) gives a relatively uncritical history of home economics.

3. Illinois Department of Agriculture 1911:283–85.

4. Ibid., 1910:182–91, 263–67, 328–35; 1911:69–81.

5. See Jellison 1993 for an in-depth analysis of farm women's adoption (and non-adoption) of "modern" technologies.

6. See ibid.; also see Fink 1992:110–13 on how New Deal programs treated farm women in Nebraska.

7. Sachs 1983, Fink 1986.

8. For a comparison of how policies affected U.S. and Third World farmers, and especially gender relations, see Flora 1988, Adams 1988.

9. Union County Agricultural Extension Service, Annual Report 1956:6, 1962:1.

10. Fink 1986:153–54.

11. This pattern was more consistent with the South, including Appalachia and the Ozarks, than with the prairie North. See, e.g., Williams 1982:156.

12. Wilson and Cash interview, 1990:4.

13. Union County Agricultural Extension Service, Home Extension Service, Annual Report 1955:4.

14. Union County Agricultural Extension Service, Annual Report 1957:7.

15. H. Kimber interview, 1990:30.

16. Throgmorton interview, 1990:35–36.

17. Walton interview, 1990:37.

18. R. Weaver interview, 1984:2.3, 2.5.

19. These figures misrepresent women's participation in paid labor, since as we have seen, farm women made up a sizable, although unenumerated, proportion of paid farm laborers. The fact that 92.5 percent of women listed in the labor force in 1940 worked in nonagricultural jobs indicates that women were simply not enumerated when they worked as agricultural laborers.

20. Salamon 1992 refers to families who valued farming enough to find ways to stay on the land as "yeoman" farmers, in contrast to more entrepreneurially oriented families who were identified as businesspeople and stayed in farming only if it paid a standard rate of return. For detailed data on the relationship between nonfarm and farm earnings, by gender, see Rosenfeld 1985.

21. U.S. Bureau of the Census 1943b: Table 32, Table 31; 1953, vol. 4, pt. 5, chap. C, Table 1; 1982, vol. 1, pt. 15, Tables 64, 188, 190. See table in Adams 1987b:187. Demographers have often drawn a direct cause-effect relationship between the structure of farming and family size, arguing that families that can economically use more hands will have larger families; as land pressure builds and the utility of more hands is outweighed by the lack of opportunity for adult children or they are simply not needed as technology replaces labor, family size falls. Others have pointed to intervening variables that may constrain changes in family size. In Union County, overall fertility started to fall while labor was still highly valued in agricultural production, although it appears to have fallen more rapidly among landowning, substantial farmers than among landless laborers and smaller farmers.

22. On trends in the larger society, see Kaledin 1984, Gatlin 1987.

Chapter 11

1. For discussions of these concepts as applied to Appalachia, see, on the concept of poverty and the "culture of poverty," Precourt 1983. See also Kirby 1987:xv–xvi on the unwarranted assumption that "progress" is inevitable.

2. See Foucault 1979. I have used his ideas in Adams 1993. See also K. Marx 1967 [1887], Thompson 1967, G. Wright 1981.

3. For discussions of Fordist economics, which combined Taylor's time-motion studies applied to manufacturing, and an understanding of the centrality of mass consumption to modern economies, see Harvey 1989: chap. 8; also Gramsci 1971.

4. Informal interview with E. Rendleman, May 2, 1992.

5. For literature on midwestern vernacular architecture, see Glassie 1975, Kniffen 1965, Montell and Morse 1976, Noble 1984: esp. 52–55, Howe et al. 1978, Stilgoe 1982, G. Wright 1981. Remarkably, Gottfried and Jennings 1988 [1985] do not list this ubiquitous type in their survey of U.S. vernacular architecture. I-houses most closely resemble a reversed "gabled-ell cottage" and their "gabled colonial cottage." On barns, see Halsted 1911 [1904], Rawson 1979.

6. Martin (1984:40, 49) documents what he calls saddlebag houses—those with two equal pens, each with an entrance—in his study of *Hollybush*. Montell and Morse (1976:91) reserve the term "saddlebag" for houses with a small central hall enclosing the fireplace. I found no houses like these in this study, although, like "dog-trot" houses (those with an open breezeway between the two pens), they were probably once common. Montell and Morse include a wide variety of floor plans under the designation I-house. See also Noble 1984:52–55, 114–18.

7. See Shapiro 1978; also see Batteau 1983, Shapiro 1983, on how Appalachia has been characterized by the national media. Brownell 1958 occasionally uses a temporalizing rhetoric to describe southern Illinois—The Other Illinois—although he is agnostic about the causes of the region's poverty (see pp. 143–48). See Fabian's 1983 extended essay on how social scientists and others have used time to construct and justify domination of the "Other." Although I focus on southern Illinois as an agricultural region, the coalfields just north of the Shawnee Hills shaped many outsiders' perceptions of the region, as coal mining did for Appalachia. Both coal and agriculture are extractive industries (see Bunker 1985 for the implications of extractive economies to long-term sustainability), but the ownership, labor, and marketing systems are very different and give rise to discrete local political and economic configurations.

8. U.S. Bureau of the Census 1947: County Table 1, pt. 1. I assume that each farm had only one primary operator, so the rest of the homes housed laborers. In reality, some farms may have had housing for both parents and resident adult children. The more common pattern before the 1950s, however, was for aging parents to live in the same house with the farming children, or for the children to establish their own farm operation.

9. Melvin 1932:8.

10. See U.S. Bureau of the Census 1943c: County Tables 22, 23, 25, 26, 27. Town rents were more in line with the state, with a median rent of $23.24 in Anna.

11. Quoted from WSIU-TV *Emphasis*, "Harvesting Farm Memories," November 1991.

12. When I spoke about the Cerny's renovation at a talk to an SIUC history department seminar, a participant remarked that he rarely saw dining room sets at local estate auctions, an indication of the general absence of formal dining rooms before the 1950s.

13. For a good description of contemporary farm homes, see Salamon 1992:43–45.

14. Basler interview 1984:5. Green's store closed in 1959.

15. Executive Committee on Southern Illinois 1949:188, 187. See also Beimfohr 1954.

16. Colby 1956:80.

17. U.S. Bureau of the Census 1964: Table 85.

18. Sennett and Cobb 1972.

19. See Walters 1949, Anon. 1946:34, *Southern Illinoisan*, August 22, 1950. Thanks to Spike DuBois for providing copies of these publications.

20. On the wood industry, see Anon. 1929, 1946; Walters 1949.

21. Southern Five Regional Planning and Development Commission [1982].

22. See Weaver 1944, Nickell 1956, Peshkin 1982; also see Union County Farm Bureau and Agricultural Extension Service 1941, Union County School Board [1935], Union County School Survey Committee 1948.

23. U.S. Bureau of the Census 1932b: Table 14; 1943a: Tables 26, 17; 1953: Tables 48, 49; 1964: Table 30.

24. On the identity of women, modernization, and health reform, see Morantz 1977.

25. The 1950 Census of Population enumerated 1,518 rural-farm females between twenty and fifty-nine years old. There is no way to determine what proportion of these women were farm owners, laborers, or renters. Two hundred sixty-six of these women were counted as employed, only thirty-nine in agricultural work (U.S. Bureau of the Census 1953: Table 49). The account of the Home Bureau's history comes from reports archived in the Union County Agricultural Extension Service office, Anna, Ill.

26. For a detailed analysis of the development of the Home Bureau in Union County, see Adams 1994.

27. A pamphlet I wrote with Judy Travelstead of the Union County Historical Society (Adams with Travelstead 1987) and an article in the *Illinois Historical Journal* (Adams 1990) provide more detailed studies of the festival. For more literature on community festivals, see Aronoff 1991, Byrne 1985, Humphrey and Humphrey 1988, Manning 1983, Rubin 1979, and Warner 1959. On queen contests, see Banner 1983, Deford 1971. See Turner 1974 and van Gennep 1960 on the significance of ritual processes in the construction of social life. On creating "communities of memory," see Bellah et al. 1985.

28. For information on the waterworks and the sewage system, see Cobden Historical Committee [1955]:23, 36, 40, 52–53; Cobden *Review*, November 27, 1936; April 17, May 2, 1957; Anna *Gazette Democrat*, August 14, 1941; April 22, 1945; March 24, 1949; July 9, 1964.

29. For a history of the Cobden Women's Club, see Miller 1976.

30. Illinois senator Paul Douglas tried to pass legislation "to help chronically depressed areas finance industrial development" (Ernst and Drake 1972:10), using the rhetoric of "Point Four" and rooted in the New Deal project to make government a partner in the nation's economy.

31. The results of this project were compiled in Cobden Community Development Committee 1956a, 1956b; Cobden Historical Committee [1955]; and other reports available in the SIUC Morris Library. The *History of Cobden* has been kept in print by the Cobden Museum, whose founders were active on the committee. See also Levin 1965, who analyzed the region as a case study of a depressed area.

32. For studies of rural clinics in Appalachia, a major thrust of the Area Redevelopment Administration, begun in 1961 and superseded in 1964 by the Economic Opportunity Act (initiating the War on Poverty), see Couto 1983, 1975.

33. The game was discontinued in 1982 when the Lions' insurance carrier refused to cover it.

34. The Union County Fair continued to draw large numbers of contestants for

queen, corroborating personal recollections that girls basically boycotted the Cobden Peach Queen contest as long as the position was bought rather than judged by relatively impartial judges.

Chapter 12

1. In some areas closer to Carbondale, relations were more strained, possibly because there were more "hippies" and they were closer to the university, so they felt less of a need or desire to establish good relationships with their older neighbors. Some older residents of Makanda, for example, tried to form a vigilante group to discourage the newcomers.

2. Local newspapers, including the *Southern Illinoisan* and, on occasion, the St. Louis *Post Dispatch*, covered these events. See also Powers 1991.

3. Anna *Gazette Democrat*, September 2, 1984.

4. Unlike in more prosperous farming areas, most rented land is locally owned because the returns are too low for investors or distant heirs to bother with. See Salamon 1992 on the effects of absentee landlords on the community she calls Wheeler.

5. Throgmorton interview, 1990:28.

6. See van Es and Bowling 1979, Wardwell 1982, Barlett 1986; see also Halperin 1990, Rodefeld 1978.

7. The Illinois South Project, a nonprofit advocacy organization now called Illinois Stewardship Alliance, organized the market. On direct marketing, see Solverson and Ellerman 1978, Sommer 1980.

8. Halterman and Halterman interview, 1983:1.

9. *Southern Illinoisan*, December 23, 1984.

10. Ibid., March 6, 1983; Bureau of Economic Analysis, Regional Economic Information System, data extracted by Sue Kohler and Scott Boehne, Office of Economic and Regional Development, Southern Illinois University at Carbondale. These data are highly "massaged," using a variety of statistical formulas to distribute state- and sometimes federal-level data to the county level. It should, therefore, be treated with some caution when applied to a unit as small as a county.

11. Kurin 1984:26. Kurin's study replicated an earlier SIUC Community Development study by Wakeley 1962.

12. The 1970s and 1980s were decades of unprecedented instability as well, with sharp rises and declines in farm income. For a summary of the events of the 1970s, see Schertz et al. 1979.

13. See, for example, *Farmline*, December–January 1986. Land prices in general outstrip their earning potential: landowning farmers are willing to pay a premium on nearby land since they expect their owned land to help subsidize the cost. Crop subsidies become factored into the price of land, leading to a crisis in the transfer of land from one generation to the next unless land stays within the family.

14. For a more detailed analysis of these trends, see Harl 1990. See also Rogers and Rogers 1989 for a bibliography of materials on the farm crisis of the 1980s. The summary given here is based on data in General Accounting Office 1986b; University of Illinois College of Agriculture Cooperative Extension Service 1986, 1985, 1984; Jolly and Doye 1985; Breimyer 1986; Lins 1985. For an analysis of the political economy of rural regions and agriculture, see Goss et al. 1980, Lobao 1990, Friedland et al. 1991. See also Friedberger 1988, 1989; Strange 1988.

15. This caused additional impoverishment in the heavily indebted countries, as governments encouraged farmers to shift from production for domestic consumption to production for export. On the debt crisis, see Cook and Sechler 1985, Schuh 1985, Lappé 1981, Lappé and Collins 1977, George 1988, MacEwan 1990.

16. Illinois Department of Agriculture 1986:78.

17. Barlett 1993:180–87.

18. General Accounting Office 1986b:28, 1986a:63.

19. U.S. Bureau of the Census 1989: chap. 2, Table 10.

20. Ibid., Table 5.

21. Derived from ibid., Table 10.

22. Illinois Department of Agriculture 1989:14. These statistics should be read with some caution. I worked as an enumerator for the Illinois Crop Reporting Service collecting this data in 1984 and 1985. The refusal rate was quite high for the survey that collected economic data, and the impression shared by enumerators with whom I spoke indicated that those farmers who appeared (from condition of house, equipment, grounds, and so forth) most stressed were the most reluctant to participate. Further, the refusal rate seemed to increase as the farm crisis deepened. As no margin of error is indicated in the statistics given, it is not possible to determine whether or not such weighting of results has been incorporated into the statistical weights given to the raw data. In any event, if the data are in error, they tend to underreport the amount of stress and underestimate debt / asset ratios.

23. See *Southern Illinoisan*, November 6, 7, 1992; Anna *Gazette Democrat*, December 3, 1992.

24. Southern Five Regional Planning and Development Commission [1982]; *Southern Illinoisan*, October 18, 1992.

25. Illinois Labor Force Report, Illinois Department of Employment Security. Thanks to Mike Vessel for providing these figures.

26. U.S. Bureau of the Census 1982: chap. 2, Tables 180, 181. *Southern Illinoisan*, October 21, 1992. Poverty rates for children in southern Illinois counties ranged from a high of 45.58 percent in Alexander County to a low of 9.51 percent in Washington County. Fifteen of the eighteen counties had child poverty rates above 20 percent. The census gives data on a number of different categories, including households, families, and unrelated individuals fifteen years and over. It distinguishes per capita income of persons in households and persons in group quarters. Since Union County has a sizable number of residents in the mental health facility, I have used only "persons in households" when citing per capita income.

27. For analyses of these trends, see Bluestone and Harrison 1982, Bowles and Gintis 1986, Harvey 1989, Navarro 1991, Singh 1992, Weisskopf 1991.

Chapter 13

1. The Hutterites appear to have adopted state-of-the-art technologies within a very different, communitarian form of organization in which elders organize the collective labor of the community. Salamon's analysis of German communities in central Illinois suggests that some ethnic communities, when located near sources of nonfarm work, may encourage the persistence of strong social networks. This may suggest that industrial technologies can be used by people through a number of

different social forms but that these are not *individual* choices; rather, they require a larger community to be effective.

2. If they had no mortgage on the farm, older farmers were able to refuse substantial innovation because they needed little cash and, at sixty-five, they could draw Social Security. Some specific groups like the Old Order Amish also avoided technical innovation and were able to sustain a satisfactory lifestyle because they maintained strong alternative communities, and a few farmers, like those who participate in programs sponsored by the Center for Rural Affairs in Walthill, Nebraska, were extremely selective in the technologies they invested in.

3. See Fink 1986, Marion and the NC 117 Committee 1986.

4. Gudeman and Rivera 1991.

5. The Amish appear to have chosen a life with few consumer conveniences, so that their need for money is small. The Hutterites, who use modern technologies, hold land in common and organize the community's labor under the management of a governing council. Among both the Amish and the Hutterites, women are excluded from arenas of formally organized power. Note that this observation to some degree counters world systems analysts who term everyone engaged in capitalist markets as "capitalist" (e.g., Wallerstein 1974) and is closer to Wolf's (1982) focus on modes of production to define capitalism. Noting the impoverishment associated with retaining some noncapitalist relations of production, this analysis is compatible, although not completely congruent, with those who see poor regions that serve as sources of resource extraction as "internal colonies" (Amin 1974, Batteau 1983, Bunker 1985, Walls 1976).

6. Pierre Bourdieu (1977) and Anthony Giddens (1979, 1984), along with Foucault (1979) and other "post-structuralist" and "post-modern" analysts, stress the centrality of these received "habits" or "structures" in determining what Giddens terms "structuration."

7. Basler interview, 1984:5.

8. The Grange involved women in its organization, but they do not appear to have been engaged in the political issues of the period.

9. See, e.g., Salamon 1992:128, 134.

10. I have not explored the role anticommunism played in cutting off alternatives, but there is no doubt it was significant. It is ironic that the bureaucratic centralization and control that people projected onto communism was being firmly institutionalized during the period of fiercest anticommunism, and that this movement virtually eliminated more egalitarian alternatives from public discourse.

Archives

Illinois Department of Agriculture, Springfield, Ill.
  Tax assessments by county and township
Illinois Regional Archives, Carbondale, Ill.
  Grantor-Grantee indexes, microfilm
Illinois State Archives, Springfield, Ill.
  Computer printout of original land entries, Union County
Union County Agricultural Extension Service, Anna, Ill.
  Annual Reports, 1918–63
  4-H Club Records, 1940–52, 1956
Union County Circuit Clerk's Office, Union County Court House, Jonesboro, Ill.
  Clear Creek Drainage District records
  Preston Drainage District records
  Court Dockets
Union County Clerk's Office, Union County Court House, Jonesboro, Ill.
  Union County Commissioners Records, Books 1, 2, 3, 4
  Union County Corporate Records, Corporate Record Books
  Union County Deed Books
  Union County miscellaneous records: Justices of the Peace and Constables, 1853–
    1868
  Union County miscellaneous records, 1889
United States Census Office
  Census of Population. Population schedules for 1850, 1860, 1870, and 1880 Census
    of Population, Illinois. Microform. Washington, D.C., National Archives.
  Census of Agriculture. Schedules for 1880 Census of Agriculture, Illinois. Micro-
    form. Washington, D.C., National Archives.

Interviews

Interviews dated 1975 or 1976 are from the Shawnee History Project. Transcripts are
archived in the Shawnee Community College Library, Ullin, Ill.
Interviews dated in the 1980s or 1990 are by the author or under her supervision.
Unless otherwise noted, transcripts and original audiotapes are archived in Southern
Illinois University, Morris Library Special Collections, Carbondale, Ill.
Aldridge, John
1976   Interview by Carla Craig, July 9, OH 83.
Basler, Al
1984   Interview by Jane Adams, March 17. Copy of transcript and au-
            diotape in SIUC Morris Library Special Collections and Union
            County Historical Society Archives.
Brimm, Ed
1990a   Interview by Ron Rich, June 29.

1990b   Interview by Ron Rich and Bonita Rubach, June 21.

Casper, Bert

1975   Interview by Michael Jackson, December 5, OH 35.

Cerny, Elizabeth

1984   Interview by Jane Adams, January 31. Copy of transcript and au-
                 diotape in SIUC Morris Library Special Collections and Union
                 County Historical Society Archives.

1976   Interview by Carla Craig, August 3, OH 101.

Davidson, Clara

1990   Interview by Julie Prombo and Troy Meyer, June 24.

Eddleman, Jacquie

1990   Interview by Troy Meyer, June 26.

Elder, David, and Clara Elder

1983   Interview by Jane Adams, January 19.

Gurley, Ada

1975   Interview by Pam Grey, August, OH 73.

Halterman, Austin, and Hazel Halterman

1983   Interview by Jane Adams, March 1. Typescript and audiotape in au-
                 thor's possession.

Hill, Mary Walton

1990   Interview by Bonita Rubach and Elizabeth Durdle, June 28.

Hindman, Ruel

1983   Interview by Jane Adams, October 12.

1975   Interview by Michael Jackson, November 14, OH 58.

Hunsaker, Bertie

1983a   Interview by Jane Adams, July 13. Typescript and audiotape in au-
                 thor's possession.

1983b   Interview by Jane Adams, June 8. Typescript and audiotape in au-
                 thor's possession.

Hunsaker, Finis

1983   Interview by Jane Adams, July 15. Typescript and audiotape in au-
                 thor's possession.

Karraker, Floyd

1983   Interview by Jane Adams, February 16. Typescript and audiotape in
                 author's possession.

Karraker, Frances

1983   Interview by Jane Adams, January 29.

Kimber, Helen

1990   Interview by Troy Meyer and Julie Prombo, June 19.

Kimber, Robert

1990   Interview by Troy Meyer and Julie Prombo, June 26.

Kinder, Ada

1975   Interview by Connie White, August 13, OH 30.

Kinder, Maude

1984   Interview by Jane Adams, March 23. Copy of transcript and au-
                 diotape in SIUC Morris Library Special Collections and Union
                 County Historical Society Archives.

Lingle, Oscar "Dutch"

1984   Interview by Jane Adams, February 9. Copy of transcript and audiotape in SIUC Morris Library Special Collections and Union County Historical Society Archives.

Miller, Clara Bell

1982   Interview by Jane Adams, March 21. Transcript and audiotape in author's collection.

Norris, Cecil

1976   Interview by Carla Craig, July 20, OH 94.

Parks, George E.

1982   Interview by Jane Adams, December 2.

1975   Interview by Jeff Kelley, August 14, OH 48.

Rendleman, Edith

1984a   Interview by Jane Adams, February 9. Copy of transcript and audiotape in SIUC Morris Library Special Collections and Union County Historical Society Archives.

1984b   Interview by Jane Adams, January 24. Copy of transcript and audiotape in SIUC Morris Library Special Collections and Union County Historical Society Archives.

Rhodes, William S. "Bill"

1984a   Interview by Jane Adams, February 8. Copy of transcript and audiotape in SIUC Morris Library Special Collections and Union County Historical Society Archives.

1984b   Interview by Jane Adams, February 7. Copy of transcript and audiotape in SIUC Morris Library Special Collections and Union County Historical Society Archives.

1984c   Interview by Jane Adams, January 30. Copy of transcript and audiotape in SIUC Morris Library Special Collections and Union County Historical Society Archives.

Sirles, Wayne, and Helen Sirles

1984   Interview by Jane Adams, March 2. Copy of transcript and audiotape in SIUC Morris Library Special Collections and Union County Historical Society Archives.

Smith, Curtis, and Faye Smith

1990   Interview by Julie Prombo and Ron Rich, June 28.

Spiller, Mrs. Lloyd (Arilla)

1983   Interview by Jane Adams, March 2. Typed notes in author's collection.

Stadelbacher, Geraldine

1983   Interview by Jane Adams, January 5.

Taylor, Grant

1990   Interview by Julie Prombo and Troy Meyer, July 3.

Thomas, Charles

1982a   Interview by Jane Adams, December 22.

1982b   Interview by Jane Adams, November 23.

Thompson, S. Earl

1976   Interview by Michael Jackson, January 6, OH 39.

Throgmorton, Barbara Walton Diefenbach

1990   Interview by Bonita Rubach and Ron Rich, June 18.

Venerable, Witt, and Mary Venerable

1983   Interview by Jane Adams, January 18.

Walton, Rosemary

1990   Interview by Bonita Rubach and Elizabeth Durdle, June 29.

Wilson, Sybil Tucker, and Agnes Tucker Cash

1990   Interview by Elizabeth Durdle and Bonita Rubach, July 1.

Weaver, George

1984   Interview by Jane Adams, January 26. Copy of transcript and au-
               diotape in SIUC Morris Library Special Collections and Union
               County Historical Society Archives.

Weaver, Ruby

1984   Interview by Jane Adams, February 1. Copy of transcript and au-
               diotape in SIUC Morris Library Special Collections and Union
               County Historical Society Archives.

Newspapers

Anna *Gazette Democrat*, Anna, Ill.
Cobden *Review*, Cobden, Ill.
Dongola *Tri-County Record*, Dongola, Ill.
Jonesboro *Gazette*, Jonesboro, Ill.
Farmer and Fruitgrower, Jonesboro, Ill.

Other Sources

Ackernecht, Erwin H.

1945   *Malaria in the Upper Mississippi Valley, 1760–1900*. Baltimore, Md.:
               Johns Hopkins University Press.

Adams, Jane

1994   Government Policies and the Changing Structure of Farm Women's
               Livelihood: A Case from Southern Illinois. In *The Economic Anthro-
               pology of the State*, ed. Elizabeth Brumfiel. Lanham, Md.: University
               Press of America.

1993   Resistance to "Modernity": Southern Illinois Farm Women and the
               Cult of Domesticity. *American Ethnologist* 20 (1): 89–113.

1992a   Agrarian Activism: Mediator between Two Worlds. *Social Science
               History* 16 (3): 365–400.

1992b   "How Can a Poor Man Live"? Resistance to Capitalist Development
               in Southern Illinois, 1870–1890. *Rural History: Economy, Society,
               Culture* 3:87–110.

1991–92   "A Woman's Place Is in the Home": The Ideological Devaluation of
               Farm Women's Work. *Anthropology of Work Review* 12 (4) and 13 (1):
               1–11.

1990   Creating Community in a Midwestern Village: Fifty Years of the
               Cobden Peach Festival. *Illinois Historical Journal* 83 (2): 97–108.

1988	The Decoupling of Farm and Household: Differential Consequences of Capitalist Development on Southern Illinois and Third World Family Farms. *Comparative Studies in Society and History* 30 (3): 453–82.
1987a	Business Farming and Farm Policy in the 1980s: Further Reflections on the Farm Crisis. *C&A: Culture and Agriculture* 32 (Spring/Summer): 1–6.
1987b	The Transformation of Rural Social Life in Union County, Illinois, in the Twentieth Century. Ph.D. diss., University of Illinois.
1986	Farmer Organization and Class Formation. *Canadian Journal of Anthropology/RCA* 5:35–42.

Adams, Jane, ed.

1995	*"All Anybody Ever Wanted of Me Was to Work": The Memoirs of Edith Rendleman.* Carbondale: Southern Illinois University Press.

Adams, Jane, Jeanette E. Stephens, and Ronald D. Rich

1990	The Economic and Social Transformation of Two Substantial Farms in Union County, Illinois. Paper given at Illinois Historic Archaeology Conference, Carbondale, Ill., September.

Adams, Jane, with Judy Travelstead

1987	*Cobden Peach Festival, 1938–1987.* Cobden, Ill.: Union County Historical Society.

Agricultural History

1990	*The United States Department of Agriculture in Historical Perspective.* Special symposium issue. Ed. Alan I. Marcus and Richard Lowitt. 64 (2).

Amin, Samir

1974	*Accumulation on a World Scale: A Critique of the Theory of Underdevelopment.* Trans. Brian Pearce. New York: Monthly Review Press.

Anna Centennial Committee

1954	*100 Years of Progress: The Centennial History of Anna, Illinois.* Cape Girardeau, Mo.: Missourian Printing and Stationery Co.

Angle, Paul M.

1952	*Bloody Williamson.* New York: Knopf.

Anon.

[1967]	Southern Illinois Electric Cooperative—How "Little Egypt" Was Electrified. Photocopy article, source unnoted, in author's collection. Supplied by Lowell Eddleman, assistant manager, Southern Illinois Electric Cooperative, 1983.
1946	Important Basket Industry 60 Years in Little Egypt. *Illinois Conservation*, Summer, p. 34.
1929	*Union County, Illinois.* Lawrenceville, Ill.: Suttle Print Shop. Promotional pamphlet in author's collection.

Aronoff, Marilyn

1991	Collective Celebration as a Source of Economic Revitalization. Paper given at Society for Applied Anthropology Annual Meeting, Charleston, S.C., March 13–17.

Atkeson, Mary Meek
1924 *The Woman on the Farm*. New York: Century.
Babbitt, Kathleen R.
1993 The Productive Farm Woman and the Extension Home Economist in New York State, 1920–1940. In *American Rural and Farm Women in Historical Perspective. Agricultural History* 67 (2): 83–101. Special symposium issue.

Balderston, Lydia Ray
1936 *Housewifery: A Textbook of Practical Housekeeping*. 5th ed. Chicago: J. B. Lippincott.

Banaji, Jarius
1980 Summary of Selected Parts of Kautsky's "The Agrarian Question." In *The Rural Sociology of the Advanced Societies: Critical Perspectives*, ed. F. H. Buttel and H. Newby, pp. 39–82. Montclair, N.J.: Allanheld, Osmun.

Banner, Lois
1983 *American Beauty*. New York: Knopf.
Barlett, Peggy F.
1993 *American Dreams, Rural Realities: Family Farms in Crisis*. Chapel Hill: University of North Carolina Press.
1986 Part-Time Farming: Saving the Farm or Saving the Lifestyle? *Rural Sociology* 51 (3): 290–314.

Barnard, Charles H., and John Jones
1987 *Farm Real Estate Values in the United States by Counties, 1850–1982*. United States Department of Agriculture, Economic Research Service, Statistical Bulletin No. 751. Washington, D.C.: U.S. Department of Agriculture.

Barnes, Donna A.
1984 *Farmers in Rebellion: The Rise and Fall of the Southern Farmers Alliance and People's Party in Texas*. Austin: University of Texas Press.

Basch, Norma
1983 Equity vs. Equality: Emerging Concepts of Women's Political Status in the Age of Jackson. *Journal of the Early Republic* 3 (3): 297–318.

Batteau, Allen
1983 Rituals of Dependence in Appalachian Kentucky. In *Appalachia and America: Autonomy and Regional Dependence*, ed. Allen Batteau, pp. 142–67. Lexington: University Press of Kentucky.

Batteau, Allen, with Phillip Obermiller
1983 Introduction: The Transformation of Dependency. In *Appalachia and America: Autonomy and Regional Dependence*, ed. Allen Batteau, pp. 1–13. Lexington: University Press of Kentucky.

Bauxar, J. Joseph
1978 History of the Illinois Area. In *Handbook of North American Indians, Northeast*, ed. Bruce C. Trigger, 15:594–601. Washington, D.C.: Smithsonian Institution.

Beauman, Guy
1899 Map of Union County, Illinois. Vienna, Ill.

Beecher, Catharine E.

1970 [1841]   *A Treatise on Domestic Economy*. New York: Source Book Press.

Beecher, Catharine E., and Harriet Beecher Stowe

1975 [1869]   *American Woman's Home*. Hartford, Conn.: Stowe-Day Foundation.

Beimfohr, Oliver Wendell

1954   *The Industrial Potential of Southern Illinois*. Southern Illinois Series
                No. 1. Carbondale: Southern Illinois University.

Bellah, Robert M., William M. Sullivan, Ann Swidler, and Stephen M. Tipton

1985   *Habits of the Heart: Individualism and Commitment in American Life*.
                Berkeley: University of California Press.

Bennett, John W., in association with Seena B. Kohl and Geraldine Binion

1982   *Of Time and the Enterprise: North American Family Farm Management
                in a Context of Resource Marginality*. Minneapolis: University of Min-
                nesota Press.

Bennett, John W., and Seena B. Kohl

1982   The Agrifamily System. In *Of Time and the Enterprise: North Ameri-
                can Family Farm Management in a Context of Resource Marginality*, by
                John W. Bennett in association with Seena B. Kohl and Geraldine
                Binion, pp. 128–47. Minneapolis: University of Minnesota Press.

Berry, Wendell

1977   *The Unsettling of America: Culture and Agriculture*. New York: Avon.

Bevier, Isabel

1907   *The House: Its Plan, Decoration, and Care*. Chicago: American School
                of Home Economics.

Bevier, Isabel, and Susannah Usher

1906   *The Home Economics Movement*. Boston: M. Barrows.

Blair, Karen J.

1980   *The Clubwoman as Feminist: True Womanhood Redefined, 1868–1914*.
                New York: Holmes and Meier.

Bloch, Ruth H.

1978   Untangling the Roots of Modern Sex Roles: A Survey of Four Cen-
                turies of Change. *Signs* 4 (2): 237–52.

Bluestone, Barry, and Bennett Harrison

1982   *The Deindustrialization of America: Plant Closings, Community Aban-
                donment, and the Dismantling of Basic Industry*. New York: Basic
                Books.

Boatman, Wm. J., D.D.

1966   History of St. John's Lutheran Church. Ms.

Boggess, Arthur Clinton

1908   *The Settlement of Illinois, 1778–1830*. Chicago: Chicago Historical
                Society's Collection. Vol. 5.

Bokemeier, Janet, and Lorraine Garkovich

1987   Assessing the Influence of Farm Women's Self-Identity on Task Al-
                location and Decision Making. *Rural Sociology* 52 (1): 13–36.

Boserup, Ester

1970   *Woman's Role in Economic Development*. New York: St. Martin's Press.

Bourdieu, Pierre
1977   *Outline of a Theory of Practice.* Translated by Richard Nice.
            Cambridge: Cambridge University Press.
Bowers, William L.
1974   *The Country Life Movement in America, 1900–1920.* Port Washington
            N.Y.: Kennikat Press.
Bowles, Samuel, and H. Gintis
1986   *Democracy and Capitalism: Property, Community, and Contradictions of
            Modern Social Thought.* New York: Basic Books.
Breimyer, Harold F.
1986   *Origins of the Rural Crisis.* AEWP 1986-16. Columbia: University of
            Missouri, Department of Agricultural Economics.
Briskin, Linda
1980   Domestic Labour: A Methodological Discussion. In *Hidden in the
            Household: Women's Domestic Labour under Capitalism,* ed. Bonnie
            Fox, pp. 135–72. Toronto: Women's Press.
Brenner, Robert
1985   Agrarian Class Structure and Economic Development in Pre-
            Industrial Europe. In *The Brenner Debate: Agrarian Class Structure
            and Economic Development in Pre-Industrial Europe,* ed. T. H. Aston
            and C. H. E. Philpin, pp. 10–63. Cambridge: Cambridge University
            Press.
Brooks, Melvin
1960   The Social Problems of Migrant Farm Laborers. Occasional paper,
            Department of Sociology, Southern Illinois University, Carbondale.
Brownell, Baker
1958   *The Other Illinois.* New York: Duell, Sloan and Pearce.
Bruere, Martha B., and Robert W. Bruere
1912   *Increasing Home Efficiency.* New York: Macmillan.
Brush, Daniel Harmon
1944   *Growing Up with Southern Illinois, 1820–1861.* Ed. Milo Milton
            Quaife. Chicago: R. R. Donnelly & Sons.
Buck, Solon J.
1917   *Illinois in 1818.* Decatur, Ill.: Review Printing and Stationery.
1913   *The Granger Movement.* Cambridge, Mass.: Harvard University Press
1910   Agricultural Organization in Illinois, 1870–1880. *Journal of the Il-
            linois State Historical Society* 3:10–23.
Bunker, Stephen
1985   *Underdeveloping the Amazon: Extraction, Unequal Exchange, and the
            Failure of the Modern State.* Urbana: University of Illinois Press.
Bush, Corlann G.
1987   "He Isn't Half So Cranky as He Used to Be": Agricultural Mechani-
            zation, Comparable Worth, and the Changing Farm Family. In *"To
            Toil the Livelong Day": America's Women at Work, 1780–1980,* ed.
            Carol Groneman and Mary Beth Norton, pp. 213–32. Ithaca: Cornell
            University Press.
1982   "The Barn Is His, the House Is Mine": Agricultural Technology and

Sex Roles. In *Energy and Transport*, ed. George H. Daniels and Mark H. Rose, pp. 235–59. Beverly Hills: Sage Publications.

Buttel, Frederick H., and Gilbert W. Gillespie, Jr.

1984   The Sexual Division of Farm Household Labor: An Exploratory Study of the Structure of On-Farm and Off-Farm Labor Allocation among Farm Men and Women. *Rural Sociology* 49 (2): 183–209.

Byrne, Donald E., Jr.

1985   The Race of the Saints: An Italian Religious Festival in Jessup, Pennsylvania. *Journal of Popular Culture* 19 (3): 119–30.

Canouts, Veletta, Ernest E. May, Neal H. Lopinot, and Jon D. Muller

1984   *Cultural Frontiers in the Upper Cache Valley, Illinois.* Center for Archaeological Investigations Research Paper No. 16. Carbondale: Center for Archaeological Investigations, Southern Illinois University.

Caraway, Charles

1986   *Foothold on a Hillside: Memories of a Southern Illinoisan.* Carbondale: Southern Illinois University Press.

Carson, Rachel

1987 [1962]   *Silent Spring.* Boston: Houghton Mifflin.

Carter, Art

1983a   The Union Army in Union County. In *History of Union County*, ed. George E. Parks, 1:283–85. Anna, Ill.: George E. Parks.

1983b   The Welch-Thompson Incident. In *History of Union County*, ed. George E. Parks, 1:300–303. Anna, Ill.: George E. Parks.

Chavira-Prado, Alicia

1992   Work, Health, and the Family: Gender Structure and Women's Status in an Undocumented Migrant Population. *Human Organization* 51 (1): 53–64.

1988   "Tienes Que Ser Valiente!": Mexicana Migrants in a Midwestern Farm Labor Camp. In *Mexicanas at Work in the United States*, ed. M. B. Melville, pp. 64–74. Houston, Tex.: University of Houston.

1987   Women, Health, and Migration: Conditions and Strategies of a Mexican Farm Working Population in the Midwest. Ph.D. diss., University of California, Los Angeles.

Chayanov, A. V.

1966   *Theory of Peasant Economy.* Homewood, Ill.: Richard D. Irwin.

Clayton, John, comp.

1970   *The Illinois Fact Book and Historical Almanac, 1673–1968.* Carbondale: Southern Illinois University Press.

Clear Creek Baptist Association

1988   *History.* Anna, Ill.: Clear Creek Baptist Association.

Clifford, James

1988   *The Predicament of Culture: Twentieth-Century Ethnography, Literature, and Art.* Cambridge, Mass.: Harvard University Press.

Cobden Community Development Committee

1956a   *Analyzing Our Organizations.* Developing Our Community Series. Carbondale: Southern Illinois University.

1956b   *Gathering the Facts about Our Population*. Developing Our Community Series. Carbondale: Southern Illinois University.

Cobden Historical Committee
[1955]   *History of Cobden*. Cobden, Ill.: Community Development Committee.

Cochrane, Willard W.
1979   *The Development of American Agriculture: A Historical Analysis*. Minneapolis: University of Minnesota Press.

Coggeshall, John M.
1984   Ethnic Persistence with Modification: The German-Americans of Southwestern Illinois. Ph.D. diss., Southern Illinois University.

Colby, Charles
1956   *Pilot Study of Southern Illinois*. Carbondale: Southern Illinois University Press.

Cole, Arthur C.
1919   *The Era of the Civil War, 1848–1870*. Vol. 3 of *Centennial History of Illinois*. Springfield: Illinois Centennial Commission.

Collins, Jane L.
1990   Unwaged Labor in Comparative Perspective: Recent Theories and Unanswered Questions. In *Work without Wages: Domestic Labor and Self-Employment within Capitalism*, ed. Jane L. Collins and Martha Gimenez, pp. 3–24. Albany: State University of New York Press.

Collins, Patricia Hill
1990   *Black Feminist Thought: Knowledge, Consciousness, and the Politics of Empowerment*. New York: Routledge.

Committee for Economic Development
[1962]   An Adaptive Program for Agriculture. A Statement on National Policy by the Research and Policy Committee of the Committee for Economic Development.
1957   Toward a Realistic Farm Program. A Statement by the Program Committee of the Committee for Economic Development.
1956   Economic Policy for American Agriculture. A Statement on National Policy by the Research and Policy Committee of the Committee for Economic Development.
[1945]   Agriculture in an Expanding Economy. A Statement by the Research Committee of the Committee for Economic Development.

Comstock, Gary
1991   Discussion of the Chapter by Dr. Thurow. In *Social Science Agricultural Agendas and Strategies*, ed. Glenn L. Johnson and James T. Bonnen, pp. I-65–68. East Lansing: Michigan State University.

Condon, Dr. Sidney S.
1987 [1871]   *Pioneer Sketches of Union County, Illinois*. Ed. and annotated by Darrel Dexter, P.O. Box 175, Ullin, Ill.

Cook, Kenneth A., and Susan E. Sechler
1985   Agricultural Policy: Paying for Our Past Mistakes. *Issues in Science and Technology* 1985 (Fall): 97–110.

Cott, Nancy F.

1978   Passionlessness: An Interpretation of Victorian Sexual Ideology, 1790–1850. *Signs* 4 (2): 219–36.

1977   *The Bonds of Womanhood: "Woman's Sphere" in New England, 1780–1835*. New Haven: Yale University Press.

Coughenour, C. Milton, and Louis Swanson

1983   Work Statuses and Occupations of Men and Womn in Farm Families and the Structure of Farms. *Rural Sociology* 48 (1): 23–43.

Couto, Richard A.

1983   Appalachian Innovations in Health Care. In *Appalachia and America: Autonomy and Regional Dependence*, ed. Allen Batteau, pp. 168–88. Lexington: University Press of Kentucky.

1975   *Poverty, Politics, and Health Care*. New York: Praeger.

Cowan, Ruth Schwartz

1983   *More Work for Mother: The Ironies of Household Technology from the Open Hearth to the Microwave*. New York: Basic Books.

1974   A Case Study of Technological and Social Change: The Washing Machine and the Working Wife. In *Clio's Consciousness Raised*, ed. Mary S. Hartman and Lois Banner, pp. 245–53. New York: Harper.

Danbom, David B.

1979   *The Resisted Revolution: Urban America and the Industrialization of Agriculture, 1900–1930*. Ames: Iowa State University Press.

Deford, Frank

1971   *There She Is: The Life and Times of Miss America*. New York: Viking.

Degler, Carl

1980   *At Odds: Women and the Family in America from the Revolution to the Present*. New York: Oxford University Press.

Dexter, Darrel, ed.

1993   Clear Creek Baptist Church Minutes, 1818–1848, Union County. *The Saga of Southern Illinois* 20 (3): 24–40.

[1987]   *Union County, Illinois, Guardianship Records, 1818–1918*, transcribed and indexed by Darrel Dexter. Carterville: Genealogy Society of Southern Illinois.

Dorst, John

1991   *The Written Suburb: An American Site, an Ethnographic Dilemma*. Philadelphia: University of Pennsylvania Press.

Doty, John Hubert

n.d.   Vancel and Lyerly Families in America. Ms.

Doyle, Don Harrison

1978   *The Social Order of a Frontier Community: Jacksonville, Illinois, 1825–70*. Urbana: University of Illinois Press.

Doyle, Jack

1985   *Altered Harvest: Agriculture, Genetics, and the Fate of the World's Food Supply*. New York: Viking.

DuBois, H. A.

1927   Cobden—High, Healthy, and Happy. In *The Spirit of Egypt: Southern Illinois*, [ed.] E. G. Lentz, p. 112. Carbondale, Ill.: H. B. Keller, L. R. Colp, and F. C. Bastin.

East, Marjorie
1980   *Home Economics: Past, Present, and Future*. Boston: Allyn and Bacon.

Elbert, E. Duane
1985   The American Roots of German Lutheranism in Illinois. *Illinois Historical Journal* 78:97–112.

Elbert, Sarah
1988   Women and Farming: Changing Structures, Changing Roles. In *Women and Farming*, ed. Wava Haney and Jane B. Knowles, pp. 245–64. Boulder, Colo.: Westview.

Eller, David B.
1987   George Wolfe and the "Far Western" Brethren. *Illinois Historical Journal* 80:85–100.

Ernst, Harry W., and Charles H. Drake
1972   The Lost Appalachians. In *Appalachia in the Sixties: Decade of Reawakening*, ed. David S. Walls and John B. Stephenson, pp. 3–10. Lexington: University Press of Kentucky.

Executive Committee on Southern Illinois
1949   *Southern Illinois: Resources and Potentials of the Sixteen Southernmost Counties*. Urbana: University of Illinois Press.

Fabian, Johannes
1983   *Time and the Other: How Anthropology Makes Its Object*. New York: Columbia University Press.

Faragher, John M.
1986   *Sugar Creek: Life on the Illinois Prairie*. New Haven: Yale University Press.

Fink, Deborah
1992   *Agrarian Women: Wives and Mothers in Rural Nebraska, 1880–1940*. Chapel Hill: University of North Carolina Press.
1986   *Open Country, Iowa*. Albany: State University of New York Press.

Finkleman, Paul
1987   Slavery, the "More Perfect Union," and the Prairie State. *Illinois Historical Journal* 80 (4): 248–69.

Fite, Gilbert C.
1981   *American Farmers: The New Minority*. Bloomington: Indiana University Press.

Flagg, Edmund
1838   *The Far West: or, A Tour Beyond the Mountains*. New York: Harper and Brothers.

Flora, Cornelia Butler
1988   Public Policy and Women in Agricultural Production: A Comparative and Historical Analysis. In *Women and Farming*, ed. Wava Haney and Jane B. Knowles, pp. 265–80. Boulder, Colo.: Westview.

Folbre, Nancy
1991   The Unproductive Housewife: Her Evolution in Nineteenth Century Economic Thought. *Signs* 16 (3): 463–84.

Foucault, Michel
1979   *Discipline and Punish: The Birth of the Prison*. New York: Vintage.

Fowler, Cary, and Pat Mooney

1990   *Shattering: Food, Politics, and the Loss of Genetic Diversity*. Tucson: University of Arizona Press.

Fowler, Melvin L., and Robert L. Hall

1978   Late Prehistory of the Illinois Area. In *Handbook of North American Indians, Northeast*, ed. Bruce G. Trigger, 15:560–68. Washington, D.C.: Smithsonian Institution.

Frederick, Christine

1919   *Household Engineering: Scientific Management in the Home*. Chicago: American School of Home Economics.

Friedan, Betty

1963   *The Feminine Mystique*. New York: Dell.

Friedberger, Mark

1989   *Shake-out: Iowa Farm Families in the 1980s*. Lexington: University Press of Kentucky.

1988   *Farm Families and Change in 20th Century America*. Lexington: University Press of Kentucky.

Friedland, William H., Lawrence Busch, Frederick H. Buttel, and Alan P. Rudy, eds.

1991   *Toward a New Political Economy of Agriculture*. Boulder, Colo.: Westview.

Friedmann, Harriet

1980   Household Production and the National Economy: Concepts for the Analysis of Agrarian Formations. *Journal of Peasant Studies* 7 (2): 158–84.

1978   Simple Commodity Production and Wage Labour in the American Plains. *Journal of Peasant Studies* 6 (1): 70–100.

Gates, Paul W.

1934   *The Illinois Central Railroad and Its Colonization Work*. Cambridge, Mass.: Harvard University Press.

Gatlin, Rochelle

1987   *American Women since 1945*. Jackson: University Press of Mississippi.

General Accounting Office

1986a   Farmers Home Administration: An Overview of Farmer Program Debt, Delinquencies, and Loan Losses. GAO/RCED-86-57BR.

1986b   Farm Finance: Farm Debt, Government Payments, and Options to Relieve Financial Stress. GAO/RCED-86-126BR.

George, Susan

1988   *A Fate Worse Than Debt*. New York: Grove Press.

Giddens, Anthony

1984   *Constitution of Society: Outline of the Theory of Structuration*. Berkeley: University of California Press.

1979   *Central Problems in Social Theory: Action, Structure and Contradiction in Social Analysis*. Berkeley: University of California Press.

Gilbreth, Lillian

1927   *The Homemaker and Her Job*. New York: D. Appleton-Century.

Glassie, Henry

1975 *Folk Housing in Middle Virginia: A Structural Analysis of Historic Ar-chitecture.* Knoxville: University of Tennessee Press.

Goldenweiser, E. A., and Leon E. Truesdell

1924 *Farm Tenancy in the United States, 1920.* Census Monographs 4. Washington, D.C.: U.S. Government Printing Office.

Goldschmidt, Walter

1978 [1947] *As You Sow: Three Studies in the Social Consequences of Agribusiness.* Montclair, N.J.: Allanheld, Osmun.

Goodman, David, and Michael Redclift

1981 *From Peasant to Proletarian: Capitalist Development and Agrarian Transitions.* Oxford: Basil Blackwell.

Goss, K. V., R. D. Rodefeld, and F. H. Buttel

1980 The Political Economy of Class Structure in U.S. Agriculture: A Theoretical Outline. In *The Rural Sociology of the Advanced Societies,* ed. F. H. Buttel and H. Newby, 83–132. Montclair, N.J.: Allanheld, Osmun.

Gottfried, Herbert, and Jan Jennings

1988 *American Vernacular Design, 1870–1940.* Ames: Iowa State University Press.

Gramsci, Antonio

1971 *Selections from the Prison Notebooks.* Ed. and trans. Quinten Hoare and Geoffrey Nowell Smith. London: Wishart.

Gray, Wood

1942 *The Hidden Civil War: The Story of the Copperheads.* New York: Viking.

Griffing, B. N.

1881 *Atlas of Union County, Illinois.* Chicago: D. J. Lake.

Groneman, Carol, and Mary Beth Norton, eds.

1987 *"To Toil the Livelong Day": America's Women at Work, 1780–1980.* Ithaca: Cornell University Press.

Gudeman, Stephen, and Alberto Rivera

1991 *Conversations in Colombia: The Domestic Economy in Life and Text.* Cambridge: Cambridge University Press.

Hadwiger, Don F., and Ross B. Talbot

1965 *Pressures and Protests: The Kennedy Farm Program and the Wheat Referendum of 1963. A Case Study.* San Francisco: Chandler.

Hahn, Steven

1983 *The Roots of Southern Populism: Yeoman Farmers and the Transformation of the Georgia Upcountry, 1850–1890.* New York: Oxford University Press.

Hall, Edward Emerson

1940 *The Geography of the Interior Low Plateau and Associated Lowlands of Southern Illinois.* St. Louis: J. S. Swift.

Halperin, Rhoda

1990 *The Livelihood of Kin: Making Ends Meet "The Kentucky Way."* Austin: University of Texas Press.

Halsted, Byron D.

1911 [1904]   *Barn Plans and Outbuildings.* New York: Orange Judd.

Haney, Wava, and Jane B. Knowles, eds.

1988   *Women and Farming.* Boulder, Colo.: Westview.

Haraway, Donna

1988   Situated Knowledges: The Science Question in Feminism and the
                Privilege of Partial Perspective. *Feminist Studies* 14 (3): 575–99.

Hareven, Tamara K.

1990   A Complex Relationship: Family Strategies and the Processes of Eco-
                nomic and Social Change. In *Beyond the Marketplace: Rethinking
                Economy and Society*, ed. Roger Friedland and A. F. Robertson, pp.
                215–44. New York: Aldine de Gruyter.

1976   Modernization and Family History: Perspectives on Social Change.
                Signs 2 (1): 191–206.

Harl, Neil E.

1990   *The Farm Debt Crisis of the 1980s.* Ames: Iowa State University Press.

Harris, Margaret

[1991]   Lawnetta Acres. Photocopied memoir, copy in author's collection.

Harris, Stanley E., Jr., C. William Horrell, and Daniel Irwin

1977   *Exploring the Land and Rocks of Southern Illinois: A Geological Guide.*
                Carbondale: Southern Illinois University Press.

Harrison, Faye V., ed.

1991   *Decolonizing Anthropology.* Washington, D.C.: American Anthropo-
                logical Association.

Hartmann, Heidi

1981   The Family as the Locus of Gender, Class, and Political Struggle:
                The Example of Housework. *Signs* 6 (3): 366–94.

Hartsock, Nancy

1989–90   Postmodernism and Political Change: Issues for Feminist Theory.
                Cultural Critique, no. 14 (Winter): 15–33.

1987   The Feminist Standpoint: Developing the Ground for a Specifically
                Feminist Historical Materialism. In *Feminism and Methodology: Social
                Science Issues*, ed. Nancy C. M. Hartsock, pp. 157–80. Bloomington:
                Indiana University Press.

Harvey, David

1989   *The Condition of Postmodernity: An Enquiry into the Origins of Cultural
                Change.* Cambridge, Mass.: Basil Blackwell.

Havens, A. Eugene

1986   Capitalist Development in the United States: State, Accumulation,
                and Agricultural Production Systems. In *Studies in the Transformation
                of U.S. Agriculture*, ed. A. Eugene Havens, pp. 26–59. Boulder, Colo.:
                Westview.

Hayter, Earl W.

1968   *The Troubled Farmer, 1850–1900: Rural Adjustment to Industrializa-
                tion.* DeKalb: Northern Illinois University Press.

Herbst, J. H.

1976   *Farm Management: Principles, Budgets, Plans.* Champaign, Ill.: Stipes Publishing.

Hightower, Jim

1973   *Hard Tomatoes, Hard Times.* Cambridge, Mass.: Schenkman.

Hoshiko, Patsy Rose (for Shawnee Library System)

1983   *Southern Illinois History Inventory: Inventory of Documents Pertaining to Southern Illinois History.* Carterville, Ill.: Southern Illinois History Project.

Howard, Robert P.

1972   *Illinois: A History of the Prairie State.* Grand Rapids, Mich.: William B. Eerdmans.

Howe, Barbara J., Dolores A. Fleming, Emory L. Kemp, and Ruth Ann Overbeck

1987   *Houses and Homes: Exploring Their History.* Nashville, Tenn.: American Association for State and Local History.

Howe, Carolyn

1986   Farmers' Movements and the Changing Structure of Agriculture. In *Studies in the Transformation of U.S. Agriculture,* ed. A. Eugene Havens, pp. 104–49. Boulder, Colo.: Westview.

Humphrey, Theodore C., and Lyn T. Humphrey, eds.

1988   *"We Gather Together": Food and Festival in American Life.* Ann Arbor: UMI Research Press.

Hunsaker, Q. Maurice, and Gwen Hunsaker Haws, eds.

1957   *Hunsaker Family History.* Salt Lake City: Hunsaker Family Organization (Desert News Press).

Illinois Central Railroad

1867   *Illinois Fruit Industry, the Egyptian Basin and Its Contents.* Chicago: Illinois Central Railroad.

Illinois Department of Agriculture

1989   *Illinois Agricultural Statistics, Annual Summary.* Bulletin 89-1. Springfield: Illinois Department of Agriculture.

1986   *Illinois Agricultural Statistics, Annual Summary.* Bulletin 86-1. Springfield: Illinois Department of Agriculture.

1911   *Sixteenth Annual Report of the Illinois Farmers' Institute.* Springfield: Illinois State Journal Co.

1910   *Fifteenth Annual Report of the Illinois Farmers' Institute.* Springfield: Illinois State Journal Co.

Illinois Sesquicentennial Commission

1969   *Illinois: Guide and Gazetteer.* Chicago: Rand McNally.

Illinois State Agricultural Society

1858   *Transactions.* Springfield, Ill.: State Journal Co.

Invisible Green, Esq.

1857   Egypt Gals Ahead—Hoosier Gals No Whar. *Yankee Notions* 6 (March): 84.

Isaac, Rhys

1985   Communication and Control: Authority Metaphors and Power Contests on Colonel Landon Carter's Virginia Plantation, 1752–1778. In

Rites of Power: Symbolism, Ritual, and Politics since the Middle Ages, ed. Sean Wilentz, pp. 275–302. Philadelphia: University of Pennsylvania Press.

Israel, Fred L.

1968   *1897 Sears Roebuck Catalogue*. New York: Chelsea House.

Jellison, Katherine

1993   *Entitled to Power: Farm Women and Technology, 1919–1963*. Chapel Hill: University of North Carolina Press.

Jensen, Joan

1986   *Loosening the Bonds: Mid-Atlantic Farm Women, 1750–1850*. New Haven: Yale University Press.

1980   Cloth, Butter, and Boarders: Women's Household Production for the Market. *Review of Radical Political Economics* 12 (2): 14–24.

Jensen, Joan M., and Nancy Grey Osterud, eds.

1993   *American Rural and Farm Women in Historical Perspective. Agricultural History* 67 (2). Special symposium issue.

Johnson, Kenneth M.

1985   *The Impact of Population Change on Business Activity in Rural America*. Boulder, Colo.: Westview.

Jolly, R. W., and D. G. Doye

1985   Farm Income and the Financial Condition of United States Agriculture. FAPRI Staff Report #8-85. July.

Jones, Jacqueline

1988   "Tore Up and a-Moving": Perspectives on the Work of Black and Poor White Women in the Rural South. In *Women and Farming*, ed. Wava Haney and Jane B. Knowles, pp. 15–34. Boulder, Colo.: Westview.

Joyce, Rosemary O.

1983   *A Woman's Place: The Life History of a Rural Ohio Grandmother*. Columbus: Ohio State University Press.

Kaledin, Eugenia

1984   *Mothers and More: American Women in the 1950s*. Boston: Twayne.

Kalmar, Tomas Mario

1983   *The Voice of Fulano: Working Papers from a Bilingual Literacy Campaign*. Cambridge, Mass.: Schenkman.

Kammlade, William G., Paul W. Rexroat, and H. A. Cate

1976   *Redeeming a Lost Heritage: The Development of the Dixon Springs Agricultural Center*. Special Publication 40. Urbana: College of Agriculture, Agricultural Experiment Station and Cooperative Extension Service, University of Illinois.

Karraker, I. O.

1947   Flaughtown and Other Union County Water Mills. Typescript. Carbondale: Southern Illinois Historical Society.

Keating, Norah, and Brenda Munro

1988   Farm Women/Farm Work. *Sex Roles* 19 (3/4): 155–68.

Kennedy, Sarah Alice
1910   *Why Did George Leave? Reminiscences of Mrs. Elizabeth Rendleman.*
            Marion, Ill.: Stafford.

Kessler-Harris, Alice
1982   *Out to Work: A History of Wage-Earning Women in the United States.*
            New York: Oxford University Press.

Kile, O. M.
1948   *The Farm Bureau through Three Decades.* Baltimore: Waverly.

Kirby, Jack Temple
1987   *Rural Worlds Lost: The American South, 1920–1960.* Baton Rouge:
            Louisiana State University Press.

Kirschner, Susan
1987   "Then What Have I to Do with Thee?" On Identity, Fieldwork, and
            Ethnographic Knowledge. *Current Anthropology* 2 (2): 211–34.

Klement, Frank L.
1960   *The Copperheads in the Middle West.* Chicago: University of Chicago
            Press.

Kniffen, Fred
1965   Folk Housing: Key to Diffusion. *Annals of the Association of American
            Geographers* 55:549–77.

Kofoid, Carrie Prudence
1906   Puritan Influence in the Formative Years of Illinois History. In *Trans-
            actions of the Illinois State Historical Society for the Year 1905.* Pub-
            lication No. 10. Springfield: Illinois State Historical Library.

Kohl, Seena B.
1988   Image and Behavior: Women's Participation in North American Fam-
            ily Agricultural Enterprises. In *Women and Farming*, ed. Wava Haney
            and Jane B. Knowles, pp. 89–108. Boulder, Colo.: Westview.
1976   *Working Together: Women and Family in Southwestern Saskatchewan.*
            Toronto: Holt, Rinehart, and Winston.

Krebs, A. V.
1992   *The Corporate Reapers: The Book of Agribusiness.* Washington, D.C.:
            Essential Books.

Kulikoff, Allen
1989   The Transition to Capitalism in Rural America. *William and Mary
            Quarterly* 46:120–44.

Kurin, Richard
1984   *The Development and Decline of Southern Illinois Communities, 1960 to
            1980.* Carbondale: Office of Regional Research and Service, Southern
            Illinois University.

Lansden, John M.
1976 [1910] *A History of the City of Cairo, Illinois.* Chicago: R. R. Donnelly and
            Sons.

Lappé, Francis Moore
1981   *Agricultural Exports: Aggravating the Crisis.* San Francisco: Institute
            for Food and Development Policy.

Lappé, Francis Moore, and Joseph Collins

1977   *Food First: Beyond the Myth of Scarcity*. Boston: Houghton Mifflin.

Laurie, Bruce

1989   *Artisans into Workers: Labor in Nineteenth-Century America*. New
            York: Hill and Wang.

Layer, Robert G.

1965   *The Fundamental Bases of Southern Illinois, 1879–1959*. Regional
            Studies in Business and Economics Monograph No. 1. Carbondale:
            Business Research Bureau, Southern Illinois University.

Lehman, David

1986   Two Paths of Agrarian Capitalism, or a Critique of Chayanovian
            Marxism. *Comparative Studies in Society and History* 28 (4): 601–27.

Lentz, E. G.

1955   *Seventy-Five Years in Retrospect: From Normal School to Teachers Col-
            lege to University, Southern Illinois University, 1874–1949*. Carbon-
            dale: Southern Illinois University.

1927   *The Spirit of Egypt: Southern Illinois*. Carbondale, Ill.: H. B. Keller,
            L. R. Colp, and F. C. Bastin.

Leonard, Lulu

[1942]   *History of Union County*. Anna, Ill.: Gazette Democrat.

Lerner, Gerda

1969   The Lady and the Mill Girl: Changes in the Status of Women in the
            Age of Jackson. *Midcontinent American* 10 (1): 5–15.

Levin, Melvin

1965   The Depressed Area: A Study of Southern Illinois. Master's thesis,
            University of Chicago.

Lins, David A.

1985   *Policy Options for Dealing with Financial Stress in Agriculture*. Urbana:
            University of Illinois Department of Agriculture Economics.

Lobao, Linda M.

1990   *Locality and Inequality: Farm and Industry Structure and Socio-
            economic Conditions*. Albany: State University of New York Press.

Lopinot, Neal H.

1984   An Environmental Model for the Upper Cache River Drainage. Ap-
            pendix C: Biotic Community Distribution Maps, and Appendix J:
            Plant Resources of the Upper Cache Valley, Illinois. In *Cultural Fron-
            tiers in the Upper Cache Valley, Illinois*, ed. V. Canouts, E. E. May,
            N. H. Lopinot, and J. D. Muller, pp. 44–67, 175–80, 203–22. Center
            for Archaeological Investigations Research Paper No. 16. Carbondale:
            Center for Archaeological Investigations, Southern Illinois Univer-
            sity.

Lord, Russell, ed.

1937   *Voices from the Fields*. Boston: Houghton Mifflin.

McConnell, Grant

1953   *The Decline of Agrarian Democracy*. Berkeley: University of California
            Press.

MacEwan, Arthur

1990   *Debt and Disorder: International Economic Instability and U.S. Imperial Decline.* New York: Monthly Review Press.

McMahan, Gale S., ed.

1988   *The Southern Baptist Churches in the Clear Creek Baptist Association.* Utica, Ky.: McDowell.

McNerney, Michael J.

1978   *A Cultural Resource Overview of the Shawnee National Forest.* Prepared for U.S. Department of Agriculture, United States Forest Service, Contract No. 01–3201. Carbondale, Ill.: Fischer-Stein Associates.

McWilliams, Cary

1969 [1939]   *Factories in the Field: The Story of Migratory Farm Labor in California.* Hamden, Conn.: Archon Books.

Mann, Susan A., and James M. Dickinson

1978   Obstacles to the Development of a Capitalist Agriculture. *Journal of Peasant Studies* 5 (4): 466–81.

Manning, Frank E., ed.

1983   *The Celebration of Society: Perspectives on Cultural Performance.* Bowling Green, Ohio: Bowling Green University Popular Press.

Marion, Bruce W., and the NC 117 Committee

1986   *The Organization and Performance of the U.S. Food System.* Lexington, Mass.: D. C. Heath and Co., Lexington Books.

Martin, Charles E.

1984   *Hollybush: Folk Building and Social Change in an Appalachian Community.* Knoxville: University of Tennessee Press.

Marx, Karl

1967 [1887]   *Capital.* Ed. Frederick Engels. New York: International Publishers.

Marx, Leo

1964   *The Machine in the Garden: Technology and the Pastoral Ideal in America.* London: Oxford University Press.

Matthaei, Julie A.

1982   *An Economic History of Women in America: Women's Work, the Sexual Division of Labor, and the Development of Capitalism.* New York: Schocken Books.

Matthews, E. M.

1965   *Neighbor and Kin: Life in a Tennessee Ridge Community.* Nashville, Tenn.: Vanderbilt University Press.

Matthews, Glenna

1987   *"Just a Housewife": The Rise and Fall of Domesticity in America.* New York: Oxford University Press.

Mauss, Marcel

1954 [1925]   *The Gift.* Translated by Ian Cunnison. London: Routledge and Kegan Paul.

May, Ernest E.

1984   Prehistoric Chert Exploitation in the Shawnee Hills. In *Cultural Frontiers in the Upper Cache Valley, Illinois,* ed. V. Canouts, E. E. May, N. H. Lopinot, and J. D. Muller, pp. 68–90. Center for Archaeological Investigations Research Paper No. 16. Carbondale: Center for Archaeological Investigations, Southern Illinois University.

Melvin, Bruce

1932   *Farm and Village Housing.* Report of the Committee on Farm and Village Housing, Albert Russell Mann, Chairman. President's Conference on Home Building and Home Ownership. Washington, D.C.: President's Conference.

Miller, Clara Bell

1976   "Through the Looking Glass": Cobden Women's Club, 1908–1976. Ms. in author's collection.

Mitchell, Theodore

1987   *Political Education in the Southern Farmers' Alliance: 1887–1900.* Madison: University of Wisconsin Press.

Montell, William Lynwood, and Michael Lynn Morse

1976   *Kentucky Folk Architecture.* Lexington: University Press of Kentucky.

Morantz, Regina

1977   Making Women Modern: Middle Class Women and Health Reform in 19th Century America. *Journal of Social History* 10 (4): 490–507.

Morgan, Dan

1979   *Merchants of Grain.* New York: Penguin.

Navarro, Vicente

1991   The Limitations of Legitimation and Fordism and the Possibility for Socialist Reforms. *Rethinking Marxism* 4 (2): 27–60.

Neely, Wayne C.

1967 [1935]   *The Agricultural Fair.* New York: AMS Press.

Newton, Milton

1974   Cultural Preadaptation and the Upland South. *Geoscience and Man* 5:143–54.

Nickell, Vernon L.

1956   Illinois Public Schools Provide Educational Opportunities to All. In *Illinois Blue Book, 1955–1956*, by State of Illinois, pp. 404–13. N.p.

Noble, Allen G.

1984   *Wood, Brick, and Stone: The North American Settlement Landscape.* Vol. 1, *Houses.* Amherst: University of Massachusetts Press.

Nobles, Gregory

1988   Capitalism in the Countryside: The Transformation of Rural Society in the United States. *Radical History Review* 41:163–76.

Nye, Russel B.

1959   *Midwestern Progressive Politics: A Historical Study of Its Origins and Development, 1870–1958.* East Lansing: Michigan State University Press.

O'Boyle, Judith

1978   An Analysis of the Needs and Problems of Female Migrant Farmworkers in Cobden, Illinois. Master's thesis, Southern Illinois University.

Ogle, George A.

1908   *Standard Atlas of Union County, Illinois.* Chicago: Geo. A. Ogle.

Osterud, Nancy Grey

1991   *Bonds of Community: The Lives of Farm Women in Nineteenth-Century New York*. Ithaca: Cornell University Press.

1987   "She Helped Me Hay It as Good as a Man": Relations among Women and Men in an Agricultural Community. In *"To Toil the Livelong Day": America's Women at Work, 1780–1980*, ed. Carol Groneman and Mary Beth Norton, pp. 87–97. Ithaca: Cornell University Press.

Otto, J. S., and N. E. Anderson

1982   The Diffusion of Upland South Folk Culture, 1790–1840. *Southeastern Geographer* 22:89–98.

Parks, George E.

1983   *History of Union County and Some Genealogy Notes*. 3 vols. Anna, Ill.: Privately printed.

[1980]   *Reaching for Riches: Rich Family Genealogy*. Anna, Ill.: Privately printed.

Parloa, Maria

1910 [1898] *Home Economics*. New and enlarged edition. New York: Century.

Pattison, Mary

1915   *Principles of Domestic Engineering*. New York: Trow.

Paul, Allen B., and William T. Manley

1970   The Marketing System for Food, Fabulous and Dynamic. In *Yearbook of Agriculture, Contours of Change*, by United States Department of Agriculture, pp. 94–102. Washington, D.C.: U.S. Government Printing Office.

Periam, Jonathan

1984 [1884] *The Home and Farm Manual*. New York: Greenwich House.

1874   *The Groundswell*. Cincinnati, Ohio: E. Hannaford.

Perrin, William Henry, ed.

1883   *History of Alexander, Union, and Pulaski Counties*. Chicago: O. L. Baskin.

Peshkin, Alan

1982   *The Imperfect Union: School Consolidation and Community Conflict*. Chicago: University of Chicago Press.

Pfeffer, Max J.

1983   Social Origins of Three Systems of Farm Production in the United States. *Rural Sociology* 48 (4): 540–62.

Phipps, Tim T., Pierre R. Crosson, and Kent A. Price, eds.

1986   *Agriculture and the Environment*. Washington, D.C.: National Center for Food and Agricultural Policy, Resources for the Future.

Plochman, George Kimball

[1957]   *The Ordeal of Southern Illinois University*. Carbondale: Southern Illinois University Press.

Power, Richard L.

1953   *Planting Corn Belt Culture: The Impress of the Upland Southerner and the Yankee in the Old Northwest*. Indianapolis: Indiana Historical Society.

Powers, Ron

1991 *Far from Home: Life and Loss in Two American Towns*. New York: An-
    chor.

Precourt, Walter

1983 The Image of Appalachian Poverty. In *Appalachia and America: Au-
    tonomy and Regional Dependence*, ed. Allen Batteau, pp. 86–110. Lex-
    ington: University Press of Kentucky.

Price, E. T.

1969 The Central Courthouse Square in the American County Seat. *Geo-
    graphic Review* 58:29–60.

Prigge, Daniel

1973 *History of the Mouth of the Cache River*. Mound City, Ill.: Mound City
    Civic and Historical Association.

Rasmussen, Wayne D., and Gladys L. Baker

1979 *Price-Support and Adjustment Programs from 1933 through 1978: A
    Short History*. Agricultural Information Bulletin No. 424. Wash-
    ington, D.C.: National Economic Analysis Division; Economics, Sta-
    tistics, and Cooperative Service, U.S. Department of Agriculture.

Rawlings, Isaac D.

1927 *The Rise and Fall of Disease in Illinois*. Springfield, Ill.: State Depart-
    ment of Public Health.

Rawson, Richard

1979 *Old Barn Plans*. New York: Bonanza Books.

Reid, Margaret Gilpin

1934 *Economics of Household Production*. New York: John Wiley and Sons.

Rendleman, Edith

n.d. The Story of My Life. Handwritten memoirs; typescript from 1976
    and 1983 versions in possession of author.

Rendleman, Ford L.

1973 *Memoirs*. N.p.: Privately printed.

Rendleman, Russel

[1959] *Union County School Report*. N.p.

Rich, Ronald

1993 From Outside the Law: Southern Illinois Women in Inheritance.
    Master's thesis. Southern Illinois University at Carbondale.

Richards, Ellen

1908 Ten Years of the Lake Placid Conference on Home Economics: Its
    History and Aims. Proceedings of the Tenth Annual Conference,
    Lake Placid, N.Y.

Rodefeld, R. D.

1978 Trends in U.S. Farm Organizational Structure and Type. In *Change
    in Rural America: Causes, Consequences, and Alternatives*, ed. R. D.
    Rodefeld et al., pp. 158–77. St. Louis: Mosby.

Rogers, Earl M., and Susan H. Rogers

1989 *The American Farm Crisis: An Annotated Bibliography*. New York:
    Garland.

Rohrbough, Malcolm J.
1978   *The Trans-Appalachian Frontier: People, Societies, and Institutions, 1775–1850.* New York: Oxford University Press.

Rosaldo, Michelle
1980   The Use and Abuse of Anthropology: Reflections on Feminism and Cross-Cultural Understanding. *Signs* 5 (3): 389–417.

Rosaldo, Renato
1989   *Culture and Truth: The Remaking of Social Analysis.* Boston: Beacon.

Rosenfeld, Rachel Ann
1985   *Farm Women: Work, Farm, and Family in the United States.* Chapel Hill: University of North Carolina Press.

Rowe, Harry R.
1940   History of Water Valley. Paper written and read at Dillow reunion. Ms. in author's possession.

Rubin, Arnold
1979   Anthropology and the Study of Art in Contemporary Society: The Pasadena Tournament of Roses. In *The Visual Arts, Plastic and Graphic*, ed. Justine M. Cordwell, pp. 669–716. The Hague: Mouton.

Ryan, Mary P.
1982   *The Empire of the Mother: American Writing on Domesticity, 1830–1860.* New York: Hayworth.
1981   *The Cradle of the Middle Class: The Family in Oneida County, New York, 1790–1865.* Cambridge: Cambridge University Press.

Sachs, Carolyn
1983   *Invisible Farmers: Women in Agricultural Production.* Totowa, N.J.: Rowman and Allenheld.

Salamon, Sonya
1992   *Prairie Patrimony: Family, Farming, and Community in the Midwest.* Chapel Hill: University of North Carolina Press.
1987   Ethnic Determinants of Farm Community Character. In *Farm Work and Fieldwork: American Agriculture in Anthropological Perspective*, ed. Michael Chibnik, pp. 167–88. Ithaca: Cornell University Press.
1985   Ethnic Communities and the Structure of Agriculture. *Rural Sociology* 50 (3): 323–40.
1980   Ethnic Differences in Farm Family Land Transfers. *Rural Sociology* 45 (2): 290–308.

Salamon, Sonya, and Karen Davis-Brown
1988   Farm Continuity and Female Land Inheritance: A Family Dilemma. In *Women and Farming*, ed. Wava Haney and Jane B. Knowles, pp. 195–210. Boulder, Colo.: Westview.

Salamon, Sonya, and Shirley M. O'Reilly
1979   Family Land and Developmental Cycles among Illinois Farmers. *Rural Sociology* 44 (3): 525–42.

Saline County Historical Society
1947   *Saline County: A Century of History.* Harrisburg, Ill.: Register Publishing.

Schertz, Lyle P., et al.

1979   *Another Revolution in U.S. Farming?* Washington, D.C.: U.S. Depart-
              ment of Agriculture.

Schuh, G. Edward

1985   Improving U.S. Agricultural Trade. In *The Dilemmas of Choice.*
              Washington, D.C.: National Center for Food and Agricultural Policy,
              Resources for the Future.

Scott, Anne Firor

1991   *Natural Allies: Women's Associations in American History.* Urbana:
              University of Illinois Press.

Scott, James C.

1990   *Domination and the Arts of Resistance: Hidden Transcripts.* New
              Haven: Yale University Press.

Scott, Roy V.

1970   *The Reluctant Farmer: The Rise of Agricultural Extension to 1914.* Ur-
              bana: University of Illinois Press.

1962   *The Agrarian Movement in Illinois, 1880–1896.* Illinois Studies in the
              Social Sciences, vol. 52. Urbana: University of Illinois Press.

1958   The Rise of the Farmers' Mutual Benefit Association in Illinois,
              1883–1891. *Agricultural History* 32:44–55.

Sennett, Richard, and Jonathan Cobb

1972   *The Hidden Injuries of Class.* New York: Random House.

Seymour, E. L. D., ed.

1919   *Farm Knowledge: A Complete Manual of Successful Farming. . . .* Gar-
              den City, N.Y.: Doubleday, Page and Co. for Sears, Roebuck and Co.

Shapiro, Henry D.

1983   The Place of Culture and the Problem of Identity. In *Appalachia and
              America: Autonomy and Regional Dependence*, ed. Allen Batteau, pp.
              111–41. Lexington: University Press of Kentucky.

1978   *Appalachia on Our Minds: The Southern Mountains and Mountaineers
              in the American Consciousness, 1870–1920.* Chapel Hill: University of
              North Carolina Press.

Simon, John Y.

1969   Union County in 1858 and the Lincoln-Douglas Debate. *Journal of
              the Illinois State Historical Society* 62:267–92.

Singh, Ajit

1992   The Lost Decade: The Economic Crisis of the Third World in the
              1980s. How the North Caused the South's Crisis. *Contention* 1 (3):
              137–59.

Sklar, Kathryn Kish

1973   *Catharine Beecher: A Study in American Domesticity.* New Haven: Yale
              University Press.

Smith, George Washington

1912   *A History of Southern Illinois: A Narrative Account. . . .* Chicago:
              Lewis.

Smith, Joan

1990   All Crises Are Not the Same: Households in the United States during

Two Crises. In *Work without Wages: Domestic Labor and Self-Employment within Capitalism*, ed. Jane L. Collins and Martha Gimenez. pp. 128–41. Albany: State University of New York Press.

Smith, Maryanna S.

1980   *Chronological Landmarks in American Agriculture*. Economics, Statistics, and Cooperatives Service, Agriculture Information Bulletin No. 425. Washington, D.C.: U.S. Department of Agriculture.

Smoot, Mildred E., and Loren Rife

1980   Dongola: Then and Now. Mimeo pamphlet.

Soady, Fred, Jr.

1965   The Making of the Shawnee. *Forest History* 9 (2): 3–16.

Solverson, Lyle, and John Ellerman

1978   *Barriers to Direct Marketing of Fruits and Vegetables in Union and Jackson Counties of Illinois: A Case Study*. Carbondale: Agribusiness Economics Department, School of Agriculture, Southern Illinois University.

Sommer, Robert

1980   *Farmer's Markets of America: A Renaissance*. Santa Barbara, Calif.: Capra.

Southern Five Regional Planning and Development Commission

[1982]   *Industrial Guide for the Counties of Alexander, Johnson, Massac, Pulaski, Union*. Anna, Ill.: Southern Five Regional Planning District and Development Commission.

Southern Illinois University, Office of Regional Research and Services

1984   SIU-C Earnings Summary for Employees Living in Southern Illinois (Including Student Wages) by County of Residence. Photocopy.

Speilbauer, Ronald H.

1976   Chert Resources and Aboriginal Chert Utilization in Western Union County, Illinois. Master's thesis, Southern Illinois University at Carbondale.

Stack, Carol B.

1974   *All Our Kin: Strategies of Survival in a Black Community*. New York: Harper and Row.

State of Illinois

1927–28   *Illinois Blue Book*. N.p.

1930   *Illinois Blue Book*. N.p.

Stephenson, John B.

1968   *Shiloh: A Mountain Community*. Lexington: University Press of Kentucky.

Stilgoe, John R.

1982   *Common Landscape of America, 1580–1845*. New Haven: Yale University Press.

Strange, Marty

1988   *Family Farming: A New Economic Vision*. Lincoln: University of Nebraska Press; San Francisco: Institute for Food and Development Policy.

Strasser, Susan
1982   *Never Done: A History of American Housework.* New York: Pantheon.
Taylor, Noel M.
1975   *The Taylor's at Devil's Kitchen.* Cassville, Mo.: Litho Printers.
Taylor, William R.
1961   *Cavalier and Yankee: The Old South and the American National Character.* New York: G. Braziller.
Thomas, Mary Martha
1992   *The New Woman in Alabama: Social Reforms and Suffrage, 1890–1920.* Tuscaloosa: University of Alabama Press.
Thompson, E. P.
1967   Time, Work-Discipline, and Industrial Capitalism. *Past and Present* 38:56–97.
1963   *The Making of the English Working Class.* New York: Vintage.
Thurow, Lester C.
1991   Agricultural Institutions under Fire. In *Social Science Agricultural Agendas and Strategies,* ed. Glenn L. Johnson and James T. Bonnen, pp. I-55–64. East Lansing: Michigan State University Press.
Tigges, Leann M., and Rachel A. Rosenfeld
1987   Independent Farming: Correlates and Consequences for Women and Men. *Rural Sociology* 52 (3): 345–64.
Tilly, Louise A., and Joan W. Scott
1987 [1978] *Women, Work, and Family.* New York: Methuen.
Tostlebe, Alvin S.
1957   *The Growth of Physical Capital in Agriculture, 1870–1950.* New York: National Bureau of Economic Research.
True, A. C.
1928   *A History of Agricultural Extension Work.* Misc. Publication 15. Washington, D.C.: U.S. Dept. of Agriculture.
Truesdell, Leon E.
1926   *Farm Population of the United States: An Analysis of the 1920 Farm Population Figures, Especially in Comparison with Urban Data, Together With a Study of the Main Economic Factors Affecting the Farm Population.* Census Monographs 6. Washington, D.C.: U.S. Government Printing Office.
Turner, Victor
1974   Social Dramas and Ritual Metaphors. In *Dramas, Fields, and Metaphors,* by Victor Turner, pp. 23–59. Ithaca: Cornell University Press.
Tweeten, Luther
1970   *Foundations of Farm Policy.* Lincoln: University of Nebraska Press.
Union County Farm Bureau and Agricultural Extension Service
1941   Survey of Rural Schools in Union County. Preliminary Report. Anna, Ill.
Union County School Board
[1935]   Union County School Districts as They Appeared in 1935. In-house report.

Union County School Survey Committee
1948   Final Report. Anna, Ill.

University of Illinois. College of Agriculture
1967   *Soils of Illinois*. Bulletin 725. Urbana, Ill.: Agricultural Experiment
              Station in Cooperation with the Soil Conservation Service, U.S. De-
              partment of Agriculture.

University of Illinois. College of Agriculture, Cooperative Extension Service
1986   *62nd Annual Summary of Illinois Farm Business Records*. Bulletin 86-1.
1985   *61st Annual Summary of Illinois Farm Business Records*. Bulletin 85-1.
1984   *60th Annual Summary of Illinois Farm Business Records*. Bulletin 84-1.

U.S. Bureau of the Census
1991   *Census of Population, 1990: Social and Economic Characteristics of the
              Population, Illinois*. Washington, D.C.: U.S. Government Printing Of-
              fice.
1989   *Census of Agriculture, 1987*. Vol. 1, pt. 13, *Illinois State and County
              Data*. Washington, D.C.: U.S. Government Printing Office.
1984   *Census of Agriculture, 1982*. Vol. 1, pt. 13, *Illinois State and County
              Data*. Washington, D.C.: U.S. Government Printing Office.
1982   *Census of Population, 1980*. Vol. 1, pt. 15, *Illinois*. Washington, D.C.:
              U.S. Government Printing Office.
1981   *Census of Agriculture, 1979*. Vol. 1, pt. 13, *Illinois*. Washington, D.C.:
              U.S. Government Printing Office.
1977   *Census of Agriculture, 1974*. Vol. 1, pt. 13, *Illinois*. Washington, D.C.:
              U.S. Government Printing Office.
1972   *Census of Agriculture, 1969*. Vol. 1, pt. 12, *Illinois*. Washington, D.C.:
              U.S. Government Printing Office.
1970   *Census of Population, 1970*. Vol. 1, pt. 15, *Illinois*. Washington, D.C.:
              U.S. Government Printing Office.
1967   *Census of Agriculture, 1964: Statistics for the States and Counties*. Pt.
              12, *Illinois*. Washington, D.C.: U.S. Government Printing Office.
1964   *Census of Population, 1960*. Vol. 1, pt. 15, *Illinois*. Washington, D.C.:
              U.S. Government Printing Office.
1961   *Census of Agriculture, 1959*. Vol. 1, pt. 12, *Illinois*. Washington, D.C.:
              U.S. Government Printing Office.
1956   *Census of Agriculture, 1954*. Vol. 1, pt. 5, *Illinois*. Washington, D.C.:
              U.S. Government Printing Office.
1953   *17th Census of the United States, Population, 1950*. Vol. 2, pt. 13, *Il-
              linois*. Washington, D.C.: U.S. Government Printing Office.
1952   *Census of Agriculture, 1950*. Vol. 1, pt. 5, *Illinois*. Washington, D.C.:
              U.S. Government Printing Office.
1947   *Census of Agriculture, 1945*. Vol. 1, pt. 5, *Illinois*. Washington, D.C.:
              U.S. Government Printing Office.
1943a   *16th Census of the United States, Population, 1940*. Vol. 1, pt. 2,
              Florida-Iowa. Washington, D.C.: U.S. Government Printing Office.
1943b   *Differential Fertility, 1940 and 1910*. Special Report of the 16th
              Census of the United States. Washington, D.C.: U.S. Government
              Printing Office.

1943c   *16th Census of the United States, 1940. Housing: Characteristics by Type of Structure.* Washington, D.C.: U.S. Government Printing Office.

1942   *16th Census of the United States, Agriculture, 1940.* Vol. 2, pt. 1, *The Northern States.* Washington, D.C.: U.S. Government Printing Office.

1936   *Census of Agriculture, 1935.* Vol. 1, pt. 1, *The Northern States.* Washington, D.C.: U.S. Government Printing Office.

1932a   *15th Census of the United States, Agriculture, 1930.* Vol. 3, pt. 1, *The Northern States.* Washington, D.C.: U.S. Government Printing Office.

1932b   *15th Census of the United States, Population, 1930.* Washington, D.C.: U.S. Government Printing Office.

1927   *Census of Agriculture, 1925.* Vol. 1, pt. 1, *The Northern States.* Washington, D.C.: U.S. Government Printing Office.

1922a   *14th Census of the United States, Agriculture, 1920.* Vol. 6, pt. 1. Washington, D.C.: U.S. Government Printing Office.

1922b   *14th Census of the United States, Population, 1920.* Washington, D.C.: U.S. Government Printing Office.

1913a   *13th Census of the United States, Agriculture, 1910.* Vol. 6. Washington, D.C.: U.S. Government Printing Office.

1913b   *13th Census of the United States, Population, 1910.* Washington, D.C.: U.S. Government Printing Office.

1902   *12th Census of the United States, Agriculture.* Vols. 5, 6. Washington, D.C.: U.S. Government Printing Office.

1901   *12th Census of the United States, Population, 1900.* Washington, D.C.: U.S. Government Printing Office.

1895a   *11th Census of the United States, Agriculture, 1890.* Washington, D.C.: U.S. Government Printing Office.

1895b   *11th Census of the United States, Population, 1890.* Washington, D.C.: U.S. Government Printing Office.

1883a   *10th Census of the United States, Agriculture, 1880.* Washington, D.C.: U.S. Government Printing Office.

1883b   *10th Census of the United States, Population, 1880.* Washington, D.C.: U.S. Government Printing Office.

1872a   *9th Census of the United States, Population, 1870.* Washington, D.C.: U.S. Government Printing Office.

1872b   *9th Census of the United States, Agriculture, 1870.* Washington, D.C.: U.S. Government Printing Office.

1865   *8th Census of the United States, Manufacturing, 1860.* Washington, D.C.: U.S. Government Printing Office.

1864a   *8th Census of the United States, Agriculture, 1860.* Washington, D.C.: U.S. Government Printing Office.

1864b   *8th Census of the United States, Population, 1860.* Washington, D.C.: U.S. Government Printing Office.

1853a   *7th Census of the United States, Manufacturing, 1850.* Washington, D.C.: U.S. Government Printing Office.

1853b   *7th Census of the United States, Population, 1850.* Washington, D.C.: U.S. Government Printing Office.

1841   *6th Census of the United States, Manufacturing, 1840*. Washington,
    D.C.: U.S. Government Printing Office.

U.S. Department of Agriculture

1990   *Agricultural Statistics, 1990*. Washington, D.C.: U.S. Government
    Printing Office.

1988a   *Economic Indicators of the Farm Sector: National Financial Summary,*
    1987. Economic Research Service, ECIFS 7-1.

1988b   *Economic Indicators of the Farm Sector: State Financial Summary,*
    1987. Agriculture and Rural Economy Division, Economic Research
    Service, U.S. Department of Agriculture, ECIFS 7-2.

1985   *Economic Indicators of the Farm Sector: State Income and Balance*
    Sheet Statistics, 1983. National Economics Division, Economic Re-
    search Service, ECIFS 3-4.

1983   *Economic Indicators of the Farm Sector: State Income and Balance*
    Sheet Statistics, 1983. National Economics Division, Economic Re-
    search Service, U.S. Department of Agriculture, ECIFS 3-4.

1940   *Yearbook of Agriculture: Farmers in a Changing World*. Washington,
    D.C.: U.S. Government Printing Office.

1936   *Yearbook of Agriculture*. Washington, D.C.: U.S. Government Print-
    ing Office.

1934   *Yearbook of Agriculture*. Washington, D.C.: U.S. Government Print-
    ing Office.

1915   *Social and Labor Needs of Farm Women*. Report No. 103. Washington,
    D.C.: U.S. Government Printing Office.

U.S. Department of Agriculture. Bureau of Home Economics

1934   *Farm Housing Survey*. Washington, D.C.: U.S. Department of Agri-
    culture.

U.S. Department of Agriculture. Soil Conservation Service and Forest Service in
Cooperation with Illinois Agricultural Experiment Station

1979   *Soil Survey of Union County, Illinois*. Illinois Agricultural Experiment
    Station Soil Report No. 110. National Cooperative Soil Survey.

van Es, J. C., and Michael Bowling

1979   Age-Related Migration in Illinois Counties. *Illinois Business Review*
    36 (6): 6–8.

van Gennep, Arnold

1960   *The Rites of Passage*. Trans. Monika B. Vizedom and Gabrielle L.
    Caffee. Chicago: University of Chicago Press.

Venerable, Mary DuBois

1974   My Years. Typescript memoirs, copy in author's possession.

Vogeler, Ingolf

1981   *The Myth of the Family Farm: Agribusiness Dominance of U.S. Agricul-
    ture*. Boulder, Colo.: Westview.

Voigt, J. W., and R. H. Mohlenbrock

1964   *Plant Communities of Southern Illinois*. Carbondale: Southern Illinois
    University Press.

Wakeley, Ray

1962   *Population Changes and Prospects in Southern Illinois.* Carbondale: Division of Area Services, Southern Illinois University.

Wallerstein, Immanuel

1974   *The Modern World System.* New York: Academic Press.

Walls, David S.

1976   Central Appalachia: A Peripheral Region in an Advanced Capitalist Society. *Journal of Sociology and Social Welfare.* 4:232–47.

Walters, C. S.

1949   *The Illinois Veneer Container Industry.* Bulletin 534. Urbana: University of Illinois Agricultural Experiment Station.

Ward, F. E.

1920   *The Farm Woman's Problems.* Circular 148, U.S. Department of Agriculture.

Wardwell, John M.

1982   The Reversal of Nonmetropolitan Migration Loss. In *Rural Society in the U.S.: Issues for the 1980s,* ed. Don A. Dillman and Daryl J. Hobbs, pp. 23–33. Boulder, Colo.: Westview.

Warner, W. Lloyd

1959   *The Living and the Dead: A Study of the Symbolic Life of Americans.* Yankee City Series, vol. 5. New Haven: Yale University Press.

Warner and Beers, proprietors

1876   *Atlas of the State of Illinois.* Chicago: Union Atlas.

Weaver, Leon H.

1944   *School Consolidation and State Aid in Illinois.* Urbana: University of Illinois Press.

Webb, Billie Sneed

1983   *Randleman Rendleman Rintleman Reunion 1981, with members of the Randleman Research Committee (Rendleman, Rintelmann).* 651 Sherwood Way, Corvalis, Or. Privately printed.

Weisskopf, Thomas E.

1991   Marxian Crisis Theory and the Contradictions of Late Twentieth-Century Capitalism. *Rethinking Marxism* 4 (4): 70–93.

Welter, Barbara

1966   The Cult of True Womanhood: 1820–1860. *American Quarterly* 18, no. 2, pt. 1: 151–74.

West, James (Carl Withers)

1945   *Plainville, U.S.A.* New York: Columbia University Press.

Williams, Thomas E.

1982   Rural America in an Urban Age, 1945–1960. In *Reshaping America: Society and Institutions, 1945–1960,* ed. Robert H. Bremner and Gary W. Reichard, pp. 147–61. Columbus: Ohio State University Press.

Wolf, Eric

1982   *Europe and the People without History.* Berkeley: University of California Press.

1957   Closed Corporate Peasant Communities in Mesoamerica and Central Java. *Southwestern Journal of Anthropology* 13 (1): 1–18.

Wright, Gwendolyn
1981   *Building the Dream: A Social History of Housing in America*. New
              York: Pantheon.
Wright, Mareena McKinley
1993   Household Division of Labor as a Family Labor Queue. Paper pre-
              sented at Midwest Sociological Society Annual Meeting, Chicago,
              April.
Zaretsky, Eli
1986   *Capitalism, the Family, and Personal Life*. New York: Harper and Row.
Zimmerman, M. M.
1955   *The Super Market: A Revolution in Distribution*. New York: McGraw-
              Hill.

Farm-based businesses, women's, 81, 88–91, 107, 113, 122, 198, 244, 249, 263 (n. 10); butter, 22, 76, 89, 90; cottage cheese, 29, 90; cream, 22, 77, 78, 90, 190; daffodils, 76, 261 (n. 9); eggs and poultry, 11, 16, 22, 24, 33, 76, 90–91, 188–89, 193; herbs and flowers, 17; sewing, 192–93; sheep and wool, 32, 229; strawberries, 85

Farm Bloc, 154

Farm Bureau. *See* Union County Farm Bureau

Farm crisis (of 1980s), xx, 24, 236–40, 276 (nn. 12, 13)

Farmers' Educational and Cooperative Union of America, 82, 125

Farmers' Home Administration (FmHA), 155, 174–75, 210, 237

Farmers' Mutual Benefit Association, 82, 123, 268 (n. 8)

Farm Extension. *See* Extension Service

Farms. *See* Cerny farm; Kimber farm; Land tenure; Rendleman farm; Rendleman Orchards; Walton farm; Weaver farm

Fertilizers, 83, 224, 246, 271 (n. 13); limestone, 39, 156

Fink, Deborah, 3, 96, 188, 263 (n. 20)

Fishing, 51

Flamm, Delores. *See* Osbourne, Delores Flamm

Floods: 1937 Ohio, 160, 271 (n. 45). *See also* Mississippi River

Foraging, 51

Foucault, Michel, 200, 210

4-H clubs, xvi, 100, 192, 220

Fraternal and sororal associations, 124, 219; American Legion, 147; International Order of Odd Fellows, 24, 124, 249; Masons, 44, 124, 249; Order of the Eastern Star, 24, 219, 221; Rebekahs, 24, 124, 219, 221; Women's Clubs, 124, 267 (n. 36)

Gender roles: crossing of, 96–97, 265 (n. 63); and cult of domesticity, 100, 105, 186–88, 198, 262 (n. 9), 272 (n. 2), 275 (n. 24); rural different from urban, 104–5, 244, 249. *See also* Division of labor

Giant City State Park, 122, 146, 151

GI bill, 210, 234, 246

Glover, Charles (county farm adviser), 174, 188, 269 (n. 14)

Government: federal, 144–61, 231; Illinois state, 145; local, 145; Union County, 43–44, 146, 241. *See also* Governmental role

Governmental role: employer, 214, 216, 231–33; redistributor of wealth, 232–34. *See also* Credit; Great Society programs; New Deal; Policy and policymaking; Social Security

Grange, 123, 124, 278 (n. 8)

Granger movement, 125, 160, 268 (n. 8)

Great Depression, 133–43, 149; economic effects of, 81, 125, 224, 248; social networks during, 33, 60, 138, 143

Great Society programs, 174, 196, 230

Green family, 12–16, 95

Green farm. *See* Cerny farm

Gurley, Ada: on clothes washing, 92; recollections, 50, 93, 104

Halterman, Austin, 226, 230, 261 (n. 9)

Health. *See* Illness

Health regulations, 188

Heffernan, Judith, 238

Herbicides, 224

Hill, Mary Walton: recollections, 89

Hidden Injuries of Class, The, 215

Hindman, Ruel: on DDT, 171–72; on Great Depression, 142; on growers' coops, 170; on livestock marketing, 179–81; recollections, 76–77, 135

Historic preservation, xvii–xviii, 150–51

History, xxii, 49, 81, 266 (n. 15); attitudes toward, xix, 1–2, 4–5; determinants of, 37–38, 248, 278 (n. 6); uses of, xxiii, 2, 4, 37–38, 40, 42, 234, 244, 251, 255. *See also* Nostalgia

for, 231; housing for, 120, 157, 174–75; Mexican and Mexican American, 175, 252; after World War II, 29, 35, 163–65. *See also* Seasonal labor

Migration into southern Illinois, 6, 32, 228–29; from Europe, 13, 43, 87, 258 (n. 19); from the northeast, 28, 46–47, 87; from the Upland South, xxi, 12, 17, 21, 43, 47–48, 86, 113

Mill Creek: population, 1900–1990, 47; on rail line between Cairo and St. Louis, 46

Miller, Clara Bell, 112

Mills and milling, 44, 51, 53, 82; carding, 19; eastern fabric, 87, 247; flour, 50, 58, 70; gristmills, 50; sawmills, 10, 12, 13, 33, 48, 140, 266; sorghum molasses, 19–20, 50. *See also* Distilleries

Mines and mining, 25; kaolin clay, 17, 140, 156; limestone, 41; silica, 41, 114, 140–41, 268 (n. 16)

Mississippi River: floods, 12, 41, 42, 158–60, 181, 237; levees, 52, 158–60, 181, 237; marijuana grown on islands in, 227–28

Mississippi River bottoms, 6, 46, 74, 83, 111, 124, 128; drainage districts in, 52, 145; draining and clearing of, 39, 181; evacuation of during 1943 flood, 158–59; grain crops in, 23, 235, 237; sizes of farms in, 109–10; timbering in, 114

Mules, 25, 79–81, 176–77; as index of commercial production, 79–80

New Deal, 144–56, 214, 224, 242, 244; agencies, 150–56, 269 (n. 13); agencies during World War II, 156–61; programs, 162, 218, 251; reformers, 183, 245. *See also* Civilian Conservation Corps; Rural Electrification Administration; Works Progress Administration

New Deal–type programs after World War II, 183, 275 (nn. 30, 32)

Nonfarm work, 233; provided by government, 231–32; in state prison, 240; trends toward, 36, 129, 191–92

Nonfarm work, men's, 33, 143; wages for, 166–67

Nonfarm work, women's, 16, 32, 34; trends toward, 36, 129, 191–92

Norris, Cecil: recollections, 50, 68–69

Nostalgia, xviii–xix, 200, 255 (n. 4)

Orchards, 26–28, 109, 135, 137, 165, 172–75

Orphans, 59, 103–4

Osbourne, Delores Flamm, 142, 221–22. *See also* Cobden Peach Festival

Osterud, Nancy Grey, 85

Outmigration from southern Illinois, 36, 129, 165, 208, 217, 256 (n. 12); to California, 165

Parks, George: on New Deal programs, 149–50; recollections, 141, 142

Pensions, 145, 215, 230, 231, 233, 252

Pesticides, 171–72, 224, 271 (n. 13); DDT, 171–72

Policy and policymaking, 2, 182–83, 188, 250; corporate, xx; governmental, xx, 183, 234–37, 246. *See also* Committee for Economic Development; Industrial models: applied to agriculture

Political parties, 57, 147, 251

Politics, 29, 48, 146

Populist movement (of 1880s and 1890s), 123, 125, 160. *See also* Farmers' Mutual Benefit Association

Poverty, 1; attitudes toward, 148, 206; of migrant workers, 29, 163–65; rural, 133, 141; of Union Countians, 156, 207, 241, 247, 277 (n. 26)

Power, social, xviii, 105, 129, 264–65 (n. 61)

Prejudice, xviii, 124

Price controls: during World War II, 26, 163

Price wars, 190

Producer associations, 82, 124–25, 174–75; women not active in, 249; *See also* Farmers' Educational and Cooperative Union of America; Union County Farm Bureau

Producer cooperatives, 136–37, 145, 170, 224, 244, 245; manure importation, 76; marketing, 48; shipping, 48, 136, 150, 170, 267 (n. 34), 268 (n. 8); wool pool, 32. *See also* Anna Producers Dairy; Illinois Fruitgrowers Exchange

Productivity, agricultural, 74, 83, 133, 177–78

Progress, ideology of, 81, 199, 204, 206, 251

Progressive movement, 154, 160, 186–87, 206. *See also* Country Life movement

Prohibition, 146, 228; repeal of, 143, 146

Property ownership, 44, 106, 125–26, 128, 264–65 (n. 61)

Railroads. *See* Illinois Central Railroad; Infrastructure

Rebekahs. *See* Fraternal and sororal associations

Reciprocity, 44, 50, 52, 60–71, 128, 143; balanced, 60; generalized, 60

Recreation, 44, 51, 78, 143, 252; croquet, 17, 67; drinking and gambling, 44, 58–59; square dancing, xvii, 12, 67, 220–21; women's, 67–68, 124. *See also* Cobden Peach Festival; Hunt clubs

Recycling, 52

Religion, 86, 252; as rarely discussed despite importance, 4, 56, 260 (n. 11); religious groups, 6, 43, 124, 221

Rendleman, Edith, 3, 4, 21–24, 187, 211–12, 220–21; on boarders, 113; on child rearing, 98–99; on flood of 1943, 42; on getting electricity, 151, 153; on her aunt leaving her uncle, 97; on her childhood, 103, 119–20,

201; on her egg and poultry business, 90–91; on her mother's charity, 22–23, 59, 120; recollections, 51, 60, 62, 67, 79, 84, 87, 89, 93, 95, 111, 128, 144, 264 (nn. 57, 60); on threshing events, 63, 66; on violence at Wolf Lake, 58–59; on women's need to earn money, 105–6

Rendleman, Edith, family, 24–28, 109, 113–14, 120, 128, 129–30, 256 (n. 15); in postwar period, 181. *See also* Bradley, Elijah

Rendleman, Edith, farm, 21–28; house, 21, 24, 211–12

Rendleman Orchards, 24–28; house, 25

Retirement, 24, 34, 36, 229, 230

Rhodes, Bill, 214, 231; on cooperative butchering, 60–62; recollections, 63, 79, 119

Rhodes farm, 17–21, 256 (n. 12); house, 17, 20, 21, 201, 202, 203, 207, 210, 212

Riverboat gambling, 240

Rivers. *See* Mississippi River; Watercourses

Rose Farms, 174

Rural Electrification Administration (REA), 24, 34–35, 151–52, 155. *See also* Southern Illinois Electric Cooperative

Rural-urban relationship, 47, 70, 123, 143, 245

St. Louis, 23; livestock market in, 180; markets in, 90; rail connection to Cairo constructed in, 45; stockyards in, 76; women's shopping trips to, 68, 124

Salamon, Sonya, 86, 246, 265 (n. 61), 277 (n. 1)

Sanitation, 157, 210. *See also* Indoor plumbing

Saratoga, 12, 41, 46, 51

Scale of production, 76–77, 130, 174; in New Deal vision, 245–47; and technology, 74, 90; trend toward increase

Waterworks, 150, 151, 221. *See also* Indoor plumbing

Wealth, disparities in, 1, 6, 50, 82–83, 119–31, 252; and immigrants, 47; reflected in built landscape, 53; values surrounding, 108

Wealth, redistribution of, 149, 232, 242

Weaver, Bruno, 11, 62, 63–64

Weaver, Ruby, 11–12; on butchering and cooking, 61–62; on farm work, 89, 96; recollections, 63, 65–66, 94

Weaver family, 7–12, 62, 156, 229

Weaver farm: house, 10–12, 202, 203, 212; rented, 229

Wolf, Eric, 37

Women's Clubs. *See* Fraternal and sororal associations

Work, 1–4, 52, 215; attitudes toward, 1–2, 148. *See also* Farm-based businesses; Labor; Nonfarm work; Work off farm; Work on farm

Work ethic, 4

Work off farm, 196–97, 229; men's, 114, 196, 214

Work off farm, women's, 161, 245; in state mental hospital, 36; teaching, 32, 95, 196; trends toward, xxi, 192–96, 214, 249, 250

Work on farm, children's, 85, 88, 100–5; and corporal punishment, 98, 186, 252; girls', 89–90, 92–93; leaving school for, 121

Work on farm, men's, 84, 104–5; hay making, 73–74. *See also* Blacksmithing; Butchering; Farm-based businesses, men's; Threshing

Work on farm, women's, 2, 3, 84–100, 122; changes in, 185–89, 244; cooking, 25, 62, 65–66; for hired hands, 106; sewing, 93, 103, 263 (n. 30); soap making, 22, 51; spinning and weaving, 19, 87; unenumerated, 273 (n. 19); washing and ironing, 92–93. *See also* Boarders; Canning; Child rearing; Farm-based businesses, women's; Housework

Works Progress Administration (Work Projects Administration) (WPA), 141, 147–51, 157, 160

World War I: period after, 5, 23, 134–36; period of, 20, 26, 133, 135, 140

World War II, 45, 215; period after, xxi, 2, 4, 5, 15–16, 20, 26–27, 29, 39, 60, 90, 100, 107, 145, 162–84, 186–98, 211, 216, 224, 241, 246, 251; period before, 2, 49–50, 185, 190, 206, 244, 248; period of, 26, 29, 35, 141, 156–61, 215, 233

Yankee, 86; and cult of domesticity, 186; as immigrant, 45, 46–47, 124, 258 (n. 23); view of southern Illinois, 44, 81, 86, 257 (n.3)